INSIDERS' GUIDE® TO
SAN ANTONIO

Help Us Keep This Guide Up to Date

Every effort has been made by the authors and editors to make this guide as accurate and useful as possible. However, many things can change after a guide is published—establishments close, phone numbers change, hiking trails are rerouted, facilities come under new management, etc.

We would love to hear from you concerning your experiences with this guide and how you feel it could be made better and be kept up to date. While we may not be able to respond to all comments and suggestions, we'll take them to heart and we'll also make certain to share them with the authors. Please send your comments and suggestions to the following address:

The Globe Pequot Press
Reader Response/Editorial Department
P.O. Box 480
Guilford, CT 06437

Or you may e-mail us at:

editorial@globe-pequot.com

Thanks for your input, and happy travels!

Insiders' Guide®
to San Antonio

By Paris Permenter and John Bigley

Guilford, Connecticut

An imprint of The Globe Pequot Press

Insiders' Guide is a registered trademark of The Globe Pequot Press.

Cover photo: SACVB/Morris Goen
Back cover photos (left to right): SACVB/Craig Stafford; Paris Permenter and John Bigley; SACVB/Al Rendon; Paris Permenter and John Bigley; Paris Permenter and John Bigley
Maps by Geografx © The Globe Pequot Press

Library of Congress Cataloging-in-Publication Data is available.
ISBN: 0-7627-1216-3

Manufactured in the United States of America
First Edition/First Printing

Contents

Acknowledgments x

Preface xi

How to Use This Book 1

Area Overview 3

Getting Here, Getting Around 17

History 29

Hotels and Motels 41

Bed and Breakfast Inns 66

Restaurants 74

Nightlife 102

Shopping 115

Attractions 133

Kidstuff 157

Annual Events and Festivals 186

The Arts 206

Parks and Recreation 215

Spectator Sports 236

Day Trips 243

Weekend Getaways 267

Neighborhoods and Real Estate 278

Education and Child Care 284

Health Care and Wellness 295

Retirement 303

Media 313

Worship 320

Military 326

Index 333

Directory of Maps

San Antonio vii

San Antonio Area viii

Downtown San Antonio ix

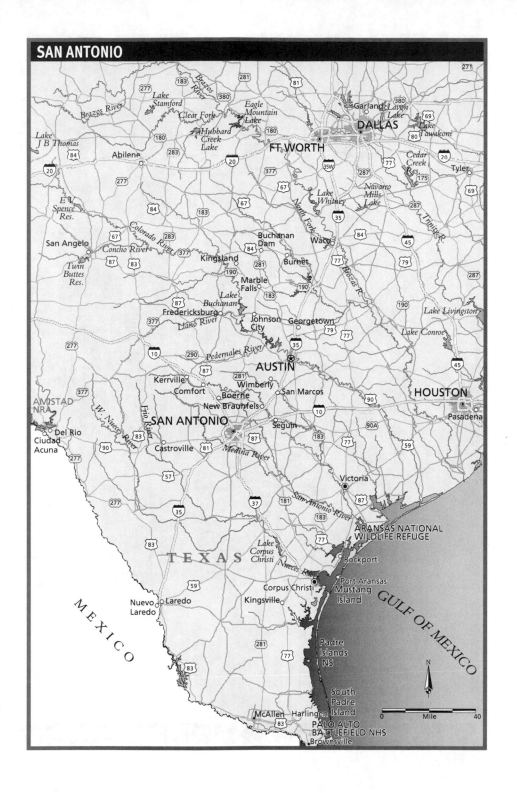

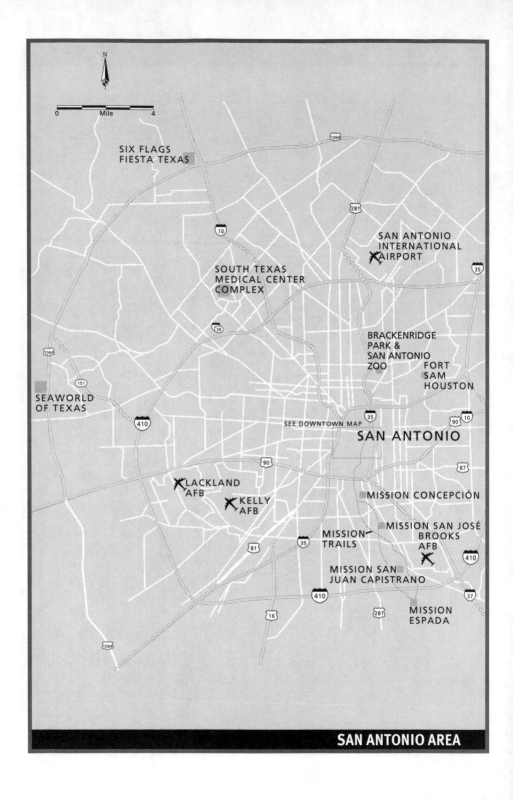

SAN ANTONIO AREA

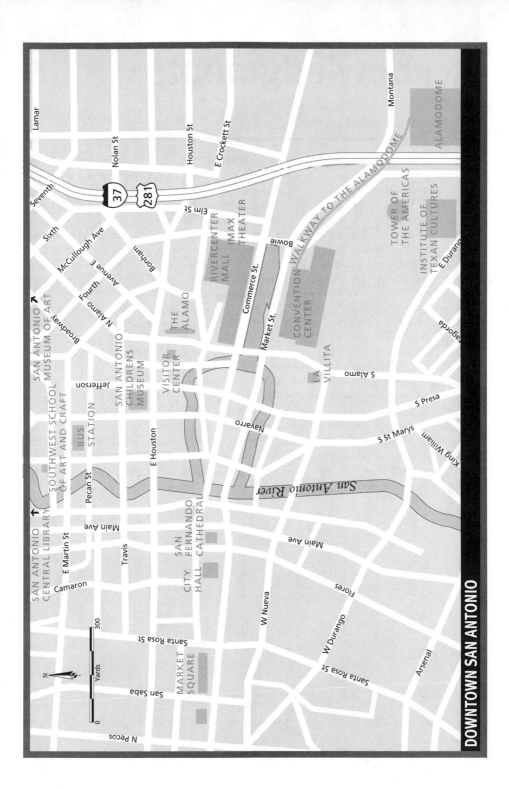

DOWNTOWN SAN ANTONIO

Acknowledgments

To help write about San Antonio, we sought the advice of two groups: long time San Antonians and San Antonio travelers. From both groups, we learned to love the city even more, and to both groups we say muchas gracias.

Our background and historical research took us throughout the city, from the public library to the resources of the San Antonio Conservation Society. We thank the librarians and volunteers who helped us search through newspaper clippings, scrapbooks, and historic documents that traced the evolution of the city's top attractions. We also relied on the San Antonio Convention and Visitors Bureau, especially Tom Bradley. We'd also like to thank Kelly Garland of Geiger and Associates Public Relations for her assistance with information on San Antonio's many attractions.

As we made our way throughout the city, we talked to shopkeepers, restaurateurs, and hoteliers about their establishments. We listened to vacationers who, as the saying goes, just wanted to have fun. We talked to folks who had come back to San Antonio, some of whom had made their first visit to HemisFair decades before, as well as visitors being introduced to the city for the first time.

Finally, we depended on the people who, on a day-to-day basis, make San Antonio tourism work: the residents themselves. They share their city with an enthusiasm and friendliness that's rare these days. To all the museum docents, the bus drivers, the waiters, the ticket-takers, and the tour guides, we give our thanks.

We'd also like to thank the folks at The Globe Pequot Press, especially editor Lynne Arany and freelance editor Mary Callahan, who helped make this book what it is today.

Finally, a big thanks to our daughter, Lauren Bigley, who helped us fact-check this massive manuscript and keep information up-to-date in an ever-changing world.

Preface

Bienvenidos to the Alamo City! Whether it's as a new home or a home away from home for a few days, you've chosen a destination that combines the best of Texas, the Southwest, and Mexico into a city that's filled with festivities and fun.

Texans, whether residents of Amarillo or Zapata, have adopted San Antonio as their second hometown. When Texans think of a vacation spot in the Lone Star State, we look to the Alamo City. It brings back memories of childhood field trips to the Alamo, romantic strolls on the River Walk, Christmases beneath thousands of tiny lights, and family fun at the theme parks.

As journalists, we've explored this city from end to end, mining the jewels we believe will help you make the most of your time in San Antonio, however long or abbreviated. Writing this book has given us the excuse to take the magnifying glass to our favorite Texas city and to seek out the tried-and-true as well as the often-overlooked. We've revisited some sites we had forgotten and discovered other locations that are truly Insiders' secrets. In these pages, we know you'll discover some gems as well, whatever your interests.

And, as you'll see from the size of this guide, San Antonio does boast a variety of attractions, from historic buildings to hair-raising thrill rides. San Antonio is the number one tourist destination in the state, according to the Texas Department of Transportation. But it's not just the number of attractions that draw visitors to this South Texas community; it's the atmosphere.

Will Rogers once proclaimed San Antonio "one of America's four unique cities." Wake up in the Alamo City with the scent of huevos rancheros in the air, the sound of mariachis filling the streets, and the sight of barges winding down the San Antonio River, and you'll know you're not in Kansas anymore, Dorothy. Even other Texas cities don't have San Antonio's unique spirit.

Along with a strong Hispanic influence, San Antonio brings together other cultures to create a unique identity all its own. For example, the influence of the city's early German residents can be seen on everything from architecture to menus. Families that trace their heritage back to the days of the earliest San Antonio merchants have proudly worked to conserve the history of this city and to preserve its buildings and historic sites.

While other cities may speed along in the fast lane, San Antonio prefers the scenic route, a perfect pace for the city's many tourists around the world. Even though there are plenty of things to do, this is the kind of town where both a siesta and a museum visit are equally acceptable ways to spend an afternoon.

At the heart of the city is the San Antonio River, winding through tropical lushness and drawing residents and visitors into its current of gaiety along the riverbanks. The San Antonio River is to this city what the Seine is to Paris, the bay to San Francisco, the delta to New Orleans. It draws both residents and vacationers to its banks to enjoy a sense of place that is unrivaled anywhere else in Texas—and few places around the globe.

When we started this book, we returned to one of our favorite San Antonio spots: the River Walk. We took a leisurely breakfast cruise along the river, reminding ourselves why this city holds such a special place in our hearts. After our cruise, we strolled to the historic La Villita for a closer look, mingling with the shoppers in San Antonio's finest crafts area, populated by weavers, glassblowers, sculptors, and boot makers.

The morning of our visit, a wedding took place in the historic Little Church. Amid beaming relatives and friends, the happy bride and groom posed for photos on the church's worn steps, just a stone's throw from the river.

Something old and something new. The promise of fresh beginnings set against the rich heritage of the past. It seemed a perfect symbol for San Antonio's comfortable marriage of history and destiny.

An old Spanish legend says, "They who drink of the San Antonio River will return." Drink up the atmosphere, soak up the sun that filters through the cypress and banana trees, and taste the excitement. And you'll be back.

How to Use This Book

This is a book for San Antonio vacationers and conventioneers—folks looking for a good meal, a good shop, a good night's sleep, and a good time in the most popular vacation spot in Texas. It's also a book for city residents, especially those who have only recently made San Antonio their home. This is not an exhaustive guide to the Alamo City, but rather one that covers places that make San Antonio unique.

This guide is divided by activity. Flying in to San Antonio International Airport? Check out the Getting Here, Getting Around chapter for information on shuttles and rental cars. In this chapter, you'll also find an explanation of the boundaries we've used to divide this city into five sections: downtown, inside Loop 410, between Loop 1604 and Loop 410, and beyond Loop 1604. These divisions will help you determine whether the restaurant you're eyeing is within easy driving distance of your hotel, or if you can combine two attractions in a single afternoon.

When you're ready to book a room, the extensive Hotels and Motels and Bed and Breakfast Inns chapters cover all price ranges. If you want to schedule your stay during a local festival—or during a quieter (and less expensive) period—read the Annual Events chapter for details on the festivals, events that San Antonio throws on a scale to rival any other Texas city.

Once you're settled, we'll guide you to attractions that range from museums to historic sights. The youngest travelers in the family will be especially interested in the Kidstuff chapter, with information on children's activities and museums. With San Antonio's excellent weather, you'll want to check the Parks and Recreation chapter to find places to enjoy the great outdoors. Nightlife and Arts chapters keep you abreast of the hottest spots in town, including theaters, galleries, and jazz clubs.

The unique character of San Antonio is due to more than its attractions, though; it's also a product of the city's rich history. This book includes a brief history of San Antonio, from its early mission days to its famous Alamo battle to its present role as a Texas cultural crossroads. You'll learn more about the Hispanic culture that makes San Antonio special as well as the diversity of other cultures that call this city home. We'll also look at the city's spiritual and religious congregations and communities as well as its educational, health care, and child care services and institutions, all important considerations if you are considering a move. The Neighborhoods and Real Estate chapter will be of special interest to relocators, too. San Antonio is also closely entwined with the military world, with five military bases within its borders. We look at the role of the military in a special chapter that takes in both the historic and the present-day impact of these bases.

We've featured several unusual spots in "Close-ups" stories sprinkled throughout the book. These are aimed at providing you with an insight into the places that make the Alamo City so special.

No guide can be everything to every reader. Your own best judgment must prevail. Keep in mind your own limits, and make your plans accordingly. Be aware of the conditions around you, and be flexible enough to adjust to meet those conditions. For example, summer in San Antonio can be downright fiery, so you'll need to adjust your schedule to take advantage of early morning and late evening temperatures during those months.

Travel is a journey of discovery that may take you down a different—and possibly more interesting—route than the one you originally intended. For instance, if your River Walk visit coincides with the city's largest event, Fiesta, your stay will be shared with hundreds of thousands of other visitors. Things will take a little longer; your total number of stops may be fewer. But at the same time, you'll be part of a celebration that makes this city distinct.

With these tips in mind, let the trip begin. Whether you're journeying from your armchair or the driver's seat, from a rental car or a moving van, we hope the following pages will help you to enjoy the Alamo City.

As you travel through San Antonio's historic streets and fast-growing outer regions, keep in mind that changes occur. The *Insiders' Guide to San Antonio* strives to keep up with the comings and goings in the Alamo City, whether the closure of a restaurant, the addition of new hotel rooms at a longtime favorite accommodation, or the rescheduling of an event from one month to another. While we have enjoyed the experiences chronicled in this book, we can't guarantee that every San Antonio visitor will have a comparable experience. If you'd like to comment on some of the sights mentioned in the book (or if you've discovered a place that we've missed), we'd love to hear from you. We update the guide periodically and keep a record of reader recommendations and advice. Check out the Insiders' Web site at www.insiders.com and send us a note from there with your picks and pans. You may also write us in care of:

Insiders' Guides
The Globe Pequot Press
P.O. Box 480
Guilford, CT 06437-0480

Area Overview

Latino Influence

African-American Culture

More Faces of
    San Antonio

Quality of Life

Tourism

Conventions

Things to Do

International Trade

Biomedical Industries

Language

Government

The term "Texas-size" is tossed around the Lone Star State to describe everything from fountain drinks to roller-coasters, but it truly sums up the sprawling metropolis that is San Antonio. This city spans 417.1 square miles, an area that ranges from a dense downtown area to quiet suburban neighborhoods.

But the description covers far more than geographic area; "Texas-size" describes everything from culture to cuisine, attractions to accommodations. Whether you're trying to decide on an afternoon activity or an afternoon meal, you'll find yourself presented with a full menu of choices. As the home of the Alamo, a symbol of Texas pride and its fight for independence, San Antonio boasts historic sites that can't be equaled. And when it's pure fun you're after—whether that translates as a museum tour or a merry-go-round—the city offers a long list of attractions that includes museums, sports, parks, children's activities, theme parks, and more.

Texas-sized really describes San Antonio's true passion: fiesta. As one local resident once said, "You can't come to San Antonio without having a fiesta!"

"Fiesta" encompasses all aspects of "party" but with a sizzle that only San Antonio parties can deliver. The Alamo City parties in a style like no other Texas destination, with year-around special events and festivals that incorporate foods, dances, and even special touches such as pastel streamers and cascarones, confetti-filled eggs that children (and the childlike) delight in breaking over any unsuspecting person's head.

Once a year, the fiesta spirit takes over the city with a ten-day celebration called Fiesta San Antonio. Dating back more than 110 years, this April celebration fills the city with parades, sporting events, live music, and a general party atmosphere.

The fiesta spirit lives year-round at the city's heart, the Paseo del Rio or River Walk. This magical place is located 20 feet below street level, nestled behind tall buildings away from street noise. With high-rise hotels and plenty of specialty shops and European-style alfresco cafes, the River Walk is easy for visitors to explore on their own. The River Walk embodies what people envision when they hear the name San Antonio: pure fun.

Latino Influence

San Antonio brings together the cultures of Texas and Mexico in a true melting pot, thanks not only to a shared history but also to shared family ties. About 57 percent of the city's residents are of Hispanic origin.

It's not surprising that practically all aspects of the city, from street names to local politics, are flavored by the cultural and historical distinctions of its dominant population.

The connection between San Antonio and Mexico is a long one; San Antonio's early history is, in fact, Mexican history. Like the rest of Texas, the city was part of Mexico until 1836. When Texas decided to break free of Mexico, several Mexican Texans took part in the historic signing of the Texas Declaration of Independence on March 2, 1836. At least seven were elected to serve at the convention; only three were able to attend. José Antonio Navarro, José Francisco Ruiz, and Lorenzo de Zavala

3

San Antonio beckons visitors with a blend of modern and historical sights. PHOTO: PARIS PERMENTER & JOHN BIGLEY

each attended the historic event, one of the most important on the long road to independence. Four days later, Santa Anna's victory at the Alamo cost seven Mexican Texans their lives.

Erasmo Seguin and son Juan dedicated the following years, as well as their personal fortune, to the development of Texas. Erasmo Seguin became an early mayor of Bexar and worked to reinforce the relationship between Texas and Mexico. His son, Juan, had been present at the battle of the Alamo but had escaped death when he was sent out with a message calling for reinforcements. Juan went on to serve in the Texas Senate until 1840, the next year becoming the mayor of San Antonio.

Hispanic involvement in Texas politics has continued into modern times. Of the five Latinos elected to the U.S. Congress in 1994, three hailed from San Antonio. Henry Cisneros, a popular mayor of San Antonio in the 1980s, was named U.S. Secretary of Housing and Urban Development by President Bill Clinton in 1993. San Antonio's present mayor, Ed Garza, also has Hispanic roots.

Throughout the city, Hispanic influences are seen in business as well. The San Antonio Hispanic Chamber of Commerce (www.sahcc.org) is the oldest Hispanic Chamber in the nation and now boasts 1,600 members and business associates. Chartered as the Mexican Chamber of Commerce in 1929, the group has continued to promote trade and cultural harmony between San Antonio and Mexico. Through the years, the groups' leaders acted as advocates for Hispanic businesses that faced discrimination in the business world.

In 1987, the Mexican Chamber of Commerce was renamed the San Antonio Hispanic Chamber of Commerce and the organization took on a more global relationship with all of Latin America. The group helped played a role in the passage and promotion of the North American Free Trade Agreement (NAFTA).

According to HispanicMarketing.com, San Antonio's Hispanic community is the

eighth-largest in the country. Of the Hispanic population, 80 percent trace their ancestry to Mexico.

Latino culture also plays an important role in the recreational side of San Antonio. The Alameda Theatre, constructed in the late 1940s as a movie palace, was the largest theater ever dedicated to Spanish-language entertainment. In 1998, the venue reopened following a refurbishment as a teaching facility for Latino arts and culture. Latin arts are the focus of the Nelson A. Rockefeller Center for Latin American Art at the San Antonio Museum of Art. Considered the most extensive collection of its kind, the exhibits include Latin American folk art as well as many historic pieces.

San Antonio also is considered the birthplace of Tejano music, a lively combination of rock, polka, and Mexican sounds. Now enjoying a global stage, top Tejano performers are recognized at annual awards held in San Antonio. In the film world, the Guadalupe Cultural Arts Center hosts an annual film festival showcasing Latino productions. In the literary world, the San Antonio Inter-American Bookfair and Literary Festival highlights Latino writers and books with Hispanic themes.

The cuisine of San Antonio is inextricably tied to that of its Hispanic history. Many Mexican delights such as *aguas frescas* (fruit drinks), *buñelos* (fried cinnamon pastries), and *raspas* (snowcones) are found at festivals throughout the city while San Antonio eateries serve dishes such as *barbacoa* (a special type of barbecue), *cabrito* (goat), and *menudo* (tripe soup).

African-American Culture

African Americans make up approximately seven percent of the total San Antonio population. The influence of the African-American community is seen throughout the city, in its festivals, its food, its booming businesses, and in its appreciation of history and tradition.

The long link between the African-American community and San Antonio dates back to the 1500s, to the days when Spaniards came to establish their claim to this region. Enslaved Africans were brought by the Spaniards; by the late 1700s, many of their descendants were freed by the Spanish. Soon the population began to intermarry with the Spanish, Mexican, and Indian residents. In 1809, Victor Blanco, a man of mixed race, became San Antonio's first and only African-American mayor.

When Mexico won its freedom from Spain in 1821, it also won claim over the Texian territory. Under Mexican law, slavery was not permitted, although many African descendants became indentured servants. In exchange for legal papers stating their freedom, these people were paid a small sum (often only a dollar) and made indentured servants—often for their entire lives.

One such indentured servant became the subject of Texas legend. Emily Morgan, a mixed-race indentured servant, captured the eye of Mexican General Santa Anna, soon becoming the military leader's confidante. After gaining his trust, she learned about the general's military plans and worked as a spy, supplying the information to Sam Houston and the Texian army fighting for independence. Emily Morgan's patriotism is remembered in a song learned by all Texas schoolchildren: "The Yellow Rose of Texas."

Emily Morgan's name is well known to Texans but the beautiful spy was only one African-American patriot in the fight for Texas independence. Several African-Americans were present at the battle of the Alamo, working as slaves to the Texan settlers.

When Texas won its independence from Mexico, settlers moved to the region from throughout the South, bringing with them a number of slaves. Following the Civil War, slavery was abolished throughout the country on September 22, 1862. Word of emancipation did not reach Texas until June 19, 1865. The day became known as Juneteenth, and today it is celebrated in San Antonio and throughout the state with an annual festival.

In the years following the Civil War, the racially segregated U.S. Army formed African-American units. In 1867 one such unit, the Ninth Cavalry, arrived in San Antonio. Stationed along the frontier to help protect against attack, the members of this cavalry were known as the "buffalo soldiers" by the Native Americans because of their strength, bravery, and curly hair. Stationed at San Pedro Springs, the soldiers protected the San Antonio–El Paso mail route and were later awarded Medals of Honor. Today many of these soldiers are buried at the San Antonio National Cemetery.

Post-Reconstruction years saw a growing influence of African Americans in San Antonio as they became active in politics and gained positions in organized labor. In 1898 St. Philip's College was established as an industrial school for girls; in 1902 an African-American woman named Artemisia Bowden took leadership of the school and elevated it to a fully accredited junior college. It was the first institution

Insiders' Tip

Bexar County is pronounced Bear County.

Famous African-American Residents of San Antonio

William Davis: If you've enjoyed instant mashed potatoes, then you've enjoyed the labors of William Davis, their inventor. Davis also worked to develop a chemical that makes machine-dispensed ice cream possible. He also helped develop mail-order blood testing for diabetes patients.

Al Freeman, Jr.: Spike Lee's film *Malcolm X* showcased the efforts of this actor, who starred as Elijah Muhammad.

Cito Gaston: Baseball fans recognize this name as that of the manager of the Toronto Blue Jays.

Gary Green: Football fans know Green as the NFL defensive back who was named All-Pro for seven out of nine years.

Dr. Bernard Harris: Harris was the first African American to walk in space.

Myra Davis-Hemmings: The Delta Sigma Theta Sorority at Howard University was established by Davis-Hemmings in 1913; she helped establish the San Antonio Delta alumnae chapter as well.

Cliff Johnson: A player for both the National and the American Baseball Leagues, Johnson is the holder of the major league record for most pinch hits.

Willie Mitchell: The first Super Bowl featured this defensive cornerback, who played for the Kansas City Chiefs.

John "Mules" Miles: Still a San Antonio resident, Miles played baseball for the Chicago American League Giants in the Negro League.

June Parker: Still performing, jazz pianist Parker is known for her work in the 1950s and '60s. Today she is a member of the San Antonio Musicians Hall of Fame.

Percy Sutton: Sutton is presently chair of Inner City Broadcasting, a national media enterprise; he served as former president of the New York Manhattan Borough.

of higher learning for African-Americans in the San Antonio region. Today the college is part of the Alamo Community College District.

Throughout the twentieth century, the number of African-American businesses in San Antonio continued to rise. The Negro Chamber of Commerce was formed in 1938; today it is known as the Alamo City Chamber of Commerce and works to assist African-American businesses. The African-American Chamber of Commerce also works for similar goals and is an affiliate of the National Association of African-American Chambers of Commerce, Inc.

The influence of the African-American community was also felt in the city's cultural life. Many African-American nightclubs entertained local audiences with traveling headliner acts. The Library Auditorium showcased many well-known performers; today the venue survives as the Carver Community Cultural Center, which has hosted such performers as Gregory Hines, Eartha Kitt, and the Dance Theatre of Harlem.

In the 1960s, San Antonio residents worked to establish racial equality at a time when retail and grocery chains were not providing equal service to black patrons and practiced discriminatory hiring practices. Boycotts and rallies brought about integration.

Today San Antonio is home to a growing number of African-American businesses and the African-American community is influential in fields ranging from medicine to politics.

San Antonio also welcomes a growing number of African-American travelers, who come to enjoy the multicultural atmosphere of the city. Several multicultural festivals are also of special interest to African-American visitors. Juneteenth Festival is a day of both family celebrations and special events, including the African-American Cultural Association Juneteenth Picnic. June also brings the Texas Folklife Festival, when the spotlight turns to the thirty-plus nationalities who helped settle this region. In January, the African-American Cultural Association presents its Joint Military Gospel Fest and its Joint Military Proclamation Ceremony. Also in January is the annual Martin Luther King March, one of the largest such marches in the country, which honors the work and the life of civil rights leader Martin Luther King, Jr. The event takes place along a 3-mile route, which extends from the MLK Freedom Bridge to the MLK statue on the city's east side. In February, the annual African-American Harmon and Harriet Kelly Art Show showcases the work of African-American artists; February is also the time of special productions, performances, and exhibits at the St. Philip's College Watson Fine Arts Center in observance of Black Heritage Month.

The San Antonio Convention and Visitors Bureau has mapped out a self-guided African-American Heritage Tour that covers 14 points of interest in the downtown area. The walk includes the Institute of Texan Cultures, where visitors can view the Black Wall, which showcases African-American contributions to the founding and building of Texas; St. Paul Square and Sunset Depot, the site of many African-American–owned businesses during times of segregation; the city cemeteries where 285 buffalo soldiers now rest; the Carver Cultural Center; St. Paul United Methodist Church, the oldest African-American church in San Antonio; and Ellis Alley, one of the first areas in the city to be settled by African Americans following the Civil War.

For more on the African-American heritage of the Alamo City, contact the San Antonio Convention and Visitors Bureau for a free copy of the *African-American Cultural Guide,* which includes a map of the self-guided tour as well as listings of many African-American–owned night-spots and restaurants.

More Faces of San Antonio

With its strong Mexican ties, San Antonio has long had an international feel but that cultural atmosphere reaches far beyond the Mexican borders. Since its earliest days, the city has been home to residents from around the globe.

San Antonio's population is approximately 57 percent Hispanic, 36 percent Anglo, and 7 percent African American, plus a smattering of other ethnic groups (Native Americans, Asians, Pacific Islanders). Census figures also report that 14 percent of San Antonians claim German ancestry while others are of Irish (8.2 percent), English (7.7 percent), Italian (1.7 percent), French (2.4 percent), and Polish (1.6 percent) descent. Although lacking the extensive ethnic neighborhoods of other cities, San Antonio does have some areas that have traditionally been home to certain groups: "Southtown" remains largely Hispanic; the Alamo Heights, Olmos Park, and other communities on the city's north and northwest are mostly Anglo; and the east side is traditionally an African-American neighborhood.

Quality of Life

Between 1980 and 1990, the population of the city rose 24 percent, compared to 19.4 percent across Texas and a 9.8-percent national average. Even with its growth, San Antonio boasts a cost of living that ranks as one of the lowest in the country for a city of its size. According to a ranking by the Association of Applied Community Researchers (ACCRA) that looks at the cost of 59 items, San Antonio scores 91.1 compared to a median cost of living in a U.S. city of 100. In Texas, Houston scored 95.7 and Dallas 99.1; out of state, Columbus, Ohio, ranked 105.3; Nashville, 95.6; Oklahoma City, 92.3; Orlando, 99.8; Phoenix, 104.3; Portland, 107; St. Louis, 98; and Tampa, 103.4.

Tourism

As the top travel destination in Texas, San Antonio's tourism business is booming; the latest figures show more than 7.7 million visitors annually. With some 60,000 residents employed in the tourism business, tourism funnels in excess of $3.5 bil-

Insiders' Tip

The largest convention in San Antonio history has been booked for 2007. The American Dental Association (ADA) will bring 50,000 attendees to the Alamo City.

lion into the local economy, according to the San Antonio Chamber of Commerce.

The lodging needs of visitors are met by numerous hotel rooms: nearly 10,000 in the downtown alone and more than 27,000 throughout the city. Nonetheless, occupancy rates average about 64.5 percent, above the national average. During peak periods such as Fiesta (April), Las Posadas (December), and anytime the San Antonio Spurs basketball team is playing on their home court, rooms can be at a premium.

Conventions

The convention business is also booming in San Antonio, increasing from 258 conventions in 1969 to 1,500 three decades later. The city has answered the demand with a recent $193.8-million expansion of the Henry B. Gonzales Convention Center. "The expansion will help us attract more and larger conventions," explained Steve Moore, executive director of the San Antonio Convention and Visitors Bureau. "It will boost hotel development. And it will keep us competitive as one of the best convention values in the country." The expansion is already encouraging hotel growth; since the beginning of 1995 some 3,000 new hotel rooms have been added throughout the city.

San Antonio's largest meeting and exhibition facility is the Alamodome, a Texas-sized structure located east of the convention center. This multipurpose building can handle groups as large as

77,000; break-out meeting space totals 30,000 square feet. With the eastward expansion of the convention center, more groups will use both the Alamodome and the convention center for their meetings and conventions.

The San Antonio Municipal Auditorium and Conference Center is another popular meeting site. With a 4,904-seat auditorium, the property includes exhibit space and break-out rooms.

The River Walk is home to some of the city's top conference hotels, including the Hyatt Regency San Antonio, with 31,000 square feet of meeting space; the Marriott River Walk, with 14 meeting rooms; and the Marriott Rivercenter, which soars up from the Rivercenter Mall and offers 60,000 square feet for meetings.

For reasons such as budget considerations, space availability, and a desire to promote group cohesiveness, meeting planners often select sites beyond the River Walk area for small to medium-size groups. Throughout the city, meeting and reception venues are available in sites of historic and cultural interest—and there are also some that are just plain fun. Market Square, Mission San José, the Lone Star Brewery, the Retama Park horseracing track, Six Flags Fiesta Texas theme park, and SeaWorld of Texas are among the unusual choices available to businesses and groups that wish to hold meetings, receptions, and other special events in San Antonio.

Things to Do

Whether travelers come as part of a group or independently, they find a full array of activities in San Antonio—all of which are explored in depth throughout this book.

For many, the first stop is the Paseo del Rio—the River Walk. The River Walk is home to high-rise hotels, shops, and European-style alfresco cafes. The best way to get an overview of the River Walk is aboard a guided river cruise; a ride on these open-air barges is a must for any first-time visitor. After a tour, stop for lunch at one of the sidewalk restaurants. San Antonio is known for its spicy Tex-Mex food, and restaurants like Rio Rio Cantina and Casa Rio offer tables along the river's edge so you can watch the activity.

From the River Walk, it's a short stroll over to Texas's best-known symbol: the Alamo. This "Cradle of Texas Liberty" plunged into history on March 6, 1836, when 188 Texas defenders died in a battle against a large Mexican army led by General Santa Anna during the Texas Revolution. Stroll through the shrine to see artifacts and arms from the fateful battle.

Just steps from the River Walk at HemisFair Plaza, the Tower of the Americas is a soaring reminder of the 1968 World Hem-

An arm of the San Antonio River takes visitors to Rivercenter Mall. PHOTO: CRAIG STAFFORD, COURTESY OF THE SAN ANTONIO CONVENTION AND VISITORS BUREAU

isFair and is today one of San Antonio's civic symbols. A one-minute elevator ride whisks you up to the observation deck at 579 feet for a great view of the city through high-powered telescopes.

Near the base of the tower stands one of the state's best museums, the Institute of Texan Cultures. Here you can learn about the more than thirty ethnic groups that settled Texas. Don't miss the dome slide show for a look at the many faces of the Lone Star State. Many days you'll find costumed docents moseying throughout the museum, ready to explain the role of a chuck wagon cook on a cattle drive or the rigors of life as a frontier woman.

Another noteworthy San Antonio attraction is the oldest section of the River Walk: La Villita. In this "little village," nestled on the east bank of the River Walk, the focus is on history and art. Dating back to the days when the Alamo served as a military outpost, La Villita developed as a temporary village of people without land title. Today it's a National Historic District that bustles with shoppers in search of one-of-a-kind items ranging from watercolors to glass creations to handmade jewelry.

West of La Villita, and easily accessible via VIA streetcar, is Market Square, a shopping area that dates back to the early 1800s. The market's real claim to fame is that it was the birthplace of chili con carne, the spicy meat and bean mixture that's now the state dish of Texas. Once young girls known as "chili queens" sold the concoction from small stands in the market.

Today the South of the Border flavor of Market Square is seen in its shops and restaurants. Shop El Mercado for the same goods found in Mexico's *mercados*—but without the bargaining. When you're ready for a break, stop by Mi Tierra, the 24-hour restaurant that's popular with locals and visitors alike. While you wait for your Tex-Mex meal, strolling troubadours take requests for Mexican ballads. Just as authentic is the adjacent panaderia, a Mexican bakery exuding the tasty aromas of fresh tortillas and polvorones, cookies topped with cinnamon and sugar.

When it's time to explore more of San Antonio's rich history, numerous options await. The Alamo may be the best known mission in town, but it's certainly not the only one. The San Antonio Missions National Historical Park stretches for nine miles along the San Antonio River and is comprised of four missions constructed by the Franciscan friars in the eighteenth century. The missions are active parish churches today, and all are open to the public.

The chain of these historic buildings begins at Mission Concepción, a site that today illustrates religious life in the missions. Mission San Juan Capistrano, once completely self-sustaining, today explains "The Mission as an Economic Center" through interesting exhibits. The reconstructed Mission Espada has displays that explain vocational education at the missions.

The most active site on the mission trail is Mission San José. The most complete structure in the tour was once called the "Queen of the Texas Missions"; today a $9.5-million visitors center is located nearby. Save time to enjoy the mission's beautiful carvings and its restored mill with waterwheel.

Finally, for families that just want to have fun, the Six Flags Fiesta Texas theme park and SeaWorld of Texas are on the northwest side of town, along loop 1604.

Insiders' Tip

Foreign currency exchange is available at Frost Bank (100 W. Houston Street) and NationsBank (300 Convent Street) any weekday.

A statue remembering the saint for whom San Antonio is named stands near the Rivercenter Mall. PHOTO: PARIS PERMENTER & JOHN BIGLEY

International Trade

The passage of the North American Free Trade Alliance (NAFTA) brought major growth to San Antonio industry thanks to increased trade with Mexico. In 1995, just a year after the passage of the alliance, more than $45 billion in trade traffic flowed south from the city to Mexico; by 2005, the Free Trade Alliance estimates that nearly $98 billion will be exported through the city. Similarly, in 1995 over $53 billion was imported through San Antonio from Mexico; by 2005 a projected $93 billion is expected. Half of all the US-Mexico trade travels through the city on highway and rail, according to the Chamber of Commerce.

To encourage international trade, San Antonio is also home to several foreign trade zones. Kelly USA, originally Kelly Air Force Base, is one of 10 locations in the city designated a Foreign Trade Zone which offer reduced customs duties and government excise taxes for foreign merchandise. The zones are not open to the public. The Free Trade Alliance (210-229-9036, www.freetradealliance.org) has International Business Development Center (IBDC) offices at Kelly designed to encourage and assist foreign companies who want to do business in the United States. This is all part of the Inland Port San Antonio project designed to make the city an inland port for international trade; the project is a joint effort of the Free Trade Alliance, the Greater San Antonio Chamber of Commerce, the City of San Antonio, the San Antonio Hispanic Chamber of Commerce, the San Antonio Economic Development Foundation, the Bexar Metropolitan Water System, and more than 600 local businesses and individual members.

Along with the Free Trade Alliance, several other international trade organizations work in San Antonio to assist import and export of goods. The International Trade Center at the University of Texas at San Antonio (210-458-2470) works to help small and medium-size businesses in the region with international trade issues. The International Affairs Department of the City of San Antonio (210-207-8100) assists in matching local companies with international markets. BANCOMEXT, the Trade Commission of Mexico (210-281-9748), works to promote investment. For San Antonio businesses interested in doing business in Mexico, and Mexican businesses interested in doing business in San Antonio, Casa San Antonio (210-297-8100) has offices in Mexico City, Monterrey, and Guadalajara to assist in the efforts.

In addition to trade with Latin America, San Antonio also has a growing trade with China. According to the Chamber of Commerce, more than 1,700 jobs in the city are directly related to trade in China. Companies in San Antonio import numerous products from China, especially eyewear, footwear, toys, and luggage.

Biomedical Industries

The health-care industry is one of the city's top employers, bringing close to $3 billion into the region every year in the form of payrolls and $10 billion (in terms of local impact).

The military health-care system includes three centers: Brooke Army Medical Center, Wilford Hall Medical Center, and the South Texas Veterans Health Care System. Brooke Army Medical Center is known throughout the state for its burn treatment and research facilities. Wilford Hall Medical Center is the largest medical facility under the umbrella of the U.S. Air Force. Not only military personnel are served by this center, however; the hospital also provides a quarter of all the emergency health care in the city.

The South Texas Veterans Health Care System is home to geriatric health-care facilities and also has one of the largest fungus-identification labs in the world. The South Texas Medical Center, located on the northwest side of the city, is one of the state's most extensive facilities, encompassing 11 hospitals, nearly 80 clinics, and many agencies.

Language

English is the official language of San Antonio but Spanish ranks a close second. Many businesses, especially in the tourism industry, have employees who speak fluent Spanish to assist the large number of tourists and business travelers who come to the city from neighboring Mexico.

Government

San Antonio operates with a council-manager form of government. Eleven elected members make up the city council; this includes 10 members elected by districts and the mayor, who is elected by the city at large.

City council members have two-year terms; they may serve up to two terms. The mayor also has a two-year term and may serve up to two terms.

San Antonio Vital Statistics

San Antonio Mayor: Ed Garza

Texas Governor: Rick Perry

Population: San Antonio: 1,192,300
Metro area: 1,606,100
State: 20,851,820

Area (sq. miles): 417.1

Nickname: The Alamo City

Average Temperatures: July: 95 degrees
January: 62 degrees

Average Annual Rain/Days of Sunshine: 28 inches/300

San Antonio Founded: 1718

Texas Achieved Statehood: 1845

Major Universities:
Our Lady of the Lake University, St. Mary's University, San Antonio College, Trinity University, University of the Incarnate Word, University of Texas at San Antonio, University of Texas Health Science Center

Major Area Employers:
Baptist Healthcare System, Bexar County, Brooke Army Medical Center, CHRISTUS Santa Rosa Health Care, Citicorp Data Systems, City of San Antonio, H.E.B. Grocery Company, Methodist Healthcare System, Northside Independent School District, Randolph Air Force Base, San Antonio Air Logistics Center, San Antonio Independent School District, San Antonio Marriott Lodging, SBC Communications, SeaWorld San Antonio, Six Flags Fiesta Texas, Southwest Research Institute, Ultramar Diamond Shamrock Corporation, United Services Automobile Association (USAA), University Health System, University of Texas at San Antonio University of Texas Health Science Center.

Famous Sons and Daughters:
Carol Burnett, Henry Cisneros, Joan Crawford, Heloise, Shaquille O'Neal, George Strait

State/City Holidays:

January 1	New Year's Day
January 19	Confederate Heroes Day
3rd Monday in January	Martin Luther King's Birthday
3rd Monday in February	Presidents' Day
March 2	Texas Independence Day
March 31	Cesar Chavez Day
March/April (varies)	Good Friday
April 21	San Jacinto Day
Last Monday in May	Memorial Day
June 19	Emancipation Day
July 4	Independence Day
August 27	Lyndon B. Johnson's Birthday
First Monday in September	Labor Day
September (varies)	Rosh Hashanah
October (varies)	Yom Kippur
November 11	Veterans' Day
Fourth Thursday in November	Thanksgiving
Friday after Thanksgiving	
December 24–26	Christmas

Resources and Visitors Centers

San Antonio Convention and Visitors Bureau
203 S. St. Mary's St., Second floor
San Antonio, TX 78205
(210) 207–6700, (800) 447–3372
www.SanAntonioCVB.com

San Antonio Convention and Visitors Bureau Visitors Center
317 Alamo Plaza
(210) 207–6748

Greater San Antonio Chamber of Commerce
P.O. Box 1628
602 E. Commerce St.
San Antonio, TX 78296
(210) 229–2100
www.sachamber.org

Major Airports/Major Interstates:

Air service is via the San Antonio International Airport. Interstate 10, Interstate 35, Interstate 37, Loop 410, and Loop 1604 provide access into and across the city. There are no toll roads in Bexar County.

Public Transportation:

San Antonio's VIA Metropolitan Transit serves the entire region. Call (210) 227–2020 for route information. VIAtrans (210–227–5371) offers transportation for mobility-impaired riders.

Military Bases:

Brooks Air Force Base, Fort Sam Houston, Kelly Air Force Base, Lackland Air Force Base, and Randolph Air Force Base

Driving Laws:

Seat belts must be worn in the front seats of cars and light trucks. Children under the age of four must be secured whether they are in the front or back seat. Infants under age two must be secured in a federally approved child-safety seat; children between ages two and four may be secured in a safety seat or with a safety belt. The fine for failure to use seat belts or child safety seats is $25 to $50. Automobile insurance is required and proof of insurance must be furnished if requested by a police officer. The maximum speed limit on Texas highways is 70 miles per hour during daytime hours, 65 m.p.h. at night.

Alcohol Laws:

You must be 21 to drink in Texas. Beer and wine purchases can be made after noon on Sunday and at any time other days of the week. Liquor can be purchased between 10:00 A.M. and 9:00 P.M. Monday through Saturday. Bars are open until 2:00 A.M. In

Texas the legal limit for blood-alcohol content for drivers is .08. Texas has a no-tolerance policy toward minors who drink and drive; while driving, minors cannot have any detectable amount of alcohol in their systems.

Daily Newspapers:
San Antonio Express-News, Daily Commercial Recorder

Sales Tax:
The hotel-occupancy tax is 15 percent. A state retail tax of 6.25 percent is levied on most retail purchases except food and drugs. The City of San Antonio levies a retail sales tax of 1 percent on all items except groceries, prescription drugs, rent, mortgage payments, and gasoline. The Metropolitan Transit Authority levies a .5 percent sales tax in the cities of San Antonio, Balcones Heights, Castle Hills, Olmos Park, Alamo Heights, Terrell Hills, Leon Valley, and others.

Time/Temperature Information:
(210) 226–3232

Getting Here, Getting Around

San Antonio lies at the gateway to South Texas, but the city is tied by interstate highways to all areas of the state and beyond. Drive to San Antonio from other regions in the state and you'll quickly get an understanding of the term "Texas-size." East of the city, Houston lies about three hours away. Austin is just over an hour's drive to the north, while Dallas and Fort Worth represent more than a five-hour haul up I-35. To the south of San Antonio lies the Gulf Coast, which can be enjoyed in getaways like Corpus Christi, just over two hours away, and South Padre Island, located in the far southern reaches of the state and more than a four-hour drive away.

West of San Antonio lies Mexico, separated from the city by miles of sparsely developed land known as the brush country. Despite its lack of development, however, the stretch of road from San Antonio to Laredo is more popular than ever, thanks to increased commerce between the United States and Mexico. The North American Free Trade Agreement (NAFTA) has resulted in not only more business for San Antonio and Mexico but also more traffic along I-35.

I-35 may be one of the most congested of the city's highways, but it is just one of four busy interstates. San Antonio's spaghetti bowl of highways can seem daunting, so take a deep breath.

Think of San Antonio as a wagon wheel, with the downtown district at its center. Four interstate highways, five U.S. highways, and five state highways form a myriad of spokes. Most of these slice through the downtown area. Two form the inner and outer rims of the wheel, however; these are the city's loops. Loop 410 (or I-410) lassoes the prime development in town, passing the San Antonio International Airport and skirting near all of the city's military bases. Loop 1604 traces the outside perimeter of the city, forming a boundary between the city and the untamed Hill Country, where white-tailed deer still roam.

Interstate highways divide San Antonio into several areas. I-35 runs an S-shaped curve through the city from northeast to southwest, skirting the downtown area. This mega-highway travels to Laredo at its southern end and reaches as far as Duluth, Minnesota, in its northern regions. I-10, which originates in Los Angeles, runs northwest to downtown before taking an easterly turn toward its final stop in Jacksonville, Florida. And I-37 defines the eastern boundary of downtown before veering off to the south and down to the coastal city of Corpus Christi. (Further confusing drivers, I-37 and I-35 are the same highway in the downtown region.)

Five U.S. highways also call on the Alamo City. U.S. 281, which originates in Hansboro, North Dakota, swings through the city near the San Antonio International Airport on its way south to McAllen, Texas. U.S.

> **Insiders' Tip**
>
> Auto insurance is required of all drivers in Texas. If stopped by a police officer, you will have to produce proof of auto insurance.

90, which starts in Jacksonville, Florida, overlaps with I-10 as it approaches the city from the east and crosses the city before branching off and heading west to Van Horn, Texas. U.S. 87, originating in Raton, New Mexico, also overlaps with I-10 in the western portion of the city before branching off to the east and making its way south to Port Lavaca, Texas. U.S. 181 (not to be confused with U.S. 281) originates in San Antonio and travels to Corpus Christi via Beeville. Finally, U.S. 81 also originates in San Antonio and travels to Laredo, overlapping with I-35.

For the purposes of this guidebook, we have divided San Antonio into sections that are defined by the highways you'll encounter on your trip. Our first section is downtown, an area bounded by I-35, I-37, and I-10. This region encompasses many of tourist highlights such as the Alamo, the River Walk, Market Square, HemisFair Plaza, and more.

The second section is the area inside and around Loop 410. This area takes in both sides of Loop 410 and everything inside, with the exception of the downtown area covered in the first section. In this area, you'll find Brackenridge Park, Fort Sam Houston, and the San Antonio International Airport.

The third section is the fast-growing region beyond Loop 410 and Loop 1604, including the theme parks and the outer fringes of San Antonio, where the city meets the country.

By Air

San Antonio doesn't rank as a hub airport (Dallas and Houston both serve as Texas hubs) but getting to the city is fairly simple, whether your chosen mode of transportation is airplane, car, bus, or train. The city is home to an international airport and, thanks to its close ties with Mexico, offers many flights to and from destinations south of the border.

San Antonio International Airport

Located 13 miles from downtown San Antonio, the San Antonio International Airport (9800 Airport Boulevard, 210-207-3450, www.ci.sat.tx.us/aviation) is where most air travelers begin their visit to the city. The airport is convenient to all areas of town thanks to its location on Loop 410, which links to I-37, the direct highway into downtown.

San Antonio International Airport sees more than seven million domestic passengers every year as well nearly a quarter of a million international passengers. The number of planes coming and going is on the increase, as is the number of passengers who travel through this busy airport.

When you deplane, you'll find yourself in one of two airport terminals, each an easy walk from the other. Terminal One is home to Aerolitoral, Atlantic Southeast, Delta, Mexicana, Midwest Express, Northwest/KLM, Southwest, and United. Terminal Two, located to the west of Terminal One, is home to Aeromar, America West, American, Continental, and TWA.

Have questions? You can ask one of the members of the SAT Ambassadors program. These volunteers are community members who donate at least four hours of their time every week to assist passengers and to welcome them to the Alamo City. The Ambassadors are easy to spot: look for a denim vest, Western hat, a

Insiders' Tip

Plan to return to the San Antonio International Airport at least one hour before your scheduled flight (two hours if you are traveling internationally).

black or beige shirt, black or khaki pants, a name tag, and a smile.

The airport will be undergoing a $27.5-million face-lift and expansion of Terminal One and Terminal Two. One of the biggest changes will be The Shops at River Landing, more than 10,000 square feet of new retail space in Terminal One with both national chains and local stores. Other Terminal One renovations include improvements to the food court, the addition of a second food court with five tenants, and revamped gate areas, ticket area, and concourse area. Terminal Two is getting a new food court, new food and beverage carts, and remodeled retail space.

Flight Times to San Antonio

From Atlanta 2.5 hours
From Chicago 2 hours
From Las Vegas 2.3 hours
From Los Angeles 2.75 hours
From Miami 3.5 hours
From Nashville 2.5 hours
From New Orleans 2.5 hours
From New York 3 hours
From Orlando 2.75 hours
From St. Louis 2.3 hours
From San Francisco 4 hours
From Seattle 4.5 hours
From Washington, D.C. 5 hours

Nonstop service makes the travel time much shorter to and from some cities; you can catch a nonstop flight to San Antonio from Atlanta, Chicago, Las Vegas, Los Angeles, New York, Orlando, and St. Louis.

Commercial Airline Telephone Reservation Numbers

Aerolitoral (800) 237–6639
Aeromar (210) 829–7482
American (800) 433–7300
America West (800) 235–9292
ASA (800) 221–1212
Continental (800) 525–0280
Delta (800) 221–1212
Mexicana (800) 531–7921
Midwest Express (800) 452–2022
Northwest (800) 225–2525
Southwest (800) 435–9792

Sun Country (800) 359–6786
TransWorld (800) 221–2000
United (800) 241–6522

Airport Parking

San Antonio International Airport has more than 6,000 parking spaces. Parking rates are divided into three categories: short-term, long-term, and shuttle or economy. Short-term parking costs a maximum of $18.00 per twenty-four-hour day; long-term parking is a maximum of $7.00 per twenty-four-hour day; and economy/shuttle parking costs no more than $4.00 per day. Transportation between the economy lot and the terminals is free; the first half hour of parking at all of the lots is also free. Airport police patrol each of the lots and can provide free battery jumps if needed; if you were in a hurry and locked your keys in your car, they'd help with that as well. Parking for disabled drivers and passengers is available in each of the lots. Payment for parking can be made with credit card; American Express, Discover, MasterCard, and Visa are accepted.

Renting a Car at the San Antonio International Airport

Several auto rental companies have booths at the San Antonio Airport; these are located near the baggage-claim area on the first level of each terminal. Restrictions vary by company but all require a current driver's license; some have an age restriction of 25 years or older. Many companies will not allow their cars to be driven into Mexico.

Many of the companies listed offer a range of compact to luxury cars and minivans; free mileage; daily, weekly, and monthly rates; and special discounts for seniors and military personnel.

Ace
**8620 Jones Maltsberger Rd., San Antonio
(210) 340–8267**

Located one mile from the airport, this rental company offers free airport pickup.

Advantage Rent A Car
(210) 341–8211, (800) 777–5500
www.advantagerentacar.com

This company has a site in the airport and offers free pickup service.

Enterprise Rent-A-Car
10150 U.S. 281 N. San Antonio
(210) 348–6806, (800) RENT–A–CAR
www.enterprise.com

With locations throughout the region, Enterprise also has an airport location. Free pickup is available; this company also offers Mexican auto insurance.

Hertz
10219 John Saunders Rd., San Antonio
(210) 841–8800, (800) 654–3131
www.hertz.com

Hertz offers airport terminal pickup and 24-hour emergency roadside assistance.

Lone Star Rent A Car
(210) 826–5551, (877) 368–2973

With locations around the city, this company, a franchisee of the Rent A Wreck company, also has a site near the airport, with pickup service available. Cash customers are welcome.

National Car Rental
(210) 824–7544, (800) CAR–RENT
www.nationalcar.com

Located at the airport, National Car Rental offers discounts to a variety of groups.

Posada Car Rental
119 N.E. Loop 410, San Antonio
(210) 349–8990, (800) 395–9227

This local company provides free shuttle-bus service to and from the airport. It also offers special discounts for stays in airport hotels including the Pear Tree Inn, Posada Ana Inn, Holiday Inn Express, Drury Inn & Suites, Staybridge Suites, and Hampton Inn.

Thrifty Car Rental
(210) 342–2097, (800) THRIFTY
www.thrifty.com

Located at the airport, Thrifty offers a number of discount rates.

Shuttle Service

Shuttle service is available to most areas of the city. Some hotels offer free shuttle service for their guests; the pickup location for these shuttles is just outside the baggage-claim area of each terminal. There are commercial shuttle services as well.

SATRANS
1331 N. Pine St., San Antonio
(210) 281–9900, (800) 868–7707
www.saairportshuttle.com

This service provides transportation between the airport and downtown hotels. A one-way ticket is $8.00; a round-trip ticket can also be purchased for $14.00. Minibuses offer ADA-accessible transportation to local hotels and other area destinations.

Taxi Service

Transportation into the downtown area is available by taxicabs, which offer metered service. The cost of a trip from the airport to the downtown area is about $14 plus tip; plan on about a 15-minute ride, depending on traffic.

The fee is based on a rate of $1.50 per mile during daytime hours (5:00 A.M. to 9:00 P.M.); there's an additional $1.00 fee at other times. Additional passengers are not charged.

Insiders' Tip

Right turn on red is permitted through the city unless otherwise indicated.

If you're traveling with a large family or a group, large minivans are also available for up to seven passengers; plan on about $15 for the one-way trip.

General Aviation

San Antonio International Airport
9800 Airport Blvd., San Antonio
(210) 207–3450
www.ci.sat.tx.us/aviation
San Antonio International Airport serves as a U.S. Point of Entry, so private planes coming into the country can make this their first stop. (Private planes once had to clear customs in Laredo or Brownsville, but a 2000 law made the facility a point of entry for airplanes whose final destination is San Antonio.) Customs facilities are available from 8:00 A.M. to 10:00 P.M.; notification must be made to the San Antonio Customs office at (210) 821-6965 no less than one hour before the aircraft enters U.S. airspace. (The penalty for failure to do so is up to $5,000.) Pilots can also fax Customs Form 178 PAES (Private Aircraft Enforcement System) to the San Antonio Customs office at (210) 821-6968 before departure. Even if San Antonio isn't a final destination, an Overnight Exemption has to be filed with the U.S. Customs office prior to a visit.

Stinson Municipal Airport
8619 Mission Rd., San Antonio
(210) 924–6634
For most travelers arriving by private plane from U.S. departure points, Stinson Municipal Airport is the port of entry into San Antonio. This airport is the second-oldest general-aviation airport in continuous operation in the country. Located south of downtown on Mission Road, it is about 10 minutes from downtown and 14 miles south of the San Antonio International Airport.

The airfield has two runways, each 100 feet long. Air-traffic control is attended from 7:00 A.M. to 9:00 P.M. daily. The Stinson Field Café is open daily except Monday for breakfast and lunch.

> ## Insiders' Tip
> Never leave children or pets inside a closed car. The interior of a vehicle in San Antonio can quickly soar to oven-like temperatures.

You might have occasion to visit Stinson even if you don't come in by private plane. The airfield is the home of the Texas Air Museum, which traces the history of aviation in San Antonio; a rare German Folke-Wulf 190 aircraft is displayed there.

By Land

Once you are in San Antonio, there are many transportation options ranging from cars to carriages. The city also offers excellent bus and trolley service; the latter is a great way to see the downtown area without the headache of finding a parking place.

Driving in San Antonio can be a challenge, especially in the downtown area, thanks to the numerous one-way streets. With some of the oldest streets in the state, San Antonio doesn't follow a grid system, but instead offers a meandering collection of byways that trace the river's passage through the city. An assortment of high-rise buildings add to the confusion—sometimes your destination is just a block away, but lies out of sight and seemingly out of reach.

What's the solution? Park and walk. Parking lots are sprinkled downtown; rates are sometimes by the day and sometimes by the hour. Don't park "just for a few minutes" without paying; you will be towed.

Covered parking garages are a blessing during the hot summer months. These are more expensive but help prevent "skillet steering wheel"—a common hazard when your car sits in that blazing sun for a few hours. (A quick look around uncovered parking lots reveals that local residents use cardboard windshield shades religiously to avoid literally being in the hot seat upon their return.) You'll find covered parking garages at many of the downtown hotels (they are available to nonguests for a fee) and at sites such as Rivercenter Mall.

Once you've parked, you'll find much of downtown is easily accessible on foot. Strolling the River Walk is a real San Antonio pleasure; temperatures there are several degrees below those at street level. By walking the River Walk, you'll be able to reach the Alamo and many of the attractions found nearby. When it's time to branch out, hop aboard a trolley; the VIA San Antonio streetcars link the main tourist sites.

For all its major highways (and, occasionally, major traffic), touring San Antonio is easily accomplished because, although the city is vast, most attractions are grouped in a few areas. Downtown sightseeing starts at Alamo Plaza, home of the Alamo and birthplace not only of Texas liberty but also of San Antonio tourism. Here you can take guided tours, a city bus or trolley, or just enjoy a stroll through the area. Behind Alamo Plaza lies the Paseo del Rio or River Walk, one of the most-visited spots in Texas. Located below street level, the river banks are lined with sidewalk cafes and specialty shops.

On one edge of the River Walk rests La Villita, the "little village" that was the original settlement in Old San Antonio. Here the wares of many of the city's artisans are displayed and sold in historic structures.

La Villita sits in the shadow of the 750-foot Tower of the Americas, where you can enjoy the best view of the city from the observation deck, a revolving restaurant, or the bar and disco. The tower was built as the symbol of HemisFair, the 1968 World's Fair. The tower is located in HemisFair Park, the fairgrounds, which now sport a fresh look following a recent facelift and the addition of restful water gardens. Nearby, the Henry B. Gonzales Convention Center, one of the state's busiest meeting facilities, hosts thousands of conventioneers each year.

Directly south of the River Walk lies the King William Historic District, home of the city's stately mansions built during the nineteenth century. This area is a favorite of bed-and-breakfast lovers.

West of the River Walk area, a quick ride by trolley or car, is Market Square, the most Mexican attraction in town. Here you can shop for imports in El Mercado (the largest Mexican marketplace in the United States), dine on a Tex-Mex feast, or tour some nearby historic buildings.

Along Broadway, north of downtown, lie many of San Antonio's museums and

Specially designated paths along the River Walk aid wheelchair users and parents with strollers.

PHOTO: PARIS PERMENTER & JOHN BIGLEY

VIA trolleys whisk visitors around downtown San Antonio. PHOTO: PARIS PERMENTER & JOHN BIGLEY

outdoor attractions. Brackenridge Park, home of the city's zoo and Japanese gardens, awaits just minutes from downtown.

If you continue north on Broadway to the intersection of Loop 410, then turn west to the intersection with U.S. 281, you come to the San Antonio International Airport, where many visitors begin and end their stay. This also is the site of some of the city's best shopping areas, from big-name department stores such as Saks Fifth Avenue and Marshall Field's to small import shops and art galleries.

South of downtown, the Mission Trail holds many attractions, especially for history buffs. Along this historic route, you can tour four Spanish missions, each still open for Sunday services.

On the northwest side of town, along Loop 1604, lie two of Texas's top family attractions: Six Flags Fiesta Texas and Sea-World of Texas. In spring through fall, these parks are filled with tourists from around the United States and Mexico who come to enjoy thrill rides, musical productions, and marine animal shows.

Trolleys

VIA Downtown Trolleys
(210) 362–2020
www.viainfo.net

Downtown trolleys, constructed like old-fashioned streetcars but with rubber tires, are a fun and inexpensive way to explore the downtown area. The red, yellow, purple, and blue trolley lines serve four routes and stop at all major downtown attractions. The fare of 50 cents is a bargain, and you also purchase a monthly streetcar pass for $10 if you think you'll be riding a great deal. You can pay by cash, with a streetcar token, or with a streetcar pass. Discounts are available for seniors, children, those with impaired mobility, and Medicare recipients. Transfers between the streetcars are free, and the lines intersect at several points in town.

If you'd like to park your car and ride the trolleys, you'll find free parking at VIA's Ellis Alley Park and Ride east of downtown at Chestnut and Ellis Alley.

From the parking lot, you can take the yellow streetcar line to the downtown area.

The Blue Line travels from downtown to the southern areas of the city. Stops include the Alamo, Blue Star Arts Complex, Central Library, Henry B. Gonzales Convention Center, HemisFair Park, the King William Historic District, La Villita, Municipal Auditorium, Rivercenter Mall, the San Antonio Information Center, and Southtown. The Blue Line runs weekdays from 7:00 A.M. to 9:00 P.M. and weekends 9:00 A.M. to 9:00 P.M.

The Yellow Line stops at the Alamodome, the Ellis Alley Park and Ride at St. Paul Square (for free parking for VIA customers), the convention center, El Mercado-Market Square, the Institute of Texan Cultures, Rivercenter Mall, St. Paul Square, Sunset Station, and the Tower of the Americas. The Yellow Line runs Monday through Thursday 7:00 A.M. to 10:30 P.M., Friday 7:00 to 12:30 A.M., Saturday 9:00 to 12:30 A.M., and Sunday 9:00 A.M. to 10:30 P.M.

Red Line stops include the Alamo, the convention center, El Mercado-Market Square, HemisFair Park, La Villita, the Rivercenter Mall, and the San Antonio Information Center. Hours for this route are weekdays 7:00 A.M. to 10:30 P.M. and weekends from 9:00 A.M. to 10:30 P.M.

The Purple Route includes the Alamodome, the convention center, El Mercado-Market Square, HemisFair Park, the Institute of Texan Cultures, La Villita, Rivercenter Mall, and the Tower of the Americas. These trolleys operate from 9:00 A.M. to 7:30 P.M. Monday through Saturday only.

Buses and Shuttles

VIA Metropolitan Transit Service
(210) 362–2020
www.viainfo.net

The metropolitan transit authority in San Antonio and Bexar County is known as VIA. Created by election in 1977, the system is funded through a one-half-cent sales tax and spans more than 1,200 square miles.

The buses operate every day from 5:00 A.M. to midnight, serving the region with more than 100 scheduled lines. The lines are divided into categories: radial, limited stop, express, crosstown, circulator, and streetcar. Radial lines buses (route numbers 1 to 99) service the central district and travel major streets. Limited-stop buses stop only at a few bus stops, even though they travel much of the same routes as the radial line buses. Express lines are nonstop; these service park and ride centers and transfer stations. Crosstown buses run (yes, you guessed it) across town; these buses have route numbers in the 500s. Circulator buses serve the residential areas and have

Many of the VIA trolleys stop at the San Antonio Information Center, across the street from Alamo Plaza. PHOTO: PARIS PERMENTER & JOHN BIGLEY

600 route numbers. Streetcars are covered in the previous "Trolley" section.

Bus fares vary by type of route. The full fare for a local or limited-stop bus is 75 cents. Express-bus service is $1.60. Bus transfers are 15 cents. Reduced fares for senior citizens age 62 and over, persons with disabilities, students, and children age 5 to 11 are 35 cents per limited-stop bus ride and 75 cents per express-bus ride. Off-peak reduced fares for senior citizens and people with disabilities are available weekdays from 9:00 A.M. to 3:00 P.M. and all day weekends; these fares are for fixed routes only.

Which bus do you want? You'll find bus information centers through town. VIA's Downtown Information Center, located at 112 Soledad Street, is open daily except Sunday. Other information centers are found at the Crossroads Park and Ride, 151 Crossroads Boulevard (210–735–3317); Ingram Transit Center, 3215 Northwestern Drive (210–509–1766); and the Randolph Park and Ride, 9400 I–35 N (210–599–3643).

You can also call VIAINFO at (210) 362–2020; it's an automated information system that has information in both English and Spanish. To speak to a live representative, call (210) 362–2020 or TDD (210) 362–2019.

More than 40 sites in the city, ranging from the airport to malls to local universities, also house computerized information kiosks. San Antonio was one of four cities in the country selected by the Federal Highway Administration to receive funding under the Model Deployment Initiative program to help reduce congestion. Part of that program is the development of kiosks with touch-screen monitors. The computers supply bus route and schedule information as well as details on fares. Printouts of the information can be produced along with route maps and the locations of the nearest bus stops. The kiosks also supply information on weather, current traffic conditions, directions, special events, airport information, and points of interest.

For riders with disabilities, VIA has some buses with ramps; most have floors at curb level. VIA also operates VIAtrans for residents with disabilities and their personal-care attendants. To apply to use this minivan service, call the VIA Accessible Services Office at (210) 362–2140; applications are also available online at www.viainfo.net/accessible services/apps. html. Once admitted to the program, riders can schedule rides on VIAtrans minivans; reservations must be made at least twenty-four hours but not more than twelve days before a trip. The fee for VIAtrans rides is $1.25 per one-way trip. If you travel outside the VIAtrans service area, there is an additional $4.00 surcharge each way. (The VIAtrans service area is inside I–410.) No fare is charged for personal-care attendants, but companions pay the $1.25 base fare and $4.00 surcharge, if applicable.

If you are approved for use of a VIAtrans-type service in your home city and you're visiting San Antonio, you will qualify for use of VIAtrans; qualified visitors may use the system for up to 21 days. Call the VIA Accessible Services Office for more information.

Greyhound Bus Terminal
500 N. St. Mary's St., San Antonio
(800) 231–2222
www.greyhound.com

This bus terminal serves several commercial bus lines: Greyhound, Kerrville, Painter, and Valley Transit. Bus service throughout the state with connections around the country is available.

The bus terminal includes a food-service facility that's open around the clock, a Western Union station, and shuttle service to and from the San Antonio International Airport. The terminal also has a military-sponsored shuttle service to the city's military facilities. These shuttles run from 6:00 A.M. to 10:00 P.M.

The second-oldest terminal in the Greyhound system, the building has an interesting history. Constructed in 1945, it showcases a 40-by-8-foot mural that illustrates the Hispanic heritage of San Antonio since the 1600s. The artwork was the collaboration of the San Antonio Cultural Arts Center and the Guadalupe Cultural Arts Center.

Taxis

Taxi service is available from the airport. Metered cab service costs $1.60 for the first mile and $1.50 for each subsequent mile. The average one-way fare from the airport to downtown hotels is about $14 plus tip. Four passengers can ride for the price of one. Outside the airport, taxis can be found at most major hotels, although you may need to call for service.

San Antonio Taxis
(210) 444–2222

This company offers citywide pickups as well as out-of-town service. Reservations are accepted, and payment can be made by credit card.

Yellow Checker Cab
(210) 222–2222

Reservations are accepted by this company, which offers around-the-clock service. Four passengers ride for the price of one in all cabs; credit cards are accepted.

Train Service

Amtrak
350 Hoefgen Ave., San Antonio
(210) 223–3226, (800) USA–RAIL
www.texaseagle.com

Amtrak is served by a new station in St. Paul's Square, located between the Sunset Station entertainment complex and the Alamodome. This convenient location makes the train an easy way to get right to the heart of the city.

The San Antonio station is a daily stop for the *Texas Eagle,* which travels between Chicago and San Antonio; stops include Ft. Worth, Little Rock, and St. Louis. Several days a week, the *Sunset Limited* pulls into the station. This train travels between Orlando and Los Angeles, with stops in Biloxi, New Orleans, Houston, El Paso, Tucson, and Palm Springs.

The *Texas Eagle* has split-level Superliner cars. You can book a coach seat or a

Amtrak passengers arrive at Sunset Station, located in downtown San Antonio. PHOTO: PARIS PERMENTER & JOHN BIGLEY

sleeping compartment. For the price of a sleeping compartment you also get complimentary meals served in your "room"; a daily newspaper each morning; baggage assistance; turn-down service; and admission to Amtrak's Metropolitan Lounge in Chicago's Union Station. The train also includes a dining car, a smoking lounge, and a lounge for sightseeing (and movies at night).

Travel on Amtrak can be booked by calling the Amtrak reservation number above (you can pick up tickets are your nearest rail station or have them mailed to you), online at reservations.amtrak.com, or through a travel agent.

Parking at the station is fairly limited, just 18 on-site spaces for pickup and drop-off only. You'll find short-term and long-term parking at the Marina Parking Garage, four blocks from station. Parking costs $4.50 per day.

The station is open from midnight to 2:00 P.M. daily.

Limos

AAA Limousine and Sedan Service
2668 Austin Hwy., San Antonio
(210) 227–5466
www.limomax.com

How would you like to tour San Antonio in a super-stretch Hummer? AAA has one for hire, along with classic limos, each equipped with a color TV, VCR, DVD, CD player, fiber optics, a mirrored ceiling, neon lighting, an intercom system, privacy partitions, and a full bar. The limos are available for everything from airport transfers to wedding parties and city touring.

Abbey Walker Executive Cars & Limousines
(210) 341–6000, (800) 341–6000
www.abbeywalker.com

Owned and operated by Star Shuttle, this company has a fleet of Lincoln Town Cars and extended limousines. All drivers are uniformed professionals, and this service is a member of the National Limousine Association. City tours and airport transfers can be arranged as well as transportation for proms, weddings, anniversaries, and other special events.

Arrow—The Limousine Co.
2403 Broadway, San Antonio
(210) 491–9555

Both classic limos and vintage Rolls Royce limos are offered by this company. Special rates are available on weekdays and for special events; corporate rates are also offered.

Carey/River City Limo, Inc.
2444 Brockton, San Antonio
(210) 525–0007

San Antonio's oldest limo company has a fleet of limousines as well as sedans, minibuses, and luxury vans. Cellular-phone rentals can also be handled through the company.

Corporate Limousine
651 Overhill Dr., San Antonio
(210) 438–9929

Affiliated with Boston Coach, this company offers airport transfers, city tours, and special-occasion transportation for weddings, proms, concerts, and more. Several employees speak Spanish.

Dunnewood Limousine, Inc.
435 Isom Rd., Suite 222, San Antonio
(210) 699–4855
www.dunnewoodlimousine.com

A member of the National Limousine Association and the Greater San Antonio Chamber of Commerce, Dunnewood offers airport pickup in limousines, sedans, vans, and minivans. City tours and Hill Country tours can be arranged, too.

Water Taxis

Yanaguana Cruises, Inc.
315 E. Commerce, Suite 202, San Antonio
(210) 244–5700, (800) 417–4139
www.sarivercruise.com

Yanaguana Cruises operates guided cruises along the San Antonio River (see "Tours" in the Attractions chapter for more information on these pleasant excursions) but they also operate the Rio Trans, a river shuttle. The shuttle is a great way for conventioneers to get to a River Walk eatery or for hotel guests on the far reaches of the River Walk to reach the more bustling areas without ever venturing up to street level. It's far more pleasant than standing on the street corner shouting "Taxi!"

The river taxis make nine stops along the route. You'll need to buy a ticket in advance, because boat drivers cannot accept cash. You can purchase a ticket from Yanaguana Cruises or at most of the businesses along and near the Rio Trans stops.

Shuttle stops are the Four Points Sheraton, IBC Center, Hyatt, Marriott Riverwalk, convention center, La Villita, Tower Life Building, Mexican Manhattan, and Adam's Mark Hotel. Rio Trans signs identify each of the water-taxi stops.

A one-way pass on the shuttle is $3.50; an all-day pass (which runs through the business day, not twenty-four hours from purchase) costs $10.00. Three-day passes are available for $25.00. Taxis run from 9:00 A.M. to 9:00 P.M. and generally come by every twenty minutes.

Horse-Drawn Carriages

Lone Star Carriage
302 Iowa St., San Antonio
(210) 533–3977, (210) 656–7527
Downtown tours as well as hotel pickups and wedding and other special-event transportation is available through this carriage company.

Yellow Rose Carriage
100 S. Alamo St., San Antonio
(210) 337–6495
www.yellowrosecarriage.com
Established in 1982, Yellow Rose Carriage provides romantic rides through the downtown district in reproduction Victorian-style carriages. Most carriages are pulled by large draft horses.

From May through September, the carriage typically operates from 7:00 P.M. to midnight; other months, rides are available from 6:00 P.M. to midnight. Special arrangements can be made for pickups at other times.

Prices vary by ride but start at $25 per couple for a short tour of Alamo Plaza, $45 for a long tour of Alamo Plaza, and $65 for a tour of King William Historic District from Alamo Plaza. With each couple, one child under the age of ten can ride free of charge.

Motorcycle Rentals

Street Eagle of San Antonio, Texas
903 E. Nakoma, Suite 102, San Antonio
(210) 496–0880, (877) 931–7433
www.streeteagle.com
This dealer has a wide selection of Harleys from which to choose. Rental periods can range from 90 minutes ($45) to a full day ($99).

Texas Motorcycle Rentals
18902 Broadway, San Antonio
(210) 805–0777, (877) 2MR–CYCLES
www.tmrentals.com
Texas Motorcycle Rentals features premium motorcycle rentals with a fleet that includes BMW, Harley-Davidson, and other motorcycles. Both half- and full-day rentals are available, and the company can provide luggage storage during the rental period.

History

The Spanish explorers and conquistadors who followed in the footsteps of Álvar Núñez Cabeza de Vaca had dreams of gold, of cities full of gold: enough gold to fund Spain's far-flung empire for years, enough to build Christian missions in the vast wilderness, enough to finance Spanish armies and navies. Cabeza de Vaca himself had not seen the fabled Las Siete Cuidades Doradas de Cibola (Seven Cities of Gold). Indeed, what the Spanish explorer had seen in eight years of wandering after being shipwrecked in Florida in 1528 was a land rich in mosquitoes and hostile inhabitants rather than precious metals.

Cabeza de Vaca and his three companions were probably the first Europeans to explore the deserts of the North American Southwest, passing through what is now Texas, New Mexico, and Arizona. The Spaniards eventually gained the trust of the natives as they undertook to heal some of the sick they encountered by invoking their faith and praying over the patients. "Our fame," he wrote, "spread throughout the area, and all the Indians who heard about it came looking for us so that we could cure them and bless their children."

Cabeza de Vaca's exact route has been debated, but by some accounts, in 1535 or so he camped in a bend of the San Antonio River where he found a friendly reception from the local inhabitants. "They indicated that they were pleased with our company and took us to their lodges . . . . The merrymaking caused by our arrival lasted three days. At the end of the three days, we asked about the country ahead." Cabeza de Vaca's band eventually found their way south to Culiacan in Mexico, where they were at last reunited with their Spanish brethren. They had found no gold, but their reports led to tantalizing rumors about vast riches to the north. One of Cabeza de Vaca's three companions, Estabanico, whom he described as a "black Arab and a native of Azamor," later volunteered to guide an expedition under Marcos de Niza to search for the treasure. Cabeza de Vaca's desultory wandering blazed a trail for several centuries of Spanish influence on the areas he visited. In some places, as in San Antonio, Hispanic influence has persisted until the present day.

The Indian village where Cabeza de Vaca tarried was not identified, but it could well have been the Payaya village of Yanaguana. It was there, in 1691, that Father Damian Masanet said Mass under the cottonwood trees for the newly installed Spanish governor, Don Domingo de Teran. The spot (and the river) were renamed San Antonio de Padua in honor of St. Anthony of Padua (as this occurred on June 13, the saint's birthday). However, the Spanish built nothing here until 1718, when Friars Antonio Olivares and Isidro Espinosa arrived to oversee the building of a new mission. It was to be named San Antonio de Valero, in honor of the Spanish viceroy of Mexico, the Marquis of Valero. At the same time, the new governor proclaimed the establishment of a new town, or villa, called San Antonio de Bexar in honor of the viceroy's brother, the Duke of Bexar, a national war hero in Spain.

They chose a lovely spot, which Padre Espinosa described as "a great shady grove of very tall pecan trees, cottonwoods, elms, and clumps of mulberries, irrigated by the water of an abundant spring."

The elegance of the Spanish colonial era surrounds visitors to the Spanish Governor's Palace.

The appeal of the location was not gold, but another precious resource in a hot, dry land: water. In addition to the river, San Antonio had numerous springs, which supported an abundance of trees and wildlife. These in turn attracted people to the area. A simple thing, but in the middle of dry, scrubby hills and rugged brush land, it seemed a miracle. To those early explorers, the spot was an oasis, and they resolved to claim it for church and crown. As Friar Olivares explained: "In this place of San Antonio there is a spring of water which is about three-fourths of a league from the principal river. In this location . . . it is easy to secure water, but nowhere else."

San Antonio was founded in 1718, the same year as was New Orleans. As French activity in Louisiana threatened to intrude upon their claims in the Southwest, the Spanish began to view the area as more than just a pleasant spot. Suddenly, the Spanish could no longer afford to ignore their hardscrabble claims north of "New Spain" (Mexico). A system of forts and missions was proposed by the Spanish crown to blockade the French from the east, to alleviate the threat of Indian attack, and ultimately, to provide the foundations for Spanish colonization of the territory. Native tribes of the area would be instructed by the friars in order to convert them to Christianity, thus making them allies of the Spanish.

San Antonio's original mission, the San Antonio de Valero, has become known as the Alamo. Since its inception in 1718, the mission has been relocated and rebuilt at least twice. The moves were conducted by Father Olivares himself; around 1720 the mission was rebuilt on the other side of the river where the soil was more fertile. After a huge storm destroyed the mission in 1724, it was again rebuilt, this time on the spot where the Alamo stands today. Although the early mission struggled, it was soon joined by several others, partly in competition, but eventually in cooperation with San Antonio de Valero. San Jose y San Miguel de Aguayo was founded in 1720, followed in 1731 by three others: San Juan Capistrano, San Francisco de la Espada, and Nuestra Señora de la Purisima Concepción. The latter three missions had been relocated from East Texas, too close to French Louisiana for comfort. At the same time that the missions were relocated, 56 colonists from the Canary Islands arrived to claim land offered by the Spanish government to encourage settlement. One family, it was said, was worth 100 soldiers in settling the frontier.

Despite numerous setbacks caused by inclement weather, disease, raids by the Apache and Comanche, and discord among the missions, the colonists, and the soldiers sent to protect them, the community of San Antonio began to grow on the bend of the San Antonio River. A visiting Frenchman, Monsieur Pages, wrote in 1768 that San Antonio was a town of some 200 houses, some constructed of stone, with the land "sloping gently to the river and commanding an agreeable prospect over the opposite grounds." Cut off from the rest of Hispanic America by hundreds of miles, San Antonio was forced to be self-sufficient in regard to food, shelter, and most everything else. In reality, the town was a collection of communities: the Canary Island colonists, the missions and the Indians they served, and the military contingent, each group more or less self sufficient, as discord prevented much cooperation.

San Antonio's most popular historical attraction is the Alamo. PHOTO: RICHARD STOCKTON, COURTESY OF THE SAN ANTONIO CONVENTION AND VISITORS BUREAU

By the 1770s, however, a serious new threat arose to encourage the town to band closer together, at least physically. The Comanche began to raid San Antonio—so effectively that they boasted that the Spanish were allowed to stay in their territory so that they could continue to raise beef and horses for the Comanche. The governor complained in 1780, "There is no time day or night when reports of barbarities and disorders do not arrive from the ranches." The Comanche were skilled fighters and raiders and could not be driven out by the small troop garrisons assigned to guard the San Antonio missions; efforts to raise more soldiers were ineffective.

In 1758, a large band of Comanche sacked the Spanish mission on the San Saba River, Santa Cruz de San Saba, killing two priests. Spanish troops pursuing the war party north were ambushed near the Red River and defeated by the Indians. The Comanche would not be pacified by payments and treaty as had the Apaches; they held the upper hand on the frontier and they knew it. Yet, somehow, the town and the missions survived and, in the face of adversity, San Antonio began to develop a character all its own.

By 1800, the town's population had reached 3,000, including more than 700 soldiers. Gradually, some of the barriers between the communities within San Antonio began to dissolve and the town's identity began to emerge: tough and self-reliant, a blend of Hispanic and Indian elements. In fact, those early inhabitants had much in common with modern-day San Antonians. But one crucial element was still missing from the melting pot and the new century would witness another invasion from the north: the coming of the Anglos.

Ironically, this movement began far to the south, where revolution brewed after centuries of Spanish rule. A parish priest in Guanajuato, Mexico, Father Miguel Hidalgo, ignited the spark by preaching revolution from the steps of his church in 1810. A long war followed, eventually drawing in even the sleepy frontier colony of San Antonio, as Royalist forces chased revolutionaries north. One such revolutionary, Benardo Gutierrez de Lara, succeeded in raising an army of American volunteers, which took San Antonio from the Spanish government forces in 1813. The revolutionaries' triumph was short-lived, however. A few months later, an army of 2000 Royalist troops crossed the Rio Grande and retook the town, destroying much of the rebel army and executing any townspeople suspected of siding with them. Many of the settlers fled to the United States to escape the purge. San Antonio's population fell drastically once again.

Eventually, even the Royalists were forced to admit that it was necessary to repopulate the area in order to stave off attacks by the still-strong Comanche. Therefore, the Royalist government was able to be persuaded when, in 1820, Moses Austin petitioned to colonize Texas with 300 American families. As Austin's son Stephen F. Austin recalled, "At the end of a week the governor and *ayuntamiento* of Bexar united in recommending a petition from my father to the [government] at Monterrey, asking for permission to introduce and settle three hundred families from the United States of America. . . . The entering wedge was thus placed for opening a legal passage for North American immigrants into Texas."

Once the petition was granted, nothing would stop the inexorable flow of immigration into Texas, not the death of Moses Austin (his son Stephen continued the project), not even a drastic change of government in Mexico (declared independent of Spain in 1821). By the early 1830s the tidal wave of new Texians (as the early settlers were called) outnumbered Hispanics by a ten to one margin. The new government in Mexico had other pressing concerns, so it allowed the Mexican colonies a high degree of self-sufficiency.

By 1835, however, that lassez-faire attitude changed as a young firebrand named Antonio Lopez de Santa Anna became president of Mexico. Santa Anna, who had earned a reputation as a tough military leader, established a stronger central government and curtailed many of the freedoms to which the Texians had grown accustomed. A showdown was inevitable, and it came swiftly as Santa Anna sent armies to deal with the rebellious colonists. On December 5, 1835, a large band of Texian volunteers led by Ben Milam attacked San Antonio, which was defended by a Mexican army under General Martin Perfecto de Cos. The fighting which lasted five days ended when the volunteers captured General Cos and forced his surrender, ending the "Battle of Bexar." The General's army was sent back to Mexico after pledging not to fight any more on Texas soil. Shortly afterward, the Texian volunteers, believing the war over, began to disperse, leaving only a small garrison of militia to guard the town.

They had not counted on Santa Anna's resolve. When General Cos's defeated army returned to Mexico, an enraged Santa Anna took personal command and promised to avenge the defeat. "I personally assembled and organized an expeditionary army of eight thousand men in Saltillo," he wrote in his autobiography. "I took command of the campaign myself, preferring the uncertainties of war to the easy and much-coveted life of the palace."

Insiders' Tip

The early settlers who came to San Antonio from the United States were called Texians by most residents as well as most Mexicans. Other names for the settlers were Texonians, Texasians, and Texicans; eventually the name was simplified to Texans.

The situation was even more uncertain for the defenders of the Alamo, numbering at most about 150, when suddenly confronted by the might of Santa Anna's army on Feb. 23, 1836. They grabbed what supplies and arms they could and took shelter behind the stone walls of the old mission, San Antonio de Valero, which had come to be known informally as "The Alamo." Thus began one of the most chronicled battles in history, a story to rival the Charge of the Light Brigade, Gettysburg, or Waterloo.

Due to the illness of Jim Bowie, sent to San Antonio by General Sam Houston of the Texian army, command of the Alamo's defenders fell to Lt. Col. William Barrett Travis, a 25-year-old volunteer from Alabama. To Santa Anna's demand for surrender, the young Travis replied, "I have answered the demand with a cannon shot and our flag still waves proudly from the wall. I shall never surrender or retreat." Travis and Bowie were joined by other volunteers, such as David Crockett from Tennessee, motivated by a love of liberty, and perhaps a taste for battle. When the threat facing the Texians was revealed, many of them could have escaped with their lives, but chose to stay and fight. James Bonham carried Travis's vain plea for reinforcements through the Mexican lines; after delivering his message, knowing it to be futile, he returned through the lines again in order to rejoin his comrades in their fight to the death.

As the third furious charge by the Mexicans at last overwhelmed the defenders, the Alamo fell at dawn on March 6, 1836. No quarter was expected by the defenders and none was extended; Santa Anna had ordered the attack under the red flag indicating that no surrrenders would be accepted. The defenders died, the Alamo fell, and a legend was born. "Remember the Alamo!" was the battle cry a few weeks later when General Sam Houston's inspired Texian army defeated Santa Anna at the Battle of San Jacinto. San Antonio's Alamo had become a shrine of liberty in a new country: the Republic of Texas.

Yet even in a new country, San Antonio inhabitants suffered from old problems. The town was still very much a frontier, subject to attack by the Comanche and by Mexican troops marauding across the new border. Two such incidents illustrate the dangers faced by residents of San Antonio at the time. In 1840, a meeting between Comanche chiefs and the military of the Texas Republic deteriorated into a fierce battle in the center of town. It resulted in many deaths on both sides and further inflamed hostilities. Two years later, a Mexican army marched on the town and captured several prominent citizens, including Sam Maverick, who were brought to Mexico and imprisoned. Despite the posting of Texas Rangers to the town, these attacks unnerved residents and many moved away, reducing San Antonio's population to around 800.

With Texas statehood in 1845, however, came a new optimism, and San Antonio grew under the protection of the U.S. military. A permanent garrison of soldiers was headquartered in barracks built by the Spanish at Military Plaza. At the western edge of the settled United States, San Antonio was as strategically important at that time as it had been during the Texas Revolution. It was the beginning of a continuous relationship between the town and the U.S. military that continues into the present. The military's presence not only made it safer for settlers and businesses to locate in San Antonio, the military itself contributed to the town's growth. It had great appetites to be fed—food, supplies, services, and all the needs of a growing army base—and San Antonio's position on the frontier, long a hindrance to its development, now became a benefit as entrepreneurs, merchants, and other camp followers moved into town.

Many of the new residents were neither Hispanic nor Anglo-American but immigrants from Western Europe, particularly Germany. Due to the concerted efforts of a number of land speculators in Germany, a sizable number of German colonies were soon located in and around San Antonio. A similar immigration campaign took place in the Alsace region, and a large Alsatian community founded the town of Castroville, a few miles west of San Antonio. In the space of a few years, the demographics of San Antonio changed drastically as the German newcomers became dominant both in numbers and in influence. German, not Spanish, was the language heard on the street. Many of the Germans were skilled craftsmen and artists; others were merchants and academics. Most were well-educated, hard-working, and determined to establish a good life for themselves in the New World. In this,

they were mostly successful. Their drive and determination made them community leaders in San Antonio. Many built substantial homes in what is now the King William District; the historic Menger Hotel was built in Alamo Plaza in 1859, the first major building to be erected there since the fall of the Alamo. It was long considered San Antonio's premier hotel, hosting such luminaries as Robert E. Lee and the poet Sidney Lanier. The town's population swelled to more than 8,000, and San Antonio surpassed Galveston as Texas's largest city. San Antonio's fortunes began to rise on the tide of German immigration and U.S. statehood.

Unfortunately, the town would still have to endure one more stern test: the Civil War. On February 6, 1861, General David E. Twiggs of the U.S. Army's Second Cavalry Regiment surrendered to a secessionist force headed by Army Major Ben McCullough. On the same day, the base's inspector-general, Robert E. Lee of Virginia, was detained by secessionists who demanded that he join them or leave town immediately. Lee refused to obey "any revolutionary government of Texas," and returned to Washington. With the coming of the war, San Antonio's

The historic Steves Homestead recalls San Antonio's age of elegance. PHOTO: PARIS PERMENTER & JOHN BIGLEY

newfound prosperity began to wither on the vine. As Vinton James, a writer of the period, described it: "Suddenly, like a bolt of lightning from a clear sky, came the firing on Fort Sumter, which shattered all the bright prospects of San Antonio. Everything was turned to ruin and despair."

Other accounts of the time indicate that the city's economy was actually in a better position than many other Southern towns. It survived partly by shipping goods to and through Mexico, thereby avoiding military blockades on the Texas coast. Forty companies of Confederate soldiers were recruited and trained in San Antonio; most were sent to faraway battles, some never returned. At the war's end, San Antonio was again occupied by the U.S. Army, this time as a conquered city. Vinton James noted that after the war, "business was at its lowest ebb, there being no money to make improvements or to keep the city clean."

Fortunately, San Antonio was quick to rebound from the depression of war and reconstruction. This was partly due to its continued strategic importance to the United States' westward expansion. Army troops located here were still needed to counter the Indian threat as settlers moved farther west. San Antonio again became an important supply depot for the Army.

Another source of wealth were the first trail drives to Kansas as entrepreneurs began to round up roaming longhorns and herd them to needy buyers in Abilene. The resulting influx of cowboys transformed San Antonio into a lively cow town filled with saloons and houses of ill-repute, often the scene of fights and even gun battles. The rigors of months spent on the trail created in the cowboys an acute need to blow off steam while enjoying the temporary luxuries of town life. "Work hard, play hard" was their rule of living, and though the more sober townsfolk may have been shocked at their ways, the town benefited financially from the cowboys and their trade. Among the unique tradespeople of the era were the "chili queens," young women who sold hot chili stew from streetside kiosks. San Antonio's era of the hard-riding, hard-drinking cowboys did not last very long; the invention of barbed wire in 1875 signaled the closing of the open range. Yet its wild and woolly Western legacy still claims a piece of the city's soul.

In 1877, San Antonio began an unprecedented decade of growth, fueled by the coming of the railroad to town. The Galveston, Harrisburg, and San Antonio Railroad arrived with great fanfare and celebration, carrying the luxuries of civilization, and, even more importantly, bringing with it the optimism of an exciting, expanding nation. No more would San Antonio be an isolated outpost on the frontier. Its role as lonely oasis was over. The town's population began to expand exponentially, growing almost 70 percent between 1870 and 1880, surpassing 20,000. Most of the new arrivals were Anglo-Americans, and thus the demographic composition of the town again changed as the solid German middle class was joined by a new crop of transplants from the Southern states.

As San Antonio grew, it also rebuilt and modernized much of its infrastructure. Brick homes began to replace adobe ones in the residential areas, while downtown, new businesses sprang up almost overnight. Streets were paved (some with stone, others with blocks cut from the hardy mesquite tree), the water supply was upgraded from dependence on open canals (the picturesque but frequently contaminated *acequias*) to a system of deep wells. Stable, massive iron bridges spanned the river at several crossings and horse-powered streetcars carried citizens through the downtown area. Electric lighting and telephones were introduced in the early 1880s and the first substantial public school system was inaugurated along with a professional police force. Santa Rosa Hospital opened its doors in 1884 and the Grand Opera House in Alamo Plaza debuted in 1886. A visiting newspaperman declared, "the magic wand of civilization has touched the city. . . . In the place of the mesquite thicket, where the coyote held his nightly revels, you see fine, broad avenues, lined on either side with beautiful and stately residences, surrounded with magnificent groves of shade trees and lovely gardens of flowers."

Almost forgotten in the frantic progress of the time was the city's heritage of missions and other historic structures. But while some priceless buildings were lost to progress, many were saved, some by chance and others quite deliberately. The Alamo was preserved thanks to the efforts of Clara Driscoll and the Daughters of the Republic of Texas, who led the fight to spare it and the adjoining Long Barrack from demolition. The Daughters purchased and renovated Texas's most beloved site and have protected it up to the present day, using private funding. Despite recent controversies and challenges to their role, the Daughters' dedication has endured. A plaque on the Alamo grounds quotes Clara Driscoll, who vowed to ensure "that the sacred shrine be saved from the encroachment of commercialism and stand through eternity a monument incomparable to the immortal heroes who died that Texas might not perish."

The Daughters were but one of many volunteer groups that sprang up in San Antonio's "Gilded Age." The German-Americans, still influential, called upon their love of music and their heritage of social clubs to build the Beethoven Maennerchor Concert Hall in 1895. The hall became the home of the city's first symphony orchestra. Another German-American club, the Turnverein, built the city's first gymnasium, Turner Halle, near the Menger Hotel. The Turnverein, known for its displays of athletic ability, also formed the basis for San Antonio's first volunteer fire department. Other societies met to discuss how best to improve various aspects of the city's cultural climate. Fiesta San Antonio and its Battle of Flowers Parade, still one of San Antonio's biggest annual events, began in 1891 as a fete for an upcoming visit by President Benjamin Harrison.

Since the days when the founding friars attempted to "civilize" the native tribes by instructing them, education has played a prominent role in San Antonio's history. Turn-of-the-century San Antonio witnessed the full flowering of that tradition as Incarnate Word College joined Our Lady of the Lake, St. Mary's Hall, and Ursaline Academy. It is worth noting that one local school, West Texas Military Institute, graduated its most famous alumni, Douglas MacArthur, in 1895.

At the end of the 1800s, San Antonio saw itself poised for greatness. The largest city in Texas was renowned for its architecture, multicultural heritage, and elegant standard of living. Although much of its economic prosperity was fueled by trade and by a considerable military presence, the city's culture was much more diversified. Hispanic, European, Anglo, and many other cultural elements created a unique society that gave San Antonio a firm foundation to face the new century with optimism and pride.

Insiders' Tip

To sound like a local, say "San Antonio," *not* "San Antone"!

In many ways, San Antonio's evolution in the twentieth century was much like that of other American cities. It experienced a burst of development in the first two decades much like it had with the coming of the railroad. This boom, however, was sparked by other inventions in transportation: the automobile and the airplane. The latter was to transform the city. In fact, the first American military flight took place at Fort Sam Houston in March, 1910. Once the war started, San Antonio's military facilities were greatly expanded and improved. By 1930, San Antonio boasted numerous bases: Kelly Field, Brooks Field, Fort Sam Houston, and Randolph Field, which was to be known as the "West Point of the Air."

Two world wars fought by the United States against Germany had a chilling effect on San Antonio's Germanic population, despite the fact that they had been Texans for more generations than many of the city's Anglo-American citizens. Street and building names were changed, and the traditional organs of German culture, the societies and their publications, were shut down. At the same time, the Hispanic population grew, fueled by refugees from the revolution in Mexico.

A catastrophic flood in 1921 destroyed much of the downtown area, initiating action to harness the San Antonio River to prevent such disasters in the future. This resulted in the building of dams to control the river and eventually in the construction of the River Walk area. Skyscrapers were constructed in the downtown area. Many of San Antonio's historical buildings were preserved, however, as by now the city was conscious of its heritage and there were organizations such as the San Antonio Conservation Society. Historic preservation was also a byproduct of the Great Depression—when the development in San Antonio, as in most American cities, stopped.

World War II pulled San Antonio out of its stagnation. The city's military bases were again enlarged, and a new base, Lackland, was constructed, eventually to train more than one-third of the air personnel serving in the war. Other research facilities sprang up: the School of Aerospace Medicine at Brooks Air Force Base opened in 1959, while the University of the Air, a college dedicated to Air Force personnel, opened at Randolph AFB. Trinity University relocated to San Antonio in 1942, and the University of Texas built a new campus here as well as a major medical center in the early 1970s.

In subsequent years, San Antonio became more dependent on a new source of revenue: tourism. The Alamo, of course, was the main draw (it remains today the Number One tourist attraction in Texas) but the city developed other attractions to increase the number of visitors, such as the River Walk, completed in 1941. This area, which remains a top tourist draw today, is a beautifully landscaped promenade along the downtown portion of the San Antonio River, flowing past alfresco restaurants, shops, and hotels. As San Antonio began to realize the potential of its unique heritage, ethnic neighborhoods such as the King William area and the old Spanish missions were beautifully restored and became part of the National Park Service. Pride in the city's heritage reached full flower in 1968 with HemisFair '68, a world's fair celebrating San Antonio's 250th birthday. The fair was held near Alamo Plaza, and its symbol was the 622-foot-tall Tower of the Americas, with its revolving observation top. The Tower, as well as other fair facilities, remain today as important city landmarks. Nearby, the San Antonio Convention Center now draws more than 500,000 conference attendees annually, making this one of the most popular convention cities in the country. Another city landmark, the Alamodome, rises near HemisFair Plaza. Completed in 1993, it hosts football bowl games and special events (The Rolling Stones recently played here) and is the home court of the National Basketball Association's San Antonio Spurs.

San Antonio has emerged from the twentieth century holding a special place in Texas. No longer the state's largest city, it remains, to many residents and visitors, its most charming. Although thoroughly modern, San Antonio is most proud of its past and eager to share its story with visitors.

San Antonio Timeline

1536 Ályar Núñez Cabeza de Vaca explores Texas.

1691 Father Damian Masanet and Governor Don Domingo de Teran hold Mass at the Payaya village of Yanaguana, dubbing the river there San Antonio.

1718 Fathers Espinosa and Olivares found the Mission San Antonio de Valero and the villa of San Antonio de Bexar.

1719 Mission San Antonio de Valero is moved to the east bank of the river.

1720 Mission San Jose y San Miguel de Aguayo is founded.

1722 San Antonio's first permanent military accommodations, Plaza de Armes, are built by the garrison.

1723 Eighty horses are stolen in a raid by the Apache.

1724 Mission San Antonio de Valero is moved again after being destroyed by storm.

1731 Missions San Juan Capistrano, San Francisco de la Espada, and Nuestra Señora de la Purisima Concepción are relocated from East Texas. Fifty-six Canary Islanders arrive to colonize area.

1734 The Spanish Governor's Palace is built.

1736 The first bridge across San Antonio River is built, connecting San Antonio de Valero mission with the town.

1738 A major acqueduct (Acequia Principia) is built to provide water to town.

1773 San Antonio de Bexar is named provincial capital.

1783 San Antonio's population is 1,392.

1793 The missions are secularized by the Spanish crown.

1810 The Mexican Revolution begins.

1813 San Antonio is captured by revolutionary army, then is retaken and decimated by Royalists.

1819 Major floods on the San Antonio River destroy much of the town.

1820 Moses Austin petitions governor for permission to colonize Texas.

1821 Mexico becomes independent of Spain; Austin's petition is granted by the new Mexican government.

1825 U.S. colonists buy land and settle in Texas.

1830 Mexico closes Texas to immigration from the United States.

1835 Texian army captures San Antonio; General Cos signs surrender.

1836 Santa Anna lays seige to the Alamo, which falls on March 6.

1840 Downtown San Antonio is the scene of a major battle with the Comanche; German immigration to the San Antonio area begins.

1845 Texas becomes part of the United States.

1848 The Rio Grande is established as the U.S.–Mexico border by the Treaty of Guadelupe Hidalgo, ending the Mexican War.

1850 San Antonio's population is 3,488.

1853 *San Antonio Zeitung,* a German-language newspaper, is first published.

1859 Menger Hotel opens.

1861 Confederate troops take the San Antonio Army fort and control of the city.

1865 The Civil War ends; the U.S. Army retakes the city.

1873 Joske's department store opens.

1876 U.S. Army begins work on Fort Sam Houston.

1877 The railroad comes to San Antonio. The water works are established.

1878 Mule-powered streetcars are introduced downtown.

1882 Telephones and electric lights are introduced.

1886 Geronimo and his band of Apache are imprisoned at Fort Sam Houston.

1890 Electric streetcars replace those drawn by mules.

1891 The Battle of Flowers parade debuts.

1898 Theodore Roosevelt trains Rough Riders in San Antonio.

1899 Brackenridge Park is dedicated. The first Mexican restaurant opens on Loyosa Street.

1910 The second Mexican Revolution begins.

1917 Brooks and Kelly airbases are established.

1921 Downtown is flooded; 50 people are killed.

1924 The Conservation Society is formed to preserve the city's heritage.

1926 Witte Museum is built. Flood-control projects are started downtown.

1928 The Milam Building, the world's first air-conditioned structure, opens.

1930 Randolph Field opens.

1936 The first River Parade is staged to honor the Texas Centennial.

1939 La Villita undergoes restoration.

1941 The River Walk is completed.

1949 San Antonio Municipal Airport opens.

1960 The world premiere of *The Alamo,* starring John Wayne, takes place at Woodlawn Theater.

1966 The Alamo is listed on the National Register of Historic Places.

1968 HemisFair '68 is held.

1973 The NBA San Antonio Spur's first season.

1981 Henry Cisneros is elected mayor.

1987 Pope John Paul II celebrates Mass in San Antonio.

1988 Sea World of Texas opens in San Antonio.

1992 Fiesta Texas opens.

1993 The Alamodome opens and hosts U.S. Olympic Festival '93.

1999 The San Antonio Spurs win the NBA championship.

Hotels and Motels

Downtown

Inside and Along
Loop 410

Beyond Loop 410

Extended-Stay
Accommodations

Resorts

Selecting accommodations in San Antonio can be difficult; the city is dotted with hotels and motels designed to appeal both to the leisure crowd and to business travelers and conventioneers. You'll find hotels sprinkled throughout the city, but most are clustered in a few high-demand areas: the River Walk, along I–35, and along I–10.

Since San Antonio has some of the highest occupancy rates in the state, obtaining a hotel room can also be a tough job, especially during peak tourist periods: the summer months, the Christmas season, Eastertime, during April's Fiesta and other festivals, and anytime the San Antonio Spurs are playing a home game. Large conventions can fill downtown and River Walk rooms at other times as well.

Even with the high demand, though, you can obtain choice rooms, especially if you book early. The city has more than 27,000 hotel rooms; nearly 10,000 are found in the downtown area. Most of these properties are family-friendly. Some allow kids to stay free in the same room as their parents; others have children's menus at on-site restaurants. Most properties can supply cribs and additional bedding, sometimes at a surcharge.

The highest demand is for rooms along the River Walk, or Paseo del Rio, the city's top tourist district. Not coincidentally, these are also the city's most expensive hotel rooms. Properties such as the Hyatt Regency Riverwalk, the Marriott Riverwalk, and La Mansion del Rio have long been favorite stops for travelers looking for luxury accommodations. These expensive hotels offer the full menu of amenities and services that you would expect to see in a first-rate property.

You will find a few moderately priced motels within walking distance of the River Walk but expect to see three-figure rates at most properties any night of the week. Remember that Friday and Saturday nights are peak times in this leisure market, although weekdays can be busy as well because of the city's excellent convention facilities, located on an arm of the River Walk.

Beyond the River Walk but still within the downtown area lie some of the city's most historic and elegant properties. These historic hotels hark back to the days when the River Walk was an undeveloped and undesirable area. The Gunter Hotel and St. Anthony Hotel were preferred addresses in the city, each within walking distance of elegant theaters. Near the Alamo, the Menger Hotel has long been one of the city's most prestigious hostelry.

If you're flying into San Antonio, you'll also find a large array of hotels, motels, and extended-stay properties near the airport. Loop 410 is home to a large concentration of accommodations, many at lower prices than those found along the River Walk. Some of these properties offer shuttle service to the airport.

Many car travelers arrive in San Antonio on I–35 and I–10. Numerous motels are located on the north side of the city along I–35, one of the state's busiest thoroughfares.

All the properties listed accept major credit cards and offer a selection of nonsmoking rooms. In observance of the American Disabilities Act (ADA), all San Antonio hotels and motels have handicapped-accessible rooms. Unless otherwise noted, the properties in this chapter do not allow pets, with the exception of service animals for disabled guests.

Price-Code Key

$	under $75
$$	$75–$150
$$$	$151–$225
$$$$	over $225

Downtown

Adam's Mark Riverwalk
111 E. Pecan St., San Antonio
(210) 362–6444, (800) 444–2326
www.adamsmark.com
$$$–$$$$

This comfortable accommodation is only steps away from the River Walk, perfect for visitors who plan to enjoy a lot of shopping and nightlife at the San Antonio landmark. Adam's Mark offers visitors same-day dry-cleaning and laundry services, an outdoor pool, and a gift shop featuring the work of Texas artists. Guests have access to the hotel's fully equipped health club and can enjoy a spectacular view of the River Walk from the sundeck with an outdoor pool and whirlpool. Each of the 410 rooms has a remote control TV with ESPN, CNN, and Headline News, in-room movies, two phones, a data port, a large desk, climate control, an iron and ironing board, electronic door locks, AM/FM clock radio, and voice mail. Restaurante Marbella is in the lobby, serving New World cuisine, steaks, pasta, and seafood. At Players Sports Bar, guests can watch their favorite teams on big-screen TVs. Tiffany Rose Lounge offers cigars and cocktails to guests while they enjoy live entertainment.

Alamo Travelodge
405 Broadway, San Antonio
(210) 222–1000, (800) 578–7878
www.alamotravelodge.com
$

This simple hotel is conveniently located fifteen minutes away from the San Antonio International Airport. Close to the low-rise structure are all of the exciting attractions of downtown San Antonio, including the Alamo, River Walk, Rivercenter Mall, and Henry B. Gonzales Convention Center. Alamo Travelodge offers modern-looking, air-conditioned rooms (for those hot Texas summers), a free *USA Today* every day during the week, an outdoor pool, and free HBO. This is the perfect accommodation for visitors looking for a modest hotel at a great location.

Courtyard San Antonio Downtown/Market Square
600 South Santa Rosa Ave., San Antonio
(210) 299–9449, (800) 648–4462
www.courtyard.com
$$

This downtown hotel has a great location. The Alamodome, downtown San Antonio, Market Square, Rivercenter Mall, the River Walk, and the Alamo are all located within a mile. The property has an outdoor pool and whirlpool, room service, complimentary parking, express check-in and check-out, and cable TV. Each guest room has a spacious sitting area for entertaining guests or just relaxing after a long day, a desk, voice mail, phones with data ports, remote-control TV with an all-news channel, in-room movies, a newspaper delivered on weekdays, in-room coffee, an iron and ironing board, a hair dryer, and an in-room safe. All rooms are positioned around the hotel's wonderfully landscaped courtyard. Cribs are available. This hotel has two meeting rooms and a total of 1,250 square feet of meeting space. Near the property, guests can find restaurants serving cuisines ranging from Cajun and Creole to Italian.

The Fairmount—A Wyndham Historic Hotel
401 South Alamo St., San Antonio
(210) 224–8800, (800) 996–3426
www.wyndham.com
$$$

This hotel calls itself "San Antonio's Little Jewel." The 37-room property pampers its guests with personal attention and style amid turn-of-the-century elegance. In 1986, the hotel earned a place in the Guinness Book of World Records when the 3.2-million-pound structure became

flavor, while the bar features live entertainment on Fridays and Saturdays.

The Fairmount couldn't be in a better location. The Alamo is only six blocks away, while the River Walk is only four. McNay Art Museum, Blue Star Arts Complex, and the Alamodome are all close by.

The Fairmount Hotel graces the downtown area and is within walking distance of many attractions. PHOTO: PARIS PERMENTER & JOHN BIGLEY

the heaviest building ever moved. The move took six days, relocating the three-story hotel just across the street from both HemisFair Plaza and La Villita. During the excavation of the basement at the new location, artifacts from the battle of the Alamo were found. Today the site is a State Archaeological Landmark.

Each guest room here has an alarm clock, hair dryer, color television with VCR, iron and ironing board, data ports, and a coffee maker with complimentary coffee. Bathrooms are equipped with a shower massager and products from Bath & Body Works. The hotel offers its guests a fitness center, laundry and valet services, 24-hour room service, and baby-sitting services.

Polo's Restaurant and Bar, located on the property, is the perfect place to end a busy day. The restaurant serves continental cuisine with a unique Southwestern

Menger Hotel
204 Alamo Plaza, San Antonio
(210) 223–4361, (800) 345–9285
www.historicmenger.com
$$–$$$

The Menger Hotel is located just next door to the Alamo. This historic hotel was built in 1859 and has remained a popular stop ever since. Some of its most famous guests include Civil War generals Robert E. Lee and William Sherman, Mount Rushmore sculptor Gutzon Borglum (who had a studio at the hotel), playwright Oscar Wilde, and author William Sydney Porter (O. Henry), who mentioned the hotel in several of his short stories. Today the Menger has been restored to its Victorian splendor. The three-story lobby features Corinthian columns, a leaded skylight, and much of its original furniture. Guests can stay in Victorian accommodations or in newer rooms. The lobby is adjacent to a tropical garden (once the home of several alligators) and shops. Directly across the street are the stores of Blum Street and the Rivercenter Mall.

The Menger prides itself on the amenities offered to guests. Among these are a complete health spa, a Jacuzzi, the largest swimming pool in downtown San Antonio, and the Colonial Room Restaurant. Nearby, guests will find the Alamo, River Walk, Rivercenter Mall, Henry B. Gonzales Convention Center, and Alamo Plaza.

Fairfield Inn San Antonio Downtown
620 South Santa Rosa Ave., San Antonio
(210) 299–1000, (800) 228–2800
www.fairfieldinn.com
$$

Cable TV, complimentary continental breakfast, laundry facilities, and complimentary newspapers are some of the extras

The Menger Hotel was one of the city's first hotels; it opened in 1859. PHOTO: AL RENDON, COURTESY OF THE SAN ANTONIO CONVENTION AND VISITORS BUREAU

available at this downtown lodging place. Guests will also find an indoor heated swimming pool, exercise facilities, and in-room movies. Each of the 110 rooms offer a desk, data ports and telephone, and remote-control TV with an all-news channel and in-room movies. Cribs are available upon request. This Fairfield is situated near the River Walk, the Alamo, the Alamodome, Market Square, and Henry B. Gonzales Convention Center. The hotel also has a 1,400-square-foot meeting room. A Planet Hollywood restaurant is located nearby on the River Walk, as is County Line BBQ, a Texas favorite.

Four Points Hotel San Antonio Riverwalk North
110 Lexington Ave., San Antonio
(210) 223–9461, (800) 288–3927
www.fourpointssanantonio.com
$$–$$$

Guests are greeted by a lobby filled with sunlight and classically elegant, comfortable furniture. The outdoor pool is a per-fect place to cool off after a long day of shopping at Market Square or seeing the historic sights of San Antonio. Looking to work off those delicious meals? Try the exercise room, equipped with a stationary bike, stair climber, and treadmill. Guests also have access to a gift shop, business center, room service, meeting facilities, laundry and valet services, and a cocktail lounge overlooking the river. The hotel's Riverside Cafe serves American cuisine on its River Terrace. Four Points offers its guests complimentary shuttle service to attractions within a three-mile radius of the hotel—the Henry B. Gonzales Convention Center, the Alamo, River Center Mall, and the River Walk all lie within that radius.

Hampton Inn San Antonio—Downtown
414 Bowie St., San Antonio
(210) 225–8500, (800) HAMPTON
www.hampton-inn.com
$$

Just two blocks from the River Walk and Alamo, this six-story, 169-room structure serves its guests' needs by offering clean rooms, a convenient location, and numerous amenities at a reasonable price. Every room is equipped with a coffee maker, iron, and television with cable. Connecting rooms are available, as are cribs and hair dryers. For an additional fee, guests can utilize meeting and banquet facilities as well as laundry and valet services. The hotel also has free parking. There are several restaurants within a mile of the hotel, including Planet Hollywood, Landry's Seafood House, Boudro's, Dick's Last Resort, and the Hard Rock Cafe. In addition to the Alamo and River Walk, the Institute of Texan Cultures, River Center Mall, Henry B. Gonzales Convention Center, and the Tower of the Americas are within walking distance.

Hawthorn Inn & Suites On the Riverwalk
830 N. St. Mary's St., San Antonio
(210) 527-1900, (800) 527-1133
www.hawthorn-riverwalk.com
$$

This property has 149 studio suites located on a quiet stretch of the River Walk, directly across the San Antonio River from the Municipal Auditorium. The long, low-rise structure, easy to spot thanks to its terra-cotta roof, has many rooms with balconies that overlook the River Walk.

Four classes of rooms are available. All rooms include coffee and coffee makers, an iron and ironing board, telephones and data ports, and voice mail. The deluxe rooms, decorated in soft tones and with plush carpeting, are equipped with a mini refrigerator, microwave, coffee maker, and wet bar. Studio suites offer up to 50 percent more space than a typical hotel room, and each includes a mini refrigerator, microwave, and wet bar. Executive suites are double the size of a traditional hotel room; each is outfitted with an expanded work area, two two-line phones, a full-size iron and ironing board, a mini refrigerator, and a microwave as well as a small kitchen/wet bar area with seating. The Jacuzzi/Honeymoon Suites include the amenities of an Executive Suite, plus a king-size bed and a Jacuzzi tub.

A complimentary breakfast buffet is available every day from 6:30 A.M. until 10:30 A.M., and Wednesday nights bring the Wednesday Night Social Hour, when complimentary beverages are served along with a light dinner. The hotel also has an outdoor pool with a sun deck and a patio with a good view of the River Walk, a convenience store where guests can buy items that they may have left at home, a guest laundry room, a fitness center, valet parking, room service every day of the week except Sunday, and cable TV with HBO and Nintendo. All of the excitement of the River Walk is only steps away.

Hilton Palacio del Rio Hotel
200 South Alamo St., San Antonio
(210) 222-1400, (800) HILTONS
www.hilton.com
$$$-$$$$

This hotel is a pre-fab structure, albeit a wonderfully elegant one. The property was constructed in just 202 days in order to be ready for HemisFair '68. Like giant children's blocks, the rooms (furnishings and all) were assembled off-site and put together here in record time. Today the hotel has a wonderful location, right in the middle of the River Walk action and just a few short steps away from La Villita and HemisFair Plaza.

The Hilton has plenty of services to offer its guests. In each of its near 500 rooms, guests will find comfortable beds, an individual thermostat to adjust the temperature of the room, and premium TV options including HBO and ESPN. In the lobby, complimentary coffee and an Advantage car rental desk are available. There are four restaurants on the property. The Ibiza Patio Bar and Restaurant serves Mediterranean and Texas-style foods for all three meals of the day, and features live music on Friday and Saturday nights. Tex's Sports Bar allows guests to watch their favorite sports teams on TV while trying Texas's microbrewed beers and appetizers. Tex's has live music on

Friday and Saturday nights and a happy hour from 5:00 P.M. until 7:00 P.M. on weekdays. Durty Nelly's is a unique Irish Pub that offers cold beer and nightly sing-a-longs. After an exhausting day seeing the sights of San Antonio, guests can have a satisfying meal at Rincon Allegre, located in the lobby.

Holiday Inn Crockett Hotel
320 Bonham, San Antonio
(210) 225–6500, (800) 292–1050
www.holiday-inn.com
$$$

Just beyond Alamo Plaza stands the Crockett Hotel, situated on grounds that were once part of the Alamo battlefield. In fact, Davy Crockett was said to have defended the southeast palisade, and the hotel is named in his honor. The original mercantile store that stood at this site was sold to the International Order of Odd Fellows, who built a lodge and hotel here in 1909. Today the 202-room hotel has been faithfully restored to its turn-of-the-century grandeur. There are modern amenities as well: Guests can enjoy a rooftop hot tub and sun deck or a land-scaped pool with its own waterfall.

The Crockett is the perfect place for guests who are looking for comfortable accommodations at a great location. Adjacent to the Alamo, River Center Mall, and the River Walk, the hotel is within walking distance of many of San Antonio's major attractions. For active guests, golf and tennis facilities are less than five miles away. For business travelers, the Crockett has photocopying, Internet, fax, and printer services. The hotel offers a restaurant and cocktail lounge, dry cleaning and laundry facilities, safe-deposit boxes, turndown service, and wake-up calls. Guests can dine either at the hotel's Landmark Restaurant or choose from any of the varied restaurants on the nearby River Walk. To finish off a busy day of shopping on the River Walk or touring the historic missions, visitors can relax in the outdoor pool or in the rooftop hot tub, which offers a beautiful view of downtown San Antonio.

Holiday Inn Express Hotel & Suites
524 S. St. Mary's St., San Antonio
(210) 354–1333, (800) 959–3239
www.holiday-inn.com
$$

Holiday Inn Hotels have a reputation for being clean, convenient, and efficient. This location is no exception. It is only a few blocks from the Alamo, Henry B. Gonzales Convention Center, the Alamodome, Hemisphere Park, and the River Walk. The building's architectural style reflects both the Mexican influence and the modern emphasis on efficiency and convenience that come together in San Antonio. For guests on business, the hotel offers photocopying, fax and PC services, and a full business center. Also available are wake-up calls, safe-deposit boxes, secretarial services, guest laundry facilities, and dry cleaning. The hotel concierge provides guests with information about air travel, rental cars, and city tours. On the nearby River Walk, guests can shop and choose from many different kinds of dining establishments serving food from all around the globe. This Holiday Inn Express is the perfect place for a busy traveler who wants convenience and a great location.

Holiday Inn San Antonio Downtown
318 W. Durango, San Antonio
(210) 225–3211, (800) 422–2419
www.holiday-inn.com
$$

Right on Market Square, this is a great lodging place for visitors who want to see the historic sights of beautiful San Antonio. The outside of the building is styled like an old mission, recalling the unique history of the city. The hotel offers a pool, an exercise room, a coin-operated laundry, concierge services, a gift shop, a newsstand, safe-deposit boxes, six meeting rooms for groups of up to 300 people, wake-up calls, photocopy and fax services, and complimentary parking. The on-site Convenience Cafe serves a speedy breakfast, lunch, and dinner for guests who are in a hurry to see San Antonio. For guests looking to relax after a long day, there's a cocktail lounge. Less than a mile from the hotel lie Market Square, the River Walk, River Center Mall, the Alamo, King William Historical District, and the Alamodome.

Holiday Inn Riverwalk
217 N. St. Mary's St., San Antonio
(210) 224–2500, (800) HOLIDAY
www.holiday-inn.com
$$–$$$

This high-rise hotel is twelve stories tall and has 313 comfortable rooms. Guest perks include a concierge, dry cleaning and laundry service, a gift shop, a newsstand, safe-deposit boxes, wake-up calls, exercise facilities, and a pool. There is a cash machine on the property, handy for shopping expeditions on the River Walk, which is located just opposite the hotel entrance. Copying, fax, and secretarial services are offered for business travelers. Guests of the Holiday Inn River Walk can stroll to many of San Antonio's main attractions. The River Walk, Hall of Horns and Fins, the Alamodome, Tower of the Americas, Market Square, River Center Mall, the Alamo, and La Villita are all less than a mile away. There is an on-site restaurant that serves casual meals and has a view of the River Walk.

Homewood Suites Riverwalk
432 West Market St., San Antonio
(210) 222–1515, (800) CALL–HOME
homewood-riverwalk.com
$$

This Homewood Suites is found in the restored historic San Antonio Drug Company building, which is listed in the National Register of Historic Places. The property offers its guests daily continental breakfast with fresh muffins, cereals, baked goods and fresh fruit. Evening social hours with full bar are held every day of the week except Sunday. A twenty-four-hour Executive Business Center is equipped with a copier, color printer, fax, and Internet access. For group travelers,

2,400 square feet of meeting space is available with projection screens, private phones, VCRs, and data ports. Guests can use the workout facilities, which include a stair climber, exercise bikes, a treadmill, and a universal weight station. Relax in the rooftop pool and spa and enjoy the view of downtown San Antonio. Valet parking with unlimited in and out privileges is also available for a daily fee. The Suite Shop is open around the clock for anyone who needs to satisfy a sweet tooth at 4:00 A.M.

Hyatt Regency Riverwalk
123 Losoya St., San Antonio
(210) 222–1234, (800) 233–1234
www.hyatt.com
$$$–$$$$

Located on the bend in the river, this elegant hotel captures all the excitement of the River Walk. Whether you enter from the street or the River Walk, you'll admire the Hyatt's soaring atrium, filled with palms and the sound of falling water. The hotel added a segment to the river to divert water through the atrium and into the water gardens beyond. The water garden area now has several small bars and a quieter atmosphere than that found on the River Walk side. Follow the steps up the water gardens and you'll find yourself facing the Alamo.

Glass elevators whisk guests to the 631 rooms above. Each room is equipped with a TV with remote control, cable movie channels and in-room pay movies, voice mail, computer hookup, climate control, electronic door locks, an iron and ironing board, AM/FM clock radio, a hair dryer, a coffee maker, and a minibar. Turndown service is available upon request. The hotel also has a heated outdoor pool and whirlpool, a health club with exercise bikes, stair climbers, and treadmills, a business center, concierge service, a gift shop, a florist, a hair and manicure salon, laundry and dry-cleaning service, room service, valet parking, currency exchange, and safe-deposit boxes. The hotel is right on the Riverwalk and a short walk from the Alamo and the Henry B. Gonzales Convention Center. On the property, Chaps Restaurant features a bistro-style cuisine with a breakfast buffet, fresh salad bar, nightly dinner specials, and delicious desserts. The River Terrace Lobby Bar is the perfect place to relax and visit with friends while enjoying cocktails and appetizers. Pets are allowed at the Hyatt; call for details.

La Mansión del Rio
112 College St., San Antonio
(210) 518–1000, (800) 292–7300
www.lamansion.com
$$$$

This elegant Spanish Colonial–style structure began as St. Mary's Academy in 1854. Eventually the campus grew and was renamed St. Mary's College, and then graduated to St. Mary's University. This location served as the law school until 1966, when the campus was relocated. At that time, the building traded in blackboards for beds, desks for dressers, and started a new life as La Mansion. Today the hotel has 337 rooms and suites, many with private balconies overlooking the River Walk.

Any visitor looking for a unique hotel that captures San Antonio's cultural charm will appreciate La Mansión del Rio. The building's Spanish Colonial architecture reflects San Antonio's roots, while the location, overlooking the River Walk, keeps guests in touch with the city's present-day personality. The past and present blend

beautifully to offer guests a distinctive home base for their trip. Many of the 337 guest rooms have a view of the River Walk, and all offer an honor bar, remote-control cable television, evening turndown service, two-line phones, and modem access. Around-the-clock room service and a concierge desk are available. The hotel restaurant, Las Canarias, serves up attractive meals, mixing regional fare with a twist of Texas. El Colegio, the piano bar, offers an extensive variety of Texas beers and wines as well as appetizers.

La Mansión del Rio Hotel is one of the River Walk area's luxury properties. PHOTO: DAVE G. HOUSER, COURTESY OF THE SAN ANTONIO CONVENTION AND VISITORS BUREAU

La Quinta Inn San Antonio Convention Center
1001 East Commerce St., San Antonio
(210) 222–9181, (800) 687–6667
www.laquinta.com
$$

Just a quick walk from the Convention Center and River Walk, this La Quinta offers its guests numerous services and amenities. Free local telephone calls, a free breakfast, cable television, in-room modem lines, an outdoor pool, overnight delivery service, laundry and valet services, free parking, express check-in, AM/FM clock radios, cribs, and safe-deposit boxes are all offered to guests, and children under 18 stay free. Rollaway beds are available, but are not allowed in the standard two-bed rooms due to fire regulations. There are 2,500 square feet of meeting space. As in all La Quinta Hotels, the rooms here are clean and well equipped. Nearby, the world-famous River Walk is bustling with excitement and is ready for shopping, dining, and sightseeing.

La Quinta San Antonio Market Square
900 Dolorosa, San Antonio
(210) 271–0001, (800) 687–6667
www.laquinta.com
$$

In one of San Antonio's best districts for shopping and learning about Mexican culture, this La Quinta has a great location for seeing the city. Each of its 122 guest rooms has television with cable, a whirlpool bath, a safe-deposit box, a modem line, and free local telephone calls. Rollaway beds and cribs are available, and kids under 18 stay free. Other pluses are free parking, express check-in, a twenty-four-hour front desk, and laundry and valet service. The accommodation also has an outdoor pool to provide relief from the hot Texas summer sun. Market Square is a few blocks from the River Walk, the Alamo, Henry B. Gonzales Convention Center, and River Center Mall. San Antonio International Airport is 9 miles from the hotel.

Marriott Rivercenter
101 Bowie St., San Antonio
(210) 223–1000, (800) 228–9290
www.MarriottHotels.com
$$$$

If you want a hotel with a great location, look no further than Marriott Rivercenter. The thirty-eight-story building towers over the River Walk and dominates the San Antonio skyline. This Marriott is connected to River Center Mall, and opens up onto the River Walk. It is less than a mile from the Henry B. Gonzales Convention Center, Hemisfair Park, Market Square, and the Alamo. The 1,000-room complex has three restaurants, twenty-four-hour room service, a coffee shop, a cocktail lounge, laundry service and self-service laundry facilities, child-care service, a gift shop, a business center, safe-deposit boxes, and a Hertz Rental Car desk. Each room has a desk, voice mail, telephones with data ports, high-speed Internet access, a newspaper delivered every weekday, a coffee maker, an iron and ironing board, a hair dryer, and remote-control TV with cable, an all-news channel, and in-room movies. There are 19 guest rooms designed specifically for business travelers and 65,000 square feet of meeting space in 36 meeting rooms. The Garden Cafe serves up continental cuisine for breakfast, lunch, and dinner. The Hanatei Sushi Bar and JW Steakhouse are open for dinner. The hotel also has an indoor and outdoor pool, a health club, a whirlpool, and a sauna; jogging, tennis, and golfing facilities are nearby.

Marriott Riverwalk
711 E. River Walk, San Antonio
(210) 244–4555, (800) 228–9290
www.MarriottHotels.com
$$$$

Like its sister property, Marriott Rivercenter, Marriott Riverwalk is on the famous San Antonio River Walk and near many of San Antonio's main attractions. Not quite as looming as its neighbor, this thirty-story building has 512 guest rooms and five suites. The Henry B. Gonzales Convention Center, River Center Mall, the Alamo, Market Square, the Mission Trail, and the San Antonio Zoo are all less than 5 miles from the hotel. Six Flags Fiesta Texas and SeaWorld of Texas are 30 and 18 miles away, respectively. Every room has a desk, voice mail, high-speed Internet access, a newspaper delivered Monday through Friday, in-room coffee, an iron and ironing board, remote-control TV with cable, an all-news channel, and in-room movies. Cribs are available upon request. The hotel has an on-site restaurant, twenty-four-hour room service, a coffee shop, a cocktail lounge, concierge service, a gift shop, a business center, and safe-deposit boxes. There is a pool and whirlpool, a health club, and a sauna; jogging, tennis, and golf are a short hop away.

Plaza San Antonio
555 South Alamo, San Antonio
(210) 229–1000, (800) 727–3239
www.plazasa.com
$$$$

Adding style and atmosphere to this elegant resort are four nineteenth-century buildings, each listed on the National Register of Historic Places, that are located directly behind the main hotel building. The Diaz House, now used for meetings and receptions, was built around 1840. Some have pointed out the similarity of the stonework in the Diaz House to that in the outer wall of the Alamo. The health club is housed in an 1850s structure that typifies the German style so popular in San Antonio during that period. Yet another house, a Victorian cottage, is now a private dining room.

But the best known of the hotel's historic structures is the German-English School. Located next to the tennis courts, this two-story building was originally built to teach the children of the German businessmen who lived in the affluent King William neighborhood. Now the hotel conference center, the school came

to national attention in 1992 when President George Bush, Mexican President Carlos Salinas, and Canadian Prime Minister Brian Mulroney met here for the initializing ceremony of the North American Free Trade Agreement.

This Marriott property prides itself on offering guests extra amenities such as overnight professional shoeshine service, chauffeured cars to San Antonio's business district, and a full business center. In-room coffee and a free newspaper are also provided. The hotel has lighted tennis courts, a health club, and an outdoor heated pool. The concierge can attend to all your needs and inquiries about the property or the city. The hotel's Anaqua Room serves the unique fare of chef Dan Freunscht. Diners enjoy Mediterranean and American-style dishes while they take in the breathtaking view of the Plaza's gardens. The Palm Terrace Lobby Bar is the perfect place to relax after a long day.

Radisson Market Square
502 West Durango Blvd., San Antonio
(210) 224–7155, (800) 333–3333
www.radisson.com
$$$

When Radisson opened this hotel, they packed it with services and amenities to satisfy all types to guests, from those who are looking for rest and relaxation to those who are seeing the sights of San Antonio from morning 'til night. Surrounded by tropical palm trees, the hotel's outdoor pool is the perfect place to cool off in the hot Texas sun; those who like to sunbathe can head for one of the lounge chairs that fill the courtyard. The exercise room is fully equipped with all types of fitness machines. Cafe

> ### Insiders' Tip
> The Plaza San Antonio Hotel incorporates three historic homes in its courtyard.

Chameleon, with indoor and outdoor seating, dishes out regional favorites and traditional fare for every meal. The lobby bar provides a quiet environment for relaxing, and the staff also serve drinks poolside. Monday through Friday, happy hour is from 5:00 to 7:00 P.M., with drinks and complimentary hors d'oeuvres. Radisson Market Square offers courtesy van service to downtown attractions such as the Alamo, the River Walk, Henry B. Gonzales Convention Center, and the Alamodome. SeaWorld of Texas and Six Flags Fiesta Texas aren't far, and San Antonio International Airport is a fifteen-minute drive away.

Ramada Inn Emily Morgan
705 E. Houston St., San Antonio
(210) 225–8486, (888) 298–2054
www.the.ramada.com/sanantonio05097
$$$

This hotel is named for the woman known in legend and song as "The Yellow Rose of Texas." General Santa Anna was enamored with Emily Morgan, a mulatto slave who acted as a spy for the Texas army. Thanks in part to her efforts, Sam Houston's troops defeated Santa Anna's men at San Jacinto on April 21, 1836, winning the Texas Revolution. The Ramada Emily Morgan offers its guests many amenities. Every room has an AM/FM clock radio, coffee maker, hair dryer, and a TV with cable. Most of the rooms also have Jacuzzis and mini refrigerators. The hotel offers baby-sitting and child-care services, a barber shop/salon, a fitness center, twenty-four-hour front desk, laundry and valet services, RV parking, indoor and outdoor pools, a restaurant, room service, safe-deposit boxes, and meeting/banquet facilities.

The best feature of this hotel is its location: Literally next door to the Alamo, it is within walking distance of River Center Mall, Henry B. Gonzales Convention Center, HemisFair Park and Market Square. Many of the guest rooms look down into the Alamo complex. The Yellow Rose Cafe is in the hotel, as is Emily's Oasis Lounge.

Residence Inn Alamo Plaza
425 Bonham, San Antonio
(210) 212–5555, (800) 648–4462
www.residenceinn.com
$$$–$$$$

An outdoor pool, exercise facilities, and a great location are just some of the tempting options at this all-suite property. Other pluses are dinner delivery service from some local restaurants, a complimentary breakfast buffet, safe-deposit boxes, and fax and copy services. Each of the attractively decorated suites has a desk, voice mail, telephones with data ports, cable TV with an all-news channel and in-room movies, a full kitchen with a refrigerator, a coffee maker, an iron and ironing board, and a hair dryer. Cribs are available upon request. There are six meeting rooms and a total of 2,275 square feet of meeting space. The Alamo, Henry B. Gonzales Convention Center, Market Square, River Center Mall, and the River Walk are all nearby. Also close to the hotel are several golf courses, and there are plenty of restaurants to choose from on the River Walk, including a Hard Rock Cafe and Morton's of Chicago.

Residence Inn San Antonio Downtown
628 South Santa Rosa Ave., San Antonio
(210) 231–6000, (800) 331–3131
www.residenceinn.com
$$$

With only 95 suites, this smaller hotel provides a more intimate feeling for its guests. Each spacious suite has separate living and sleeping areas, a desk, a two-line phone with voice mail and data ports, remote-control TV with an all-news channel and in-room movies, a full kitchen with a refrigerator and microwave, a coffee maker, and an iron and ironing board. Cribs are available upon request. The property offers a complimentary continental breakfast; laundry service as well as self-service laundry facilities; fax, printer, and copy machine access; secretarial services; safe-deposit boxes; and dinner delivery from some local restaurants. For guests looking for something active to do, there is an outdoor pool, an exercise room, and a whirlpool on-site, and golfing nearby. Make sure to partake in the traditional weekly barbecue held on the premises. For meals the rest of the week, the numerous restaurants of the River Walk are only a half-mile away. Also close by are the Alamo, Market Square, the Alamodome, Henry B. Gonzales Convention Center, and the San Antonio Zoo.

Riverwalk Plaza Hotel Resort & Conference Center
100 Villita St., San Antonio
(210) 226–2271, (800) 554–4678
www.riverwalkplaza.com
$$

Just steps from the River Walk, Market Square, La Villita, the Alamo, King William Historic District, Henry B. Gonzales Convention Center, and the Alamodome, this hotel prides itself on its personal touches and amenities. The private swimming pool is surrounded by a tropical courtyard where guests can enjoy cocktails or cold drinks. There is a twenty-four-hour fitness center with the latest exercise equipment. Every room features either a king-size or full bed, remote-control TV with HBO, a hair dryer, an AM/FM clock radio, and a coffee maker. In the hotel lobby, the El Mercado Gift Shop is the perfect place to find presents for friends and family, or pick up a memento of your trip. The award-winning and refined Cascades on the River Restaurant and Cocktail Lounge serves hotel guests fine cuisine and has a hand-selected wine list.

St. Anthony Hotel
300 E. Travis St., San Antonio
(210) 227–4392
www.stanthonyhotel.com
$$$

Now part of the Wyndham Historic Hotel group, the St. Anthony has certainly seen its share of history and probably even made some at the same time. Construction began on the hotel in 1909, when San Antonio was just a Texas cow town. Soon after its opening, it was rated in the same category as New York City's Waldorf-Astoria by some visitors. The property was bought in 1935 by entrepreneur Ralph W. Morrison, who initiated many changes, including the addition of a ten-story tower and air conditioning. Since 1909, the St. Anthony has been the place for celebrities and dignitaries to stay while in the Alamo City. First Lady Eleanor Roosevelt stopped here, as did General Douglas MacArthur, President Dwight D. Eisenhower, Prince Rainier and Princess Grace of Monaco, Judy Garland, Lucille Ball, Fred Astaire, John Wayne, Gregory Peck, and Rock Hudson. More recently, Arnold Schwartzenegger and Maria Shriver, Bruce Willis, George Clooney, and many others have stayed at this elegant lodging place.

The St. Anthony pampers all its guests—famous or not. Each room is equipped with a hair dryer, coffee maker, telephone with data port and voice mail, and an iron and ironing board. The business center has copy, binding, shipping, laser-printing, and secretarial services as well as rental computers, typewriters, and cellular phones. The hotel is a short walk from the River Walk, the Alamo, Henry B. Gonzales Convention Center, La Villita, the Alamodome, San Antonio Children's Museum, and Hemisfair Park. If you'd like to dine where the stars eat, look no further than The Madrid Room, found on the

Insiders' Tip
Suite 884 at the St. Anthony Hotel was renamed for actor John Wayne. The star of *The Alamo* film stayed at the hotel in 1960 and again in 1978 for the National Entertainers' Conference.

grounds of the St. Anthony. The Madrid Room serves breakfast, lunch, and dinner in an Old World Spanish atmosphere and features Italian cuisine with a Southwestern twist. Also on the property, Pete's Pub offers guests drinks and light meals. Don't miss the St. Anthony's Sunday brunch, regarded as one of the best weekend brunches in San Antonio.

San Antonio/Riverwalk Drury Inn & Suites
201 N. St. Mary's St., San Antonio
(201) 212–5200, (800) DRURY–INN
www.drury-inn.com
$$

This Drury Inn, right on the River Walk, is a historical landmark. The building was erected in the 1920s and has since been restored to its original beauty. To the delight of visitors, the period architecture of the building has been maintained. Nonetheless, the guest rooms are equipped with such modern amenities as voice mail, coffee makers, and irons and ironing boards. Guests have access to a twenty-four-hour business center, an exercise room, fax service, laundry services, meeting rooms, and a rooftop pool. Hotel parking is available for a fee. The Alamodome, the Buckhorn Museum, the Children's Museum, the Convention Center, the Empire Theatre, La Villita, the Majestic Theatre, Market Square, the River Walk, River Center Mall, and the Alamo are all within walking distance of the hotel. A Texas Land & Cattle Company Steakhouse is on the premises, and the many restaurants of the River Walk are only a few steps away.

Sheraton Gunter
205 E. Houston St., San Antonio
(210) 227–3241, (888) 999–2089
www.gunterhotel.com
$$–$$$

Dating back to 1909, when Jot Gunter turned the Frontier Hotel into the Gunter Hotel with the aim of creating the definitive lodging place for the booming city of San Antonio, the Gunter recently celebrated its 91st anniversary with a rededication ceremony and an $8-million renovation project. The guest rooms, lobby, and meeting areas have all been beautifully restored.

Guests will find many extras here. A fitness center, outdoor heated pool, twenty-four-hour room service, a pub with a big-screen TV, a barber shop, and a whirlpool are all on-site, as is Barron's Restaurant, which serves breakfast, lunch, and dinner every day. Barron's well-known pasta bar is open for business for lunch during the week. The Sheraton Gunter Bakery bakes mouthwatering treats for guests and visitors. Breads, pastries, cookies, cheesecake, and delicious chocolate-covered strawberries are among the selections found here.

Gunter's hospitality continues into the guest rooms, where visitors will find comfortable appointments and generous amenities. Every room has an alarm clock; voice mail; private bath; remote-control television with 35 channels, pay-per-view movies, and Nintendo; irons and ironing boards; and vintage-style furniture. For guests looking for extra room, Sheraton Gunter suites have the same amenities as the guest rooms, but include a separate parlor.

Villager Lodge
1126 E. Elmira St., San Antonio
(210) 222–9469, (800) 584–0800
www.villager.com
$

Rooms at Villager properties can be rented by the day or for extended stays. Each of the 70 rooms at this property has a microwave and refrigerator and a television with satellite programming. There is a pool where guests can cool off in the hot Texas summers, and a cocktail lounge. The front desk is available around the clock to take care of any needs that guests may have, and coin-operated laundry facilities can be found on-site. A golf course and other San Antonio attractions are nearby. The Villager has free parking as well as space for RV and truck parking.

The Westin Riverwalk
420 Market St., San Antonio
(210) 224–6500, (800) WESTIN–1
www.westin.com
$$$$

Looking for a hotel that has as much to offer as San Antonio itself? Then head to the Westin Riverwalk. Each of the 474 guest rooms has two-line telephones with data ports, a hair dryer, an iron and ironing board, a coffee maker, hypoallergenic pillows, and in-room safe, and remote-control color TV with in-room movies and on-command video. Westin recently introduced what it calls "The Heavenly Bed," with cozy down bedding that is sure to satisfy any fatigued guest. The hotel also features twenty-four-hour room service, concierge service, safe-deposit boxes, wake-up calls, a daily newspaper, a health club, an outdoor swimming pool, dry cleaning, and nightly turndown service. The hotel's Caliza Grille serves Mediterranean fare with a Spanish twist in an ideal environment for a romantic dinner or relaxing and conversing with friends. Rincon de Maria offers a full bar and music. This property is the perfect choice for travelers who want to make their accommodations another attraction on their trip.

Inside and Along Loop 410

AmeriSuites San Antonio Airport
7615 Jones Maltsberger Rd., San Antonio
(210) 930–2333, (800) 833–1516
www.amerisuites.com
$$

Only a mile from San Antonio International Airport, this nice hotel offers many amenities. Each of the 128 colorful suites offers such conveniences as an iron and ironing board, a hair dryer, a refrigerator, a microwave, a wet bar, a coffee maker, a TV with pay-per-view options, a VCR, telephones with data ports and voice mail, and Internet access. Other extras: complimentary breakfast buffet, laundry facilities, valet service, a free daily newspaper, a fitness center, free local transportation,

an outdoor heated pool, and a cutting-edge business center. There are two meeting rooms on the property, totaling 1,200 square feet; facilities can accommodate up to 50 people.

Comfort Inn Airport
2635 Northeast Loop 410, San Antonio
(210) 653–9110, (800) 228–5150
www.comfortinn.com
$

Each of this comfortable hotel's rooms has air conditioning, a coffee maker, an iron and ironing board, and a remote-control TV with cable and free movies. The property also offers free airport transportation, bellhops, free continental breakfast, meeting rooms, an outdoor seasonal pool, safe-deposit boxes, a copy machine, a fax machine, guest laundry facilities, and valet cleaning services. A 24-hour Denny's restaurant is on-site. Nearby, guests can find a public baseball field, basketball courts, the Henry B. Gonzales Convention Center, a health club, shopping, outdoor lighted tennis courts, a beauty shop, bowling, a convenience store, and a golf course. All of the major attractions of San Antonio are not far away.

Comfort Inn East
4403 I–10 East, San Antonio
(210) 333–9430, (800) 456–9345
www.comfortinn.com
$$

Comfort Inn properties usually offer clean rooms at a good price, and this location does just that. The staff is very friendly and is ready to help guests with any requests that they may have. In addition, the hotel offers generous amenities to sweeten the deal. Free continental breakfast, a playground, an outdoor seasonal pool, safe-deposit boxes, meeting rooms, copy- and fax-machine access, guest laundry facilities, a newsstand, and a tour desk are available, and each guest room has an iron with ironing board, AM/FM radio, and cable TV with free movies. Near the hotel are a beauty shop, a car rental company, a convenience store, a barber shop, fishing, a gift shop, a golf course, and shopping.

Comfort Suites Airport North
14202 U.S. 281 North, San Antonio
(210) 494–9000, (888) 727–8483
www.comfortinn.com
$$

With only 65 guest rooms, this Comfort Suites provides guests with an intimate atmosphere in the middle of a bustling, fast-paced city. A mile from San Antonio International Airport, the hotel is less than 15 miles from the Alamodome, Six Flags Fiesta Texas, HemisFair Plaza, and the Alamo. Cascade Caverns, Natural Bridge Caverns, and SeaWorld of Texas are less than 20 miles away. In addition to its great location, this property offers an array of services and amenities. Every room has air conditioning, a clock radio, a coffee maker, an iron and ironing board, free local phone calls, remote-control cable TV with free movies, a VCR, and voice mail. The hotel also offers its guests free airport and mall shuttles, a free full breakfast, an exercise room, a business center, fax machine, copy machine, lighted parking areas, an outdoor heated pool and Jacuzzi, safe-deposit boxes, guest laundry facilities, valet cleaning service, a cocktail lounge, and a gift shop.

Courtyard San Antonio Airport
8615 Broadway St., San Antonio
(210) 828–7200
www.courtyard.com
$$

This reasonably priced hotel takes care of all a traveler's needs. The on-site restaurant is open for breakfast, and there's also room service, a cocktail lounge, and complimentary coffee in the lobby. Other conveniences include laundry service and guest laundry facilities, free parking, fax and copy services, and safe-deposit boxes available at the front desk. Each of the 145 comfortable rooms has a desk with a lamp, voice mail, telephones with data

ports, high-speed Internet access, remote-control cable TV with an all-news channel and in-room movies, a newspaper delivered on weekdays, a coffee maker, an iron and ironing board, and a hair dryer. Each room also has a spacious sitting area that provides guests with the perfect setting for chatting with friends and relaxing following a day of sightseeing. Cribs are available upon request. For more active guests, this Courtyard has an outdoor pool, an exercise room, and a whirlpool, and jogging, tennis, squash, and golf are close by.

Days Inn Northeast
3443 I–35 N., San Antonio
(210) 225–4040, (800) 548–2626
www.daysinn.com
$$

This two-story structure has 125 guest rooms, each opening onto exterior corridors for easier access. Every standard room at this Days Inn has a king-size or double bed, free local telephone calls, and cable TV with HBO. The Executive King Suites and Family Suites have a living room, sleeper sofa, and private bedroom. The Honeymoon Suite, the perfect place for a romantic evening, has a king-size bed, heart-shaped Jacuzzi, and sleeper sofa. All suites have a refrigerator, microwave, coffee maker, hair dryer, and Jacuzzi tub. The River Walk (the perfect place for a night on the town or a day of shopping), the Alamo (a good place to visit for a history lesson), and Six Flags Fiesta Texas and SeaWorld of Texas (for lots of family fun) are all only a few miles away.

Doubletree Club Hotel San Antonio Airport
1111 Northeast Loop 410, San Antonio
(210) 828–9031, (800) 731–1379
www.doubletree.com
$$

This Doubletree, with its tall palm trees and high-rise structure, is reminiscent of a classic Las Vegas hotel in the 1950s. But luckily for San Antonio visitors, it isn't found in Nevada, but in the Lone Star State, only a few minutes from San Antonio International Airport. Nearly all of the 227 units here have air conditioning; cable TV with premium channels like HBO, CNN, and ESPN; electronic locks; an iron and ironing board; telephone with voice mail; a desk; a coffee maker; an adjustable thermostat; and Monday through Friday delivery of *USA Today*. Open for every meal, the hotel's restaurant, Au Bon Pain, serves delicatessen-style fare such as soups, salads, and sandwiches. Golf, bowling, jogging, basketball, a walking track, and tennis courts are all only five miles away, and there is a fitness center and indoor pool on the property. Many of the sites of San Antonio are close by, too.

Doubletree Hotel San Antonio Airport
37 Northeast Loop 410, San Antonio
(210) 366–2424, (800) 535–1980
www.doubletree.com
$$

Only five minutes from San Antonio International Airport, this hotel, built in 2000, has an abundance of amenities to offer its guests. The exterior is Spanish Colonial in style, while inside, traditional Texas hospitality reigns. The hotel's 290 guest rooms have twenty-four-hour housekeeping; clock radios; hair dryers; electronic locks with a secondary lock; irons and ironing boards; telephones with auto wake-up, voice mail, and data ports; adjustable thermostats; desks; air conditioning; cable TV with HBO, CNN, ESPN, and pay-per-view; coffee makers; Internet access; and a free *USA Today* Monday through Friday. Some rooms also have balconies and a sofa bed. Use of the property's computers, software and printers is complimentary. The hotel's Cascabel Restaurant, the seven-time winner of the AAA Four Diamond Award, serves Southwestern fare in a comfortable atmosphere. The Cascabel Bar is a great place to have a quiet drink, and the Lobby Bar offers live piano music.

Fairfield Inn San Antonio Airport
88 Northeast Loop 410, San Antonio
(210) 530–9899, (800) 228–2800
www.fairfieldinn.com
$$

The friendly attitude of the staff is one of this 120-room hotel's highlights. Guests here are met with a smile and a hospitable atmosphere. Each guest room has a desk with a lamp, phones with data ports, and cable TV with in-room movies and an all-news channel. Other conveniences include laundry service, self-service laundry facilities, fax and copy services, and safe-deposit boxes. Complimentary continental breakfast is yet another plus. Active guests can take advantage of the hotel's indoor pool and whirlpool, and the nearby health club and golf facilities. Instead of room service, the hotel offers dinner delivery service from area restaurants. For guests who want to eat out, Applebee's Neighborhood Grill & Bar, Pappadeaux's Red Lobster, and Texas Land and Cattle Steakhouse are close by and serve lunch and dinner. Pets are only allowed as service animals for disabled guests.

Hampton Inn San Antonio Airport
8818 Jones Maltsberger Rd., San Antonio
(210) 366–1800, (800) HAMPTON
www.hampton-inn.com
$$

Have tickets to a San Antonio Spurs game? This hotel is 7 miles from the Alamodome. Looking for a good restaurant that won't drain your budget? Luby's, Shoney's, and La Margarita are all a short drive away. What about a place for a nice romantic or business dinner? Old San Francisco Steak House is 5 miles away, and Pappadeaux and Red Lobster are both less than a mile from the hotel. The hotel has a pool, and every room has remote-control television with cable, a hair dryer, and an iron. Cribs are available upon request, and for an extra charge, guests can use the meeting and banquet facilities, and laundry services.

Hilton San Antonio Airport
611 Northwest Loop 410, San Antonio
(210) 340–6060, (800) HILTONS
www.hilton.com
$$$

Each of the 386 guest rooms at this posh hotel has a Texas theme, perfect for visitors who want to immerse themselves in the rich history and culture of the Lone Star State. Amenities include twenty-four-hour housekeeping, clock radios, a newspaper delivered Monday through Friday, cable TV with premium channels like HBO, CNN, and ESPN, a telephone with data port, an adjustable thermostat, air conditioning, a coffee maker, and a desk with lamp. Guests on the Executive Level receive a daily newspaper, complimentary breakfast, and bathrobes to use during their stay. The hotel has a fitness center, indoor pool, table tennis, and a video arcade as well as complimentary airport shuttle service. For business travelers and groups, there are 16,000 square feet of meeting space, including two ballrooms. Tex's Sports Bar has several televisions broadcasting games via satellite while serving guests drinks and dinner from a full menu. One of the property's prime assets is its location, not only close to the airport but also within a five-minute drive of North Star Mall and Central Park Mall. In less than 20 minutes, guests can find themselves at a golf course, driving range, bowling alley, playground, basketball court, tennis courts, or horseback riding.

Holiday Inn Express San Antonio Airport
91 Northeast Loop 410, San Antonio
(210) 308–6700, (800) HOLIDAY
www.holiday-inn.com
$$

This hotel offers all the amenities that guests have come to expect from the Holiday Inn chain. Each spacious room has either one king-size or two double beds, a desk, and a full complement of conveniences: coffee maker, TV with premium cable channels like HBO and ESPN, telephones with data ports, an iron and ironing board, and an AM/FM clock radio.

The hotel also offers on-site guest laundry facilities, safe-deposit boxes, wake-up calls, copy and fax services, and free parking. Within a mile, guests can find golf, tennis, shopping—and the San Antonio International Airport. Looking for a bite to eat? Several chain restaurants are within walking distance.

Holiday Inn Select San Antonio International Airport
77 Northeast Loop 410, San Antonio
(210) 349–9900, (800) HOLIDAY
www.holiday-inn.com
$$

Like most hotels in the Holiday Inn chain, this one offers guests tidy, efficient rooms at a good price. Also on the premises are two restaurants, a cocktail lounge, a gift shop, a newsstand, guest laundry facilities, and a cash machine. The full business center has copy and fax machines as well as PCs and printers, and secretarial services are available. The hotel also has 10,000 square feet of meeting space. For guests with shopping on the agenda, North Star Mall is just a quick walk away.

Homegate Studios & Suites San Antonio Airport
11221 San Pedro Ave., San Antonio
(210) 342–4800, (888) 456–GATE
www.homegate.com
$$

The 115 roomy suites here are equipped with full-size kitchens with most appliances, remote-control cable TV, two telephone lines with voice mail, and irons and ironing boards. Guests can enjoy the pool and Jacuzzi, or work out at the on-site fitness center. Guest laundry and valet services are available.

La Quinta Airport East
333 Northeast Loop 410, San Antonio
(210) 826–0781, (800) 531–5900
www.laquinta.com
$$

Just a short drive from both San Antonio International Airport and downtown San

Antonio's attractions, this 200-room property has an outdoor pool and offers the full roster of hotel amenities. Rooms include cable television, modem lines, and AM/FM clock radios. Children under 18 stay free in their parents' room, and cribs and rollaway beds are available. Other perks and services include free local telephone calls, complimentary breakfast, free parking, express check-in, overnight delivery service, safe-deposit boxes, and laundry and valet service. The property also has 800 square feet of meeting space.

La Quinta San Antonio Airport West
219 Northeast Loop 410, San Antonio
(210) 342–4291, (800) 598–3828
www.laquinta.com
$$

Only a half-mile from San Antonio International Airport, this 100-room La Quinta is a good choice for visitors who want to be close to the airport—and to have all the amenities of a downtown hotel. Built in 1996, the property has an outdoor pool and offers free breakfast every day, courtesy van service daily from 5:00 A.M. until 1:00 A.M., free local telephone calls, free parking, express check-inn, safe-deposit boxes, laundry service, and a twenty-four-hour front desk. Each guest room has cable TV with movies and video games, modem lines, and an alarm clock. The hotel has a number of family units, and children under 18 stay free in their parents' room; cribs are available upon request. For business guests, the hotel has 500 square feet of meeting space.

Microtel Inn & Suites
1025 South Frio St., San Antonio
(210) 226–8666, (800) 771–7171
www.microtelinn.com
$$

This is a good home-base for visitors who want to pack in all of the San Antonio sights in just a few short days. Market Square, the Alamo, the River Walk, River Center Mall, and the Convention Center

are all nearby. SeaWorld of Texas is 10 miles away, as is San Antonio International Airport, and Six Flags Fiesta Texas is 20 miles from the hotel. Every room is equipped with a remote-control TV with premium channels like ESPN, CNN, and HBO. Children under 16 can stay free when they are accompanied by an adult; cribs are available upon request. Several fast-food chain restaurants are nearby—great for families with young kids and visitors looking to maximize their sightseeing time.

Residence Inn San Antonio Airport
1014 Northeast Loop 410, San Antonio
(210) 805–8118, (800) 331–3131
www.residenceinn.com
$$

Each of the one- and two-bedrooms suites at this three-story Residence Inn has a full kitchen—complete with refrigerator, microwave, and coffee maker—and separate living and sleeping areas furnished with a desk, remote-control cable TV with an all-news channel and in-room movies, a telephone with voice mail, and an iron and an ironing board. Some rooms even have a fireplace. Parking and a daily breakfast buffet are free, and guest laundry facilities, fax and copy services, and safe-deposit boxes are available. The hotel has an outdoor pool, tennis court, exercise room, and whirlpool, and there are three golf courses within a 20-mile radius. There are several restaurants nearby, including Veladi Ranch Steakhouse and Water Street Oyster Bar.

Rodeway Inn Downtown
900 North Main Ave., San Antonio
(210) 223–2951, (800) 228–2000
www.rodeway.com
$$

The best thing about this Rodeway Inn is its location. The Alamodome, the Alamo, San Antonio Botanical Gardens, Hemis-Fair Park, an IMAX Theater, the Japanese Sunken Gardens, Brackenridge Park, Market Square, River Center Mall, the

River Walk, San Antonio Zoo, and Splash-town USA are all within a 5-mile radius, and San Antonio International Airport is just 7 miles away. The modest property has a multilingual staff, an outdoor pool, and an on-site restaurant, and it offers the usual services and amenities: free continental breakfast, wake-up service, access to a fax machine, laundry service, and safe-deposit boxes. Most of the rooms have a coffee maker, full-length mirror, alarm clock, and cable TV.

San Antonio Airport Pear Tree Inn
143 Northeast Loop 410, San Antonio
(210) 366–9300, (800) 282–8733
www.drury-inn.com
$

Right in the heart of San Antonio's Business District, this hotel's clean rooms and affordable prices make it a good choice for business travelers. It's also a handy for shoppers and golfers: North Star Mall is only two blocks away, and the Quarry Golf Course is just a mile down the road. The property also boasts friendly, helpful staff members and a number of perks: free continental breakfast, free evening drinks Monday through Thursday from 5:30 P.M. to 7:00 P.M., free local telephone calls, and a complimentary airport shuttle. Guests also have access to an outdoor pool, fax services, laundry facilities, and on-site meeting rooms. Several restaurants are only a short walk away.

San Antonio Airport Posada Ana Inn
8600 Jones Maltsberger Rd., San Antonio
(210) 342–1400, (800) 378–7946
www.drury-inn.com
$$

Less than a mile from San Antonio International Airport, this Drury Inn property treats its guests like family. Every morning, a complimentary cooked-to-order full breakfast is served, and in the evenings, popcorn and cookies are available in the lobby. Other extras include an outdoor pool, free local telephone calls, an airport courtesy van, fax services, and

guest laundry facilities. For business guests, there are meeting rooms on-site. Many of San Antonio's top attractions are very close to this inn. The Alamo, Alamodome, River Walk, and Henry B. Gonzales Convention Center are 6 miles away; the San Antonio Zoo, Quarry Market, Quarry Golf Course, and North Star Mall lie closer still. Six Flags Fiesta Texas is 10 miles away, and SeaWorld of Texas is only a 14-mile drive. There are several dining options within a block of the property, including Applebee's Neighborhood Grill & Bar and Texas Land and Cattle Company. This is a good choice for families who want a good location, but not a high price.

Beyond Loop 410

Best Western Continental Inn
9735 I–35 N., San Antonio
(210) 655–3510, (800) 451–3510
www.bestwestern.com
$$

One of the highlights of this property is its landscaped pool area; the many large palm trees and other tropical plants create a relaxing and exotic atmosphere. Part of the largest lodging chain in the world, the hotel offers numerous special services and facilities. Two outdoor pools, four heated whirlpools, and a playground are on the premises, and guests enjoy such extras as complimentary shuttle service from 9:00 A.M. until 5:00 P.M., a twenty-four-hour front desk, express check-in and check-out, free parking, and complimentary newspapers in the lobby. Each of the 160 guest rooms offers cable TV with HBO, a hair dryer, free local telephone calls, room service, and air conditioning. The Continental Inn Restaurant is open daily for breakfast, lunch, and dinner; its varied menu includes everything from fried chicken to Mexican entrees. Shops and Retama Park are just 2 miles away; downtown San Antonio, including the River Walk and Alamo, is 8 miles away; and SeaWorld of Texas and Six Flags Fiesta Texas are each a 20-mile drive from the hotel.

Comfort Suites
6350 I–35 N., San Antonio
(210) 646–6600, (800) 519–3442
www.comfortsuites.com
$$

For families traveling on a budget, Comfort Suites is a dream come true. The suites are reasonably priced and accommodate several people quite comfortably. Each has remote-control cable TV and an iron and ironing board, and an exercise room, whirlpool, outdoor pool, and a newsstand are on the premises. Other services include a free newspaper on weekdays, outdoor parking, free local telephone calls, and safe-deposit boxes. Market Square, La Villita, and the River Walk are all 6 miles away.

Embassy Suites San Antonio International Airport
10110 U.S. Hwy. 281 North, San Antonio
(210) 525–9999, (800) EMBASSY
www.embassy-suites.com
$$

The major advantage of this comfortable hotel is its location near the airport. Hotel facilities include a pool, Ellington's Restaurant and Lounge, a game room, an exercise room, and meeting rooms; laundry facilities; guests may also use a microwave and a refrigerator. Each room comes equipped with a coffee maker, hair dryer, iron, and cable TV; cribs are available upon request. Other amenities include free newspapers, a free airport shuttle, room service, laundry service, safe-deposit boxes, and express checkout.

San Antonio Days Inn
9401 I–35 N., San Antonio
(210) 650–9779, (800) DAYS–INN
www.daysinn.com
$

Built in 1996, this motel is only 5 miles away from the airport and offers simple but comfortable rooms and moderate rates. Each of the 60 units is furnished with either a king-size or double bed, remote-control cable TV with HBO, in-room safe, AM/FM clock radio, and modem lines; rollaway beds and cribs are available upon request. The property also features an outdoor pool and meeting facilities, and offers free continental breakfast, express checkout, free parking, free local phone calls, a twenty-four-hour front desk, guest laundry services, and fax and copy services. It's is a good choice for families on a budget.

Super 8 San Antonio Airport
11355 San Pedro Ave., San Antonio
(210) 342–8488, (800) 800–8000
www.super8.com
$

Not the most elegant lodging place in town, but certainly not the shabbiest, this modest motel offers guests clean rooms for a good price. Extras include an outdoor pool, cable TV, complimentary continental breakfast, free local telephone calls, a twenty-four-hour front desk, and laundry service. There is also a meeting room, and a fax machine is available. San Antonio International Airport is very close to this property, and all of the excitement of downtown San Antonio and the River Walk is a short drive away.

Extended-Stay Accommodations

Are you staying in San Antonio for more than a week or two? Or are you traveling with children and in need of more space than the average hotel room provides? If so, you may want to look into business lodging hotels. These are properties that provide fully-furnished and -equipped apartments to guests who are planning a long stay, whether they are vacationing, relocating to the area, or in town on business. Nino Corporate Lodging, Inc. (12079 Starcrest Drive, San Antonio, 210-494-1008, 800-949-0703, www.relo-nino.com/NCL.htm) provides corporate lodging at several locations around the city. Nino offers one- or two-bedroom furnished apartments with fully-equipped kitchens, many with washers and dryers; most properties will even allow the family pet to stay. Prices vary from property to property, but generally, a one-bedroom apartment will be around $100 per night for fewer than 30 days and around $60 per night for more than 30 days. A two-bedroom apartment is about $129 per night for less than 30 days and about $75 per night for more than 30 days. There is a five-night minimum stay at all Nino properties. Call the Nino telephone numbers above for additional information about any of the nine complexes listed below.

Cadillac Lofts
317 Lexington Ave., San Antonio
www.relo-nino.com/cadillaclofts.html

Each of the 153 loft-style apartments at this Nino property has a unique floor plan. Guests can catch some sun on the rooftop terrace, or enjoy the outdoors at the two parks within walking distance of the property. Fast-food eateries, a YMCA, grocery stores, and other convenient businesses are also nearby. Cadillac Lofts is on the trolley line, so guests can reach downtown San Antonio without driving.

The Crescent
340 Treeline Park, San Antonio
www.relo-nino.com/Crescent.html

This Nino apartment complex is located in the Lincoln Heights area, providing quick access to Loop 410. It's a gated community, which means more security.

Communal facilities include an exercise room, pool and patio area, and a clubroom with a full kitchen. Each unit has 9-foot ceilings in the living area, and each bedroom has a ceiling fan. Guests also have the option of using a parking garage.

Indian Hollow
12701 West Ave., San Antonio
www.relo-nino.com/IndianHollow.html

Built on land that may at one time have been the site of a Payaya Indian settlement, this community has preserved the natural beauty of the San Antonio region. Native plants can still be found on the grounds thanks to thoughtful landscaping. Near the airport, this Nino property has an many luxury amenities, including an elegant pool area, a clubhouse with a business center, a full fitness center, and tastefully decorated units with ceiling fans and full kitchens. Some units also offer a garage or covered parking, fireplaces, and washer and dryer connections.

Lakeside Villas
8555 Laurens La., San Antonio
www.relo-nino.com/lakesidevillage.html

Located in the elegant Oakwell Farms area, this Nino site offers beautiful and comfortable accommodations. Each units features walk-in closets, an enclosed balcony, full washer and dryer, ample storage areas, and access gates. Guests may use the complex's three swimming pools, Jacuzzi, private lake, and 3 miles of jogging trails.

Promontory Point
4114 Medical Dr., San Antonio
www.relo-nino.com/Promontorypoint.html

Guests have their choice of five different floor plans at this limestone and stucco-surfaced complex, which offers outstanding views of the Texas Hill Country. The property features an outdoor pool and spa, a heated lap pool, an athletic facility offering aerobics classes, a putting green, a sand volleyball court, a full business center, lighted assigned covered parking, and washers and dryers.

Sterling Heights

Lincoln Heights, San Antonio
(210) 494–1008, (800) 949–0703
www.relo-nino.com/SterlingHeights.html

This Nino location's easy access to San Antonio's business district make it ideal for business travelers. The River Walk and River Center Mall can also be reached rapidly for a night out or day of shopping. The property offers an outdoor swimming pool and a fitness center, and guests traveling with kids will be glad to find a playground on-site. Each unit features a private balcony or patio, a full kitchen, walk-in closets, and security alarms. Card-controlled access gates are an additional safety measure.

Towers at the Majestic

222 E. Houston St., San Antonio
www.relo-nino.com/towersmagestic.html

Originally office buildings, these downtown towers were transformed into apartment buildings in 1993. Units feature large windows with wonderful views of downtown San Antonio. The property is within walking distance of the exciting nightlife of the River Walk and all of the historic sights of downtown San Antonio. Rivercenter Mall is nearby, and the Alamodome is a short walk away. Safety measures include coded security cards, surveillance cameras at entrances, and a covered parking garage.

Turtle Rock

3333 Oakwell Court, San Antonio
www.relo-nino.com/turtlerock.html

Located in Oakwell Court, the center of the Oakwell Farms community, Turtle Rock provides its guests with many amenities not found at a typical hotel. In addition to large and comfortable units, the property offers access gates, covered parking, a drive-through mail drop-off, and extensive recreational facilities. Guests can swim in the pool; play racquetball, billiards, tennis, basketball, and sand volleyball; and relax in the sauna and spa.

The Vintage

7733 Louis Pasteur, San Antonio
www.relo-nino.com/TheVintage.html

With architecture reminiscent of a Spanish square, this Nino property gives guests the feeling that they've been transported to the era of the Texas Revolution. The enclosed gardens are nice for a stroll at dusk, and the landscaped pool area is perfect for catching some sun. Units include washer and dryer connections, built-in bookcases, formal dining areas, and fully-equipped kitchens. For added security, the complex offers parking garages and gates with closed-circuit cameras.

Resorts

Hyatt Regency Hill Country Resort

9800 Hyatt Resort Dr., San Antonio
(210) 647–1234, (800) 233–1234
sanantonio.hyatt.com
$$$$

This elegant resort is situated in the rolling hills of the beautiful Texas Hill Country. The ranch house–style property's exposed wood beams and wooden porches with breathtaking views of the Hill Country give it a homey feel. The resort offers a wide range of recreational facilities, but it is an especially great choice for golf lovers. Hyatt Hill Country's 18-hole championship course has been rated one of the best in the United States by Golf Magazine. Private lessons are available for guests. Three tennis courts also are available for guest use, and a tennis pro is on hand for lessons or just a few tips. Guests can rent equipment from the pro shop. Ping-Pong, volleyball, croquet, and horseshoes can all be played at the health club, which also features the latest exercise equipment. Guests can pamper themselves with a variety of spa services, including massages, reflexology, facials, manicures, and pedicures.

Guests of all ages love Hyatt Hill Country's Ramblin' River, a 950-foot landscaped river where swimmers and floaters can drift along and enjoy the sun. Near the

The Hyatt Hill Country Resort's Lazy River ride cools summer visitors. PHOTO: HYATT REGENCY HILL COUNTRY RESORT

Ramblin' River, guests will find two swimming pools separated by a waterfall. Little guests will also enjoy Camp Hyatt, open to children between the ages of three and twelve; kids can participate in games, nature walks, and other activities.

The resort has several categories of rooms. Each of the 500 guest rooms offers cable TV with in-room movies, telephones with voice mail and computer hookup, video check-out, climate control, electronic door locks, an iron and ironing board, an AM/FM clock radio, a hair dryer, a refrigerator, and a coffee maker. Suites offer an additional room, a dining table and chairs, and a sofa bed, while VIP suites have two bedrooms and two bathrooms. Some of the suites are decorated in a Texas or Old West theme. The most deluxe accommodations option here is the Sunday House, a lovely two-story guest house with a charming covered porch where guests can admire the view from wooden rocking chairs. Constructed in the style of a traditional Texas ranch house, the house includes two bedrooms, three bathrooms, a formal dining room, a living room, a full kitchen, and a fireplace.

There are several restaurants on the property that offer a range of cuisines. Springhouse Cafe serves up a buffet and á la carte menu with Texas specialties. Don't miss the Hill Country Quesadillas; Texas favorites, they are flour tortillas filled with beef, chicken, or chorizo. The Cactus Oak Tavern serves grilled burgers, salads, and sandwiches at the clubhouse, where there's a pool table and the two TVs are always tuned to the Sports Channel. Pets are allowed at the resort; call for details.

Westin La Cantera
16641 La Cantera Parkway, San Antonio
(210) 558–6500, (800) WESTIN–1
www.westinlacantera.com
$$$–$$$$

Guests will find just about everything they could ever want in a resort at this

Arnold Palmer designed this golf course at La Cantera. PHOTO: WESTIN LA CANTERA RESORT

300-acre, $115-million property on the northwest side of San Antonio. Thirty-six holes of golf, six swimming pools, three hot tubs, spa services, a full fitness center, a kids' club, numerous restaurants, and magnificent views of the Texas Hill Country are all part of the package here.

The Traditional Rooms offer two double beds or one king-size bed with all of the standard amenities: a large desk, two telephones with voice mail, modem jacks, an in-room safe, two closets, a coffee maker, a mini refrigerator, cable TV with in-room movies, an iron with a full-size ironing board, a hair dryer, and a makeup mirror. Deluxe Rooms offer the same features as Traditional Rooms, but with a view of either the Hill Country, the pool, or the city; some have balconies or patios. Deluxe Rooms on the Royal Hacienda

Level offer such additional perks as concierge service, evening cocktails, continental breakfast, and access to the club lounge with beautiful views of the natural Texas landscape. Junior Suites have a separate sitting area with a sleep sofa for extra guests. The top-of-the-line Executive Suites are more than 1,000 square feet. The main feature of these suites is a parlor area that is equipped with a wet bar, entertainment center, fold-out couch, and coffee table. A balcony presents amazing views of the city.

Among the many restaurants on property, Francesca's at Sunset offers gourmet Southwestern fare, accompanied by a gorgeous view. The La Cantera Grille serves three meals a day; steak is the specialty of the house, but fish and chicken dishes are also popular choices. The Gantry is at the

Lost Quarry Pools, and guests can eat while lounging in the sun; seasonal Texas-style cookouts here are not to be missed. A fun and easygoing atmosphere make Brannon's Cafe a popular choice for meals. The menu is varied and the views are remarkable. For in-room dining, room service is offered around the clock. Looking for a place to unwind after a long day? Stop in at Tio's Lobby Lounge or Steinheimer's Bar.

The facilities at La Cantera are outstanding. Castle Rock Health Club provides guests with a wide range of spa services, including pedicures, manicures, facials, and many types of massages. Enchanted Rock Kid's Club, for guests between the ages of five and twelve, offers organized activities such as arts and crafts, outdoor sports like volleyball and swimming, games—and a chance to play with other kids. Rates for Enchanted Rock Kid's Club vary, so check with the resort.

The health club, numerous dining options, and the kids' activities all may sound wonderful, but the pride of this resort is the golf. Two 18-hole golf courses make up the property's backyard. The Resort Course at La Cantera was designed by golf course architect Jay Morrish and PGA Tour pro Tom Weiskopf. The Palmer Course at La Cantera was developed by Arnold Palmer, his first in the area.

Pets are allowed at the resort; call for details on restrictions.

Bed and Breakfast Inns

To experience San Antonio in a special way, stay in one of its many bed and breakfast properties. These one-of-a-kind accommodations offer a home-away-from-home experience that's tough to beat, especially if you'd like the chance to meet local residents, other travelers, and immerse yourself in the local atmosphere. San Antonio's B&Bs, many located in historic homes, are intimate properties that only host a handful of guests at a time. Often the owners of the inn reside right on-site, so you'll receive plenty of personal attention.

The capital of San Antonio's bed and breakfast world is the King William Historic District. This region, located on a quiet bend of the river, is a far cry from the bustling River Walk but still within easy walking distance of the restaurants and shops of the tourist area. Rich in nineteenth-century atmosphere, King William is dotted with historic homes that have been transformed into unique accommodations.

You'll also find bed and breakfast properties in some of San Antonio's other exclusive neighborhoods such as Monte Vista, a historic district that was first granted by King Philip of Spain as public land.

Days at these hostelries typically begin with a special breakfast, often one that showcases a favorite recipe of the house. Guests can chat with fellow travelers and ask the innkeeper for tips on exploring the city.

Local residents often turn to San Antonio's bed and breakfast properties for special occasions, whether it's a romantic weekend in their own hometown or a wedding or special party. Many of the bed and breakfast properties host weddings, and the innkeepers will even act as wedding coordinators, handling all the details.

If you are considering a stay in a bed and breakfast property, you'll want to ask more questions than you might at a traditional hotel or motel. These aren't cookie-cutter properties but instead unique lodging places, each with its own set of rules and its own way of doing business. A B&B may offer limited services and may be more restrictive in its policies. If applicable, be sure to ask: Is smoking permitted indoors? Are children allowed as guests? Is breakfast served at one time or as guests wander in? Are intimate tables available or are meals served family style? Are special dietary considerations met? Is there a minimum stay? What is the cancellation fee?

This chapter includes an array of bed and breakfast inns in San Antonio. Unless otherwise noted, each of these properties accepts major credit cards. Because they are small, most B&Bs are not required to comply with the same Americans with Disabilities Act regulations that govern hotels and motels; many do not have wheelchair-accessible guest rooms.

Insiders' Tip

Some bed and breakfast inns can be entirely rented by groups, such as people attending a reunion or wedding. Arrangements for such a takeover must be made many months in advance.

A Beckmann Inn and Carriage House
222 East Guenther St., San Antonio
(210) 229–1449, (800) 945–1449
www.beckmanninn.com
$$

Built in 1886 by Albert Beckmann for his bride, this Greek Revival home stayed in the Beckmann family for seventy years. The beautiful house is now owned by Betty Jo and Don Schwartz, who have turned it into an elegant bed and breakfast inn. Since opening the B&B, Betty Jo and Don have done everything possible to restore the original charm of the house and to make each guest as comfortable as possible. The wraparound porch invites guests to enjoy its shade, and the house's other porch is furnished with wicker chairs and love seats, so guests can unwind and enjoy complementary chocolates, cookies, and tea.

The interior is decorated with Victorian-style furniture that gives the house a dignified, elegant atmosphere. Each of the five spacious guest rooms has a colorful floral decor and is equipped with a ceiling fan, a television, a phone, a refrigerator, and a large armchair. The focal point of each room is an elaborately carved, queen-size Victorian bed. Adjacent to the main house, the Carriage House has been converted from the Beckmanns' maid's quarters and horse and carriage shelter into two mini-suites for guests seeking more privacy. They feature shuttered windows, gardens, balconies, and colorful flowers.

Guests are served a gourmet, two-course breakfast every morning in the house's formal dining room. Fresh-ground coffee, teas, juices, fresh fruit, muffins, pastries and a main entree are served at tables set with china, crystal, and silver. Betty Jo and Don guarantee that no guest will be served the same breakfast twice during their stay.

Adams House Bed & Breakfast Inn
231 Adams St., San Antonio
(210) 224–4791, (800) 666–4810
www.san-antonio-texas.com
$$

Nora Peterson and Richard Green opened the Adams House to visitors in 1997. Nestled in San Antonio's King William Historic District, it has five guests rooms, each with a different look and feel and each decorated with antiques. Every room has all the comforts of home, including cable TV with HBO and Showtime, a telephone, a queen-size bed, and private bath. The Texas Room is the largest; it opens onto a private porch and is outfitted with early-1900s Texas oak furniture, wildlife art, and American Indian rugs. Though writer O. Henry is not known to have ever visited the Adams House when he lived in the King William District, one of the guest rooms bears his name. A quiet, sunny room, perfect for visiting business guests or writers, it has large windows that look out over the courtyard. A collection of O. Henry's works can be found in the room. Guests looking for a quiet weekend getaway should stay in the Verandah Room, which features a verandah (of course) overlooking the shady backyard. This room has a private entrance and a luxurious two-person Jacuzzi. The 1902 Carriage House is the perfect place for honeymoon or anniversary couples. A newly installed two-person Jacuzzi sets the mood for romance in this private apartment suite. The Rose Sitting Room is available for the third person in a party of three. It is furnished with a twin day bed, and guests in this room share the bath in the room that the rest of the party is in. When the sitting room has no occupants, it is open to other guests as a quiet retreat for reading or resting.

B&Bs are Starting to Mean Business

Many companies are finding that bed and breakfast inns make excellent meeting sites, offering employees the chance to bond in a family atmosphere. Individual business travelers are also turning to these homey properties. At the end of another long day on the road, they are happy to enjoy an evening at "home," reading magazines or watching TV in a comfortable living room, enjoying some friendly conversation, or perhaps sitting out on the front porch sipping a glass of wine or iced tea.

As B&Bs have become more aware of the business traveler's needs, they have added features such as separate phone lines for individual rooms, faxes, photocopying service, and desks in guest rooms.

It's a trend that's taking place nationwide. The Professional Association of Innkeepers International (PAII) reports that 45 percent of its members offer blackboards and flip charts, 42 percent have meeting rooms, 32 percent own audiovisual equipment, 77 percent offer fax services, and 50 percent offer copying services.

Business travelers are turning to these nontraditional accommodations for several reasons. "First, B&Bs are getting more accommodating to the needs of the business traveler. They're getting adequate phone service, they're serving early breakfast, they're doing the things business travelers want them to do," explains Pat Hardy, co-executive director of PAII. "Second, they're becoming more mainstream. You can find B&Bs in big cities as well as small towns."

But for many business travelers, it's the chance to be recognized as an individual that makes the B&B increasingly attractive. "Anyone who's on the road a long time gets tired of seeing the same room and of being a number," explains Hardy. "The

The Bonner Garden
145 E. Agarita St., San Antonio
(210) 733–4222, (800) 396–4222
www.bonnergarden.com
$$

Located in what is now San Antonio's Monte Vista neighborhood, the Bonner Garden was built in 1910 by architect Atlee Ayers for Louisiana aristocrat Mary Bonner. Bonner's four previous homes all burnt down, so Ayers answered her concerns by erecting a 4,000-square-foot concrete Italian villa, reinforced with steel, cast in iron, and cased in stucco. Bonner became famous for her artwork, much of which is now displayed in the house. Jan and Noel Stenoien purchased the home, which opened in 1989 as Bonner Garden Bed and Breakfast, in 1993. They made

several improvements to the property, adding central air conditioning and heat, and off-street parking, to make their guests' stays as comfortable and happy as possible.

Each of the six guest rooms at the Bonner Garden has its own style and atmosphere. Guests looking for privacy and seclusion should reserve The Studio. The original studio of Mary Bonner, this stone-walled building is detached from the main house. Guests can relax in its queen-size canopy bed and Mexican-imported furniture. The Studio has modern amenities, too, including a television and VCR, a telephone, and a private bathroom. The popular Ivy Room features a queen-size sleigh bed, a Louis XVI armoire, English bedside tables, and a

opportunity to be a human being and not someone's number is one of the big draws of the B&B."

The corporate world is also turning to B&Bs as meeting sites. For some groups, the added security of a B&B is a plus. By renting the entire inn, meetings can be held without security worries that might be faced in a hotel, whether those worries take the form of corporate espionage or simple eavesdropping.

Security is an asset that draws individual business travelers as well. Since resident innkeepers know who is supposed to be on property and who is not, some people feel safer staying in a B&B.

Here are some tips for business travelers considering a stay at a San Antonio bed and breakfast:

•Look into the phone service. Is phone service available in all guest rooms? Do the guests rooms each have separate lines?

•Confirm meal times. Breakfast at B&Bs may range from a simple continental buffet to a massive sit-down feast. Some innkeepers put out the food for guests to enjoy at their leisure; others stick to a set meal time. Check to see that the inn serves early breakfast so you can be out and on the road.

•Check fax availability.

•Ask if the rooms are computer friendly. More and more B&Bs are providing modem hookups, but check first. Also, see if the guest rooms include a work space, either a table or desk.

•Recognize that B&Bs are not hotels. Don't look for twenty-four-hour room service, laundry service, and twice-a-day maid service.

colonial-era writing desk. The bathroom has both a bathtub and shower, and the imported tile floor gives it a certain flair. For honeymoon couples, the Bridal Suite is the obvious choice. It features a blue porcelain tile fireplace, a Louis XVI armoire, a queen-size mahogany canopy bed, and delicate Battenburg lace balloon drapes. A two-person Jacuzzi bathtub is the highlight of the private bath. The upstairs Garden Suite overlooks the property's gardens and swimming pool. Guests can lounge on the love seat by a sizable fireplace, or rest in the room's king-size four-poster bed. The bathroom has a Jacuzzi tub for relaxing after a long day of sightseeing or shopping. The Portico Room has its own entrance to the pool and gardens, making it a good choice for

guests who want to get some sun, or who just like a little extra privacy. The focal point of this room is the hand-painted, imported porcelain fireplace, though the mural on the ceiling by San Antonio artist John Crawford certainly deserves attention, too. The private bath has a shower and a mosaic tile floor. Though the Ancestors Room is the property's smallest, its collection of antiques, including ancient Chinese woodcarvings and a French armoire make it a special place to stay.

Brackenridge House
230 Madison, San Antonio
(210) 271–3442, (800) 221–1412
www.brackenridgehouse.com
$$–$$$$

Retired Air Force Colonel Bennie Blansett and his university administrator wife, Sue, bought this intimate inn in 1995. Since then, they've decorated it with comfortable antiques and quilts to make their guests feet right at home. Every room comes equipped with a king- or queen-size bed, cable TV with premium movie channels, a coffee maker, a mini refrigerator, a private telephone, and a microwave. Each also has a private bath with a claw-foot tub.

The Blansetts took much pleasure in decorating each of the six guest rooms in their new home. Monica's Suite, done in peaches and greens, has a sitting area and kitchenette. It opens onto the front porch near the wicker swing and rocking chairs that allow guests to relax and enjoy the beautiful King William neighborhood. A door connects Monica's Suite to Charlie's Room. It can be opened when two couples are traveling together; otherwise, the door remains locked. Decorated in shades of red, Charlie's room features a queen-size brass bed and a garden entrance that is only a short distance from the hot tub. Similar to Monica's Suite is Benet's Suite, but it color scheme is mauve and blue. The iron bed is covered in a beautiful turn-of-the-century-style yo-yo spread.

Another connecting door joins Benet's Suite to Karla's Room. A butterfly quilt and crocheted bedspread cover a beautiful iron king-size bed in this room, whose predominant color is a soft teal. Honeymoon or anniversary couples will feel at home in the Bride's Room, on the second story of house. The private verandah overlooking the garden and hot tub is just the spot for a romantic tête-à-tête. Decorated in shades of white, and with a king-size bed and lovely Victorian love seat, this room is the perfect place for couples who want to get away for a weekend. For families, or couples planning on a longer stay, the Carriage House has two bedrooms, a private bath, a full kitchen, and separate living and dining rooms. Monthly rates for the Carriage House are available.

The Ogé House on the Riverwalk
209 Washington St., San Antonio
(210) 223–2353, (800) 242–2770
www.ogeinn.com
$$$–$$$$

Guests staying at the Ogé House (pronounced "OH-jhay") are sure to be impressed by all the work that owners Patrick and Sharrie Magatagan have done to restore this pre–Civil War home. Set on 1.5 acres of the King William Historic District and overlooking the River Walk, the house was built in 1857 by Texas ranger and cattle rancher Louis Ogé. The Magatagans bought it in 1991 and have since made major renovations. It now has 10 guest rooms and suites. Each room was equipped with premium cable TV and a telephone, bathrooms were modernized, and the house was put in tip-top condition. It's furnished mostly with early American Victorian furniture, but there are some Texas-style items, mainly found in the Bluebonnet Room. Every room here has something special to offer, but guests looking for a great view should stay on the third floor, where each suite has access to the veranda or a private balcony. Sharrie prepares a continental breakfast usually consisting of croissants, sweet rolls, and cereals, served in the formal dining room or on the veranda.

Insiders' Tip

The VIA trolley is an excellent way for bed and breakfast guests in the King William district to reach major tourist attractions without the hassle of driving and parking.

Guests at the Ogé House are close to many of San Antonio's attractions. PHOTO: PARIS PERMENTER & JOHN BIGLEY

Riverwalk Inn
329 Old Guilbeau St., San Antonio
(210) 229–9422, (800) 254–4440
www.riverwalkinn.com
$$–$$$

This inn is a truly unique lodging place. A far cry from the typical B&B, the property consists of five two-story log homes, each moved from Tennessee, where they were first erected in 1842 and then had fallen to ruin. Owners Jan and Tracy Hammer had the cabins moved and restored and hope that they will help guests relive the history of San Antonio.

To help remind visitors of the history of the city, each of the 11 guest rooms is named for a hero of the Alamo. Antique country furniture, stone fireplaces, four-poster beds, soft quilts, and overstuffed armchairs are found in every room, and the Hammers hope that these will help transport their guests to the 1840s. If the old-fashioned rooms don't do the trick, then surely Storytelling Sunday will. Every

Sunday morning, storytellers come to the grounds, each representing a Texan in the mid-1800s. Some are specific people, such as Davy Crockett, but others simply portray a typical resident of early San Antonio.

Innkeepers Johnny Halpenny and Tammy Hill are sure to keep guests satisfied with a delicious breakfast served on an astounding 80-foot porch that overlooks the River Walk. French toast and ham and cheese kolaches (Czech pastry) are Johnny's specialties, and they keep guests coming back for more.

The Royal Swan
236 Madison, San Antonio
(210) 223–3776, (800) 368–3073
www.royalswan.com
$$

In the King William Historic District, this 1892 Victorian home is the perfect picture of what a B&B should be. The front and back porches, gabled roof, and verandas

queen-size bed, the other a comfortable twin day bed. The Texas Rose Room's yellow and rose decor is perhaps meant to recall Emily Morgan, today remembered as the "Yellow Rose of Texas." The room features a queen-size bed, a television, and a wardrobe, as well as a modern bathroom. With its own private entrance, the Garnet Room is perfect for guests who plan on enjoying San Antonio's nightlife, or who just want some extra privacy. Furnished with a king-size bed or two twins, a large claw-foot tub, and access to the back deck, this is a good choice for couples on a quiet weekend getaway.

Terrell Castle
950 E. Grayson St., San Antonio
(210) 271–9145, (800) 481–9732
www.terrellcastle.com
$$–$$$

While serving as ambassador plenipotentiary to Belgium under President Benjamin Harrison, Edwin Terrell saw many grand European castles, and when he returned home to San Antonio in 1894, he had his own built on a 1-acre site. Hard to miss, this grand mansion is now a unique B&B.

The main floor boasts amazing architectural details. Much of the library is in its original state, including the cabinetwork. The library's fireplace is the best of the nine in the house and features unique molded brickwork. The French chandelier in the parlor accents the magnificent round front window, the highlight of the room. The formal dining room still maintains the original detailed woodwork. The impressive curved windows at one end of the room even feature curved glass. Be sure to note the original border of the floor, which is an unusual design. The Central Hall features the remarkable main staircase, with carved, rounded newel posts. Unfortunately, a previous owner of the house destroyed much of the staircase during renovations.

The home's ten guest rooms are on the second and third floors. Each has a different ambience. On the second floor, the

beckon guests to come inside. There, the crystal chandeliers, claw-footed tubs, hand-carved woodwork, and cozy fireplaces entice them to stay.

A full home-cooked breakfast is served every morning at 9:00 A.M. in the dining room. It might consist of fresh bacon, spicy sausage, tasty muffins, fluffy pancakes, and homemade quiche. Breakfasts are planned ahead so that no guest has the same meal twice during their stay. An assortment of snacks and drinks is always available to guests who may need a quick bite before heading into San Antonio, or who want to sip something before bed.

There are five guest rooms here, and each one has something special to offer visitors. The Crystal Room's mahogany four-poster bed and velvet love seat bring out the romantic side of guests. Its private bath features a bathtub and shower, as well as an elegant crystal chandelier and lace shower curtain. A small balcony is accessible through French doors. The spacious Emerald Room contains a unique mahogany four-poster bed, rocker, and wardrobe. The private bath, with a claw-foot tub, is located just across the hall. The Emerald Room opens onto a veranda with wicker furniture, perfect for viewing the lovely Texas sunsets. Sharing access to the veranda with the Emerald Room is the Veranda Suite. This two-room unit has its own sitting room and can accommodate up to three people. One room features a

Yellow Rose Room features a king-size canopy bed, a television, three enormous windows; its own private bath, with shower, is just across the hall. A curved glass window with a window seat gives the Oval Room its name. Guests in this room are treated to a king-size bed, cozy chairs, a fireplace, a television, and a private bath with shower. Located at the back of the house, the Victorian Room is done in dark-toned woods and features a king-size bed, attached bath with shower, a television, and lots of privacy. The octagonal Colonial Room's highlight is a lovely fireplace. The room has both a twin and king-size bed, large windows, and a private bath. Rooms on the second floor include the Terrell Suite, with a large bay window facing north. A fireplace, comfortable chairs, an oversize closet, an antique bed, a sitting area, and a sunroom make this a special place. The room's private bath features an antique claw-foot tub, a dressing room, and a wet bar. One of the property's larger suites, the Giles Suite is a good choice for families. The main room has a four-poster king-size bed and the two attached rooms have a double bed and a single bed respectively. The private bathroom includes a shower/tub unit and there is a TV and a wet-bar area.

The third floor of the house has two suites and two guest rooms. The Tower Room has a posh king-size bed and a twin. The octagonal room features three large windows and comes equipped with a television set. The angles of the towers create the unique shape of the Moffat Room. It has a king-size bed and two twin beds, as well as a television and a wet bar. The Tower Room and Moffat Room share a bath. The Tower Suite is made up of the Tower Room and Moffat Room, the hallway connecting the two, and the shared bath. The Tower Suite can sleep up to seven guests, making it a good choice for large groups.

Decorated in an oriental motif, the Ballroom Suite has a king-size bed in the main room and a twin bed in each of the two adjacent chambers and is the largest suite in the house. An attached private bath

has a shower, and a separate bathing room features a large claw-foot tub.

A Yellow Rose
229 Madison St., San Antonio
(210) 229–9903, (800) 950–9903
www.ayellowrose.com
$$–$$$

Tucked away in the quiet King William Historic District, this elegant B&B is in a 130-year-old Victorian structure. Innkeepers Deb and Kit Walker have attended to every detail in an effort to make each guest's stay as comfortable and memorable as possible.

Each of the five spacious guest rooms is decorated with art and fresh flowers. There are beverages in the refrigerator, and as an added bonus, Godiva chocolates seem to find their way onto the pillows at night. A private entrance and porch, an en suite bath, a queen-size bed, as well as traditional amenities such as a radio, premium cable TV, a hair dryer, and an iron and ironing board make these rooms even more tempting.

Deb and Kit do everything they can to make sure your stay at A Yellow Rose is memorable, whether you're celebrating a special occasion such as a birthday or anniversary, or just out for a relaxing weekend. For a small additional fee, guests can arrange to have a bouquet of roses or a basket filled with goodies like champagne or chocolate waiting in their room upon arrival. The Walkers also offer special weekend packages that include such extras as massages and flowers. They'll even work with you to create a custom package—one that will surely make your visit unforgettable.

Restaurants

American

Asian

Barbecue

Breakfast

Cajun/Creole

Coffeehouses

Continental

Delis

French

Greek

Italian

New American

Southwestern

Steak

Texas

Tex-Mex

While Easterners were sitting down to meals seasoned with imported spices and served on fine china, Texas was still a frontier. Throughout much of its history as part of Mexico, then an independent republic, and finally as a state, Texas remained a vast land sparsely populated by cowboys and hardy pioneer types who learned to cook using the ingredients they had at hand, including prickly pear pads and rangy beef that was as tough as shoe leather.

Today San Antonio boasts some restaurants whose haute cuisine and continental fare have been lauded by national publications. But many people think the best food in San Antonio is served up at the small diners, the neighborhood cafes, and the smoky barbecue pits across the city. That's where you'll find reminders of that frontier ingenuity in dishes like fajitas and chicken-fried steak, plus ethnic favorites such as German sausage and Tex-Mex tacos and enchiladas.

Texas specialties have two things in common. First, most Texas dishes can trace their roots to harder times, when it was a necessity to use every cut of meat, even some that more gentrified diners might consider scrap. Fajita marinade was created to break down tough-as-hide skirt steak. Chicken-fried steak, tenderized to the point where the meat had to be breaded and fried just to hold it together, was a way to improve cheap steak cuts. And sausages use meat that the butcher just couldn't sell.

Another characteristic that Texas dishes have in common (along with enough cholesterol to harden any artery) is a reliance on beef. Cattle are king here, and beef makes an appearance on every menu and at every backyard cookout.

Those early cowboy cooks knew that not all meat was steak; some of it was tough and even stringy. They used Western ingenuity to turn what could have been waste into dishes that award-winning restaurants are now proud to serve. Chicken-fried steak is such a dish, using one of the toughest cuts of meat: the round steak. It's tenderized (the cook just beats the meat into submission) then dipped in an egg and milk batter, floured, and fried to a golden crispiness. The chicken-fried steak is the equivalent of white bread in Texas cuisine. Folks feel comfortable with chicken-fried steak. It's not spicy, so even those who can't handle the fiery heat of other local dishes love this one.

When you're ready for something spicier, order up the state dish of Texas: chili. More than a century ago, young girls known as "chili queens" sold chili con carne from kiosks in San Antonio's Market Square. When the dish went to the Chicago World's Fair in 1893, chili caught on and the rest, as they say, is history.

For all its variety, San Antonio's best-loved cuisine remains Tex-Mex. While you will find delightful dishes from the interior of Mexico on some menus, the standard enchilada, tamale, and taco offerings of the Tex-Mex restaurant rule. This cuisine was imported from the Monterrey region of Mexico, an area rich with cattle. Tex-Mex favorites feature lots of beef and plenty of cheese. Side dishes of refried (pinto) beans and

Spanish rice are standard, along with hot tortillas, either corn or flour. Baskets of fried tortilla chips accompanied by hot sauce (which is either green or red and can range from mild to fiery) are also standard fare.

Fajitas are a favorite "trash to treasure" Tex-Mex treat. Fajitas were a brainstorm of chuckwagon cooks who learned that marinating the tough skirt steak in lime juice broke down the meat into chewable consistency. Sliced in narrow strips and grilled, the meat is now served with cheese, salsa, and guacamole, and rolled into a flour tortilla.

You can find great chicken enchiladas with a flavorful verde tomatillo sauce, as well as vegetarian dishes or even shrimp enchiladas. But the real Tex-Mex favorite, known affectionately as Regular Plate No. 1, is an order of beef enchiladas, refried beans, and Spanish rice. If you're lucky, leche quemada, a sugary pecan praline, will be brought out with your check.

Tamales, both mild and spicy varieties, are also found on every Tex-Mex menu, but they're most popular during the Christmas season. Stores sell tamales by the dozen during the holidays, when it's popular to bring them to office parties and home get-togethers.

Making tamales at home is a time-consuming job, one traditionally tackled by large families. Tamales start with the preparation of a hog's head, boiled with garlic, spices, peppers, and cilantro. After cooking, the meat is ground and then simmered with spices. As the filling is prepared, other family members ready the hojas (corn husks) used to wrap the tamale. Others prepare the masa, a cornmeal worked with lard and seasonings, that is spread thinly on the shucks before filling with meat. Finally, the tamales are steamed in huge pots.

As you venture further south in Texas, you'll find a larger variety of Tex-Mex dishes, including some that are sold primarily in Hispanic neighborhoods. One of these dishes is cabrito, tender young goat usually cooked over an open flame on a spit. Cabrito is a common dish in border towns, where you can often see it hanging on spits in market windows.

Although San Antonio's cuisine borrows heavily from the Mexican culture, it also draws from other ethnic groups that settled this land. People of more than thirty nationalities, from Alsatians to Czechs to Poles, settled communities throughout Texas, bringing their own culinary styles and adjusting them to fit the food supply they found on the frontier.

The Germans, one of the city's largest immigrant groups, settled the area northwest of San Antonio and founded the towns of New Braunfels and Fredericksburg. A New Braunfels museum explains that when German farmers butchered a pig, they "used everything but the squeal." Some shoppers preferred not to see all those pig parts looking back at them across a meat counter, so the German meat markets used whatever didn't sell to make sausage. Today the central Texas town of Elgin is the capital of the sausage world. Barbecue joints throughout the state sell Elgin sausage, a spicy, greasy concoction that's now all beef.

Barbecue is big business here. At last count there were over 90 smokin' pits across San Antonio. The state itself boasts

Insiders' Tip

Pick up a free copy of *San Antonio Food and Leisure* magazine. The bimonthly is published by Food and Leisure Publications (210-590-2921, www.food-leisure.com); copies are available at the San Antonio Convention and Visitors Bureau downtown visitors center.

about 1,300 barbecue joints, but that statistic only hints at the seriousness with which Texans take their task. The business of barbecue rings up over a half-billion dollars annually, a cobweb of commerce that connects an otherwise diverse, sprawling state with a common mission: Go forth Texans to cook and consume good barbecue.

Beef rules most of the Texas barbecue pits in the form of brisket, ribs, sausage, and chopped beef. But you'll find plenty of chicken and pork, plus an occasional offering of mutton.

Every Texas barbecue joint, whether the jukebox is playing Cajun or conjunto tunes, features beef brisket. Following the brisket, menus might involve some regional variation. Cabrito or barbecued goat is often spotted in the western portion of the state while lamb is a more common offering in East Texas. Cooking styles can vary as well.

Barbecue got its start in this region in the meat markets and butcher shops. These pioneer merchants were determined to find a use for cuts that weren't selling. On the weekends, they began smoking those quickly aging meats, hoping to make them more palatable with an infusion of smoke. It worked. Like a gaseous billboard, the smell of barbecue soon permeated the small towns and captured the attention of those doing their Saturday marketing. Farmers and ranchers in town for weekend trading came by the meat market and found an inexpensive lunch served up on the only plate a butcher had on hand: butcher paper.

Alfresco dining on the River Walk is enjoyed almost year-round. PHOTO: PARIS PERMENTER & JOHN BIGLEY

Eventually, farm and ranch families began making the meat market a regular weekend stop, dining off the back of their wagons. Soon some meat markets began to put up a few picnic tables for customers. Today the best joints still have a picnic table or two. Some still serve their product on butcher paper.

The rules of Texas barbecue are few, whether produced in a smoky restaurant, a backyard cooker, or a competitor's rig. First, take your time. Professional pitmasters spend as long as 18 to 20 hours to cook a brisket to smoky perfection, even when thermometers top 100 degrees. Cookoff competitors are known to stay up through the night stoking their smokers.

Second, Texan barbecue is always smoked, never grilled. True Texas barbecue is accomplished in a closed smoker, a treasure chest that seals in the meats with the smoke to ensure the union of the two. (Just how the smoker should be arranged, however, is the topic of yet another 'que controversy. In the community of Llano, north of San Antonio, pitmasters use an indirect barbecuing method. Wood, primarily mesquite, is placed in the firebox and allowed to burn down to coals, then it's transferred to the main section of the pit beneath the meat. Here it flavors and cooks the meat to perfection, imparting a delicate smoky taste that is subtler than that achieved through ordinary smoking.)

But with those ground rules in place, it's a cook's free-for-all when it comes to the preparation and presentation of the meal. In researching barbecue across this vast state, we also saw a myriad of ingredients tossed into rubs and sauces. Beer, cider vinegar, mustard, Worcestershire, brown sugar, Chinese chili oil, celery seed, white vinegar, soy sauce, pancake syrup, honey, apple jelly, gin, rum, Creole mustard, cayenne pepper, molasses, chipotles, Jamaican PickaPeppa sauce, orange juice, and even cranberry sauce have made appearances in Texas barbecue sauces and marinades. One pitmaster explained his varying recipe by, "It depends what I've got on hand" while another said his recipe "depends on how much beer I've had to drink that day."

One point that cooks will agree on, however, is that the barbecue sauce should be held back until the last stages of barbecuing to prevent burning. While many cooks continue to mop the meat with a spicy marinade during the smoking process, the actual barbecue sauce sees the meat only during its final minutes in the flames, if at all. Instead, cooks baste the meat with flavorful marinades to keep the meat moist in its trial by fire and to impart a unique taste. Many barbecue joints dish up their meat right of the smoker, sans sauce, with the tomato-based concoction served on the side, usually accompanied by a shaker of hot peppers soaking in vinegar to add a tangy kick to the meal. Rub recipes are similarly eclectic. These mixtures of dry ingredients, often heavy with garlic powder, chili powder, and black pepper, complement the meat's tastes without overpowering it.

Wood is another matter of personal choice—and controversy. Oak, hickory, pecan and mesquite chips are the choices of many Texas pitmasters, often in combination.

Barbecue ranks with state politics when it comes to provoking heated discussion between Texans. One barbecue joint has a sign over its counter that says it best: "Bar-b-que, sex and death are subjects that provoke intense speculation in most Texans. Out of the three, probably bar-b-que is taken most seriously."

Whatever cuisine you select, you'll find that most San Antonio restaurants are casual eateries. During the summer months, shorts and T-shirts are the uniform at many restaurants, especially those in tourist-frequented areas such as the River Walk. Some restaurants are "dress-up" establishments by Texas standards, places where diners would feel more comfortable in a jacket; we've indicated these restaurants in the listings.

Our restaurant listings are arranged by cuisine. We haven't included chain restaurants as a rule except for those properties that are especially unique or those chains that are headquartered near San Antonio.

Most restaurants are open for lunch and dinner and remain open between meals; we've indicated if restaurants deviate from this practice. You'll find that the majority of restaurants in San Antonio don't serve into the wee hours. Most close up around 10:00 P.M.

Thanks to the American Disabilities Act, restaurants are wheelchair accessible for the most part.

Smokers will find specially designated smoking sections in many restaurants; places that forbid smoking anywhere on-site are identified in the listings.

Some larger restaurants accept (and encourage) reservations; we've indicated these in the listings. Often, however, you'll just need to show up and get your name on the waiting list, especially at River Walk area restaurants. Waiting time varies, but expect long waits on Friday and Saturday evenings. Outdoor tables are especially popular anytime the mercury dips below the mid-90s during summer months and any time winter days are sunny and clear. Most River Walk restaurants also have indoor seating, popular with those in search of a little air-conditioned relief.

Most restaurants accept major credit cards; we've indicated those that deviate from this practice.

Price-Code Key

The price key symbol found in each listing is the approximate price for a meal for two including an entree and nonalcoholic beverage as well as appetizer and dessert. Some restaurants have a wide variety of entrees, so some listings have a price range.

$ . . . . Less than $20
$$ . . . . $20 to $40
$$$ . . . . $41 to $60
$$$$ . . . . More than $60

American

Blue Star Brewing Company
1414 South Alamo St., San Antonio
(210) 212–5506
www.bluestarbrewing.com
$$–$$$

Located in the Blue Star Arts Complex in the historic King William District, this was the city's first full-scale brew pub. Owned and operated by Joey and Maggie Villarreal, it stands across from Pioneer Flour Mill on a quiet stretch of the river. Although it may be San Antonio's first brew pub, the structure has a long history with hops: it first served as a beer warehouse.

Patrons can dine inside or on the outside deck and beer garden. The menu is extensive: Lunch specialties include burgers, soups, and salads as well as many deli sandwiches; dinner options include fresh catch of the day, chicken-fried chicken breast, chicken fajita plate, jerk chicken, and often a mixed grill. Vegetarians find plenty of options as well—a tasty black bean soup, veggie burgers, and more. And what other pub do you know that has its own pastry chef?

All this is served up with the real specialty of the house: beer. Among the brews on tap are European Pilsner, King William Ale, Pale Ale, Golden Ale, and others.

The pub is open for lunch and dinner Monday through Saturday.

Bullpepper's Old Towne Café
9903 San Pedro, San Antonio
(210) 348–7377
www.bullpeppers.com
$–$$

Like a traditional cafe, Bullpepper's offers diners a little bit of everything: some German dishes, a few steaks, a little Italian fare, and, most of all, plenty of good old-fashioned American cuisine. This family-friendly restaurant features specials like the No Bull Schnitz, a tenderloin of pork jaeger schnitzel in brown gravy and mushrooms, and O'Brien's whiskey-roasted corned beef and cabbage. Southwestern cuisine gets a share of the limelight, too, with dishes such as blackened catfish and the smoked jalapeño grill, which is smoked sausage and fresh jalapeño peppers skewered and charbroiled. Southern dishes make an appearance as well. Try the frog legs in a spicy breading. Save room for dessert if you can—selections are tempting. The specialty is Bull Mousse On The Loose, a chocolate mousse in a chocolate candy cup, but a favorite is App-Bull Dumpling, a cored apple filled with cinnamon, pecans, golden raisins, and butter caramel, all baked together to create a decadently delicious treat.

Dick's Last Resort
406 Navarro St., San Antonio
(210) 224–0026
$$–$$$

Dick's is known as the most wisecracking restaurant and bar on the river. The waiters and waitresses like to make jokes and toss out matchbooks decorated with old photos of topless women, and the ladies' room is decorated with photos of scantily clad hunks and vending machines offering fluorescent condoms. The restaurant offers both inside and outside seating. If you dine inside, you'll sit at huge communal tables and enjoy blues played by some of the area's finest musicians. The menu here leans toward barbecue, but includes choices from burgers to chicken to shrimp. Everything is served in small tin buckets on a table covered with white butcher paper. Main dishes arrive with a bucket of french fries and bread. Save room for the desserts: Mississippi mud pie, cheesecake, and that Texas favorite, pecan pie.

Gazebo at Los Patios
2015 Northeast Loop 410, San Antonio
(210) 655–6171
www.lospatios.com
$–$$

For more than three decades, this northside restaurant has served diners just five minutes from the San Antonio International Airport. The restaurant lies just below the traffic of Loop 4101, offering a quiet retreat in the heart of the hustle and bustle of the Loop. Gazebo is located in the heart of a 20-acre open-air mall filled with specialty shops.

The menu offers light fare, primarily salads, chicken, and shrimp. But the real charm of Gazebo lies in its setting. Located on the banks of Salado Creek, the restaurant is nestled among majestic live oaks and exotic plants.

Hard Rock Cafe San Antonio
111 Crockett St., San Antonio
(210) 224–7625
www.hardrockcafe.com
$$–$$$

Part of the South Bank development project, the Hard Rock Cafe offers rock 'n' roll memorabilia, good old American food, and, of course, the Hard Rock Cafe gift

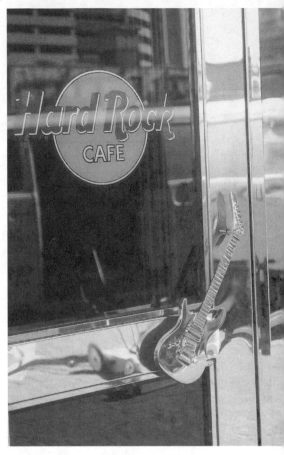

The world-famous Hard Rock Cafe draws a crowd on the River Walk. PHOTO: PARIS PERMENTER & JOHN BIGLEY

shop selling the requisite T-shirts. This popular restaurant has both indoor and River Walk dining (our favorite); the outdoor tables are nestled beneath shade trees so it's not too toasty even on summer days. But even if you eat outside, save time for a peek at the indoor collection of rock 'n' roll artifacts; Southeby's says that Hard Rock Cafe has the most extensive collection of rock memorabilia in the world.

Jim's Restaurant
8520 Crownhill Blvd., San Antonio, and
numerous other locations
(210) 828–1493
www.jimsrestaurants.com
$

Texans know Jim's, but they may not be familiar with the success story that lies behind this popular chain of family restaurants. Jim Hasslocher began his entrepreneurial endeavors by renting bikes and selling watermelon slices in Brackenridge Park in 1946. A few years later, he opened the Frontier Drive-In, with carhops dressed like cowgirls.

Today the cowgirl remains on the Jim's Restaurant logo, one that's seen in 20 locations in San Antonio alone. Started in 1963, the popular chain serves excellent breakfasts—everything from traditional eggs and bacon to an array of waffles—as well as lunch and dinner. Most of the locations are open around the clock and appeal to travelers as well as families and shift workers.

After Jim's took off, Jim Hasslocher branched out, opening other San Antonio eateries. The Tower of the Americas Restaurant, perched high atop the downtown tower, and the Magic Time Machine Restaurant, popular with kids of all ages, were founded by Hasslocher, past president of the National Restaurant Association. The entrepreneur also started the Biloxi Belle Casino Resort.

Kangaroo Court
512 River Walk, San Antonio
(210) 224–6821
www.kangaroocourt.com
$$

The Kangaroo Court is a combination oyster bar, restaurant, and pub, with something to make everyone happy. Daily

entrees include temptations such as shrimp served in a red-pepper cream sauce on angel-hair pasta; Appellate Court Shrimp, featuring skewered, bacon-wrapped shrimp with chipotle tartar sauce; and Flowing River Ribeye, dotted with fresh ground peppercorns and sweet bourbon cream. In keeping with its pub theme, the restaurant also features a wide selection of imported beer.

You can dine inside or along the River Walk (just look for the British flag table umbrellas). During the evening, guitarist Rusty Martin entertains diners.

The restaurant offers two hours of free parking in the River Bend and Mid-City Garages; just get your parking ticket validated by your server.

If you'd like to enjoy the restaurant's fare on a river barge, check with the restaurant about river dining.

Little Hipps
1423 McCullough Ave., San Antonio
(210) 222–8114
$

This noisy, immensely popular burger joint is something of a San Antonio legend. Although it's basically a dive located in a small tin building, its interior completely covered in old license plates, Little Hipps is popular with many downtown professionals as well as students from San Antonio College. The burgers are the draw: Texas-size creations that range from large to "giant," all served with your choice of toppings. The menu also offers other items such as grilled chicken sandwiches and shypoke eggs (tortilla chips piled with jalapeños topped with cheese).

Magic Time Machine Restaurant
902 Northeast Loop 410, San Antonio
(210) 828–1470
www.magictimemachine.com
$$

Started in 1973, this fun-loving restaurant offers more than a meal: It's an experience. Start with the waitstaff dressed as cartoon and movie characters: you might be seated by Ace Ventura or Braveheart, it's just the luck of the draw. And the seat you'll receive is no Formica table or corner booth, either. You might be assigned the Jail Cell, the Orgy Pit, or the Mine Shaft, depending on the crowd that night.

The brainchild of Jim and Veva Hasslocher (who also founded the Jim's Restaurants and the Tower of the Americas Restaurant), this unique eatery has spawned similar restaurants in Dallas. The menu features a mix of seafood, steaks, and grilled items, but the highlight is the Roman Orgy, a massive meal consisting of brisket, chicken, corn on the cob, and more. You'll serve yourself from the salad bar, set in an authentic 1953 MG Roadster. This restaurant is open daily for dinner only.

Malt House
115 South Zarzamora St., San Antonio
(210) 433–8441
$

The Malt House has been a San Antonio institution for more than half a century, serving up classic dishes like the quarter-pound Fat Boy burger with the obligatory order of fries. Other options include enchiladas and fried fish. But the real centerpiece of the Malt House menu is, predictable enough, its malts. Save room for one of these creamy creations (chocolate is an all-time favorite) and enjoy a taste of the 1950s, San Antonio-style. This restaurant is often selected by San Antonians as a favorite for budget watchers, a place where you can dine for less than $2.00 per person. It's open daily for breakfast, lunch, and dinner.

Olmos Pharmacy
3902 McCullough Ave., San Antonio
(210) 822–3361
$

It's rare these days to find an honest-to-goodness, old-fashioned drugstore soda fountain, but that's just what Olmos Pharmacy offers. This luncheonette is a San Antonio landmark serving up burgers, BLTs, and the like. It's open for breakfast and lunch daily.

Asian

Fujiya
9300 Wurzbach Rd., San Antonio
(210) 615–7553
$–$$

Located between I-10 West and Fredericksburg Road, this eatery holds the title as San Antonio's oldest authentic Japanese restaurant. You'll feel like you've taken a quick trip to Japan in the authentic tatami dining room, with seating on mats. The restaurant serves favorites such as sukiyaki, along with numerous seafood, vegetarian, and noodle dishes; more than 50 varieties of sushi are also available. Open daily for lunch and dinner.

Hunan River Garden
506 River Walk, San Antonio
(210) 222–0808
$$

Located right on the River Walk, this longtime local eatery offers up traditional Chinese fare, from sweet-and-sour pork to Kung Pao chicken, with a view that's definitely nontraditional. Szechuan, Hunan, and Cantonese cuisines are featured. This is the only Chinese restaurant on the River Walk and, as such, is always crowded. Daily lunch specials draw many office workers in the area as well as tourists. Open daily for lunch and dinner.

Kabuki Japanese Restaurant
15909 San Pedro Ave., San Antonio
(210) 545–5151
$$

This restaurant is located in the Galleria Oaks Shopping Center, just off U.S. 281 North at the Thousand Oaks exit. The elegant eatery features teppanyaki hibachi cooking as well as the creations of a Japanese sushi chef. Popular menu selections include sashimi, chirashi, sukiyaki for two, shabu shabu for two, tempura, teriyaki chicken, and teriyaki beef. The restaurant offers a happy hour special on Tuesday, Wednesday, Thursday, and Sunday nights from 5:00 to 7:00 P.M. with

San Antonio boasts restaurants of all kinds, many found along the River Walk. PHOTO: PARIS PERMENTER & JOHN BIGLEY

$1.00 sushi. Open Tuesday through Friday for lunch and dinner (closing between 2:00 and 5:00 P.M.) and weekends for dinner only.

Barbecue

Bill Miller Bar-B-Q
2750 Bill Miller La., San Antonio
(210) 533–5143
$

The largest barbecue chain in the nation is headquartered in San Antonio. Bill Miller Bar-B-Q has over three dozen locations in San Antonio alone. It might be considered the fast food version of barbecue joints, with a product milder and

more geared to family tastes than some of its competitors. But nevertheless the offerings here are plentiful and inexpensive. Take the whole family and order anything on the menu—brisket, chicken, sausage, or ham followed by an excellent slice of homemade pie—and you still won't break the family budget.

Bun 'N' Barrel
1150 Austin Hwy., San Antonio
(210) 828–2829
$

If you're nostalgic for the 1950s, visit the Bun 'n' Barrel. Founded in 1950, this diner is a genuine product of those happy days, complete with car hops, frothy malts, and a lunch counter. The walls are dotted with photos of classic cars, and a bulletin board by the cash register is dotted with ads offering classic cars and parts for sale. Every Saturday night, vintage-car enthusiasts fill the Bun 'n' Barrel parking lot, swapping stories and making deals on those old jalopies.

But the best reason to visit the Bun 'n' Barrel is the barbecue—and the buns. Order the chopped beef sandwich, a finely chopped mixture devoid of fat, seasoned with tangy sauce. It's served up on a homemade braided roll dotted with poppy seeds. If you're in the mood for something other than beef, try the pork ribs, beef sausage, ham, or turkey breast served with potato salad and ranch-style beans.

Carranza Grocery and Market
701 Austin Hwy., San Antonio
(210) 223–0903
$–$$

With a name like Carranza in downtown San Antonio, you might expect Tex-Mex fare from this two-story limestone restaurant. Wrong. This popular eatery is considered by many locals to be the source of some of the city's finest barbecue, all mesquite smoked and lovingly prepared. Carranza also serves Italian fare as well as steaks and seafood. Open for lunch weekdays, dinner Monday through Saturday.

Glossary of Texas Barbecue

Baby back ribs—Ribs from a young hog; usually the most tender of the rib cuts.

Barbacoa—The Spanish took the Indian word barbacoa, the basis for our own word barbecue, to describe this smoky meat. You will find barbacoa on the menu in many South Texas restaurants, especially Tex-Mex. It refers to a special type of barbecue: the head of a cow wrapped in cheesecloth and burlap, slow-smoked in a pit.

Beef clod—Part of the shoulder or the neck near the shoulder; used like brisket.

Brisket—Chest muscle of a cow. This typically tough cut requires a long, slow cooking period to break down to fibrous meat. When many Texans say they're eating barbecue, they mean brisket. Every joint probably serves up this barbecue dish of Texas.

Cabrito—Young goat.

Country-style pork ribs—Backbone of a hog. These ribs contain large chunks of meat and sometimes resemble a pork chop.

Marinade—A seasoned liquid mixture in which meat is soaked prior to cooking. Acidic marinades such as those containing lime juice help tenderize meat. (Note: Acidic marinades should never be used in aluminum containers.)

Rub—Dry ingredients rubbed onto meat to season it during cooking.

Sauce—The flavored liquid used as a condiment after the meat has cooked. In Texas, most sauces are tomato-based.

Skirt steak—Diaphragm muscle of a cow. This tough cut is usually used for fajitas after marinating.

Slab of ribs—A whole side of the rib cage.

Smoke ring—The telltale pink ring in meat that authenticates it as barbecue.

Sop—A basting sauce applied during the barbecuing process.

Spare ribs—The lower portion of a hog's ribs.

Texas hibachi—A used 55-gallon drum used as a barbecue cooker.

The Club House Pit Bar-B-Q
2218 Broadway, San Antonio
(210) 229–9945
$

This is one of the real treasures of San Antonio. This family-owned and -operated joint serves up slow-cooked barbecue prepared in a brick pit. All the meats are prepared without tenderizers or MSG—what you see is what you get, with lots of tangy sauce. You can choose from ribs (both pork and beef), all-beef sausage, chicken, pork, and beef brisket. Can't decide? Choose the "Super Platter" with a combination of five meats, potato salad, beans, and white bread. It's the best buy in the house and truly Texas-size. Finally, if anyone has saved room, there's a good supply of desserts. Offerings vary, but you'll usually find peach cobbler, brownies, bread pudding, and even sweet potato pie.

Paul Bunyan appetites should come by on Tuesday or Friday evenings for the all-you-can-eat special. On Friday nights there's live jazz, too, usually with no cover charge.

County Line Smokehouse and Grill
111 West Crockett St., San Antonio
(210) 229–1941
10101 I–10 W., San Antonio
(210) 641–1998
www.countyline.com
$$

The County Line is an institution among Texas barbecue lovers—folks who know good barbecue. With locations around the state, this restaurant is a step above the usual BBQ joint; it's the kind of place where you might go to celebrate a special event with some special food.

The River Walk location is tucked next door to the Hard Rock Cafe in the South Bank Complex and offers indoor and outside dining. The restaurant has a roadhouse atmosphere, casual and fun. Like the other locations, this County Line specializes in slow-cooked barbecue. Have your table order the all-you-can-eat extravaganza and you'll feast on beef ribs, brisket, and sausage served family style, with huge bowls of sour cream potato salad, crunchy coleslaw, and tasty pintos. The side dishes are made from scratch daily. There's even homemade bread that rises twice before baking.

One extra this location offers that other County Line's can't boast is its party barges. Call to reserve a private barge if you'd like to take your barbecue and beer cruising on the river.

This other San Antonio County Line is located just three miles from Fiesta Texas and is the newest in the chain. With its position right on the edge of the Hill Country, this location has a genuine country atmosphere, complete with a big breezy country porch and a landscaped patio. Like the chain's other locations, this restaurant serves up 'que in the finest Texas tradition. Open for lunch and dinner daily.

Fatso's Sports Garden
1704 Bandera Rd., San Antonio
(210) 432–0121
www.fatsossportsgarden.com
$

Known primarily as a recreation center, this eatery serves up lots of 'que in the form of mesquite-smoked chopped or sliced brisket, baby back ribs, smoked sausage, and grilled chicken. You can order the meat alone or with appetizers such as hot wings served with celery and chunky bleu-cheese dressing, potato skins and bacon, or nachos. Tacos are also available, filled with brisket or sausage. The atmosphere here is pure fun, with volleyball courts, pool tables, and eight big-screen televisions. The restaurant is open for lunch and dinner nightly and is a good choice if you've got a case of the late-night muchies.

Grady's Bar-B-Que
4109 Fredericksburg Rd., San Antonio
(210) 732–3571
7400 Bandera Rd., San Antonio
(210) 684–2899
6919 S. Zaramora St., San Antonio
(210) 932–2684
$

Grady Cowart's restaurants have been keeping the folks in San Antonio happy with big plates of barbecue since 1948. His restaurants serve up some of the most inexpensive offerings in the region, in large, comfortable dining rooms decorated with cowboy art.

Insiders' Tip

Several River Walk restaurants offer free parking in designated garages; check with your intended restaurant before heading out for the evening.

You can choose from beef, sausage, ham, or rib plates. We opted for brisket and ribs and couldn't have been happier. The brisket was tender and thinly sliced, served with a tangy sauce. The ribs were also cooked to tender perfection. All the plates arrive with a corn muffin plus a choice of two side dishes: French fries, potato salad, coleslaw, or beans.

Pig Stand
1508 Broadway, San Antonio
(210) 222-2794
801 South Presa St., San Antonio
(210) 227-1691
3054 Rigsby Ave., San Antonio
(210) 333-8231
$

This chain of coffee shops rose to prominence in the 1930s, calling itself the "world's first drive-in." Along with chicken-fried steak and breakfast dishes, it serves up barbecue, plus sandwiches, salads, and soups. Its first location was in Dallas, built in 1921, and the San Antonio site opened shortly after on Broadway. When the highway interchange project took place a while back, the original building was condemned and the restaurant was moved a few hundred yards away, but they're still serving the pig sandwiches, burgers, and malts that made them famous. The original Pig Stand neon signs proudly hangs at the Broadway location, which serves as a gathering place for classic-car owners every Friday night. All the locations serve the famous Pig Sandwich, barbecued pork with a secret relish and sauce, as well as chicken-fried steak, fried Gulf shrimp, burgers, seafood platters, enchilada dinners, and daily plate lunches. Open twenty-four hours daily.

Rudy's Country Store and Bar-B-Q
24152 I-10 W., Leon Springs
(210) 698-2141
$-$$

Rudy's calls itself "the worst bar-b-q in Texas." You sure wouldn't know that from the taste of their product, or from the crowds that flock to this sprawling joint just north of San Antonio in Leon Springs. Mention barbecue in the Alamo City and you'll hear Rudy's name. You can't miss the place—if the smell of smokin' meats doesn't lead you off the interstate, then the fluorescent pink letters atop the joint will. Once you arrive, you'll find an old-fashioned meat market with indoor seating plus an always-packed outdoor area filled with picnic tables holding bottles of vinegar and sauce.

Rudy's has an extensive menu: pork, baby back, St. Louis, and beef short ribs, plus chicken, prime rib, pork loin, chopped beef, sausage, turkey, and even rainbow trout.

Tom's Ribs
121 North Loop 1604 W., at Stone Oak Pkwy., San Antonio
(210) 404-7427
2535 Northwest Loop 410, at Vance Jackson Rd., San Antonio
(210) 344-7427
13323 Nacogdoches Rd., San Antonio
(210) 654-7427
www.tomsribs.com
$$

If it's ribs you crave, then head to Tom's Ribs. When San Antonians go out for a nice family barbecue dinner, many head to this eatery, north of Loop 410. It's plusher than most, with a bar, carpet, and booth and table service.

Tom's mascot is a lip lickin' pig with a bib around his neck and silverware in each front foot. Be prepared to feel like that pig when you place an order for a slab of baby back pork ribs. The waitress will robe you up with a plastic bib (sporting none other than the Tom's pig). Chicken and sausage are available as well, served up with two side dishes selected from a list of twelve. Besides the usual, diners can feast on Italian green beans and new potatoes, hot buttered carrots, sweet potatoes, or Tom's own Whiskey River Baked Beans.

The waitstaff wear T-shirts proclaiming "Praise the Pig and Pass the Napkins."

With ribs this good, what's a little mess?

The restaurant offers takeout as well as dining on the premises. It's open daily for lunch and dinner.

Fay Willie's
119 Heiman St., San Antonio
(210) 222–0887
www.FayWillies.com
$–$$

This Sunset Station barbecue restaurant, just steps from the Alamodome, is the creation of Fay Moore, a longtime caterer in San Antonio. Set in a two-story brick building, it is filled with smoky wonders ranging from brisket to sausage to lamb ribs. This is the kind of barbecue joint that you'll feel equally comfortable in whether you're wearing cowboy boots or a three-piece suit. Nothing is better with barbecue than potato salad, and you'd have a tough time finding a better one that Fay Willie's. Save room for the cobbler if you can. If you fall in love with Fay Willie's smoky creations but wonder what you'll do when your San Antonio trip is just a memory, have no fear. This restaurant sells barbecue on the Internet, available in vacuum-packed pouches cooled by dry ice. The restaurant is open for lunch and dinner Monday through Saturday.

Breakfast

Earl Abel's
4200 Broadway, San Antonio
(210) 822–3358
$

This longtime favorite has been serving folks for over half a century. Like an old pair of sneakers, there's something comfortable and reassuring about this no-frills diner and its dependable menu, which starts with a good old-fashioned scrambled egg and pancake breakfast and continues with Texas favorites such as burgers, chicken-fried steak, pot roast, and fried chicken. Meals are topped off with desserts sure to blow any diet—like triple-layer German cake and coconut cake to

name just two. Along with in-house dining, the restaurant offers food to go; for orders, call (210) 822–7333. Open for breakfast, lunch, and dinner daily.

Guenther House Restaurant
205 E. Guenther St., San Antonio
(210) 227–1061
$$–$$$

Located in the former home of Carl Guenther, founder of Pioneer Flour, this restaurant features, not too surprisingly, plenty of biscuits and gravy, sweet cream waffles, and pancakes. After a morning of looking at King William's elegant homes, you can stop here to enjoy a light lunch of salad, a sandwich, or soup. There are outdoor tables, cooled by misters, and an elegant but small dining room. This eatery is very popular with San Antonians who work nearby and gets busy during the lunch hour.

Kangaroo Court
512 River Walk, San Antonio
(210) 224–6821
www.kangaroocourt.com
$$

Known as a popular dinner restaurant and pub (see American restaurants, above), The Kangaroo Court also offers a breakfast menu, something of a rarity among River Walk eateries. Start your day with the Magistrate's Mushroom, a roasted Portobello mushroom topped with sun-dried tomato pesto, fresh tomato slices, scrambled eggs, sautéed bell peppers, and melted mozzarella and parmesan cheese. In the mood for something a little sweeter? Order the River Barge Belgian Waffle, a creation topped with maple pecan syrup, strawberry and banana slices, and whipped cream. The restaurant offers two hours of free parking in the River Bend and Mid-City garages; just get your parking ticket validated by your server.

Magnolia Pancake Haus
13444 West Ave., San Antonio
(210) 496–0828
$

If you don't have the time or inclination to get up in the morning and make a big breakfast, then just head to the Magnolia Pancake Haus. Just about everything, from the pancakes to the sausage to the corned-beef hash, is made from scratch. Specialties of the house include the Munich apple pfannekuchen and the omelet Monterrey. This smoke-free restaurant offers a children's menu as well as take-out service. Open for breakfast and lunch from Tuesday through Sunday.

Cajun/Creole

The Bayous Riverside
517 North Presa St., San Antonio
(210) 223–6403
$$-$$$

If you're hungry for file gumbo or oysters on the half shell, The Bayous Riverside is your destination. This restaurant is located right on the banks of the river, and serves up spicy Cajun and Creole fare, including shrimp remoulade, frog legs, crawfish étouffée, and more. This restaurant has been operated by the Cace family for three generations and is known for its attention to detail and consistency. You can dine indoors or out (it's tough to beat the view on the River Walk), and the upstairs Overlook Saloon makes a good place to start the evening. Open for lunch and dinner daily.

Wahooz Seafood Kitchen
9802 Colonnade Blvd., San Antonio
(210) 690–9100
www.wahooz.com
$$

Upscale Cajun dining is the order of the day at this northside eatery, which also has a location in Corpus Christi. Decorated in New Orleans style, this fun-loving restaurant brings the spirit of the Big Easy to the Alamo City not only with its decor but also with its extensive menu. Entrees include étouffée, jambalaya, and plenty of po' boys. Specialties of the house include snapper Pontchartrain, charbroiled salmon, and blackened tchoupitulas. If you're looking for a little less spice, you'll also have your choice of numerous fried seafood dishes: shrimp, catfish, oysters, and crawfish. Dishes are accompanied by your selection from a good wine list. Wahooz is open daily for lunch and dinner.

Coffeehouses

Bawdsey Manor British Tea Room
124 Schertz Pkwy., San Antonio
(210) 659–8766

You may think of British tea as a stuffy occasion, but the Bawdsey Manor British Tea Room has a casual atmosphere. Serving traditional British tea, this is a fun place to spend an hour for lunch or an afternoon break. The beverages here taste very good, and are authentic enough to make you think you're in jolly Old England. There is a menu of sandwiches and finger foods to accompany your tea. Bawdsey Manor also does catering, so keep them in mind for your next special event or party. The tea room is open Tuesday through Thursday from 11:00 A.M. to 2:00 P.M., Friday from 11:00 A.M. to 8:00 P.M., and Saturday from 11:00 A.M. to 4:00 P.M. for lunch only.

Beignets Coffee House
245 Losoya St., San Antonio
(210) 224–7484

Serving hot and iced coffee, Beignets Coffee House offers some excellent food choices, too. Predictably enough, the beignets here are excellent. They're also very cheap; for less than $2.00 you can have three (or a dozen for less than $6.00). The texture is very light and the taste is as sweet as can be. We recommend them covered in powdered sugar for an after-coffee treat. Have a seat on the outdoor sidewalk tables to soak in the San Antonio atmosphere. Beignets is open Sunday through Thursday from 7:30 A.M. to 2:00 P.M., and Friday and Saturday from 7:30 A.M. to 9:00 P.M.; breakfast and lunch foods are served all day.

Bestpresso's
1900 N.W. Military Hwy., San Antonio
(210) 348–8210

Bestpresso's is a drive-thru, but that doesn't mean that the coffee, smoothies, and pastries that you get here aren't as good as those found at sit-down joints in the city. It's actually pretty convenient—there aren't many places where you can get a specialty coffee like Bestpresso's fabulous White Mocha when you're late for a meeting or on your way to Six Flags Fiesta Texas. There is one table at Bestpresso's, but you'll have to get there pretty early in the morning to get a shot at it, especially on the weekends, when the place can get pretty busy. It's open weekdays from 6:00 A.M. to 6:00 P.M., Saturday from 7:00 A.M. to 6:00 P.M., and Sunday from 8:00 A.M. to noon.

Calcutta Coffee House
7920 Fredericksburg Rd., San Antonio
(210) 692–9600

It's a little hard to find Calcutta Coffee House, but once you do locate it, you're sure to find something that tickles your taste buds. The coffee here is a little on the strong side and can be enriched with a shot of syrup, which comes in a variety of different flavors (our personal favorite is coconut). If you don't like coffee, but enjoy the coffeehouse atmosphere, you can order up a chai or another drink. Have a seat at one of the iron tables on the outdoor deck and have a conversation with a friend, or just enjoy the scene. Calcutta Coffee House is open Monday through Friday from 9:00 A.M. to 10:30 P.M., and Saturday 9:00 A.M. to 3:00 P.M.; sandwiches and light fare are served all day.

Candlelight Coffeehouse
3011 N. St. Mary's St., San Antonio
(210) 738–0099

Found on the St. Mary's Strip, this cafe is one of the most popular coffeehouses in San Antonio. A cup of joe here promises to be rich and not too strong. Candlelight Coffeehouse also is known for its menu.

Insiders like to design their own sandwiches, selecting from the variety of gourmet breads and fillings. Other light fare such as soups and pastas are also served, along with desserts and wine. This favorite hangout is open from 4:00 P.M. to 1:00 A.M. Friday and Saturday, and from 4:00 P.M. to midnight the rest of the week.

Espuma Coffee and Tea Emporium
928 S. Alamo St., San Antonio
(210) 226–1912

In the elegant King William Historical District, Espuma Coffee and Tea Emporium is one of San Antonio's favorite coffeehouses. Folks come from all around the city to enjoy its casual atmosphere and good drinks. If you want a little food to go with your coffee, you're in luck. Espuma serves light fare such as soups and sandwiches with a special twist (don't miss the tomato, mozzarella, and pesto sandwich). Gracing the brightly painted walls is original art by local artists. There is live music here on most Friday nights, so call ahead to see if you'll be able to catch an act. Espuma closes at 7:00 P.M. Sunday through Thursday, and at midnight on Friday and Saturday.

Lighthouse Coffee and Cafe
18730 Stone Oak Pkwy., San Antonio
(210) 495–5099

This quaint cafe serves some of the best coffee in San Antonio, according to some loyal locals. Fresh fruit smoothies and light meals also can be enjoyed here. Chef Eric Rocca, a graduate of the Culinary Institute of America in New York, personally prepares each plate. Many people enjoy the Lighthouse's blackened turkey sandwich. For a unique treat, try the mango pancakes. The comfortable atmosphere is ideal for families with children. The owners try to convey Christian themes in the cafe. Call ahead to see if there is live music scheduled. Lighthouse is open Monday through Thursday from 7:00 A.M. to 9:00 P.M., Friday and Saturday from 7:00 A.M. to 10:00 P.M.

Madhatter's Tea
320 Beauregard, San Antonio
(210) 212–4832

Only a quick walk from San Antonio's famous Witte Museum and in the city's Alamo Heights District, this funky tea joint is composed of three small sitting rooms and an outside deck. The inside is decorated with peculiar signs and quirky decorations. This place is known for its breakfast, so if you have a free morning, stop by. (For something different, try the tea waffles.) The Madhatter serves light fare Monday from 7:00 A.M. to 3:00 P.M., Tuesday through Thursday from 7:00 A.M. to 9:00 P.M., Friday from 7:00 A.M. to 10:00 P.M., Saturday from 9:00 A.M. to 10:00 P.M., and Sunday from 9:00 A.M. to 9:00 P.M.

Olmos Coffee House
518 Austin Hwy., San Antonio
(210) 829–4546

Though it still bears the name of its previous location in Olmos Park, this coffeehouse is now in the Alamo Heights neighborhood. Espressos, lattes, and yes, even drip coffee, can be found here, as can hot and iced tea. The menu includes homemade ice cream, sandwiches, and other quick bites. Saturday mornings feature a full breakfast menu until 11:00 A.M. Enjoy your drink or meal on the outdoor patio. Olmos Coffee House is open weekdays from 7:00 A.M. to 11:00 P.M., Saturday from 7:30 A.M. to 11:00 P.M., and Sunday from 8:00 A.M. to 4:00 P.M.

Continental

Crumpets Restaurant
3920 Harry Wurzbach Rd., San Antonio
(210) 821–5600
www.crumpetsa.com/
$$

For more than two decades, this restaurant has offered diners a relaxing place to enjoy continental fare as well as elegant baked goods. Many, especially during the lunch rush, come for the lighter fare such as chicken salad with toasted almond slices and celery, or Crumpets' special salad, a bed of lettuce topped with sliced charbroiled chicken breast, Canadian shrimp, and pecans. The entree list is extensive and includes fresh rainbow trout, sautéed medallions of veal, a daily quiche, and tenderloin of beef, charbroiled with Bordeaux mushroom, Bearnaise, or a green-peppercorn sauce. The restaurant is also home to a European-style bakery, with baguettes, flans, French pastries, and more. Reservations are recommended for five or more people and during holiday periods. Crumpets is open daily for lunch and dinner.

Fig Tree Restaurant
515 Villita St., San Antonio
(210) 224–1976
www.figtreerestaurant.com
$$$$

One of the most elegant and pricey restaurants at La Villita, and indeed in the city, is The Fig Tree, where continental cuisine is the order of the day. Dining here is at linen-topped tables set with china and crystal.

Fig Tree Restaurant was the 1998 recipient of the DiRoNA (Distinguished Restaurants of North America) Award. It has long been considered a place to celebrate special occasions. The restaurant is housed in one of the last private buildings in La Villita—the building was purchased in 1970 by the Phelps family as a residence but the family opened it as a restaurant one year later.

The menu here reflects the elegant style of the dining room, starting with appetizers such as Russian Beluga caviar, foie gras, escargot, and smoked salmon sautéed in white wine and herbs. Entrees include chateaubriand for two, rack of lamb, beef Wellington, filet mignon, venison loin, duck breast, and veal chop. Desserts are equally impressive: a delicate crème brûlée with seasonal fruit, Bananas Foster flamed table-side, and baked Alaska are among the choices. This restaurant is open for dinner only, and reservations are recommended.

The Fig Tree Restaurant, located near La Villita on the River Walk, hosts many special-occasion dinners.
PHOTO: PARIS PERMENTER & JOHN BIGLEY

Delis

Schilo's Delicatessen
428 E. Commerce St., San Antonio
(210) 223–6692
$

Just around the corner from Casa Rio, this deli is located on the street, not on the River Walk. What it lacks in atmosphere, it definitely makes up for in history. The deli was founded by Papa Fritz Schilo, a German immigrant. He opened a saloon in 1917, but when Prohibition came along he converted the operation to a deli. It was a lucky break for diners; mere suds could never match the subs and sandwiches that keep this deli packed with locals. Try a Reuben or a ham and cheese, or go all out for dinner with entrees like Wiener schnitzel or bratwurst. The homemade root beer is a must. Open for breakfast, lunch, and dinner Monday through Saturday.

French

Cafe Soleil
5800 Broadway, San Antonio
(210) 805–8866
$$

Cafe Soleil is a little different than your typical French restaurants. For starters, you'll find Internet terminals at the bar so you can check your e-mail before sitting down to dinner. (What would the French think of this intrusion into the meal?)

The menu is also not typically French. Although you will find some Provencal dishes, look for plenty of Texas favorites like steak and seafood at this eatery as well. Open Tuesday through Friday for lunch and dinner.

Chez Ardid
1919 San Pedro Ave., San Antonio
(210) 732–3203
$$$–$$$$

When it's time to pull out all the stops, whether to impress or to celebrate, this tony eatery is just the place to go. Serving classic French cuisine with a Spanish accent, this romantic dining spot is especially known for its herb-crusted rack of lamb and pheasant stuffed with veal and wild boar sausage. If you're in the mood for something with a little more punch, the paella is outstanding. There are excellent wines to accompany your selection. Jackets are required at this restaurant, and reservations are recommended. Open for dinner only Monday through Saturday.

L'Etoile
6106 Broadway, San Antonio
(210) 826–4551
$$$

Its name declares that this restaurant is "The Star," and many San Antonians agree.

Schilo's (pronounced she-lows) Deli has been feeding San Antonians for 100 years. PHOTO: PARIS PERMENTER & JOHN BIGLEY

L'Etoile is the city's longest-running French eatery, a casual restaurant with fancy dishes like escargot and baked oysters. Meat lovers can try the New Zealand rack of lamb or calf liver flavored with caramelized onions. The menu also includes pasta and a variety of seafood dishes such as Norwegian salmon and poached lobster. The restaurant is open for lunch and dinner Monday through Saturday.

Greek

Kostas' Greek Food
12606 Nacogdoches Rd., San Antonio
(210) 590–6969
$

Decorated with posters of Greek villages, this cafe is nothing fancy but nevertheless fun. Greek dishes are the order of the day, ranging from the traditional gyro, made with strips of lamb and beef rolled in tender pita bread, to spanakopita (spinach pie). Meals are accompanied by Greek salads topped with feta cheese. Be sure to save room for the real show stopper: the homemade baklava, a honey and nut creation that's the perfect complement to the spiciness of the main dishes. For even greater decadence, Kostas frequently prepares a chocolate chip–filled baklava.

Mina and Dimi's Greek House
7159 U.S. 90 W. and Military Dr.,
San Antonio
(210) 674–DIMI, (877) 671–3464
$

A mural of a whitewashed Greek village sets the scene at this popular Greek restaurant. Casual and fun, the eatery offers gyro sandwiches in chicken, beef, or lamb. A specialty of the house are the dolmathes, seasoned beef and rice in rolled grape leaves. Meat lovers often select the lamb chop platter, featuring charbroiled lamb chops with pita bread, fried okra, oven-baked potatoes, and a Greek salad. Others opt for moussaka, a Greek eggplant casserole with potatoes and seasoned ground beef with bechamel sauce.

The restaurant, located in Gateway Plaza, also hosts special events including a wine tasting on the first Thursday every month. Friday and Saturday nights bring belly dancing to the family-friendly place. Open for lunch and dinner Monday through Saturday.

Italian

Aldo's Ristorante Italiano
8539 Fredericksburg Rd., San Antonio
(210) 696-2536
$$

Located in a century-old house, this Italian eatery is a favorite for romantic occasions. Decorated with antiques, the restaurant is filled with the soft sounds of live piano music on weekend evenings. The menu offers a wide variety of Italian dishes such as snapper di Aldo (with crabmeat and artichoke hearts), and chicken gorgonzola. A good wine list offers plenty of selections to accompany your meal. Aldo's is open for lunch on weekdays and dinner nightly.

Boccone's Italian Restaurant
17776 Blanco Rd., San Antonio
(210) 492-2996
www.boccones.com/
$$

A dinner at Boccone's is a little like a trip to Italy. The dining room is filled with reminders of the Old Country, from the full-size replica of Leonardo da Vinci's flying machine that's suspended over the main dining room, to the hand-painted artwork that decorates the walls. This charming restaurant, located just inside Loop 410, has an extensive menu. Riccota gnocchi, pasta and pepperoni, chicken stuffed with green peppers and served in an iron skillet, and veal parmigiana are just a few of the house specialties. For real fire eaters who would like to test their ability to down hot peppers, the pasta arrabiata ("angry pasta") presents a real challenge. The Sicilian dish is prepared with hot peppers, black olives, whole garlic cloves, cabbage, penne pasta, and

more. Diners are warned that no refunds are given! The restaurant is completely smoke-free. Boccone's is open for lunch and dinner daily (closing between lunch and dinner except on Saturdays). There's live music on Friday, Saturday, and Sunday nights.

Italia Ristorante
504 River Walk, San Antonio
(210) 227-5902
www.italiariverwalk.com
$$-$$$

This elegant restaurant is located in the historic Casino Club Building. One of its most unusual features is the Chef's Gourmet Pasta Table, offering fresh pastas (the chef is so picky about pasta that he designed his own pasta boiler so it could be guaranteed to be al dente) and four kinds of sauce as well as sausage, shrimp, chicken, clams, and vegetables. The restaurant also serves a wide array of entrees including manicotti, lasagna prepared six different ways, eggplant parmesan, cannelloni, and many seafood dishes. It's open daily for lunch and dinner.

Michelino's
521 River Walk, San Antonio
(210) 223-2939
$$

The taste of Italy, from calamari to capellini with shrimp and scallops, comes to the River Walk at this popular eatery. Pasta dishes and pizzas are offered along with more elegant fare, such as grilled pork tenderloin with foccacia and fine wine. The outdoor tables, sheltered and shady, are the most popular but well worth the wait. Open daily for lunch and dinner.

Paesanos
555 E. Basse Rd., San Antonio
(210) 828-5191
Paesanos River Walk
111 West Crockett St., San Antonio
(210) 227-2782
http://paesanos.citysearch.com/
$$

This restaurant has two locations; the River Walk location is tops with tourists, while locals tend to gravitate to the Basse Road location, which overlooks The Quarry golf course. Both restaurants are well known for the signature dish: shrimp paesano, a delicate blend of angel-hair pasta and seasoned shrimp. But if you don't like seafood, don't despair—plenty of other options await. First-course selections include vegetable ravioli with pesto, spinach and chicken with tomatoes and cream, and cappellini with vegetables. Main courses range from pizza (the Margherita with cheese and fresh basil is tough to beat) to red snapper to veal shank.

The downtown location is considered to have one of the River Walk's most extensive wine lists. You'll also find an extensive martini menu at both locations. Both locations are open for lunch and dinner daily.

New American

Anaqua Grill
555 South Alamo St., San Antonio
(210) 229–1000
www.plazasa.com/
$$$–$$$$

The Plaza San Antonio is home to this often-lauded restaurant. Located just off the lobby, the sunny eatery has indoor and outdoor seating. The cool Saltillo tile floor lends a colorful accent to the outdoor seating area (where you may be joined by Chinese pheasants that roam the grounds). It's shaded and cooled by surrounding tropical foliage and ivy-covered columns. The menu features New American cuisine, ranging from Mediterranean-influenced pastas to Tex-Mex selections to Pacific Rim infusion dishes. Innovative presentations make for an adventurous experience with creative dishes such as masa-battered shrimp and orange-jicama salad. Open for breakfast, lunch, and dinner (closing between lunch and dinner).

Biga's on the Banks
203 S. St. Mary's St., San Antonio
(210) 225–0722
www.biga.com
$$$

Biga's chef and owner Bruce J. Auden has been nominated for the James Beard Foundation Award, one of the dining world's highest honors. One of San Antonio's most lauded restaurants, Biga's was also recently named one of "America's Best Restaurants" by *Gourmet Magazine*. These recognitions come as no surprise to San Antonio residents, who have long enjoyed the elegant eatery's innovative fare and events.

Located on the River Walk at street level, the contemporary style restaurant boasts natural lighting, river views, and a sophisticated loft-like atmosphere.

An eclectic menu awaits diners, who find that the New American cuisine of Biga's reflects the flavors of both Mexico and Asia. The menu changes daily. Typical appetizers include seared Hudson Valley foie gras with black trumpet mushrooms and grapefruit-duck glaze; duck confit with celery root, tart apples, and blackberry jus; and plain old Beluga caviar. Entree selections might include phyllo-wrapped sea bass with Serrano ham, creamy mustard leeks, and pinot noir sauce; sesame-tempura–crusted swordfish; Hunan-style barbecue-rubbed natural veal chop; rice wine–braised duck leg; and smoked cinnamon guinea hen breast.

One of Biga's most innovative concepts is its Table 31. Situated with a view of the kitchen, this table is available for parties of six to eight guests who enjoy a

Insiders' Tip
Restaurant reviewers at the *San Antonio Express-News* have voted Biga's "Best Brunch in the Alamo City."

prix-fixe tasting menu. Participants select a menu of six, seven, or eight courses, paired with wine. Price for the six-course dinner without wine starts at $59 per person. The menu varies but a typical meal might include lobster ravioli on arugula with lobster sauce and soft fennel; Szechuan pepper–cured salmon with orange chili noodles and sweet mustard; boudin-stuffed quail with pears and blackberry jus on a zucchini cake; veal and beef medallions with a chanterelle demi-glacé, mint marigold béarnaise, and truffled fries; Pavlova with marscapone; and orange muscat fruit. Don't have six or eight people in your party? Tables of two and four can also be accommodated at a private screened table. Reservations are required for Table 31, which is offered Sunday through Thursday evenings only. The restaurant also offers many special events throughout the year, from jazz brunches to international tastings.

Reservations are recommended for all dining. You can call the restaurant, reserve online at www.biga.com/reservations. html, or send an e-mail to perny@ biga.com. Biga's is open for dinner nightly and for Sunday brunch.

Polo's at the Fairmount
401 South Alamo St., San Antonio
(210) 224–8800, (800) 642–3363
www.wyndham.com/Fairmount/default.cfm
$$$–$$$$

The most highly acclaimed restaurant in the downtown area (and one of the most praised in San Antonio) is Polo's. *Esquire* magazine called this eatery "one of the most innovative in the country" and *The New York Times* lauded it as "the chicest in San Antonio." But judge for yourself at breakfast, lunch, or dinner. Give the seafood pizza a try or, if you're in a Texas mood, nibble on the venison sausage pizza. The dinner menu takes on an international flair with choices such as New Zealand lamb, grilled Norwegian salmon, and good ol' barbecued quail in raspberry chipotle barbecue sauce.

Southwestern

Antlers Lodge
9800 Hyatt Hill Country Resort Dr.,
San Antonio
(210) 520–4001
$$$

The Hill Country Golf Club, located at the Hyatt Hill Country Resort near Fiesta Texas, is home to Antlers Lodge, a restaurant featuring Southwest cuisine that boasts an atmosphere casual enough to enjoy after a day of sightseeing in downtown San Antonio but special enough to celebrate a birthday, anniversary, or other occasion. The restaurant, with views of the greens, is lit by giant chandeliers made from deer antlers, appropriately enough, and the warm woodsy colors further enhance the lodge atmosphere. The eclectic menu offers some unique items such as San Antonio rattlesnake fritters, buffalo ribeye, and Texas Axis deer. Tamer fare, including steaks and potato-crusted salmon steak, round out the options. Antlers Lodge is open for dinner Tuesday through Sunday.

Boudro's
421 River Walk, San Antonio
(210) 224–8484
www.boudros.com
$$$

Located right on the River Walk between the Hyatt and the Hilton hotels, this steak and seafood restaurant is always packed. It offers the finest in Southwestern cuisine, usually with a twist that makes it unique even among San Antonio's plethora of excellent eateries. Start with a cactus margarita, a frozen concoction with a jolt of red cactus liqueur. Follow that eye-opener with an appetizer of smoked chicken or crab quesadillas or crab and shrimp tamales. Save room, though, for Boudro's specialties—coconut shrimp, pecan-grilled fish fillet, or the specialty of the house, blackened prime rib. Seating is available on the River Walk or in the dining room. Boudro's is open daily for lunch and dinner.

Zuni Bar and Grill
511 River Walk, San Antonio
(210) 227–0864
www.joesfood.com
$$$

This River Walk restaurant serves Southwestern cuisine to River Walk diners, with selections that start with blue corn nachos and andouille and brie quesadillas and then progress to specials such as roasted poblano pepper filled with shrimp and mozzarella, and spicy fajitas served with black beans. It's open daily for lunch and dinner.

Steak

Crystal Steak House
1039 Northeast Loop 410, San Antonio
(210) 826–2371
www.crystalsteakhouse.com
$$

Located on the north side of town, this restaurant is set in what was originally the Crystal Baking Company. Today the building is filled with Victorian furnishings that provide the backdrop for an elegant steak house.

Owned and operated by Jon Dennison and Achim Barrow, the restaurant aims to provide elegant meals without the sting of a high-priced steak house. Lunch options start at $5.95 and early bird specials, served from 4:00 to 7:00 P.M., also keep prices low.

This is one of San Antonio's most unique dining spots, showcasing one-of-a-kind fixtures from around the country. The exterior is lit by Victorian park lamps originally from Jacksonville, Illinois. The windows of the entryway are covered in 23-karat gold leaf and inlaid mother of pearl, while the hand-carved bar and mirror over the bar have been relocated from the Blind Pig Saloon in Beardstown, Illinois. The bar's stained-glass skylights hail from a Buffalo, New York, church while two 600-pound bronze chandeliers in the bar recall the turn-of-the-century elegance of a Pueblo, Colorado, courthouse.

The restaurant is open for lunch and dinner weekdays and Sundays, for dinner only on Saturdays. Reservations are suggested.

Grey Moss Inn
19010 Scenic Loop, Helotes
(210) 695–8301
www.grey-moss-inn.com/
$$$$

This steak house began as a tearoom in 1929. Located near Six Flags Fiesta Texas, the restaurant is about a forty-five-minute drive from downtown San Antonio, but well worth the trip thanks to its romantic, candlelight atmosphere and excellent food. You can choose from indoor or patio seating. Along with a full selection of mesquite-grilled steaks, the Grey Moss Inn also serves non-beef dishes such as free-range chicken and lamb chops with fresh rosemary cabernet sauce. The extensive wine list has been cited by *Wine Spectator* magazine.

The Grey Moss Inn is one of San Antonio's favorite wedding spots. The entire property is available for rental, or smaller groups can be accommodated in the 1929 cottage on the property; the inn's Garden Room, with its wood-burning stove; or the Veranda Room, which has a fireplace.

Reservations are recommended at this popular restaurant, which is open for dinner nightly. Monday through Thursday evenings, the inn offers specials for diners who arrive before 6:00 P.M.

Little Red Barn Steakhouse
1836 South Hackberry, San Antonio
(210) 532–4235
www.little-red-barn.com
$$

The Little Red Barn Steakhouse has been serving San Antonio residents and guests since 1963. The Western decor is as authentic as this Texas steak house itself (which serves more than 1,000 steaks every day). Brands dot the walls, creating a mural of Texas ranch history. The Western theme is carried out in the waitstaff's uniforms as well: denim-skirted, red-scarfed "cowgirls" and cowboy-hat-bedecked "cowboys" serve the tables with friendly efficiency. The restaurant prides itself in freshness, serving beef that is butchered daily and homemade salad dressings made fresh every morning. Menu offerings range from T-bone steaks (in sizes from 12 to 20 ounces), porterhouse, sirloin, club steak, prime rib, chopped sirloin, and hamburger steak. Beef liver with onions, chicken-fried steak, shrimp, catfish, fried chicken breast, and other offerings round out the menu. This restaurant is also very popular with groups, thanks to its seating capacity of up to 600 diners. The restaurant is open for lunch and dinner daily (closing between lunch and dinner on weekdays).

Little Rhein Steak House
231 South Alamo St., San Antonio
(210) 225–2111
www.littlerheinsteakhouse.com
$$$

Serious beef lovers should make plans to dine at the Little Rhein Steak House. Located where La Villita meets the River Walk near the Arneson River Theatre, this restaurant offers an excellent selection of fine steaks served on terraces overlooking the river. On less pleasant days, you may choose to dine inside the historic structure, built in 1847, which witnessed the development of San Antonio under six flags. The stone building also survived the battle of the Alamo only a few blocks away. In later years, the neighborhood was called the Little Rhein District because of its many German immigrants, and the restaurant took its name from that early title. In 1967, Frank W. Phelps (also the owner of the Fig Tree Restaurant) opened the Little Rhein Steakhouse, filling it with collectibles such as a 1907 bar and a light fixture that once illuminated President Theodore Roosevelt's Pullman car.

The extensive menu offers all types of beef, from T-bones to ribeye to porterhouse steak, all served with Texas caviar, a mixture of black-eyed peas and chopped onion.

Reservations are recommended. The restaurant is open daily for dinner only.

Morton's of Chicago Steakhouse
849 E. Commerce St., San Antonio
(210) 228–0700
www.mortons.com
$$$–$$$$

Located in the Rivercenter Mall, this steak house is part of the Morton's of Chicago chain of elegant eateries. The restaurant specializes in USDA prime aged beef as well as fish, lobster, veal, and chicken entrees. The house specialty is a twenty-four-ounce porterhouse; other top choices are the twenty-ounce New York sirloin and a fourteen-ounce double cut filet. The restaurant is open for dinner only; reservations are suggested.

Stockyards Cafe
1716 South San Marcos St., San Antonio
(210) 271–9471
$$

This restaurant, located a mile south of downtown west of the I–10 at the South Laredo exit, holds the record as Texas's oldest continuously open cafe, serving diners since 1889. Decorated with Western artifacts, the restaurant still feels like a slice of the 19th century. If you eat here on Monday or Wednesday, you can see beef at its source during the cattle auction, which starts about 9:00 A.M. in the adjacent Union Stockyards. The Stockyards Cafe serves all the usual cuts of beef; other options include chicken-fried steak, fried catfish, pork chops, and more. Breakfast tacos are favorites with early-morning diners. The cafe is open Monday and Wednesday from 7:00 A.M. to 1:00 P.M.; Tuesday, Thursday, and Friday 7:00 A.M. to 2:00 P.M.

Tower of the Americas Restaurant
222 HemisFair Plaza, San Antonio
(210) 223–3101
www.toweroftheamericas.com
$$$

For the best view of the city, head up the Tower of the Americas to the Tower

Restaurant. Steaks, Southwestern dishes, and seafood are the specialties of the house, all enjoyed in a revolving dining room (it makes one complete revolution per hour). Top choices include roast prime of beef, filet mignon, New York Strip, grilled salmon filet with lobster cream sauce, and baked shrimp. The High in the Sky Lounge has live jazz piano on Friday and Saturday nights. This restaurant is also popular with groups (up to 300 people can be accommodated in the restaurant and 150 in the lounge). Diners enjoy free parking and complimentary shuttle service to downtown hotels, the convention center, and the Alamodome. Reservations are recommended. The restaurant is open for lunch Monday through Saturday (then closing until 5:30 P.M.) and for dinner nightly.

Texas

Lone Star Cafe
237 Losoya St., San Antonio
(210) 223–9374
$

This popular River Walk restaurant serves up plenty of good old-fashioned country cooking. Look here for chicken-fried steaks, fried chicken, and some Tex-Mex dishes. The restaurant is located at street level, not at the level of pedestrian traffic on the River Walk, so it's a little away from the hustle and bustle. The tables on the porch, nestled under tall cypress trees, are a great place for people-watching.

Republic of Texas
526 River Walk, San Antonio
(210) 226–6256
$

Search for the table umbrellas that look like the Lone Star flag, and you'll have found the Republic of Texas. This restaurant serves up a little of everything, from fajitas to catfish to burgers, in a building that was once the office of River Walk architect Robert H. H. Hugman. The building still bears his name and the title

"Architect" still appears on the former river-level office. Hugman once wrote, "As soon as the river walkway was finished, I opened my office at water level. When I did this, people said, in essence, 'I knew you were a dreamer, but now I know you are also a fool. You'll be drowned like a rat in your own hole.'"

Tex-Mex

Alamo Café
14250 U.S. 281 North, San Antonio
(210) 495–2233
100600 I–10 West, San Antonio
(210) 691–8827
$$

Since 1981, this restaurant has been a favorite of many San Antonio residents. Although the name might make you think it would offer traditional Texas food, don't look for barbecue or chicken-fried steak here: this is the land of enchiladas, tacos, and tortillas. The restaurant also has several specialties including *carne guisada* (a stew of beef, chili peppers, and tomato), fajitas, and, that winter favorite, tortilla soup. Open daily for lunch and dinner.

Café Ole!
527 River Walk, San Antonio
(210) 223–2939
$

Located one level up from pedestrian traffic, this restaurant is right on the banks of the River Walk. From the covered porch you can watch the continual conga line of sidewalk activity that parades through this stretch of the walk—all while you've got your hands wrapped around a frozen margarita or a sizzling fajita. Other Tex-Mex favorites are served here, too. Café Ole! is open daily for lunch and dinner.

Casa Rio
430 Commerce St., San Antonio
(210) 225–9718
$

A Tex-Mex Primer

Here are some traditional Tex-Mex dishes that you're sure to see on San Antonio restaurant menus.

Bunelos—cinnamon crisps served as a dessert.

Botanas—appetizers.

Cabrito—young, tender goat.

Cerveza—beer.

Chalupa—fried, flat corn tortilla spread with refried beans and topped with meat, lettuce, tomatoes, and cheese; an open-faced taco.

Chicarrones—fried pork cracklings.

Chile rellenos—stuffed peppers.

Chorizo—spicy pork sausage.

Enchilada—corn or flour tortillas wrapped around a filling and covered with a hot or mild sauce; varieties include beef, chicken, cheese, sour cream, and shrimp.

Fajita (pronounced fa-he-ta)—grilled skirt steak strips, wrapped in flour tortillas and usually served still sizzling on a metal platter with condiments (pico de gallo, sour cream, cheese) on the side.

Flauta—corn tortillas wrapped around beef, chicken, or pork and fried until crispy; may be an appetizer or an entree.

Frijoles Refritos—refried beans.

Guacamole—avocado dip spiced with chopped onions, peppers, and herbs.

Huevos Rancheros—ranch-style eggs, spicy and made with tomatoes and chiles.

Leche Quemada—a pecan praline made with burnt sugar; the No. 1 dessert in Tex-Mex restaurants.

Margarita—popular tequila and lime drink, served in a salted glass either over ice or frozen.

Menudo—soup made from tripe.

Migas—eggs scrambled with torn strips of corn tortillas.

Molé (pronounced mole-ay)—a sauce made with nuts, spices, and chocolate; served over chicken enchiladas.

Picante Sauce—red sauce made from tomatoes, peppers, and onions and used as a dip for tortillas chips; ranges from mild to very hot.

Pico de Gallo—hot sauce made of tomatoes, chopped onions, peppers, and cilantro.

Quesadilla (pronounced kay-sa-dee-ya)—a tortilla covered with cheese and baked.

Salsa Verde—green sauce made with tomatillos, green chiles, garlic, and cilantro; used as a dip or on enchiladas.

Sopapilla—fried pastry dessert served with honey.

Tamale—corn dough filled with chopped pork, rolled in a corn husk, and steamed; served with or without chile sauce.

Tortilla (pronounced tor-tee-ya)—flat bread-like disc made of flour or corn; used to make many main dishes, and also served as an accompaniment to the meal, with or without butter.

Tostada—fried tortilla.

For more than fifty years, this restaurant has been best known as a tourist stop catering to folks eager to try some traditional Tex-Mex right on the banks of the river. But, hey, what's wrong with being popular with the tourist trade? Sure, your fellow diners may say "jal-a-peeno" instead of "hal-a-pen-yo" or (shudder) "fa-ji-tas" instead of "fa-hee-tas," but even diners brand new to Tex-Mex soon learn what tastes good. There's a real reason behind Casa Rio's long-running popularity—the food. The green chicken and the cheese enchiladas are especially tasty, both served with sides of good ol' cholesterol-laden beans, rice, chips, and tortillas.

The choicest tables at Casa Rio are at riverside, and you may have to wait a while for one of these seats. It's worth the wait. With tables right on the edge of the river (many of the River Walk restaurants are located about 10 feet back from the water's edge), you'll have an unbeatable view of the action up and down the river. This restaurant dates back to 1946, when it was built by Alfred F. Beyer on land first granded title in 1777 by the King of Spain. A hacienda was built here during the city's Spanish Colonial period and today it remains the core of the restaurant; cedar doors, cedar window lintels, a fireplace, and thick limestone walls are evidence of that early dwelling.

This restaurant was the first business in San Antonio to take advantage of its setting on the riverwalk. The owner used canoes, gondolas, and paddleboats, which eventually evolved into tours and dinner boats, San Antonio's first river cruises.

Even the menu is historic. The "regular plate"—a combo that includes a cheese enchilada, tamale, chili con carne, rice, and beans—was introduced in San Antonio in the 1800s and has been appearing on Casa Rio's menu since 1946. Today it's joined by the "deluxe dinner," which adds a crispy beef taco and guacamole to the mix. Lighter eaters might prefer La Senora, a plate with one cheese enchilada, guacamole, chili con queso, rice, and beans. On cooler days, Poblano El Rio soup, a combination of poblano peppers, corn, tomatoes, and chicken, is a flavorful choice. Any time of year, the Casarita, a twenty-ounce margarita, is a popular drink. Casa Rio is open for lunch and dinner daily.

Jacala Mexican Restaurant
606 West Ave., San Antonio
(210) 732–5222
www.jacala.com
$–$$

This restaurant, located on the north side of San Antonio about twelve minutes from downtown, holds the distinction of being the oldest originally owned Mexican restaurant in San Antonio. Since 1949, the Quinones family has owned and operated this popular eatery.

The restaurant offers a weekday lunch special for $4.99 that includes an enchilada, a taco, rice, beans, and iced tea. Although the enchiladas and tacos are local favorites, the restaurant is also known for its *caldo* (chicken soup) as well as its *menudo* (tripe soup) and tortilla soup. Other options include chile rellenos, chicken mole, chalupas, tamales, and more. You can dine indoors or outside in the courtyard. If you want to take a taste of San Antonio home with you, purchase a jar of Jacala's salsas or its jalapeño jelly; meals are also available to go. The restaurant is open daily for lunch and dinner.

La Fogata Mexican Restaurant
2427 Vance Jackson Rd., San Antonio
(210) 340–1337
www.lafogata.com
$$

When it comes time to relax and enjoy a meal in a setting that is a bit out of the ordinary, La Fogata is the place. Built like a Mexican hacienda, this restaurant has patios filled with tropical plants. Splashing fountains make for gentle background music and cantera stone pillars outline the dining area.

Although it offers many Tex-Mex specialties such as enchiladas and fajitas, La

Fogata also serves more traditional Mexican dishes. One specialty of the house is the *carne adobada* plate, pork marinated with bay leaves, cinnamon, and red peppers and served with rice and beans. Chicken mole, a chicken breast topped with La Fogata's own mole sauce, is especially popular. Another specialty is *chile poblano al carbon,* a poblano pepper stuffed with chicken and cheese then flamed over charcoal. This restaurant is open for lunch and dinner daily and for breakfast on weekends only.

La Margarita Mexican Restaurant and Oyster Bar
120 Produce Row, San Antonio
(210) 227–7140
$–$$

Mi Tierra is a restaurant that never closes. It serves Tex-Mex for breakfast, lunch, and dinner.

PHOTO: PARIS PERMENTER & JOHN BIGLEY

Just around the corner from Mi Tierra (see below) is its sister restaurant, La Margarita. This place was established to accommodate the huge overflow of Mi Tierra customers, but today it draws a regular clientele of its own. Styled like a New Orleans restaurant with outdoor patios, the often-noisy eatery has a definite Mexican feel, thanks not only to the food but to wandering mariachi musicians. Fajitas are the specialty of the house, and they're served with spicy pico de gallo, a mixture of chopped onions, cilantro, and peppers strong enough to wake up any palate. If you choose alfresco dining, you can enjoy watching shoppers stroll among the many specialty shops and vendor carts. The restaurant is open for lunch and dinner daily.

Mi Tierra Cafe and Bakery
218 Produce Row, San Antonio
(210) 225–1262
$

This restaurant never sleeps. Twenty-four hours a day, 365 days a year, this San Antonio institution serves up some of the city's best Tex-Mex fare. No matter when you visit, Mi Tierra is packed with locals and visitors. They crowd into the festive eatery, into booths garnished year-round with Christmas decorations, to enjoy Tex-Mex specialties.

Breakfast is a busy time, and locals start their day here with *huevos rancheros, chiliquiles* (scrambled eggs mixed with cheese, onions, and strips of corn tortillas, served with refried beans), or breakfast tacos. All feature the best tortillas in San Antonio. For lunch and dinner, Tex-Mex delights include enchiladas, carne asada (grilled beef prepared with an olive oil and garlic rub), quesadillas. Strolling troubadours take requests for Mexican ballads and give the restaurant a truly authentic air. Just as authentic is the adjacent *panaderia,* a Mexican bakery exuding its own tasty aromas: fresh tortillas and *polvorones,* cookies topped with cinnamon and sugar. Mi Tierra is open twenty-four hours daily.

The Original Mexican Restaurant
528 River Walk, San Antonio
(210) 224–9951
$

The original Mexican restaurant lives up to its name: it dates back to 1899 (although not at this location). Enjoy a seat right on the riverbanks and dine on Tex-Mex fare: enchiladas, fajitas, and tacos washed down with a Mexican *cerveza* or a cold margarita. Mariachi musicians play on Friday and Saturday nights, so stop by for an authentic San Antonio experience. The restaurant is open daily from 11:00 A.M. to midnight.

Rosario's Mexican Cafe y Cantina
910 South Alamo St., San Antonio
(210) 223–1806
$

This cafe and cantina is popular with the arts community in King William, but it's also known for its specialties: tortilla soup, enchiladas de mole, chiles rellenos, and *carne de puerco cascabel* (pork tips in red chile sauce). Decorated with original art and lots of terra-cotta pots, this funky restaurant offers live music on the weekends. It's open daily for lunch and dinner.

Tomatillos Café y Cantina
3210 Broadway, San Antonio
(210) 824–3005
www.tomatillos.com
$–$$

This casual and family friendly restaurant serves up grande proportions of Tex-Mex favorites. Start with quesadillas, marinated beef fajita taquitos, or nachos topped with beef or chicken fajita strips. The restaurant has several specialties, including the puffy taco (like the name says, puffed tortillas filled with spicy beef or chicken). An original dish is Tomatillos's enchiladas rellenos: one beef enchilada and one chicken enchilada with sour cream sauce, each stuffed with sautéed onions, bell peppers, and mushrooms and served with rice and beans. This restaurant is open daily for lunch and dinner.

Nightlife

Bars
Brewpubs
Comedy Clubs
Country/
 Western
Dance Clubs
Live Music
Movie Theaters
Piano Bars
Pubs
Sports Bars
Tejano Clubs

From clubs where you can wear your boots and learn to line dance to places where you can sip a martini in a quiet corner and enjoy the smooth sounds of a jazz ensemble, San Antonio has a varied nightlife scene. This chapter covers the highlights, including some of the city's best night spots and some of our personal favorites. Although not every nightclub in San Antonio is listed, it is a pretty good start.

There are a few things you should know before venturing out into the night in San Antonio. Some places, especially those that offer live music, have a cover charge. This is only the fee for getting through the door—drinks or meals are not included. Cover charges can vary greatly from place to place, but the typical cover runs from $3 to $8. If a big-name musician is playing at the club, the fee may be higher, and in some cases, tickets may need to be bought in advance.

Most San Antonio bars and clubs close at 2:00 A.M. on the weekends and earlier on weekdays. Every joint has its own hours, so if you're planning on hitting the town, call ahead to find out the closing times and plan your evening accordingly. Lastly, most of the places in this chapter are 21-and-over bars. The legal drinking age in Texas is 21, and minors are not even allowed in most places. If a bar or club admits those who are 18 and over, or is an all-ages spot, this information is included in the listing. In other words, if our listing doesn't mention a minimum age, assume that it is only for those 21 and older.

Unlike some Texas cities such as Austin, where liquor cannot be carried off premises, San Antonio does allow open containers of alcohol to be taken out of bars. Many sidewalk cafes along the River Walk sell margaritas, cold beer, and piña coladas to go.

Bars

Baramerica
723 South Alamo St., San Antonio
(210) 223-7462

What do most people picture when they hear the words "Texas bar"? Cowboys with big boots and bigger hats drinking beer, playing pool, and listening to their favorite tunes on a jukebox—in other words, Baramerica. Okay, so maybe some of the cowboys are really college kids, and the boots and Stetsons are sneakers and baseball caps, but the picture is basically the same. The prices at Baramerica can't be beat, less than $2.00 for a beer and under a dollar for a game of pool.

Blanco Tavern
7210 Blanco Rd., San Antonio
(210) 341-0405

This comfortable all-ages bar offers what most native Texans look for: a no-frills spot to relax and grab a drink. The comfortable environment is ideal for any type of patron from businessmen stopping in after a long day, to the Thursday night dart-leaguers who make this bar a weekly tradition, to the karaoke fans who crowd the place on Monday night. Several televisions broadcast sporting events, while pool tables are available for experts or those looking to learn. Blanco Tavern serves finger foods to tide patrons over until dinner, and Fat Tire, Shiner, Guinness, Paulaner Oktoberfest, Bass, Amstel Light, Bud, and Miller are on tap.

Cadillac Bar & Restaurant
212 South Flores St., San Antonio
(210) 223-5533

The restaurant part of the Cadillac Bar & Restaurant serves full meals on a quaint outdoor patio, but the real attraction here is the bar and dance floor. Because of its close proximity to Bexar County Courthouse and San Antonio City Hall, you may find this place full of lawyers and city officials during the week—it's a favorite afterwork spot for folks who work in those buildings. On the weekends, though, the place is hopping with local thirty-somethings out for a good time. On Wednesday and Saturday nights, a DJ provides the music, but on Fridays it's all live. Local groups with sounds ranging from soul to modern rock play at the Cadillac.

Fat Tuesday
111 West Crockett St., San Antonio
(210) 212-7886

If your last trip to New Orleans Mardi Gras was canceled, then head to Fat Tuesday while you're in San Antonio. This River Walk place has the fun party atmosphere of New Orleans' biggest festival every night. What else would you expect from a place that's surrounded by River Walk party spots like the Hard Rock Cafe? Fat Tuesday's daiquiri bar claims to offer the world's largest selection of premium frozen drinks. The menu here consists of salads, sandwiches, and other light fare.

Hills & Dales Ice House
15403 White Fawn Dr., San Antonio
(210) 695-2307

On the outside of Loop 1604, this dive is a favorite with the college-age crowd due to its close proximity to the University of Texas at San Antonio. The single-room establishment is lined with long picnic tables where patrons kick back with their choice of beer—and what a choice it is. Hills & Dales has more than eighty varieties of beer for the choosing, ranging from Abita to Shiner. A pool table provides recreation for those who are interested; a jukebox plays the latest favorites.

Houston Street Alehouse
420 E. Houston St., San Antonio
(210) 354-4694
www.houstonalehouse.com

Only a short distance from the River Walk, this ale house is a fun spot to spend a Friday night with friends. It offers twenty-five beers on tap and a large selection of mixed drinks, as well as a variety of cigars. While this may look like a place for college kids, older folks should give it a try. With so many choices, you're sure to find something that pleases you here.

Mark's on the River
245 Commerce St., San Antonio
(210) 222-2444

If you're looking for a place on the River Walk that's not filled with neon lights and college kids, then Mark's on the River may be just the spot. It's the kind of place where you can enjoy a martini while listening to some soft jazz. If you're planning on stopping by Mark's, you may want to call ahead to see if there is a swing night planned. Big band music and discounted drinks make for a great time.

Martini's
8507 McCullough Ave., Suite A9, San Antonio
(210) 344-4747

This funky little bar gets very crowded on the weekends—cars pack the parking lot and patrons squeeze in to drink and dance. The place looks a little like a Vegas lounge; the guitars and neon martini glasses on the walls provide a fun atmosphere, while the small stage hosts a few musicians who provide mood music. If you're feeling active, head to the dance floor; it may be small, but that never stops the patrons here! If it's your first trip to Martini's, leave a little extra time to find the place; it's hard to spot unless you know exactly where you're going.

The Menger Bar
204 Alamo Plaza, San Antonio
(210) 223–4361

This historic bar is found at the Menger Hotel, where many famous figures have stayed while visiting the Alamo City. Decorated to look like the House of Lords Pub in London, this popular place is equally as legendary. It is said that Teddy Roosevelt enlisted some of his Rough Riders in this very bar during the Spanish-American War. The cherry-wood ceilings and decorative glass cabinets provide an elegant atmosphere, perfect for socializing with friends.

Mix Night Club
2423 N. St. Mary's St., San Antonio
(210) 735–1313

This is definitely a place for a younger bunch, or for older folks who don't mind mixing with the pierced and tattooed crowd. That's not to say that the Mix isn't a fun place to be. The loud music and pool tables keep the fans coming, especially those who attend the nearby San Antonio College. Cheap drinks are probably the main appeal of the bar, but whatever it is, it works. The Mix is nearly always packed, especially on the weekends.

Niles Wine Bar
7319 Broadway, San Antonio
(210) 826–8463

Niles Wine Bar knows its wine. And why shouldn't it? Owner and founder Niles Chumney is a former wine salesman who brings his experience with the beverage to this new business venture. Most of the patrons of this bar also are very familiar with wine, and that only makes Chumney try harder to find the very best to put on his wine list. That's not to say that customers who may not know much about wine can't enjoy this place. They just have more to learn—and will hopefully enjoy the learning experience as much as Niles Wine Bar staffers enjoy teaching would-be oenophiles. Jazz ensembles perform Thursday, Friday, and Saturday nights. Hours vary with the day, so call for closing times.

Polo Lounge
40 South Alamo St., San Antonio
(210) 224–8800

The drinks at Polo Lounge may be a little more expensive than at other places in town, but the atmosphere is worth the extra price. A three-piece ensemble recalls the far simpler decade of the 1950s, playing jazz and swing music on Friday and Saturday nights. The leather couches here are so comfortable that you won't want to leave them. Order a drink at the marble-top bar, which serves all the traditional favorites.

Swig
111 West Crockett St., San Antonio
(210) 476–0005

If you think that all of the bars on the San Antonio River Walk are for college kids and the Spring Break crowd, then you haven't been to Swig. Though the clientele is mostly in their twenties, these aren't the same kids that you'll find just down the river at techno dance clubs. You won't find this crowd with beers in their hands, either. More upscale drinks are served here, and the patrons enjoy them while listening to a jazz ensemble and basking in their undeniable coolness. Swig can be a little pricey, so those on a tight budget shouldn't plan on spending too much time at this trendy spot.

Zinc Champagne & Wine Bar
207 North Presa St., San Antonio
(210) 224–2900

This is not a place to go if you're pinching pennies, but if you want to experience a real upscale bar in San Antonio, this is your spot. Parchman Stremmel, one of the city's most acclaimed art galleries, is right next door. The drink list here isn't limited to wine and champagne, but they are the most popular choices. A metal bar area gives the place a modern look and feel. A small menu of snacks offers escargot, pâté and the like. There are televisions in the bar, but an adjoining room provides a TV-free environment.

Brewpubs

Blue Star Brewing Company Restaurant & Bar
1414 South Alamo St., at the Blue Star Arts
Complex, San Antonio
(210) 212–5506

Toward the back of the Blue Star Arts Complex sits the funky building that houses Blue Star Brewing Company. This is a real brew pub that makes its own beer—to the delight of patrons. It's a very popular place and draws an eclectic crowd. Students from the University of Texas at San Antonio and customers of the adjoining arts complex all come here to have a good meal and an even better beer. Blue Star Brewing Company is a great place to spend a Saturday night, and you can make an evening of it by visiting the mixture of art galleries and shops in the rest of the complex.

Laboratory Brewing Co.
7310 Jones Maltsberger Rd., San Antonio
(210) 824–1997

Lots of live music and a brewery in the back make this a great spot to hang out. Mainly aimed at the singles crowd, Laboratory Brewing Co. has some pretty cheap deals during the week. Mondays and Tuesdays bring pints for $1.00, and happy hour takes $1.00 off Texas's favorite drink, the frozen margarita. Head for the outdoor patio if you want a place to chat. Check the newspaper or call to find out who's playing here; the music is generally funk, blues, or soul. If you're planning on going to the Lab, you may want to dress up a bit so you fit in with the bar's cruising crowd.

Comedy Clubs

The Rivercenter Comedy Club
849 E. Commerce St. at Rivercenter Mall,
San Antonio
(210) 229–1420
www.hotcomedy.com/rivercenter.htm

On the top floor of Rivercenter Mall, this club is the best place in town for live comedy. Operated by Hot Comedy Productions, which also runs comedy clubs in Austin and Tulsa, Oklahoma, it is one of the hottest tickets on the River Walk. Performers featured on HBO, Showtime, and *The Tonight Show with Jay Leno* have come here to entertain the San Antonio crowds. The air-conditioned space is a great place to get out of the city's sweltering heat. Showtimes are usually at 8:30 and 10:45 P.M., and there is a box office at the top of the escalators in the mall. Make sure to call ahead to confirm times, performers, and prices, because they can change.

Along with traveling acts, the club hosts several regular shows. The Oxymorons play at 10:30 P.M. every Sunday while an adult-oriented late night revue, *After Midnight Madness,* is scheduled for Saturday nights starting about 12:20 A.M. and running until 2:00 A.M.

The club also sponsors the annual Latino Laugh Festival, held every June. In previous years, the nationally broadcast event has featured talents such as Cheech Marin, Daisy Fuentes, Paul Rodriguez, Edward James Olmos, Maria Conchita Alonso, and Jimmy Smits.

Reservations for all shows are suggested; you can call the number above or fax in your reservation to (210) 229-9233. Ticket prices range from $9.00 to $12.00 for most acts (highest prices apply on Friday and Saturday nights).

Insiders' Tip

Brewpubs are a fairly new addition to the San Antonio scene; the Texas Legislature only voted to permit them in 1993.

Country/Western Clubs

Midnight Rodeo
12260 Nacogdoches Rd., San Antonio
(210) 655-0040

You saw all the movies before you came to San Antonio, and now you're wondering: Where are all the cowboys? They're here. So dust off the boots and break out the Stetson—at Midnight Rodeo, you can learn the latest line dances and sip a beer by the jukebox that blares country music non-stop. Dinner is served at a small buffet, but the main attraction is the bar, especially on Thursdays when all drinks are $1.25. There's live music on the weekends. Hours vary every day, so call ahead to find out what time the fun begins and ends.

Dance Clubs

The Atrium
8505 Broadway, San Antonio
(210) 822-1912

With six clubs, each with a different theme, you're sure to find a night spot you like at this 18-and-over complex. Slightly older patrons, or younger ones who can only wish they had been around to see *Saturday Night Fever* on the big screen, will enjoy the disco's beats. The karaoke bar is always a favorite, and Azteca is the best place to dance to Latin

sounds. Don't miss the Mirage, where a DJ plays the latest dance tunes in an Egyptian-styled room, or Red Square, where live music keeps dancers hopping. Be advised that the Atrium has a dress code, so make sure you're looking neat.

Banana Joe's Island Party
315 E. Houston St., San Antonio
(210) 224-4200

Do you miss the laid-back days of Spring Break? Then head to Banana Joe's Island Party. This is a place where everyone has a good time and there are (or perhaps because there are) plenty of drinks decorated with bright little umbrellas. If you dislike the fruity mixtures, there's beer on tap. Banana Joe's dance floor is always hopping, and tunes from the 1970s on to current hits make for great dancing. The casual atmosphere at Banana Joe's makes it ideal for socializing with friends new and old.

Bonham Exchange
411 Bonham, San Antonio
(210) 271-3811

Housed in a building that during World War II was the U.S.O., today the Bonham Exchange is one of San Antonio's hottest 18-and-over night spots. Popular with the gay crowd, this isn't just a club, it's a dance experience. Five bars and three dance floors let patrons get loose and boogie, while several special nights, such as "college and straight night," make everyone feel welcome. Sometimes the place doesn't get hopping until past midnight, so don't be in a rush to get there. This is a great spot that shouldn't be missed by anyone who enjoys the dance club scene.

Cabaret Dance Hall
801 Main St., San Antonio
(830) 796-8166

This dance hall is guaranteed to provide a good time for all visitors. The full bar includes more than forty domestic and imported beers with Guinness, Lone Star, Shiner Bock, and other Texas favorites on tap. Mixed drinks are also available. The

Cabaret Cafe offers gourmet food and takes special pride in the preparation of its burgers, chicken, steaks, and shrimp dishes. While the bar and the food may be appealing, the main draw of this spot is the music. Live music is scheduled regularly, and certain nights have special themes. Wednesdays are open-mike nights, for amateur rockers. Bigger shows are on Fridays and Saturdays, and occasionally Thursdays and Sundays. Shows usually start at 9:00 P.M. and advance tickets are available. Shows are for all ages. The Cabaret Cafe is open for lunch and dinner Tuesday through Sunday and closed Monday.

Club Agave
1174 E. Commerce St. at Sunset Station, San Antonio
(210) 222–9481
www.sunset-station.com

This dance club pulsates to a Latin beat. The club features live salsa as well as merengue music; if you don't know how to dance to a Latin groove, you can even take dance lessons here. The dance floor, a multicolored terrazzo, is an attraction in itself, lit by a state-of-the-art system.

Observatory Night Club
13307 San Pedro, San Antonio
(210) 494–1036

One cover fee buys admission to this three-dance-room experience. The first nightclub has a distinctive Latin feeling. It is a good spot to relax and maybe dance a little salsa. The second room is the main dance room, where you can dance under moving lights or belly up to the bar for a drink. The Spider Room is next and is the main draw of this club. Droves head for the warehouse-style space for its rave-like atmosphere.

Polly Esther's Culture Club
212 College St., San Antonio
(210) 220–1972

With three stories of dance floors, Polly Esther's has something for everyone. A '70's disco lets dancers shake their groove thang, the Culture Club blares the hippest hits from the '80s, and techno beats pound at Generation DVD. Planning on visiting Polly Esther's? Be prepared for skin-tight clothes and sweaty dancers. A restaurant on the first level serves dinner starting at 5:00 P.M. The

Polly Esther's may just be the funkiest dance club on the River Walk. PHOTO: PARIS PERMENTER & JOHN BIGLEY

location on the River Walk guarantees that there is never a shortage of patrons. The dance floors get crowded, especially on the weekends, but places like this were made for closely pressed bodies. The fun ends at 3:30 A.M.

The Saint
1430 North Main Ave., San Antonio
(210) 225–7330

If your idea of a good time involves drag shows and dancing iron men in Speedos, then The Saint is the perfect place for you. Mostly attracting men in their twenties (some in drag, some not) this club always provides a good time. The decor here is all about fun. The walls are painted with depictions of angels and fairies (perhaps not the kind for children's eyes) and balloons hang from the ceiling, giving the whole place a New Year's Party feeling. Tuesday nights bring the Amateur Drag Show, and there are male dancers on Wednesday and Saturday nights. There is no cover at The Saint before 11:00 P.M.

Studio 794
1174 E. Commerce St. at Sunset Station, San Antonio
(210) 222–9481
www.sunset-station.com

This 18-and-over club is a favorite with the under-21 crowd. With its flashing light and dance cages, it's probably not the best place to go if you're looking for a quiet drink. But if your idea of a good time includes the pounding rhythms of techno and hip-hop music, then this is the place to be. Two bars serve drinks to

those who are old enough to enjoy them. There is a small video arcade for when your feet start to hurt. Studio 794 is closed on Sundays.

2015 Club
2015 San Pedro Ave., San Antonio
(210) 733–3365

This dark club serves a mostly gay clientele. The large dance floor is usually filled with dancers, most of whom are in their thirties. The pool tables, video poker machines, and the bar are also popular. The drink prices aren't too expensive, so it's a good place to spend an evening. Don't worry about stopping for cash on the way, there's an ATM machine right at the club.

Live Music

Casbeers
1719 Blanco Rd., San Antonio
(210) 732–3511

Originally opened in the 1930s as a small bar where locals could grab a beer, today Casbeers is a San Antonio music must-

Rustic Gruene Hall in the nearby community of Gruene has become a favorite for boot-scootin' fun.
PHOTO: PARIS PERMENTER & JOHN BIGLEY

see. Its stage hosts some of the most popular local and regional bands, playing music ranging from rock to bluegrass. If you're planning on making a stop at Casbeers, make sure you don't spoil your dinner before you come; the food here is almost as legendary as the music. Heaping portions of enchiladas, burgers, and other hearty fare make this a very popular spot. Try to stop by on Saturday nights for a plate of some of the best chicken and dumplings in town. The drink menu here is limited to only beer and wine.

Floore Country Store
14464 Old Bandera Rd., San Antonio
(210) 695–8827

This is one of the best places in town to hear good country music. Some of Texas's favorite country performers have called this place home for at least one night. Lyle Lovett and Robert Earl Keen have played here to crowds of noisy fans. Don't eat before you come—spicy barbecue, frosty beer, and cold soft drinks are all waiting for you here, but you may have to stand in

quite a line to get them. Patrons can sit at picnic tables and enjoy the show, or stand near the stage for a better view.

Gruene Hall
281 Gruene Rd., New Braunfels
(830) 606–1281
www.gruenehall.com

North of San Antonio, on the north side of New Braunfels in a former ghost town called Gruene, a forty-six-star U.S. flag hangs over a steamy dance hall. Advertisements from the 1930s decorate the walls, and the only air conditioning is a breeze through the wide front door. Burlap bags, suspended from the ceiling, dampen the sounds of shuffling feet and country and western bands.

Although it may sound like another Hollywood version of small town life in Texas, this is Gruene Hall, the oldest dance hall in the Lone Star state. Since 1878, this joint has shook to the sounds of Texas music—from gutbucket country to folk to blues. Over the years, the dance and music styles may have changed, but Gruene Hall, like a good pair of boots, is as dependable as ever. The place has rocked to all sorts of music performed by a variety of both Texas- and nationally-known artists, including Guy Clark, the Fabulous Thunderbirds, Joe Ely, Nanci Griffith, Jimmy Gilmore, John Hiatt, Tish Hinojosa, Townes Van Zandt, and many more.

The dance hall is also home to one of Texas's most unique events: Gospel Brunch with a Texas Twist in Gruene Hall. Like a New Orleans–style gospel brunch, this special event fills the historic hall with the sounds of gospel, served up with an expansive buffet. The brunch is scheduled for the second Sunday of the month throughout the year. During the holiday season, there are also special performances featuring traditional, cowboy, and Christmas gospel tunes. Dress is as casual or as nice as you'd like it to be.

All ages are welcomed at the dance hall. Tickets for concerts and special events can be purchased by phone, online, or at the dance hall. Ticket prices vary by performer; tickets for the Gospel Brunch are $19.50 for adults, $8.50 for children. Seating is at large tables for parties of 12.

Jim Cullum's Landing
123 Losoya St., San Antonio
(210) 223–7266
www.landing.com

Established in 1963, Jim Cullum's Landing is the place to be for jazz on the River Walk. Located at the Hyatt Regency, this is a casual and fun spot to have a drink and hear some great music by the Jim Cullum Jazz Band. Bandleader Jim Cullum and his crew are well-known in San Antonio, delighting crowds with jazz primarily from the World War II era. The sounds of Jelly Roll Morton, Louis Armstrong, and other jazz greats often fill the air of the Paseo del Rio. Band members play vintage instruments in keeping with their historic sound; Cullum plays a 1927 Conn Victor model cornet.

Each circular table here is made to look like a classic LP, and hanging from the umbrellas atop the tables are trumpets, saxophones, and other instruments.

Jim Cullum's Landing at the Hyatt: a San Antonio jazz tradition. PHOTO: PARIS PERMENTER & JOHN BIGLEY

If you enjoy the sounds of The Landing and want to hear more, tune in to "Riverwalk, Live from The Landing," a 52-week radio series co-hosted by Cullum. Since 1988, the series has been bringing the sound of jazz across the country via Texas Public Radio. Presently the show is heard on more than 200 U.S. radio stations; for a list of the stations, see www.riverwalk.org. Cullum and his crew have also appeared on the big screen in *Still Breathing,* a 1996 film in which they play themselves. Their music can also be heard on the soundtrack of *The Newton Boys,* a 1997 movie shot in San Antonio and Austin.

Live jazz music can be heard every night of the week at The Landing, which is also open for lunch and dinner serving Tex-Mex fare: wines, liquors, beers, and coffee drinks are available at the bar. The Landing also offers special jazz cruises on the river for a minimum of 15 people.

Salute International Bar
2801 N. St. Mary's St., San Antonio
(210) 732–5307

Any kind of live music you could imagine can be heard at Salute International Bar. Local and regional bands play everything from heavy metal to blues to alternative rock at this dive. It's a local favorite, so be prepared for big crowds packed in to a very small space, especially on Thursdays. The cheerfully painted walls invite patrons to relax and enjoy the show. The club is only open Wednesday through Saturday nights.

Tequila Mockingbird
245 E. Commerce St., San Antonio
(210) 226–2473

This River Walk spot hosts bands and singers nearly every night of the week, so if you want to hear live music, head on over. Despite the name, it's not Latin sounds that you'll hear here. Most of the performers are of the blues persuasion, and the laid-back style of the music is reflected in the club itself. Tequila Mock-

ingbird has a casual attitude and a no-frills atmosphere. This is a great place to go if you want to have an informal drink and hear some good live music.

Taco Land
103 West Grayson St., San Antonio
(210) 223–8406

It may not look like much from the outside, or even on the inside, but didn't your mother tell you not to judge a book by its cover? If you can get past the low ceilings and dark spaces, you'll find a real Texas treasure. Pool tables, cheap beer, and good music make Taco Land a San Antonio staple. This 18-and-over alternative rock club hosts local and touring groups. If you want to find out who's playing, stop by and ask bartender Ram, a local legend himself, for a schedule.

White Rabbit
2410 N. St. Mary's St., San Antonio
(210) 737–2221

Appealing to mostly the younger crowd, this is a great place to hear live music, if you prefer hard rock and the like. This all-ages club attracts touring and local bands who love to play loud and fast. Try to show up early, because the place can get crowded and seats are scarce. Despite the packed room, the sound system here is hard to beat, though you may lose your hearing from the volume. Call ahead to find out who is playing if you don't want to get stuck listening to some local teenagers pound out hard-rock riffs.

Movie Theaters

Seeing a movie in a cool, dark theater is a nice way to beat the Texas heat. San Antonio has numerous movie theaters, most of which show first-run films. There are three major theater chains in the city: AMC, Regal, and Cinemark Theaters combined own 14 movie theaters in San Antonio. Ticket prices may vary by chain, but will be around $5.00 for matinee shows (films that start before 6:00 P.M.) and $8.00 for an evening show. There are discounts for children, students, and seniors at most locations.

AMC Theaters

There are two AMC Theater locations in San Antonio, and they are among the most popular theaters in the city. Each offers stadium-style seating, high-tech sound systems, and multiple screens. Recently AMC has created MovieTickets.com, allowing moviegoers to buy movie tickets and find out information about films online.

AMC Huebner Oaks 24
11075 I–10 W. at Huebner Oaks Shopping Center, San Antonio
(210) 558–9988

AMC Rivercenter 9
849 E. Commerce St. at Rivercenter Mall, San Antonio
(210) 558–9988

Cinemark Theaters

There are two Cinemark Theaters in the San Antonio. They show second-run movies for a discounted ticket price of $1.50.

Cinemark Dollar Movies 16
5063 Northwest Loop 410, San Antonio
(210) 523–1294

Cinemark Movies 9
4100 S. New Braunfels Ave., San Antonio
(210) 532–8886

Regal Cinemas

Regal has 10 locations around San Antonio, more than any other theater chain. They all show first-run movies, with the exception of Regal Crossroads, which is a good place to see art pictures, independents, foreign films, and documentaries. Several Regal Cinemas in San Antonio offer stadium seating.

Regal Alamo Quarry 14
255 E. Basse Rd., in the Alamo Quarry Market, San Antonio
(210) 333–3456, ext. 267

Regal Century Plaza 8
1215 Grosvenor Blvd., San Antonio
(210) 333–3456

Regal Cielo Vista 18
2828 Canyon Ridge Dr., San Antonio
(210) 680–7469

Regal Crossroads
4522 Fredericksburg Rd., San Antonio
(210) 333–3456, ext. 255

Regal Embassy 14
13707 Embassy Row, San Antonio
(210) 333–3456

Regal Fiesta 16
12631 Vance Jackson Rd., San Antonio
(210) 333–3456

Regal Galaxy 10
2938 Northeast Loop 410, San Antonio
(210) 333–3456

Regal Live Oak 18
7901 Pat Booker Rd., San Antonio
(210) 657–4480

Regal Northwest 10
7600 I–10, San Antonio
(210) 333–3456

Regal Northwoods 14
17640 Henderson Pass, San Antonio
(210) 333–3456

Special Movie Theaters

You can always see a movie at home, so why do it on vacation? San Antonio has two unique theaters that you can't find everywhere.

San Antonio IMAX Alamo Theatre at Rivercenter
849 E. Commerce St., in Rivercenter Mall, San Antonio
(210) 247–4629
www.imax-sa.com

This six-story theater is home to *Alamo...The Price of Freedom,* one of the best accounts on film of the fateful battle for Texas independence. This film has been playing at the San Antonio IMAX for about a decade, but never ceases to please moviegoers. The theater also shows 2- and 3-D IMAX features, which usually run about one hour. Occasionally, the theater shows first-run films that are particularly thrilling and thus well-suited to the extra-big screen (for example, *Jurassic Park* and *The Mummy Returns*).

Mission 4 Drive-In
3100 Roosevelt Ave., San Antonio
(210) 532–3258

Yes, this is a real drive-in movie theater, just like the ones folks used to go to in the 1950s and '60s. Recently bought by Cinemark Theaters, the Mission was first opened in 1947. The season for the theater runs from April through October. Whether the kids are in the backseat in their PJs or it's just two on an old-fashioned date, a night at the drive-in means nostalgic fun. Show times vary here, so make sure to check the *San Antonio Express-News* for what's showing.

Piano Bars

Howl at the Moon
111 West Crockett St., San Antonio
(210) 212–4695

Probably the most popular piano bar on the River Walk, Howl at the Moon is a San Antonio institution. Two bars serve patrons while a pianist plays old favorites and invites the audience to sing along. The piano players take requests for an extra "tip." Musicians at Howl at the Moon have been known to drag unsuspecting patrons to the piano, creating a slightly embarrassing situation, but it's all in good fun. Even if piano bars aren't usually your cup of tea, Howl at the Moon is worth a stop just so you can see a classic one in full swing.

Pubs

Brew Moon Cafe & Pub
16350 Blanco Rd., San Antonio
(210) 479–0066

If you're looking for a pub that doesn't feel like a pub, then head to the Brew Moon. Though Irish drinking songs may not blare from the speakers, this place does serve up some good brews. Murphy's Irish Stout and Guinness are popular choices with some patrons; others prefer Texas favorites like Shiner. Hungry? Good news: Brew Moon also serves up basic American fare. When a patron drinks 100 different beers at the pub, he gets his name on a plaque at the bar. What more could you ask for?

Durty Nelly's Irish Pub
200 South Alamo St., San Antonio
(210) 222–1400

With a great location, right in the middle of the River Walk at the Hilton Palacio del Rio hotel, Durty Nelly's is a very popular night spot for visitors and locals alike. Better still, it has one of the best beer selections around. The bar can get very crowded, especially on weekends, but it's all part of the experience. Some may find the prices a little high, but many say it's worth it. Visitors shouldn't miss this spot if they want to really experience the River Walk.

Sports Bars

Fatso's Sports Garden
1704 Bandera Rd., San Antonio
(210) 432–0121

A sports bar that lets you play—as well as watch—your favorite games, this is a great hangout no matter what the season (baseball, football, basketball, or hockey). If watching is your preference, 16 satellite receivers pick up any sporting event that you could think of, and there is only a cover charge on pay-per-view nights. Want to play? There are pool tables and volleyball courts, with volleyball league games every night from March through December. Don't miss karaoke on Wednesday through Friday or happy hour every day from 11:00 A.M. to 7:00 P.M.

Tejano Clubs

Planeta Mexico
3830 Parkdale St., San Antonio
(210) 593–0411

The most influential culture in San Antonio is no doubt the Hispanic culture, and no other nightclub delivers a Latin atmosphere like Planeta Mexico. You may want to brush up on your Spanish before you visit this hot spot, or at least learn how to order your favorite drink or ask someone to dance *en espanole*. And dance you will—salsa music is the preferred type every night. If you're looking for a place to cool off after hitting the dance floor, head for the backyard, which has a bridge that overlooks a pool. This is a very popular club and with good reason—it's a very fun place to be.

Shopping

Malls and Shopping Areas

Antiques and Fine Art

Bookstores

Boutiques/Gift Shops

Comic Books/Collectibles

Flea Markets

Clothing

Imports and Handicrafts

Music Stores

Sporting Goods

Outlet Shopping

Specialty Food Stores

Thrift Stores and Resale Shops

Western Gear

Mexican Mercado

San Antonio has been a shopping destination since its founding as a Spanish outpost. Along with the missionaries, soldiers, and colonists came the traders and merchants, determined to sell their products for the best price. During the Civil War, San Antonio became a center of commerce with Mexico, a distinction it still enjoys. El Mercado on Produce Row is the largest Mexican market north of the border and has operated on the same site for more than 100 years. Although the "chili queens" no longer sell their wares from rudimentary carts in Haymarket Square and Military Plaza, you can still eat a good meal there when you are tired of shopping. Much of San Antonio's shopping now takes place in that modern marketplace, the mall, and the city has a great many from which to choose, in all parts of town. But it's not all modern glitz. Strip shopping centers and mom and pop establishments make up a large percentage of San Antonio retail space. A little dated, these may not be the hippest places to shop, but they are comfortable and somehow reassuring, just like the city itself.

Malls and Shopping Areas

La Villita
Bounded by South Alamo, East Nueva, South Presa, and River Walk Streets, San Antonio

While this may be a major shopping area today, La Villita has an extensive history. It was the site of some of the first houses built by the Spanish after they discovered the area; the earliest were erected circa 1722. A few years later, colonists from the Canary Islands resided here. The area also marks the spot where General Cos of the Mexican Army surrendered his army in 1835 and ceded independence to the colonizing Texans, an emancipation soon revoked with a vengeance by Mexican President Santa Anna by his attack on the nearby Alamo. Eventually, the historic area fell into disrepair and ruin as the town grew in other directions. It remained a slum area until 1939, when a city ordinance called for its restoration. As a result it became a center for crafts and recreation as part of the National Youth Administration Program. In 1972, twenty-seven structures here were added to the National Register of Historic Places. Each year, La Villita is the scene of one of the city's biggest celebrations, Night in Old San Antonio. During the day, the picturesque area is filled with shoppers looking for handicrafts and artwork.

Alamo Quarry Mall
255 E. Basse St., Alamo Heights
(210) 255-1000

Alamo Quarry is definitely an upscale shopping destination. Located in the ritzy Alamo Heights area, it is built on the site of an old factory. In fact, the original

Crafts, including many Southwestern designs, tempt San Antonio shoppers. PHOTO: PARIS PERMENTER & JOHN BIGLEY

cement plant's smokestacks still remain, lending character to the mall's steel-and-glass exterior. Inside you'll find the usual array of mall shops (Old Navy, Borders Books, Whole Foods Market) and eating establishments, and the Quarry Cinema. There is also a Bally's Health Club here.

Central Park Mall
622 Northwest Loop 410, San Antonio
(210) 344–2236

A popular shopping destination on the north side, Central Park Mall has something for visitors of all ages. Besides the usual mall shops, it features the Little Theatre Off Broadway, which stages children's plays, as well as the Park Place nightclub, which draws a late-night crowd. And for seniors, it has a local affiliate of the American Association of Retired People and a Luby's Cafeteria.

Crossroads Mall
4522 Fredericksburg Rd., San Antonio
(210) 735–9137

This westside property houses more than 70 shops, including major retailers such as the Burlington Coat Factory and Stein Mart. It also boast a Regal theater with six screens, with some dedicated to art, indie, and foreign films.

The Forum
8320 Agora Parkway, Selma
(210) 566–7610

The Forum is a Texas-size outdoor mall with several major stores such as Best Buy, Target, and Home Depot. There are a number of chain eateries, too, including Chili's, Outback Steakhouse, IHOP, and Romano's Macaroni Grill. Selma is directly north of San Antonio on I–35.

Huebner Oaks
11745 I–10 W., San Antonio
(210) 225–1000

This is another large, outdoor shopping center with several national chain stores such as Borders Books, Old Navy, and Banana Republic. It also has an admirable slate of restaurants including La Madeleine and the Saltgrass Steakhouse. A twenty-four-screen AMC movie theater shows first-run releases.

Ingram Park Mall
6301 Northwest Loop 410, San Antonio
(210) 684–9570

Located on the city's northwest side, this mall has all the offerings one expects from a large, modern mall: large anchors (Dillard's, Sears), chain specialty shops (Victoria's Secret, Gap), and restaurants such as Chelsea Street Pub and Luby's Cafeteria.

Los Patios
2015 Northeast Loop 410, San Antonio
(210) 655–6171

Los Patios is a quiet retreat in the heart of the hustle and bustle of the Loop. This 20-acre open-air mall is filled with specialty shops, from Tejas Gifts for Texas souvenirs to Tienda for Mexican jewelry and South of the Border items. The shopping area also has three indoor/outdoor restaurants. But, as excellent as its shopping is, the real charm of Los Patios lies in its setting. Located on the banks of Salado Creek, the retail area is nestled among majestic live oaks and exotic plants, making for a pleasant shopping experience—whether you buy something or not.

McCreless Mall
4100 South New Braunfels Ave., San Antonio
(210) 534–8831

One of the few malls on the south side of the city, McCreless is best known for its most distinctive feature, the full-size carousel at its center. Kids love it. But parents come for the many discount clothing stores. Bealls Department Store and Learner New York are among the most popular shopping stops at this mall, which also has a food court and the Cinemark 9 Movie Theater.

North Star Mall
San Pedro Ave. and Loop 410, San Antonio
(210) 340–6627

Shopping is more cosmopolitan at this, the priciest mall in town. With anchor stores such as Saks Fifth Avenue, Marshall Field's, and Foley's, you'll find the best money can buy here. North Star Mall is easy to spot on the Loop—just look for the boots. The 40-foot-tall pair of cowboy footwear was the creation of sculptor Robert Wade.

Rivercenter Mall
849 E. Commerce St., San Antonio
(210) 225–0000
www.shoprivercenter.com

This popular mall contains more than 125 specialty shops and big-name department stores, as well as many restaurants. The Marriott Rivercenter Hotel soars from one arm of the structure. One of the most attractive shopping malls in the nation, Rivercenter is over one million square feet of retail space encased in aqua-colored glass, giving shoppers a lovely

Insiders' Tip

Membership in the Rivercenter Concierge Club is free to visitors from out of town, who need only show a hotel room key or out-of-town ID upon application at the mall. Members receive a free gift as well as special offers at mall shops.

Rivercenter Mall is a favorite with travelers thanks to its convenient location, food court, and variety of shops. PHOTO: PARIS PERMENTER & JOHN BIGLEY

view of the River Walk. Although the shopping is nice, the real attraction here is the river. A new branch of the San Antonio River was actually dug so that the river and the River Walk could be brought right into the U-shaped mall. The two sides of the mall are connected by the Bridge Market. Patterned after Italy's Ponte Vecchio in Florence, this area of the complex is filled with artisans selling their work.

Entertainment takes place throughout the day at the mall's outdoor performance island. As river taxis lazily cruise past, singers and dancers entertain shoppers and diners. On weekends, visitors can look forward to anything from lively mariachi music to singers performing rousing Texas tunes.

Rolling Oaks Mall
6909 North Loop 1604 E., San Antonio
(210) 651–5513

In addition to the usual mall stores such as Dillard's, Foley's, and Sears, Rolling

Oaks is the site of Games Unique, a game store that hosts gaming tournaments each week. They draw a number of dedicated role-players, mostly youths.

South Park Mall
2310 Southwest Military Dr., San Antonio
(210) 921–0534

A mall located southwest of downtown, off of I–35, South Park features more than ninety stores, including Sears, JC Penney, Zales Jewelers, and Foley's.

Westlakes Mall
1401 Southwest Loop 410, San Antonio
(210) 674–0222

Westlakes features national retailers such as Target, Waldenbooks, and Payless Shoes.

Windsor Park Mall
7900 North I–35, San Antonio
(210) 654–1760

Another mall featuring a kid-pleasing carousel, this northeast side shopping center includes several department stores as well as a host of typical mall specialty shops such as Spencer's Gifts, Radio Shack, and Gordon's Jewelers. It has many food choices such as Applebee's and The Olive Garden.

Antiques and Fine Art

A King's Attic/About Antiques and Art
951 South Alamo St., San Antonio
(210) 212–5533

This quaint store is housed in one of San Antonio's oldest Victorian mansions, a proper setting for an antiques shop. It specializes in both art and high-end antiques. The store also buys antiques, so head here if you've got some collectibles that you'd like to sell.

The Antique Center
11345 West Ave., San Antonio
(210) 344–4131

The Antique Center has a very good selection of items for collectors. Many kinds of jewelry and china can be found here, most with what seem to be reasonable prices. Objects of Americana, like old slot machines and jukeboxes, are also sold. This is a good stop on the antique-hunting trail.

Antiques at 115 Broadway
115 Broadway, San Antonio
(210) 222–1265
www.antiquesat115broadway.com

From the outside, Antiques at 115 Broadway looks like it was erected by the Romans. Its large columns remind shoppers of ancient times, and the shops inside this antiques mall are no different. While they may not have collectibles dating back as far as the Roman, Greek, or Egyptian civilizations, this collection of stores does have jewelry, art, and furniture that qualify as antiques—or at least collectibles. You'd need to spend a good part of the day to visit all of the shops here.

Charlotte's Antiques and Clocks
2023 Austin Hwy., San Antonio
(210) 653–3672

This antiques shop has such a variety of items and collectibles that nearly every shopper will find something they like. From fine china to pottery to jewelry, Charlotte's has it all. If you'll be in San Antonio for a while, try to make a few trips to this store—they get new items in every week.

Galleria II
218 South Presa St., La Villita, San Antonio
(210) 227–0527

This artists' cooperative is housed in a Victorian building that dates back to 1873. You'll see artists at work creating pottery, stained glass, and watercolor paintings.

J. Adelman Antiques
7601 Broadway, San Antonio
(210) 822–5226
204 Alamo Plaza, at the Menger Hotel, San Antonio
(210) 225–5914

Selling mainly one-of-a-kind pieces, this place can be pricey—but you'll be getting top-notch items. Much of the jewelry, silver, porcelain, and fine art are from estate liquidations. J. Adelman Antiques also has a good selection of furniture, imported mostly from England and France.

Marshall's Brocante
8505 Broadway, San Antonio
(210) 804–6320
www.marshallsbrocante.com

Furniture from Europe and America, silver, and fine art can all be found at Marshall's Brocante. If you're looking for Western or Texas art, then this is your place, too. Are you a collector of antique slot machines or poker chips? Marshall's has those, too. Louis and Beth Marshall have set up a nice store that has an amazing variety of antiques and collectibles.

The River Art Group was founded in 1947, making it the city's oldest art group. PHOTO: PARIS PERMENTER & JOHN BIGLEY

River Art Group Gallery
510 Paeso De La Villita, La Villita, San Antonio
(210) 226–8752

Located next to the Little Church, the River Art Group Gallery represents 500 artists and craftsmen. The River Art Group was founded in 1947, making it the city's oldest art group. Its members sponsor the annual River Art Show in October and display their works year-round in the gallery, which is open daily. If you're looking for a watercolor of the Paseo del Rio, you'll find one here. Fireplace pokers, branding irons, foot scrapers, and bootjacks are other popular purchases.

Bookstores

Barnes and Noble Booksellers
18030 Hwy. 281 N., San Antonio
(210) 490–0411
12635 West I–10, San Antonio
(210) 561–0205
321 Northwest Loop 410, San Antonio
(210) 342–0008

6065 Northwest Loop 410, San Antonio
(210) 522–1340
www.bn.com

This chain bookstore has four locations in San Antonio. Offering a very large selection of books and magazines, these stores are good places to find what you're looking for and curl up on a comfortable chair to read. Each also has a full-service coffee bar and a wide variety of compact discs for sale.

Borders Books and Music
11745 W. I–10 at the Huebner Oaks Center, San Antonio
(210) 561–0022
255 E. Basse Rd., at Quarry Market, San Antonio
(210) 828–9496
www.borders.com

With two locations in the San Antonio area, Borders Books and Music carries fiction and nonfiction books, magazines, and a good selection of music. If you find something you'd like to read, you can feel free to find a comfortable chair and enjoy your book and a coffee from the coffee bar and cafe.

Half Price Books Records Magazines
3207 Broadway, San Antonio
(210) 822–4597
7959 Fredericksburg Rd., San Antonio
(210) 692–8868
4919 Northwest Loop 410, San Antonio
(210) 647–1103
125 Northwest Loop 410, San Antonio
(210) 349–1429
www.halfpricebooks.com

Half Price Books is a uniquely Texas institution that began in Dallas back in the counterculture days of 1972. Since then, the stores have spread to ten states, but the basic idea remains the same: they sell used books at (approximately) half their cover price. And they will buy almost any books you bring in, though you may not always get as much for them as you hoped. Most of the stores are located in retail storefronts that were designed for other businesses, so each Half Price store is funkily different from the others.

LandM Bookstore
1716 North Main St., San Antonio
(210) 222–1323
15503 Babcock Rd., San Antonio
(210) 695–UTSA
www.lm-bookstore.com

This is a great spot to find college textbooks for those heading back to school. LandM has new and used textbooks, educational software for good prices, and an especially good selection of nursing texts and reference books and contractor code books. School supplies are also sold.

Lifeway Christian Stores
125 Northwest Loop 410, San Antonio
(210) 349–6376
www.lifewaystore.com

Christian materials such as Bibles, inspirational books, and music can all be found here. Whether it's for a gift or for yourself, if you're looking for religious products, you'll probably find something suitable here.

Mexican-American Cultural Center Bookstore and Gift Shop
3115 West Ashby Place, San Antonio
(210) 732–2156

The Mexican-American Cultural Center Bookstore and Gift Shop has a variety of books, videos, and gifts that reflect the cultural diversity of the city of San Antonio. This is the place to buy bilingual (Spanish/English) religious materials, videos, and language-education books. The store will place special orders for customers who can't find exactly what they're looking for.

R and R Bookstore
1107 San Pedro Ave., San Antonio
(210) 225–1107

This bookstore is a great place to find college textbooks. Both new and used texts are stocked.

Boutiques/Gift Shops

Bering's
8502 Broadway, San Antonio
(210) 824–8040
berings.com

Looking for some nice gifts for the folks back home? In business for more than sixty years, Bering's has a wide selection of items, from gourmet coffee, candy, and tea to home accessories and gift baskets to fine silver and crystal. Take a break from shopping in the store's tea room, or register for bridal gifts on the Bering's Web site.

Bless Your Heart Gift Shop
18771 FM 2252, at Bracken Village, San Antonio
(210) 651–1000

This quaint shop has many gifts that will delight you or your friends and family. Items from Mary Engelbreit and Vera Bradley line the shelves, along with greeting cards, novelty bath products, and good-smelling candles. There is a variety of jewelry, too.

Collector's Gallery
13500 West Ave., San Antonio
(210) 497–2525

This gallery calls itself the "area's largest and finest gift shop" with good reason. The large shop has collectibles from such names as Armani, M.I. Hummel, Swarovski, and David Winter. Boyds Bears, Precious Moments, Fenton Glass, Cherished Teddies, and other collectible lines also can be found here.

Cositas Gift Shop
514 West Commerce St., San Antonio
(210) 224–0282

This gift shop is found in the Market Square shopping area and is a great place to find turquoise and sterling silver jewelry made by American Indians. There is a large selection of necklaces, earrings, rings, and other pieces to choose from. Don't miss this unique shop.

Grandma's Attic
18771 FM 2252, at Bracken Village, San Antonio
(210) 651–3090

Located in the Bracken Village shopping center, this gift shop sells unique handcrafted gifts, including quilts, painted glass, and porcelain dolls. Want something for the cat-lover in your life? Grandma's Attic also has a wide variety of feline-oriented gifts.

The Pink Giraffe
250 E. Houston St., San Antonio
(210) 227–8851

The Pink Giraffe has a varied selection of collectibles and figurines, greeting cards for any occasion, many types of candy, and lots of other gifts. You won't miss this gift shop—it's on Houston Street, by the famous Majestic Theater.

Comic Books/Collectibles

Alien Worlds
7319 San Pedro Ave., San Antonio
(210) 341–8860
3203 Wurzbach Rd., San Antonio
(210) 681–0701
13909 Nacogdoches Rd., San Antonio
(210) 590–6310
www.alien-worlds.com

This comic-book store has much more than just comics. Alien Worlds is a great source for role-playing games, collectible card games, action figures, and collectible cards. It also carries rare and not-so-rare Star Wars, GI Joe, Pokémon, and Transformers figurines.

Excalibur Comics and Video
7959 Fredericksburg Rd., San Antonio
(210) 615–1229

Here you'll find a good selection of old and new comic books and collectibles as well as other toys, games, models, collectible cards, and Japanese anime. There are also game rooms available for rent.

Heroes and Fantasies
226 Bitters Rd., San Antonio
(210) 545–9063
7103 Blanco Rd., San Antonio
(210) 340–0074
6780 Ingram Rd., San Antonio
(210) 522–9063
8425 Bandera Rd., San Antonio
(210) 681–1114
914 Pat Booker Rd., San Antonio
(210) 945–4376

This store claims to have more than a million comic books, and once you step inside you may not doubt it. In addition to new and used comics, Heroes and Fantasies also stocks a variety of role-playing games, card games, action figures, sports memorabilia, posters, T-shirts, gifts, and models. Collectors of Japanese anime or Pokémon, Dragonball, Star Wars, Archie, or Spiderman stuff will be happy here.

Ike and J's Comics
2373 Austin Hwy., San Antonio
(210) 590–4534
www.ijcomics.com

Ike and J's has more than 10,000 comic books for a quarter and an additional 10,000 for less than $1.50. If you've got some comics that you'd like taken off your hands, this shop may buy them from you. Ike and J's has a wide variety of rare comic books, so stop in if you're looking for something special.

Flea Markets

Bussey's Flea Market
18738 I–35 N., New Braunfels
(210) 651–6830

This flea market is located 6 miles north of San Antonio, almost to the town of New Braunfels. Situated on more than 20 acres, Bussey's has more than 500 dealer spaces. Buyers will find items here to add to their antique collections or to begin new collections. Bussey's is open on Saturday and Sunday only.

Eisenhauer Road Flea Market
3903 Eisenhauer Rd., San Antonio
(210) 653–7592

Eisenhauer Road Flea Market is one of the largest indoor flea markets in America, making it a must for flea-market aficionados. A wide variety of antiques and collectibles is available. Admission to the market and parking are both free. Note that the market is closed on Monday and Tuesday.

I–37 Flea Market
I–37 at the Southton Rd. exit, San Antonio
(210) 633–2220

South of San Antonio, I–37 Flea Market is more than 37 acres of antiques, collectibles, jewelry, and more. There are some 500 seller's booths, so everyone is sure to find something to buy here. Live band music adds a festive air. This market is only open on Saturday and Sunday.

Mission Flea Market
707 Moursund Blvd., San Antonio
(210) 923–8131
www.missionfleamarket.com

This open-air market has hundreds of sellers on 40 acres of space. Whether you're looking for antiques or new merchandise, this is a worthwhile place to check out. An enormous variety of items make this a great spot to poke and browse. Mission Flea Market is only open on Wednesday, Saturday, and Sunday.

Clothing

Kids' Clothing

Around The Carousel
999 E. Basse Rd., San Antonio
(210) 805–0101

This is a good place to shop for kids of all ages, from infants to preteens. Around The Carousel carries a variety of shoes and clothing for special occasions such as christenings and formal parties, and for outdoor activities and sports.

Best Friends and Best Buddies
1931 Northwest Military Hwy., San Antonio
(210) 349–9233
www.bestfriendsbestbuddies.com

Featuring specialty clothing for boys and girls of all ages, this place is sure to have something unique for your little ones. If you're planning on visiting the store on Sunday, make sure to call first and make an appointment.

Growing Room For Kids
355 E. Basse Rd., San Antonio
(210) 930–8833

Growing Room For Kids is a one-stop shop for children. Fashions for kids sizes 0–14 are available, as are custom-made bedding, furniture for kids' rooms, and toys for all ages. This is a good stop for children's gifts.

Men's Clothing

Casual Male — Big and Tall
5392 Walzem Rd., San Antonio
(210) 590–0686
7334 San Pedro Ave., San Antonio
(210) 344–6409
5755 Northwest Loop 410, San Antonio
(210) 521–8904, (800) 844–6524
www.casualmale.com

As the name might suggest, Casual Male is a great stop if you're looking for nice clothing for a big and/or tall man. The store carries sizes 1X to 6X and XLT to 5XLT. If you need large shoes to go with your new big-guy clothes, they've got those, too. Sizes 11 to 16W are carried here in many major brand names. The staff at both San Antonio locations are friendly and ready to answer your questions.

Penner's
311 West Commerce St., San Antonio
(210) 226–2487

This store carries designer clothing for men of all sizes. Bill Blass, Hugo Boss, Nautica, Levi's, Dockers, Tommy Hilfiger, Stetson, Johnston and Murphy, Rockport, and Florsheim are among the brands you'll see here. Penner's can also handle same-day alternations if your new suit needs a little adjustment. There is free parking for customers behind the store.

Satel's
5100 Broadway, at Alamo Heights,
San Antonio
(210) 822–3376
9801 W. I–10, at The Colonnade, San Antonio
(210) 794–0944

Clothing with recognizable names like Oxxford, Hickey-Freeman, Tallia, and Ralph Lauren can be found at this men's store. Satel's has a wide selection of designer clothing and a knowledgeable staff to make sure that you get the clothes that fit you best. The store at The Colonnade has more items for big and tall men than the Alamo Heights location.

Women's Clothing

Adelante Boutique
6414 North New Braunfels Ave., San Antonio
(210) 826–6770

The thatched roofs may give you the impression that you're entering an imports store, and in a way you are. Adelante Boutique features the latest trends, which are usually inspired by cultures all over the globe, particularly India and China. In business in San Antonio for twenty-five years, this shop provides the Alamo City women with comfortable clothes that look great and don't put a big dent in their bank accounts. Women of all ages flock here in seach of the latest trends, and they find them—and not just the ones that only look good on fifteen-year-old girls. Make sure to check out the sales rack; good deals can almost always be found.

Kathleen Sommers Retail Store
2417 North Main Ave., San Antonio
(210) 732–8437

As the name suggests, this shop specializes in Kathleen Sommers clothing. The relaxed yet trendy natures of the Sommers line is a big hit with San Antonio women, who shop here for themselves and for their daughters. That's right, Kathleen Sommers has clothing for females of all ages, infant to adult. The shop also features an array of accessories: bath products with relaxing scents can be found through the store, as can purses, shoes, and books.

Imports and Handicrafts

Angelita's
208 South Presa St., La Villita, San Antonio
(210) 224–8362

Angelita's is the oldest import boutique in the city, offering a mixture of clothing and jewelry from Mexico, Guatemala, and several other Central American countries. The shop is housed in an adobe building that dates back to the mid-1800s (watch out for the low doorway!).

Casa Manos Alegres
418 Villita St., La Villita, San Antonio
(210) 224–5107

This import gallery, located near Angelita's, features Latin American folk art, from tin art to *milagros* (miracle charms) to Nativity sets.

The Tequila Tree
202 Produce Row, San Antonio
(210) 224–6202

This three-story shop sells imports from around the world, from scarves made in Nepal to religious figures from Guatemala. Nearly forty countries are represented here through jewelry, clothing, and artwork.

The Village Gallery
418 Villita St., La Villita, San Antonio
(210) 226–0404

This shop specializes in hand-blown glass, plus stoneware and pottery.

Villita Stained Glass
418 Villita St., La Villita, San Antonio
(210) 223–4480

Original designs in stained glass and glass ornaments are featured in this shop. Visitors are invited to watch the craftspeople at work.

Village Weavers
418 Villita St., La Villita, San Antonio
(210) 222–0776

Handwoven clothing, placemats, rugs, and other textile items are the specialties of the Village Weavers. This shop handles the work of artists from both San Antonio and many Latin American countries. Blankets, skirts, sweaters, and more abound in this interesting shop.

Music Stores

Backstage CDs
7319 San Pedro Ave., San Antonio
(210) 342–4700

Backstage CDs is a great place to find used CDs in good condition at a fair price. You can also find rock memorabilia here if you're looking for something to add to your collection. If you prefer vinyl, there is a wide selection of classic LPs as

Crafts fill many shops in the La Villita area. PHOTO: PARIS PERMENTER & JOHN BIGLEY

well. Backstage CDs has listening stations posted throughout the store, so you can check out your music before you buy it. They also buy albums here, so bring the music you don't listen to anymore and make a bit of money.

CD Exchange
2325 Northwest Military Hwy., San Antonio
(210) 342–3472
2950 Thousand Oaks Dr., San Antonio
(210) 545–3472
5442 Evers Rd., San Antonio
(210) 680–3472
8246 Marbach Rd., San Antonio
(210) 674–5200
3611 Broadway, San Antonio
(210) 828–5525
6900 San Pedro Ave., San Antonio
(210) 826–2662
5201 Walzem Rd., San Antonio
(210) 650–3472

At any of the many CD Exchange locations, you'll find a good selection of music for good prices. Mostly used CDs are sold, but they tend to be in very good condition. If you've got some old albums that you'd like to get off your hands, bring them down and they'll pay you for them.

Flip Side Record Parlor
1445 Southwest Military Dr., San Antonio
(210) 923–7811

Flip Side is a one-stop record shop. In addition to a wide selection of domestic and imported albums in LP, CD, and cassette format, there is a variety of videos, T-shirts, stickers, and jewelry.

Hogwild Records Tapes and CDs
1824 North Main St., San Antonio
(210) 733–5354

This record shop specializes in Texas music, heavy metal, reggae, blues, dance music, and imports. In addition to a large selection of music, it stocks music paraphernalia like T-shirts and posters. They also buy used records and CDs.

Sporting Goods

A-1 Sports Center
1027 Bandera Rd., San Antonio
(210) 433–1246

A-1 Sports Center carries everything you might need to join the team. Whether you play basketball, baseball, football or soccer, A-1 has the uniforms, jackets, caps, and equipment that you'll be wanting. They can also do custom silk-screening and computerized monogramming so you can personalize your purchases.

Gassman's Archery and Air Gun Headquarters
102 Jackson Keller Rd., San Antonio
(210) 822–7131

This is San Antonio's hunting supplies store. Gassman carries a good selection of bows (including crossbows) and arrows and bow accessories. It also stocks air guns from America and Europe, blow guns, camouflage clothing, and game calls.

Racquetball Pros of San Antonio
5504 Bandera Rd., San Antonio
(210) 680–8800

This is the place to shop in San Antonio when you're looking for racquetball supplies. Here you'll find racquets, eyeguards, gloves, and shoes that could help improve your game. The store carries such brand names as Head, Wilson, and E-Force, to name a few. It also offers services like racquet regripping and restringing.

Soccer Locker USA
15124 San Pedro Ave., San Antonio
(210) 490–9070
6487 Blanco Rd., San Antonio
(210) 349–5021

Many kids today are involved in team soccer, and Soccer Locker USA has the supplies they need for the coming season. The store has a large selection of soccer balls, shin guards, and cleats. It offers team discounts, takes special orders, and even does printing and silk-screening to personalize the equipment.

Soccer World
903 Bitters Rd., San Antonio
(210) 495–8929
3703 Fredericksburg Rd., San Antonio
(210) 734–7906

Soccer World calls itself "The Most Complete Soccer Store In Town" with good reason. They have a huge selection of practically anything connected with the sport, including uniforms and equipment. Soccer World also offers team discounts and in-house monogramming. This is a great place to shop for anything soccer.

Outlet Shopping

Prime Outlets
Exit 200 off I–35, San Marcos
(800) 628–9465

This open-air mall features more than 125 shops that sell direct from the factory. Luggage, shoes, leather goods, outdoor gear, china, kitchen goods, and other specialty items are available. Along with stores, shoppers find plenty of special features: a food court, a children's playground, free stroller and wheelchair loans, and tourist information. Moyer Winery provides guided tours and tastings, and there's even a miniature golf course to distract non-shoppers. Chartered buses from as far away as Dallas and Houston stop here regularly. San Marcos is a forty-five-minute drive north of San Antonio.

Tanger Factory Outlet Center
Exit 200 off I–35, San Marcos
(800) 408–8424

Just south of Prime Outlets lies the expansive Tanger Factory Outlet Center. Here you can shop for name-brand goods ranging from housewares and footwear to home furnishings and fine perfumes. More than seventy-five shops are located in this open-air mall.

New Braunfels Marketplace
Exits 187 and 189 off I–35, New Braunfels
(888) SHOP–333

What started out as a factory store for West Point Pepperell has become a destination for busloads of shoppers from Houston and Dallas. The stores, which often sell new product lines, are owned by the factories, but unlike some factory outlets, this mall does not feature second or discounted merchandise.

Specialty Food Stores

Blum Street Cellars
Rivercenter Mall at Blum St., San Antonio
(210) 222–BLUM

Wine enthusiasts should save time for a stop at this wine store. It specializes in Texas wines plus an assortment of Lone Star State specialty foods and gift items. It even offers chilled wines, so you can take a bottle back to your hotel room or enjoy it with a picnic lunch.

Rivera's Chili Shop
109½ South Concho, El Mercado, San Antonio
(210) 226–9106

Rivera's Chili Shop recalls Market Square's early chili connection with chili peppers, dried chiles, chili-themed clothing, and even chili Christmas decorations. Look for Texas cookbooks and specialty foods here as well.

Thrift Stores and Resale Shops

Goodwill Stores, San Antonio
727 Northwest Loop 410, San Antonio
(210) 341–6809
3401 Fredericksburg Rd., San Antonio
(210) 736–1373
13909 Nacogdoches Rd., San Antonio
(210) 655–6009
3822 Pleasanton Rd., San Antonio
(210) 923–9410
www.goodwillsa.org

Goodwill has several locations in the San Antonio area and all of them have the same low prices. At most stores, you'll be able to

Shopping in Los Dos Laredos

The two sisters have always lived side by side. They share a proud heritage, though each asserts her individual personality. The older of the two has a passion for history and architecture, while the younger bubbles over with enthusiasm for good food and good times.

But, oh boy, do both sisters love shopping.

The sister cities of Laredo, Texas, and Nuevo Laredo, Mexico, attract visitors from both sides of the border for some spirited Christmas shopping. Located just over two hours from San Antonio on I-35, these communities are magnets for shoppers. Though they lie on opposite sides of the Rio Grande, little else divides them.

Physically, international bridges connect the cities. However, the link between these sister cities was forged long before the building of the bridges. Originally, only a single city—Laredo—occupied the north bank of the Rio Grande. Following the Mexican War in the early 1840s, some families wishing to protect their divided land holdings made the decision to split, leaving some family members in Texas and sending others splashing across the newly drawn border. There they founded Nuevo Laredo, literally New Laredo.

Today in downtown Laredo, Zaragoza Street is a route that serves as a sort of foyer into Old Mexico. Near the international bridge, wholesalers along Zaragoza Street entice shoppers with electronics, clothing, shoes, jewelry, and other goods. This area has the feel of a Middle Eastern bazaar, with deals to match on perfumes, purses, and jewelry as well as Italian gold. (Italian gold can't be imported directly into Mexico; it has to come through the United States. Many of these Texas shops sell wholesale to Mexican jewelry retailers.)

For Mexican imports such as pottery and wrought-iron furniture, try the markets of the San Bernardo area a few blocks north of Zaragoza. The stores along San Bernardo are a good place to shop for larger import items if you won't be driving into Mexico. Vegas' Imports, at 4002 San Bernardo, offers Mexican home furnishings for every room of the house. Much of the furniture in this well-stocked store is hand-carved.

Laredo is also the site of an expansive mall: Mall del Norte, at 5300 San Dario. It's home to chain stores such as Foley's, the Disney Store, Bath and Body Works, and others. The city also has several high-end shops that offer one-of-a-kind items. Polly Adams, offering exclusive lines of women's clothing and accessories, is located at 101 Calle Del Norte in Laredo (956–723–2969). Frequented by many Mexican movie stars as well as discerning shoppers from around Texas, Polly Adams can provide meals for shoppers with advanced notice and always has several seamstresses on hand to guarantee a perfect fit.

But as enticing as the Laredo stores can be, the charms of its sister city act as a magnet for the dedicated shopper. Nuevo Laredo boasts an amazing procession of shops along its avenues. Here the sights and sounds of the Mexican holiday season bombard the visitor: the air fills with the scent of roasted ears of corn sold from steaming carts; the sunlight glints off a jumble of silver-plated necklaces on a vendor's arm; a tablecloth salesman waves his poinsettia-dotted wares like a bullfighter's cape.

In Nuevo Laredo, prices run the gamut, from a dollar for trinkets such as yarn bracelets and hologram necklaces sold by street vendors to thousands of dollars for fine jewelry at top-of-the-line shops. Want a Mexican memento? Your selection is limited only by your pocketbook.

The main shopping district is along Avenida Guerrero, located just steps across the International Bridge. Two of Nuevo Laredo's finest stores occupy spots along Avenida Guerrero. Marti's, well-known to shoppers throughout South Texas, has offered fine clothing, jewelry, and furniture for four decades. The three-level department store, which has been called the "Neiman Marcus of Mexico," is a compendium of all things Mexican, including ribbon-knit clothing from Mexico City and gold-coin jewelry. Fine Mexican jewelry and housewares also fills several neighboring shops. Look for elegant gifts such as colorful wooden flowers made in Puerto Vallarta, stoneware pottery from Tonala, and aluminum serving platters from Mexico City.

Just beyond Marti's on Avenida Guerrero, the Nuevo Mercado, or the New Market, is the most popular spot in town. The block-long, open-air market is always filled with shoppers searching through the 100-plus small shops and street vendors displays that explode with colors and textures. Be prepared to bargain at all the market shops. *Negociacion* is a friendly game here, and both merchant and shopper usually come away happy.

Mexican crafts are sold throughout the market and the adjoining streets. Currently, silver jewelry, much of it produced in Taxco, shines as the hottest item in the market. Display cases bulge with dangle earrings, bangle bracelets, rope necklaces, and belt buckles. Jewelry stamped with the numbers "925" is high-quality. Unless you see the 925 stamp, assume you are looking at silver plate. Colorful serapes also fill the Nuevo Mercado, as well as fringed blankets sporting bright stripes and other typical Mexican designs. Leather goods like belts and wallets are always popular, as are hand-embroidered dresses, onyx bookends, and tin mirrors. Men, completely covered by their merchandise, hawk brilliantly striped baskets, some from the Toluca region. And on the streets, you'll be met by salesmen peddling woven hammocks.

Don't forget the kids on your Christmas list during your shopping excursion. Nuevo Laredo overflows with children's merchandise: friendship bracelets, piñatas of every description, miniature cup and saucer sets, tiny kitchen implements—the list goes on and on. Women on the curbsides making colorful yarn dolls and yarn bracelets personalized with the name of the wearer. Fringed leather jackets, child-size guitars, and charro hats bring home the flavor of Old Mexico as well.

Save time for a trip deeper into Nuevo Laredo to El Cid, the city's only glass factory, located at 3861 Avenida Reforma. You'll need to drive or catch a taxi to this store, but the shopping here makes the effort worthwhile. Colorful glassware—everything from traditional glasses and bowls to delicate Christmas ornaments—is sold here.

When your Nuevo Laredo shopping expedition is complete, you must cross through U.S. Customs, located on the American side of the International Bridge. Certain items cannot be carried back into the United States. These include fruits, vegetables, animals and birds, and meats (including canned items). Fireworks, switchblade knives, firearms, liquor-filled candy, lottery tickets, and items made from endangered species will be confiscated. Although you can go to a Mexican farmacia and buy any item without a prescription, you must have a doctor's prescription to bring Mexican pharmaceuticals into the United States. Be careful of counterfeit trademark items, such as $40 "Rolex" watches sold in many shops. These can be seized, and you must forfeit them if stopped by a customs official.

You may return with $400 worth of merchandise without paying duty. Every person in your party, regardless of age, has this $400 exemption. If you've made large purchases, save your receipts. There's a 10-percent duty on goods that cost more than $400 but less than $1,400. You must also pay tax on imported liquor and cigarettes. If you are 21 or older, you may bring back one liter of liquor and 200 cigarettes. For more information on customs, obtain Publication 512, Know Before You Go, by writing to: U.S. Customs Service, P.O. Box 7407, Washington, DC 20044.

find blouses for under $5.00, jeans for under $6.00, and dresses for under $10.00. Look for sale signs around the store to get up to 50 percent off on certain items.

Kirby Senior's Thrift Shoppe
5070 Old Seguin Rd., San Antonio
(210) 666–3600

Retro clothing for adults, clothes for kids, and household items including furniture and cookware, books, and collectibles are all sold here. Kirby Senior's also has a military memorabilia selection. As with all thrift shops, inventory fluctuates as donations increase and decrease.

Texas Thrift Store
6776 Ingram Rd., San Antonio
(210) 521–3336
3606 Fredericksburg Rd., San Antonio
(210) 733–1707

With two locations in the San Antonio area, Texas Thrift Store claims to have some 4,000 new items every day. Leave a generous amount of time to explore these stores, because there is a lot to sort through.

Western Gear

Boot Hill
849 E. Commerce St., at Rivercenter Mall, San Antonio
(210) 223–6634
8023 Callaghan Rd., San Antonio
(210) 341–4685

If you want to outfit the whole family to look like John Wayne, then you'll want to make a stop here. Jeans from Wrangler and other Western brands can be found, as can tops and shirts. The prices at Boot Hill are reasonable.

Boot Town Western Wear
2803 Northeast Loop 410, San Antonio
(210) 590–9229

This store carries brand names such as Levi's, Wrangler, and Rockies. If you want to dress like a cowboy, whether you're heading to a dude ranch on the outskirts of San Antonio, a rodeo, or just for everyday wear, you'll find the clothes you're looking for here.

Cavender's Boot City
8640 Four Winds Dr., San Antonio
(210) 590–2668
5075 Northwest Loop 410, San Antonio
(210) 520–2668
303 Northwest Loop 410, San Antonio
(210) 377–4241

Cavender's Boot City sells name-brand clothing at good prices. There is a large selection here, so if you're looking for jeans, boots, or cowboy hats, head on over. The sales staff is always knowledgeable and friendly.

Lucchese Boot Company
255 E. Basse Rd., San Antonio
(210) 828–9419

Every cowboy needs boots, and this shop has been making Western boots for more than a century. Many are made with exotic leathers such as alligator and ostrich.

Paris Hatters
119 Broadway, San Antonio
(210) 223–3453

If you want to look like a real cowboy, you'll need a Western hat. Since 1917, Paris Hatters has outfitted cowboys and cowboy wanna-bes with Stetsons and other authentic headgear.

Mexican Mercado

Market Square
514 West Commerce St., San Antonio
(210) 207–8600
tavernini.com/mercado/

One of the neatest things about shopping in San Antonio is the opportunity to buy great Mexican made items. Although there are scores of small boutiques and shops throughout the city that sell Mexican goods, there's one place where virtually every conceivable kind of Mexican

Stock up on handmade gifts at El Mercado. PHOTO: AL RENDON, COURTESY OF THE SAN ANTONIO CONVENTION AND VISITORS BUREAU

Mexican piñatas are popular souvenirs of the Alamo City. PHOTO: PARIS PERMENTER & JOHN BIGLEY

meats, hay and firewood, clothing, hammocks, chess sets, musical instruments—you name it.

Clothing and textiles are always best-sellers at El Mercado. The traditional Mexican dress, complete with an embroidered bodice and short sleeves, starts at about $35. To make sure you're getting a high-quality garment, look for tight embroidery stitches. Men's shirts, called guayaberas, are found in many stores as well. These solid-color, short-sleeved shirts, decorated with pleating and stitching, are worn outside the pants.

Blankets are another popular item. Many stores sell striped ones in a variety of sizes and colors, most made from a wool blend. A 5-by-7-foot blanket typically costs $7.00 to $8.00; panchos and serapes sell for $10.00 to $12.00.

Piñatas are found throughout Market Square. At Mexican birthday parties, one of these colorful paper creations is filled with candy and hung from a tree. Blindfolded children take turns swinging at the vessel with a stick until someone finally breaks it and the loot spills all over the ground. Look for piñatas in the shapes of watermelons, clowns, donkeys, and even parrots.

Cascarones, dyed eggshells filled with paper confetti and covered with tissue paper, are sold in many stores. They're especially popular during the annual Fiesta, when children break them over the heads of their friends (or sometimes complete strangers).

handicraft is represented. It's the largest Mexican market in the United States, known variously as El Mercado or Market Square. A few blocks from downtown, this market is where generations of San Antonians have come to buy and sell everything under the sun: vegetables and

Attractions

Downtown

In & around Loop 410

San Antonio Missions

Outside Loop 410

Historic Districts

Tours

For many San Antonio visitors and residents, this city means history. You find historic buildings, historic homes, even sites where the food is historic! While most of Texas is still a babe compared to Eastern destinations, San Antonio traces its roots back over half a millennium and has the attractions to prove it.

The most recognized building in the city is Alamo; the former mission is surrounded by Alamo Plaza, a site that is at one time historic and hysterical, the ultimate shrine to Texas history alongside shrines to the Texas tourist. The Alamo, the mission that represents the fight for freedom and the spirit of Texas, is a place where tones are hushed and respectful, a destination to which every true Texan makes a pilgrimage at least once in his or her life. In juxtaposition, Alamo Plaza is the home of the city's most tourist-oriented businesses: souvenir stands, a wax museum, and a bounty of tour companies. But both solemnity and souvenirs somehow work together to create a memorable destination.

But not all the attractions in San Antonio are man-made. The natural beauty of the city is readily apparent after just a quick look around. From the cypress-lined River Walk to beautiful Brackenridge Park, San Antonio has plenty of destinations for a shady stroll. Don't miss our chapter on Parks and Recreation, which lists lots of options for everything from a jog to a picnic. You'll also find more things to see and do in the chapters covering Nightlife, Kidstuff, The Arts, Spectator Sports, and The Military.

To help you maneuver through the many attractions of San Antonio, we've divided this chapter into sections: Downtown, In and Around Loop 410, Beyond Loop 410, San Antonio Missions, Historic Neighborhoods, and Tours.

You'll find that these attractions—and the city itself—are most crowded in the summer months. Other peak times are in April during Fiesta and at Christmastime. In planning your itinerary during a summer visit to San Antonio, keep the heat in mind. Do what residents do: plan outdoor and strenuous excursions in the morning hours, then head for indoor or shady attractions during the heat of the day.

Price-Code Key

The price ratings below are for an adult admission fee during the summer high season. Keep in mind that many attractions offer significant discounts for children, seniors, and military personnel.

$	less than $5
$$	$5–$10
$$$	$11–$20
$$$$	more than $20

Downtown

Alamo
300 Alamo Plaza, San Antonio
(210) 225–1391
www.thealamo.org
Free

If you visit only one San Antonio attraction, make it the Alamo. The most famous sight in Texas, this mission is now a symbol of the fight for freedom in the battle for independence from Mexico. It's often referred to as the "cradle of Texas

133

liberty," and even today, conversation is hushed here, men remove their hats, and photography is prohibited. It stands as a reminder of the Spanish colonization of this area and of the bloody battle that was fought so valiantly.

Although today it is primarily known as the Alamo, the mission was originally called San Antonio de Valero. The mission was abandoned in 1793, and the buildings began to fall to ruin. Troops from San Jose y Santiago del Alamo Parras in northern Mexico converted the building to a fort in 1801, and the structure took the name of the troops' hometown. Since that moniker was a real mouthful, the name was later shortened to simply "El Alamo." And just what is the English translation of Alamo? Cottonwood.

The Alamo was originally a large compound. Today all that remains of the mission is the original church and the Long Barrack. When you enter the Alamo, you'll be struck by the quietness of the complex. It retains a chapel-like atmosphere in spite of the hundreds of thousands of visitors who tour it each year. The Alamo operates under the care of the Daughters of the Alamo, a conservation group that protects and guards the mission, many say, as fiercely as the Texian troops did a century and a half ago.

First-time visitors should budget about two hours for a look at the chapel and its displays, the barrack, and the film that tells the story of the historic battle. Gardens behind the chapel are also well worth a visit.

The story of the Alamo is a tale taught to every young Texan: it's the account of fewer than 200 brave volunteers who faced nearly 10 times as many Mexican troops in a battle whose outcome was predetermined. To further the cause of Texas independence, they gave their lives but won a place in the history of the Lone Star State.

The battle of the Alamo was preceded by battles in Gonzales, Goliad, and in San Antonio itself. Mexican troops led by General Martin Perfecto de Cos had taken refuge in the Alamo and surrendered in early December. The surrender had angered Mexican President Antonio Lopez de Santa Anna. He vowed to get rid of the Anglos and also to punish the Tejanos, the Mexicans living in Texas who had taken part in the battle.

After the surrender by General Cos, the Texas army floundered without a leader for several months, and its numbers dwindled. Simultaneously, Santa Anna was rallying his troops for the long journey from Mexico City to San Antonio.

Texas troops still occupied the Alamo, joined by volunteers such as Davy Crockett from Tennessee. The troops believed they would be joined by reinforcements before Santa Anna would arrive, but they were wrong. Santa Anna's advance troops first arrived in San Antonio on February 23, 1836. The revolutionaries scrambled inside the protective walls of the mission, bringing along cattle and supplies that commander William Travis thought could sustain them until help arrived.

Travis quickly made another appeal for more troops, knowing that the brunt of Santa Anna's army was only days away. The help so desperately needed did not arrive, and on March 3 Travis allegedly drew a line in the earth with his sword. All men who wanted to stay and defend the Alamo crossed the line—exhibiting their dedication to independence even at the cost of battling an enemy that vastly outnumbered them. Only one man did not cross the line.

The battle began with bombardments from Mexican cannons, but the real surge took place at about 5:30 the morning of March 6. Perhaps as many as 1,800 Mexican soldiers stormed the mission, fighting first with guns and finally hand to hand as they progressed up the walls. By 7:00 A.M., the battle was over. All the Texas revolutionaries died or were executed, but Santa Anna's troops permitted several women and a slave of William Travis's to live. The most famous survivors were Suzanna Dickinson and her daughter, Angelina, the family of an Alamo officer. They were left to spread the word of the Alamo defeat. And spread the word they did. "Remember the Alamo" was the battle cry months later, when finally the Texans defeated Santa Anna at the Battle of San Jacinto and Texas became an independent republic.

Visitors who are in San Antonio on March 6 can watch an early morning reenactment of the fateful battle.

The Alamo is open Monday through Saturday, 9:00 A.M. to 5:30 P.M. and Sunday, 10:00 A.M. to 5:30 P.M. The facility is closed December 24 and 25.

Alamo Cenotaph
Alamo Plaza, San Antonio
Free

Directly in front of the Alamo stands the Alamo Cenotaph, a memorial to the men who lost their lives in the battle. The marble monument, designed by Italian-born and Texas-adopted sculptor Pompeo Coppini, was erected in 1939 by the Texas Centennial Commission and includes all the names of the Alamo defenders. Vehicles are no longer permitted in this area, a gesture of respect for the Native Americans buried in a cemetery found in front of the chapel.

Bolivar Hall
418 La Villita St. in La Villita, San Antonio
(210) 224–6163
Free

Operated by the San Antonio Conservation Society, this museum contains exhibits on the society's work as well as its "A Night in Old San Antonio" (NIOSA) annual event. Photographs trace the evolution of this annual event and of Fiesta. The exhibit is open Monday through Saturday from 10:00 A.M. to 5:00 P.M.

Buckhorn Saloon and Museum
318 E. Houston St., San Antonio
(210) 247–4000
www.buckhornmuseum.com
$$

In 1881 the Buckhorn Saloon opened as a Texan watering hole. Soon hunters and trappers were stopping by, and eager for a cold brew, they traded in furs and horns. Owner Albert Friedrich collected the horns, some which his father made into horn chairs. Today you can see the heads, hides, and horns on a guided tour of the Buckhorn Hall of Horns, one of four unusual museums housed here. The tour also includes the Buckhorn Hall of Fins

Visitors of all ages will enjoy the Buckhorn Saloon and Museum. PHOTO: AL RENDON, COURTESY OF THE SAN ANTONIO CONVENTION AND VISITORS BUREAU

(marine trophies and fishing lures) and the Buckhorn Hall of Feathers (mounted birds).

But not all the exhibits here are stuffed—some are wax. The Hall of Texas History Wax Museum features a re-creation of the Battle of the Alamo and other important Texas events.

Buckhorn Saloon and Museum is open daily except Christmas and New Year's Day.

Canary Islands Descendants Museum
100 Main Plaza, San Antonio
(210) 534–8579
Free

If you've already visited the Institute of Texan Cultures, you know the diverse groups of people who founded and settled this town. Among the first groups were the Canary Islanders. This small museum, located on the second floor of the building, contains artifacts of the original 16 families who founded Villa de San Fernando and the community's first civil government in 1691. The museum is open Tuesday through Sunday from 1:00 to 5:00 P.M.

Casa Navarro State Historical Park
228 S. Laredo St., San Antonio
(210) 226–4801
$

This small home was once the residence of Jose Antonio Navarro (1795–1871), a signer of the Texas Declaration of Independence. The adobe and limestone structure includes an office used by Navarro, who was a lawyer. Navarro was a member of the Texas legislature under Mexico, the Republic of Texas, and the United States; he also served as a mayor of San Antonio. This home is considered one of the few remaining dwellings that provide a picture of what residences were like during the years of independence. Casa Navarro is open Wednesday through Sunday from 10:00 A.M. to 4:00 P.M.

IMAX Theater at Rivercenter Mall
849 E. Commerce St., at Rivercenter Mall, San Antonio
(210) 247–4629, (800) 354–4629
www.IMAX-sa.com
$$

Located at the Crockett Street entrance of Rivercenter Mall, this IMAX theater is the home of *Alamo—The Price of Freedom*. The story of the fall of the Alamo comes to life on this six-story screen several times daily. The 45-minute docudrama is one of the best film versions of the 13-day siege, giving viewers a real sense of participation in the action. The film was produced at Alamo Village in the West Texas town of Brackettville, using a replica of the Alamo built for the John Wayne film of the same name. From a rolling thunderstorm over the rugged Texas landscape to the daybreak siege by Santa Anna's troops, this movie makes viewers feel as if they are witnessing the fateful battle and the days leading up to it. When not running *The Price of Freedom,* the IMAX Theater shows other films produced especially for the big screen.

Institute of Texan Cultures
801 S. Bowie Rd., San Antonio
(210) 458–2300
www.texancultures.utsa.edu
$

Operated by the University of Texas, this museum explores the 30-plus ethnic cultures that settled Texas. Most days you'll find costumed docents throughout the museum, ready to educate visitors about the role of a chuck-wagon cook on a cattle drive or the rigors of life as a frontier woman. Along with an outdoor interpretive area, the focal point of the museum is the dome slide show, which utilizes 36 screens to display the many faces and places of Texas. The show is presented four times a day.

The museum is open Tuesday through Sunday, 9:00 A.M. to 5:00 P.M.

Market Square
514 W. Commerce St., San Antonio
(210) 207–8600
Free

Bounded by I-35 and Santa Rosa, Dolorosa, and Commerce Streets, this two-block area embraces three special shopping centers: Farmer's Market Plaza, a renovated former produce market now ripe with crafts and imports after a $2.1-million renovation; an open-air consortium of specialty boutiques; and El Mercado, the largest Mexican market in the United States.

The history of Market Square dates back to the early 1800s, to a time when Mexico ruled the settlement of San Antonio de Bejar. Fresh produce and meats were sold in the Farmer's Market, and pharmaceutical items were available at Botica Guadalupana, today the oldest continuously operated pharmacy in town. However, the market's real claim to fame lies in the fact that it was the birthplace of chili con carne, the spicy meat and bean mixture that today is generally considered the state dish of Texas. In the early 1800s young girls known as "chili queens" sold the concoction from small stands in the market.

El Mercado offers the kinds of items that shoppers typically find in a Mexican border town. Styled after a traditional Mexican mercado (market), albeit one that is enclosed and air conditioned, El Mercado has merchandise piled to the ceiling. Look for onyx chess sets, ashtrays, painted pottery, silver jewelry, sombreros, and charro hats. The prices here are slightly higher than those found in Mexican border towns, and unlike the fare offered in traditional mercados, the merchandise carries set prices. Prices vary from store to store within the market, and most shops accept major credit cards. (For more on Market Square see the Shopping chapter.)

The stores of Market Square are open 10:00 A.M. to 8:00 P.M. during the summer months, closing at 6:00 P.M. during the winter. Restaurants keep longer hours. Expect most stores to be closed Thanksgiving, Christmas, New Year's Day, and Easter.

Plaza Wax Museum
301 Alamo Plaza, San Antonio
(210) 224–9299
www.plazatheatreofwax.com
$$$

This museum depicts the famous, from Jesus to John Wayne, reproduced in wax. The sculptures are well done and many are displayed in elaborate sets depicting movie scenes. Alamo visitors will appreciate the "Heroes of the Lone Star" exhibits on the fateful battle. See the Kidstuff chapter for more details.

The theater is open daily, but hours change by the season, so call ahead. The ticket box office closes one hour prior to closing time.

Ripley's Believe It or Not!
301 Alamo Plaza, San Antonio
(210) 224–9299
www.plazatheatreofwax.com
$$$

Located in the same facility as the Plaza Theatre of Wax, Ripley's Believe It or Not! houses more than 500 oddities, including freaks of nature and miniatures. The collection is open daily; hours vary by season, so call ahead. See the Kidstuff chapter for more details.

River Walk (Paseo del Rio)
Downtown, San Antonio
(210) 227–4262
Free

The Paseo del Rio, or River Walk, is a magical place 20 feet below street level. Nestled behind tall buildings, away from traffic and street noise, the River Walk is the most popular spot in town, lined with specialty shops and alfresco cafes. Visitors stroll the walkways that follow the winding river. Some sections throng with shoulder-to-shoulder crowds; others have a quiet, almost park-like atmosphere.

The River Walk is the heart of the city. Tourists from around the world pack the hotels here. Military personnel from San Antonio's five military bases enjoy a few hours off duty at the outdoor cafes. And

The River Walk winds through downtown below street level. PHOTO: STEVE MOORE, COURTESY OF THE SAN ANTONIO CONVENTION AND VISITORS BUREAU

locals come to the area to enjoy a respite from the hustle and bustle of the city.

But the popularity of this riverside goes back far before the days when people came here for sizzling fajitas and frozen margaritas. Payaya Indians called this river Yanaguana, or "refreshing waters." It also had a less elegant nickname that meant "a drunken old man going home at night"—a reference to its numerous twists and turns. Indians camped along the river banks and hunted on the rich land nearby.

On June 13, 1691, the feast day of San Antonio de Padua, the Spanish renamed the Yanaguana. The change was just a hint of the many transformations the river would soon witness as Spanish domination came to the area.

In the early 1700s, the Spaniards constructed several missions on the river's bends. The northernmost one was built first: San Antonio de Valero, later known as the Alamo. It was followed by four other missions to the south. The Indians who lived in the missions dug ditches or acequias from the river to their fields to irrigate crops of beans and corn.

Soon settlement began on the riverbanks. When the missions were secularized and later occupied by military troops, camp followers and tradesman built temporary houses near the river to serve those stationed at the Alamo. After Texas became a republic, permanent settlements developed on the riverbanks. As the population rose, bathhouses sprang up along the water's edge.

The condition of the river declined, and for many residents its only characteristics were bad ones. The river was untamed and it wreaked havoc in the downtown area after heavy rains. In 1921, a devastating flood killed 50 people, and talk was that the river should be covered with concrete and converted to a storm sewer. But on March 22, 1924, the San Antonio Conservation Society stepped in.

The river was saved with a puppet show called "The Goose That Laid the Golden Egg." Cloth puppets resembling city officials dramatized the tale and helped San Antonians realize that their river really could be an attribute to the city. A flood-control program was started, and dams were built to protect the horseshoe bend during floods.

While the river was saved, the real gold came later, thanks to a visionary named Robert H. H. Hugman. As part of WPA program, Hugman was commissioned to develop the scenic walkway. He pictured a festive area he called "The Shops of Aragon and Romula," named for the cities of Old Spain. The River Walk was completed in 1941.

But development along the River Walk remained minimal until the World Hemis-Fair in the late 1960s. As it prepared for global visitors to the fair, the city beautified the park, investors opened businesses along the walkways, and the River Walk, as visitors today now know and love it, was born.

No matter what day of the week, no matter what time of the year, activity abounds along the River Walk. This is where city residents come to party, where conventioneers come to meet, and where vacationers come to taste the flavor that is San Antonio.

The River Walk spans from Municipal Auditorium to the north to King William Historic District to the south. For the best overview, take a river cruise, a narrated tour that provides a look at stretches most pedestrians never see. (See "Yanaguana Cruises" in the Tours section, below.)

San Fernando Cathedral
115 Main Plaza, San Antonio
(210) 227–1297
Free

For many years, folks believed the San Fernando Cathedral was the final resting place of the defenders of the Alamo. A Spanish church was built at this site in 1738 by the city's Canary Island colonists. Here Santa Anna raised a flag of "no quarter" before he stormed the Alamo, signifying to the Texians that he would take no prisoners. In 1873, following a fire after the Civil War, the chapel was replaced with the present-day structure. Although a tomb holds the remains of some unknown soldiers, modern historians do not believe these were the bodies of the Alamo defenders because evidence of military uniforms, never worn by the Texians, has turned up among the remains. The cathedral is open to the public Tuesday through Friday 9:00 A.M. to 1:00 P.M. and 2:00 to 4:45 P.M.

Southwest School of Art and Craft
300 Augusta St., San Antonio
(210) 224–1848
www.swschool.org
Free

The Southwest School of Art and Craft (formerly known as the Southwest Craft Center) offers a good overview of the San Antonio arts and crafts scene. The school is housed in the former Ursuline Academy, which in 1851 became the first girls' school in the city. The long halls of the once-busy dormitory are now filled with photography, jewelry, fiber art, paintings, and the like. The Ursuline Gift Shop sells handcrafted items, including silver Southwestern jewelry, hand-painted plates, and wooden Christmas ornaments. Grab a sandwich or salad at the on-site Copper Kitchen. The school is open to visitors Monday through Friday, 10:00 A.M. to 5:00 P.M. For additional details, see The Arts chapter.

Spanish Governor's Palace
105 Plaza de Armas, San Antonio
(210) 224–0601
$

Located just down the street from Market Square, this historic site was once home of the officials of the Spanish Province of Texas. Today it's the only remaining

> ## Insiders' Tip
> The National Geographic Society has called the Spanish Governor's Palace "the most beautiful building in San Antonio."

example in Texas of an early aristocratic Spanish home. Completed in 1749, the structure is now open for self-guided tours of its antique-furnished rooms and cobblestone patio.

Don't expect a palace in the usual sense of the word—turrets and towers are replaced by a simple patio and courtyard here. Remember, this building dates back to the early eighteenth century, a time when the area was wild and unsettled, and this house was considered quite ornate, comparatively speaking.

The palace is open Monday through Saturday from 9:00 A.M. to 5:00 P.M. and Sunday from 10:00 A.M. to 5:00 P.M.

Texas Adventure
307 Alamo Plaza, San Antonio
(210) 227–8224
www.texas-adventure.com
$$

This unique theater calls itself the world's first "Encountarium F-X Theatre," using state-of-the-art film technology to tell a historic tale. Here you can see a version of the fall of the Alamo played out with animatronics and holographic figures. Guests are first ushered into a room for a six-minute introductory presentation that uses excellent dioramas to explain the events that led up to the famous battle. Next, visitors take seats on benches in the theater, where the story of the Alamo comes to life, complete with holographic versions of Crockett, Travis, and Bowie. The presentation lasts just under 30 minutes and is suitable for anyone except very young children. (When Jim Bowie "appeared" out of thin air, a young child seated near us let loose a scream the likes of which may not have been heard in these parts since that fateful battle.)

The theater is open daily from 8:30 A.M. to 8:00 P.M.

Tower of the Americas
600 HemisFair Park, San Antonio
(210) 207–8615
www.toweroftheamericas.com
$

Regardless of which direction you approach San Antonio from, you'll see the Tower of the Americas looming over the skyline. This symbol of the 1968 World HemisFair remains a landmark for downtown San Antonio. Visitors view the city from the observation deck at 579 feet. Close to three decades after its construction, this is still one of the tallest free-standing structures in the Western hemisphere—87 feet taller than the Seattle Space Needle and 67 feet higher than the Washington Monument.

Since its construction, the Tower and its grounds have undergone many changes. In April 1988, HemisFair Park was rededicated after a $12-million reno-

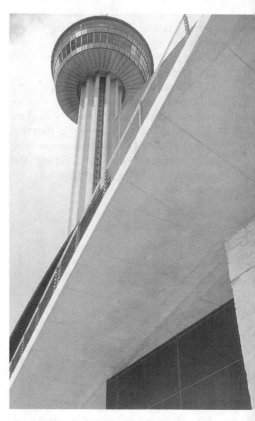

Centerpiece of Hemisfair '68, the Tower of the Americas rises above San Antonio. PHOTO: PARIS PERMENTER & JOHN BIGLEY

vation of the grounds. In March 1990, a $1.2-million restoration was completed on the Tower. Today you can enjoy a one-minute elevator ride (traveling 7 miles per hour) to the observation deck, where high-powered telescopes provide a bird's-eye view of the city's sights. Eight panoramic photo panels help visitors locate major attractions. There are both enclosed and open-air observation decks, and at night the view is especially breathtaking.

The tower is open Sunday through Thursday from 9:00 A.M. to 10:00 P.M.; on Friday and Saturday, it stays open until 11:00 P.M.

In and around Loop 410

Brackenridge Park
2800 Broadway, San Antonio
(210) 736–9534
Free

The largest park in the city, Brackenridge sprawls across 433 acres shaded by majestic oaks. A popular picnic destination, the park is also home to the San Antonio Zoological Garden and Aquarium (see below), housed in a former rock quarry. Nearby the Japanese Tea Gardens (see below) showcases lush flowers, climbing vines, and tall palms alongside many koi-filled ponds. For more details on the park, see the Parks and Recreation chapter.

Japanese Tea Gardens
3800 N. St. Mary's St., San Antonio
(210) 207–8480

San Antonio's semitropical climate encourages the lush flowers, climbing vines, and tall palms found inside this quiet, serene place, part of the San Antonio Zoological Garden and Aquarium. The ponds, with beautiful rock bridges and walkways, are home to koi (large goldfish).

This limestone quarry was transformed into a garden with fish ponds and a palm-thatched arbor in 1918. Later, a pagoda was added and a Japanese-American couple operated a tea room nearby. During World War II, public pressure forced the family to move; when the tea room was taken over by a Chinese family, the attraction was renamed the Chinese Tea Gardens. Recently, descendants of the original owners of the tea room, along with the Japanese ambassador to the United States, were in attendance when the gardens were officially renamed the Japanese Tea Gardens. The gardens are open daily from 8:00 A.M. to dusk.

Marion Koogler McNay Art Museum
6000 N. New Braunfels Ave., San Antonio
(210) 824–5368
www.mcnayart.org/
Free

This Spanish Mediterranean–style mansion (designed by Atlee B. and Robert M. Ayres in 1926 and remodeled in 1954) was the home of the late art collector Marion Koogler McNay, heiress to an oil fortune and an artist herself. The 24-room house, which was converted to a museum in the 1950s, is now home to a collection of European and American art. Works of Picasso, Van Gogh, Matisse, and Gauguin are found in the permanent collection. After a look at the impressive artwork, visitors can stroll the palm-shaded grounds, popular with picnickers. The museum is open Tuesday through Saturday from 10:00 A.M. to 5:00 P.M. and Sunday noon to 5:00 P.M. For additional details see The Arts chapter.

Insiders' Tip

The Marion Koogler McNay Art Museum— better known around town as "the McNay"— was the first museum in Texas devoted to modern art.

San Antonio Botanical Gardens and Halsell Conservatory
555 Funston Pl., San Antonio
(210) 207–3255
www.sabot.org/
$

Separate gardens for roses, herbs, and native plants are found within these 38-acre gardens. The centerpiece here is the Lucile Halsell Conservatory, designed by Emilio Ambasz, formerly curator of design at New York's Museum of Modern Art. To take advantage of the cooling effect of the earth during hot Texas summers, the greenhouse is built 16 feet underground. Separate structures showcase palm trees from around the world, desert plants, and tropical foliage. The gardens are open daily except Christmas and New Year's Day. From March through October, the gardens are open 9:00 A.M. to 6:00 P.M.; during the winter months, the hours are 8:00 A.M. to 5:00 P.M. For additional details see the Parks and Recreation chapter.

San Antonio Zoological Garden and Aquarium
3903 N. St. Mary's St., San Antonio
(210) 734–7183
www.sazoo-aq.org
$$

Widely considered one of the best zoos in the nation, the San Antonio Zoological Garden is located at the headwaters of the San Antonio River. Surrounded by limestone cliffs (this was once a rock quarry), the exhibits include animals from habitats around the world.

The zoo is best known for its excellent collection of African antelopes and other hoofed species. You'll find many other interesting creatures, too, including African lions and Asian elephants, snow leopards and giant armadillos. More than 3,500 animals representing 750 species live here. Birds, including many housed in open-air exhibits, make up a large part of the collection. San Antonio holds the distinction of being the only zoo in the nation

with a pair of whooping cranes that have successfully bred in captivity. Other notable accomplishments include the first Caribbean flamingos hatched and reared in a zoo, the first white rhino born in North America, and a breeding program for the rare snow leopard. The zoo also includes an aquarium that exhibits species ranging from tiny seahorses to deadly red piranha. The zoo is open daily starting at 9:00 A.M. to 6:00 P.M. in summer; 9:00 A.M. to 5:00 P.M. the rest of the year.

San Antonio Museum of Art
200 W. Jones Ave., San Antonio
(210) 978–8100
www.sa-museum.org/
$$

This expansive museum is housed in the buildings of the former Lone Star Brewery and maintains its factory feel with skywalks and glass elevators. Collections include Egyptian, Greek, and Roman antiquities; Asian art; and eighteenth-, nineteenth-, and twentieth-century American work. Recently the museum opened the three-story Rockefeller Center for Latin American Art, considered one of the nation's best collections of Latin art. For additional details, see the museum's entry in The Arts chapter. The museum is open Tuesday 10:00 A.M. to 9:00 P.M.; Wednesday through Saturday 10:00 A.M. to 5:00 P.M.; and Sunday noon to 5:00 P.M. Admission is free every Tuesday from 3:00 to 9:00 P.M.

Splashtown
3600 N. Pan Am Expwy., San Antonio
(210) 227–1400
www.splashtownsa.com
$$$$

San Antonio's closest waterpark lies on the north side of the city and provides cool relief on hot summer days. Spanning 18 acres, this park offers a variety of rides whose pace varies from relaxing to thrilling. For more information on this park, see the Kidstuff chapter.

Texas Air Museum—Stinson Chapter
8406 Cadmus, San Antonio
(210) 977–9885
www.texasaviationmuseum.org
$

If you're a private pilot, you're probably familiar with Stinson Field, the country's second-oldest continuously used airfield. Other visitors to the city might be more familiar with Stinson as the home of this new museum, which showcases vintage and replica World War I and World War II aircraft. The facility also displays an astronaut rotational simulator from Brooks Air Force Base. The museum is open Monday through Saturday, 10:00 A.M. to 4:00 P.M.

Texas Highways Patrol Association Hall of Fame Museum
812 S. Alamo St., San Antonio
(210) 231–6030
Free

One of San Antonio's small treasures, this often-overlooked museum honors the highway patrol officers who have fallen in the line of duty. Some of the first officers to lose their lives were those shot by bank robbers Bonnie Parker and Clyde Barrow. Additional exhibits are concerned with motor safety. The museum is open Tuesday through Saturday 10:00 A.M. to 4:00 P.M.

Texas Pioneer Trail Drivers and Rangers Museum
3805 Broadway, Brackenridge Park, San Antonio
(210) 822–9011
$

This museum traces the role of the Texas Rangers on the frontier, with exhibits covering badges to saddlebags. The museum was created for the 1936 Texas Centennial to showcase the work of the Texas Rangers, which held the distinction as the first law-enforcement group in the nation with statewide jurisdiction.

A more peaceful side of Texas is explored in the collection housed in the Pioneer Room, dedicated to the hardworking pioneers who settled the Lone Star State. Western art is displayed here as well. Have a look at the statues in front of the museum featuring trail drivers and a ranger; one was sculpted by Gutzon Borglum, creator of Mount Rushmore. The museum is open daily 10:00 A.M. to 5:00 P.M. during summer months; 11:00 A.M. to 4:00 P.M. at other times of the year.

Texas Transportation Museum
11731 Wetmore Rd. at McAllister Park, San Antonio
(210) 490–3554

Train and antique-car buffs enjoy this museum whose exhibits include antique pedicabs, horse-drawn vehicles, model railroads, and more. Train rides are offered Saturday afternoons from noon to 3:00 P.M. The exhibits are open Thursday, Saturday, and Sunday from 9:00 A.M. to 4:00 P.M.

Yturri-Edmunds Historic Site
257 Yellowstone at Mission Trail, San Antonio
(210) 534–8237
www.saconservation.org
$

When the missions were secularized, this land was granted to Manuel Yturri-Castillo, and he built an adobe home here. It was later given to the San Antonio Conservation Society by his granddaughter, Ernestine E. Edmunds. Today you can tour the residence and its shady grounds and have a look at the acequia (aqueduct), the only one of its kind still in use in the country. The site is open by appointment only.

Witte Museum of History and Science/ H-E-B Science Treehouse
3801 Broadway, San Antonio
(210) 357–1900
www.wittemuseum.org
$$

This exciting interactive museum covers all things Texan, from the area's early dinosaur inhabitants to the white-tailed deer that roam the region today.

The museum collection is extensive. One of the best exhibits is "Texas Wild: Ecology Illustrated," a look at the ecology of this diverse state. Nearby, a display takes a look at the ancient Texans who roamed the region as hunter-gatherers more than 8,000 years ago.

After a look around the museum, step out back to see the historic homes that have been relocated to the courtyard. Here you'll also find the H-E-B Science Treehouse, a four-story collection of interactive exhibits on science concepts. Perched in concrete "trees," this museum is a favorite with children. (For more details, see the Kidstuff chapter.)

The museum is open Monday and Wednesday through Saturday from 10:00 A.M. to 5:00 P.M. and Tuesday from noon to 5:00 P.M.

and the widespread malaria that resulted from settling in the swampy woodlands. In 1731, three missions were relocated to San Antonio, forming the densest concentration of Spanish missions in the New World.

The Indians who lived in the missions were Coahuiltecan, hunter-gatherers from South Texas and northeastern Mexico. Because European diseases had taken their toll on the native population and nomadic tribes were moving in on their lands, the Indians allowed themselves to be recruited by the friars. By the late 1700s, however, the missions had become secularized, and the Indians moved to neighboring land. Many of the mission buildings began to fall to ruin.

In the 1920s the citizens of San Antonio began to preserve the deteriorating

San Antonio Missions

Mention "San Antonio" and "mission" in the same sentence, and the Alamo will come to most travelers' minds. The Alamo was, however, just one in a chain of missions built by the Spanish to convert the Indians to Catholicism. But the Spanish had political as well as religious reasons for building the missions: they wanted to stake a claim on lands in which their rival, France, was showing little interest.

While the Alamo is fascinating for its historic story, visiting the missions park is a better way to get a full picture of the roles of these complexes played in this area. Once these missions covered many acres, land that was irrigated with an ace-*quia* (aqueduct) fed by the San Antonio River. Today one historic purpose, from religions to agriculture, is showcased at each of the park's four missions.

The first San Antonio mission, the Alamo, was built to serve as a way station between missions in East Texas and those in Mexico City. Seven years later, San José y San Miguel de Aguayo Mission was built south of the Alamo. The East Texas missions subsequently proved unsuccessful, due to the French influence in Louisiana

Mission Espada is part of the National Park Service's Mission Trail. PHOTO: AL RENDON, COURTESY OF THE SAN ANTONIO CONVENTION AND VISITORS BUREAU

structures, then in 1978 the San Antonio Missions National Historic Park was established to protect and operate the four sites. (The Alamo is a separate entity, operated by the Daughters of the Republic of Texas.) The cooperative effort between the Park Service, the San Antonio Conservation Society, the State of Texas, the City of San Antonio, and Bexar County was later expanded to include a cooperative agreement with the Archdiocese of San Antonio that keeps the mission churches open for regular religious services.

Today the missions are each open to the public free of charge, with a suggested donation of $1 for adults and 25 cents for children. When planning your visit, remember that these are active parish churches (unlike the Alamo). Services are conducted every Sunday, and respectful visitors are welcome. Mission San Juan has a Mariachi Mass every Sunday at noon; it is very popular with visitors.

A free National Park Service brochure with a map showing all sites and how to get to them is available at the Missions National Historical Park Visitors Center at Mission San José, (6701 San Jose Dr.). The map is also available at the Visitors Information Center in Alamo Plaza. The San Antonio Convention and Visitors Bureau also distributes the Mission Trails Map; call (800) 447-3372 to request it. The map also may be downloaded in PDF format at www.nps.gov/saan/.

Even with the map, getting to the missions can be a little tricky (the National Park Service brochure warns that "the route that connects the four missions can be confusing for visitors"). The way is marked with brown National Park signs, but it twists and turns among residential neighborhoods and parks. Further complicating matters, during heavy rains two low-water crossings are closed, necessitating an alternate route. The National Park Service brochure outlines both the traditional Mission Trail as well as alternate routes to take during inclement weather. The mission trail is currently undergoing a $17-million improvement project to enhance signage and improve its foot and bicycle trails.

To reach Mission Concepción, the first stop for most travelers, travel south on South St. Mary's Street; the road turns into Roosevelt Avenue. Turn right on Lone Star Boulevard and continue to Mission Road. Mission Concepción is located south of the I-10 overpass.

The drive from downtown to the Mission Concepción (pronounced "con-cep-see-OWN") takes about 15 minutes. This site is tucked into a quiet residential neighborhood, far different from the bustling Alamo area. The mission was moved here in 1730. Its full name is a mouthful: Mission of Nuestra Señora de la Purisma Concepción de Acuna.

For your tour of the missions, be sure that you wear some type of sturdy walking shoes. All the sites have irregular staircases and stone walkways that are especially slippery on rainy days. The missions are open daily 9:00 A.M. to 5:00 P.M. but are closed Thanksgiving, Christmas, and New Year's Day.

Mission Concepción
807 Mission Rd. at Felisa St., San Antonio
(210) 534-1540
$ donation

Mission Concepción is especially notable for its wall paintings. Geometric and religious symbols in ochre, blue, and brown decorate the ceilings and walls of several rooms. The most striking is the "Eye of the God," a face emanating rays of light. Displays at each of the four missions illustrate different aspects of mission life. At Concepción, the theme is "The Mission as a Religious Center," appropriate for one of the oldest unrestored stone churches, and the oldest unrestored Catholic church, in the nation.

Like the Alamo just over 2 miles to the north, Mission Concepción has seen some bloodshed. On October 28, 1835, Colonel James Bowie and 20 Texans were surprised by a detachment of the Mexican army. They fought well and forced the Mexicans, with 60 dead and 40 wounded, to retreat.

The oldest intact church in Texas, Mission Concepción was relocated to San Antonio from East Texas in 1731. PHOTO: TOM BECKER, COURTESY OF THE SAN ANTONIO CONVENTION AND VISITORS BUREAU

The Texans only suffered one loss, further bolstering their spirits. Less than five months later, however, Bowie and his men would again fight the Mexican army, with far less success.

Mission San José
6539 San Jose Dr., San Antonio
(210) 932–1001
$ donation

The second stop on the mission trail is the grandest in terms of size and architectural detail, so much so, in fact, that more than 200 years ago it was termed "Queen of the Missions." Founded in 1720 by Fray Antonio Margil de Jesus, in its heyday Mission San José boasted 300 residents, a granary that held 5,000 bushels of corn, and elaborate ornamentation. Its full name is Mission San José y Miguel de Aguayo, named for the Governor of Texas at that time.

You may find yourself humming "Do You Know the Way to San Jose?" while making your way to this second site. The route mapped by the Park Service is the most scenic but not the most direct. Just follow the signs and be patient; San José is worth the effort. Thanks to an extensive renovation in 1936 for the Texas Centennial, this mission is in spectacular condition. The elegant structure echoes with reminders of an earlier time, when Texas was a frontier and this mission was a haven in an unsettled land. The most famous detail here is the rose window. Legend has it that an architect named Pedro Huizar created the window for his lost love, Rosa. (When you're downtown, look at Dillard's exterior window displays at the Rivercenter Mall. These are copies of "Rosa's Window.")

Begin your visit with a stop at the modern visitors center adjacent to Mission San José to pick up a free Park Service brochure (a necessity for driving the Mission Trail) then start your self-guided tour of the chapel. The flagstone floor has borne thousands of worshippers, from barefooted Native Americans two centuries ago to tennis-shoed tourists today.

Walk around the grounds to get an idea of the size of this former community. Indians lived in rooms along the outside wall, and the priests lived in the two-story convento. The land in the quadrangle was used for crops. The theme of San José's exhibits is "The Mission as Social Center and a Center for Defense." Displays show that Indian residents were instructed in the use of guns and lances to help defend the mission against Apache and Comanche raiders. The mission also shows a 23-minute film about early mission life.

Mission San Juan Capistrano
9101 Graff Rd., San Antonio
(210) 534–0749
$ donation

This mission was once completely self-sustaining. San Juan grew enough crops to meet the needs of the mission and also supply other communities in the area with food. Skilled artisans made ironwork and leather goods and wove cloth in the mission workshops.

To appreciate the natural richness of this area, take a hike on the San Juan Woodlands Trail. In about a third of a mile, the trail winds along the low river bottom land and gives you a look at many of the indigenous plants used by the mission.

The chapel, with its bell tower and elaborate altar, was destroyed by a storm in 1886. In 1909 the building was repaired and in the 1960s it underwent an extensive renovation. Today it is an active parish church and a good example of how San Antonio continues to use its historic structures both for tourists and for the local community.

San Juan also has a small museum featuring items found at the site and artifacts typically used by missionaries in Texas. The theme of San Juan's exhibits is "The Mission as a Economic Center," and displays show how this self-sufficient mission worked with others to obtain the food and goods it needed.

Insiders' Tip

In 1777 Mission San Jose was dubbed the "Queen of the Missions" by Fray Juan Augustin Morfi, known as the first historian of Texas.

Mission Espada
10040 Espada Rd., San Antonio
(210) 627–2021
$ donation

From Mission San Jose, head west on Mission Road to Ashley, turn left, then right on Espada Road. This will take you to the most remote spot on the trail: Mission Espada. Located about 9 miles from the downtown area, this mission was named for St. Francis of Assisi, founder of the Monastic order of Franciscans. The mission's full name is Mission San Francisco de la Espada (de la Espada means "of the sword," referring to St. Francis's decision to be a "soldier of God").

This mission's theme is "The Mission as a Vocational Education Center," and its displays focus on the education of the local Indians in blacksmithing, woodworking, and other vocational areas.

The park occasionally opens Rancho de las Cabras, located near the town of Floresville. The fairly recent addition to the parks system once served as a ranch that supported the residents of Mission Espada. If you would be interested in visiting Rancho de las Cabras, check with the park rangers for opening dates and times.

Outside Loop 410

Natural Bridge Caverns
26495 Natural Bridge Caverns Rd., at exit 175 on I–35, San Antonio
(210) 651–6101
www.naturalbridgecaverns.com
$$$–$$$$

The largest cave in Central and South Texas is Natural Bridge Caverns, reminiscent of New Mexico's Carlsbad Caverns. Imagine the surprise of four spelunkers from San Antonio's St. Mary's University when they discovered the gargantuan halls of limestone in 1960. After the cave was discovered, developers worked to carve passages from room to room, resulting in a comfortable walk through this long cavern.

Natural Bridge Caverns takes its name from a rock bridge between two sinkholes, the original entrance to the mouth of the cavern. Local residents had known of the sinkholes since the 19th-century, but there is evidence of much earlier visitors. Bones of a grizzly bear at least 8,000 years old have been discovered, as well as human bones and stone weapons and other Indian artifacts.

Today the cave offers two separate tours. The North Cavern Tour is the traditional guided tour; it departs at least every 30 minutes and lasts about 75 minutes. The tour takes visitors through enormous rooms that look like the playing fields of prehistoric dinosaurs. The rooms have been given fanciful names like "The Castle of the White Giants."

The latest addition to the cave's offerings is the South Cavern Tour, an adventure excursion for which participants are outfitted in spelunking gear. The mile-long tour descends to a depth of 230 feet below the surface and is rated moderate to hard in terms of difficulty. Activities range from rappelling to crawling through passageways to view rarely seen cave features such as a 14-foot "soda straw," one of the largest such formations in North America. You'll need to make reservations for this tour.

Natural Bridge Wildlife Ranch
26515 Natural Bridge Caverns, San Antonio
(830) 438-7400
www.nbwildliferanchtx.com
$$

Located next to the Natural Bridge Caverns, this ranch holds the title of Texas's most-visited safari park (and the state's oldest). Established on a family's century-old ranch, the park boasts species from around the globe; more than 500 animals roam these fields. You'll receive a bucket of food when you arrive, and the animals come right up to the car to greet their guests—and get a bite to eat. Don't miss the expanded rhinoceros facility, a specially designed building that helps the rhinos endure the chilly winter days. The park is open daily, although hours change seasonally.

Schlitterbahn
305 W. Austin St., New Braunfels
(830) 625-2351
$$$$

Texas's largest water park is located just about a half hour north of San Antonio. This family-oriented park is not just a leader in the world of Texas parks, but a worldwide innovator with numerous water-park products. The park offers one- and two-day passes, which offers a hint at the size and incredible number of rides in this expansive park. For more on Schlitterbahn, see the Kidstuff chapter.

SeaWorld of Texas
Ellison Dr. and Westover Hills Blvd. off Rte.
151 between Loop 410 and Loop 1604,
San Antonio
(210) 523-3611, (210) 523-3618
www.seaworld.com
$$$$

Located 16 miles northwest of downtown, this 250-acre park is the largest marine-life adventure park in the world. Displays and shows featuring orcas, dolphins,

Insiders' Tip

Traveling with your dog? Check with Six Flags Fiesta Texas and SeaWorld to arrange kennel space during your visit.

seals, and otters are featured, along with an enjoyable amusement and water park. The star of SeaWorld is Shamu, the 2.5-ton orca who engages in graceful swimming exercises with his human partners. There's room for 4,500 onlookers in this stadium, and most of the seats are safe from the huge splashes that Shamu produces as he leaps and dives in his 7-million-gallon tank. Nearby an impressive 300,000-gallon coral reef display contains the world's largest collection of Indo-Pacific coral reef fishes in a simulated coral reef environment.

SeaWorld also offers numerous rides, including two roller coasters and several cool (literally) water rides. More than 25 shows and rides keep families happy. Lost Lagoon water park is one of SeaWorld's most popular spots on hot summer days (see the Kidstuff chapter for details). Shamu's Happy Harbor adventure play area is tops with younger visitors. The Clydesdale Hamlet is home of the renowed Anheuser-Busch Clydesdale horses.

The park is open daily from the end of May through November. Hours vary but are usually 10:00 A.M. to 10:00 P.M.

Six Flags Fiesta Texas
17000 I–10 W., San Antonio
(210) 697–5050
www.sixflags.com
$$$$

Fiesta Texas operates in a former limestone quarry. The white, chalky stone used to build homes throughout Central and South Texas was mined from this and similar sites, leaving behind tall limestone cliffs that make dramatic backdrops for the park. San Antonio has a long history of reusing its quarries: the San Antonio Zoo and the Japanese Tea Gardens also occupy a former quarry, using the walls to contain animals and grow subtropical vines.

Fiesta Texas showcases music, from 1950s rock 'n' roll and local Tejano sounds to oompah German tunes. The award-winning shows are interspersed with thrill rides, sure to bring a squeal to even the most jaded amusement-park aficionados.

You'll enter the park through Los Festivales, where stucco buildings add to an atmosphere that recalls Texas's closest neighbor. Wandering musicians play festive mariachi music and open-air shows feature Tejano and conjunto music. You won't find rides in this section, but you will see the park's largest theater: Teatro Zaragoza. A great place to go in the heat of the afternoon, the theater is home to the Festival Folklorico show, with swirling Mexican dances and traditional songs.

Los Festivales also provides a taste of Old Mexico. Pick up some churros (deep-fried dough doused with sugar) and roasted corn, or if you're ready to take a break, enjoy a meal in the Mi Pueblito restaurant (reservations are accepted).

If you are a roller-coaster fan, then you know about Crackaxle Canyon. This western section of the park is the home of "The Rattler," the world's tallest wooden roller coaster. Lines can be long for this popular ride, so head here early for a jump on the crowds. The latest addition to the thrill ride offerings is the Superman Krypton Coaster, the largest steel and only floorless coaster in the Southwest. The ride takes passengers through 400-plus feet of spiral loops and corkscrew turns at a speed of more than 70 miles per hour. There are tamer rides for tiny tots, too (see the Kidstuff chapter).

A good place to escape the heat is Waterpark at Six Flags Fiesta Texas, which is entirely devoted to water rides. (For more information on the waterpark, see the Kidstuff chapter.) The park is open daily 10:00 A.M. to 9:00 P.M. in summer and on weekends in the fall.

Historic Districts

Dignowity Hill Historic District

Located on the east side of town, north of Commerce Street, this historic neighborhood is named for Michael Dignowity, a Czechoslovakian immigrant. Dignowity served as a medical doctor in San Antonio after his arrival in the mid-1800s. The doctor had to flee the city for his life because of his outspoken views against secession; he didn't return until 1869 and at that time set about trying to recover his property, which at one time extended for blocks. Much of the surrounding land was sold to German businessmen and the neighborhood quickly became a wealthy enclave. The neighborhood is known for its numerous cemeteries. More than 30 dot the historic district, one of the densest collections of cemeteries in the United States. It's also the site of the Hays Street Bridge, a whipple-style iron-truss bridge brought here from Louisiana between 1908 and 1910.

Ellis Alley

Located east of I–35 just beyond the Alamodome on Chestnut Street, this section of the city was one of the first to be settled by African-Americans following the Civil War. Today it's primarily a residential neighborhood, but the area was once best known for its live entertainment. The focal point of the district was an auditorium that first opened in 1905 as the Colored Community House, serving as a library for the African-American population of the area. A new building was constructed in 1930 and named the Colored Library Auditorium; it soon grew to host graduations, live concerts, and debutante balls. During its peak years, Ella Fitzgerald, Duke Ellington, Nat King Cole, Paul Robeson, and many other nationally known performers appeared here. The auditorium later was renamed the Carver Library Auditorium in honor of Dr. George Washington Carver. Following desegregation, use of the auditorium declined and eventually the facility was abandoned and slated to be demolished. Local community activist Norva Hill lay in the path of the bulldozers and stopped the destruction of the historic landmark. The auditorium was saved, and Hill was awarded the lease on the facility. In 1977, the building reopened as the

Carver Cultural Community Center and is today known for its art galleries and diverse performances. (See The Arts chapter for details.)

Government Hill

Located on the north side of town just west of I–35 around Fort Sam Houston, Government Hill is one of the most historic neighborhoods in the city. Approximately 27 percent of the neighborhood contains historic buildings.

The site is rich with military history and is known as the home of the "soldier medic." Military medical personnel from more than 30 countries around the globe train at Fort Sam Houston, which is the world's clearinghouse for military combat medicine. The base is adjacent to the original site of the West Texas Military Academy, established in 1893. The academy's most famous graduate was General Douglas MacArthur in 1897.

One of the most unique historic buildings on Government Hill is Terrell Castle (see the Bed and Breakfast chapter for more details). The castle looks out at what was once called General's Row, a street lined with the elegant homes of the fort's military leaders.

King William Historic District

If there's a preferred address in San Antonio, it's most likely in the King William Historic District. Just a stone's throw south of the River Walk, this neighborhood boasts elegant homes, stately shade trees, and an atmosphere of grace and gentility.

Its status as a superior neighborhood goes back to the mid-1800s, when this district was populated by the Alamo City's most successful businessmen and their families. Many of these frontier citizens were German immigrants with names like Guenther, Wulff, and Heusinger. With their wealth gained in merchandising and

San Antonio's German merchants built stately homes in the King William District. PHOTO: DAVE G. HOUSER, COURTESY OF THE SAN ANTONIO CONVENTION AND VISITORS BUREAU

investing, they set about building the most lavish homes in the city, most in the grand Victorian style.

One of the most opulent of these residences is the Steves Homestead, positioned right on the banks of the river. Besides a natatorium (indoor swimming pool) and a carriage house, the home also boasted the finest furnishings and detail work of its era. Today it's open for public tours, as is the Guenther House, next to Pioneer Flour Mills (see below for details on both). The old mill still churns out some of the best flour gravy mix found on grocery shelves, along with cornbread, pancake, and similar mixes. The San Antonio Art League Museum is also located in a historic home in this district (see below).

Other historic homes in King William are privately owned, but residents are accustomed to tour buses and pedestrians sight-seeing in the area. You can enjoy a self-guided tour by picking up a brochure ("King William Area—A Walking Tour") in front of the San Antonio Conservation Society headquarters in the Anton Wulff

House at 107 King William Street (210–224-6163) or at a visitor center in town. The walk takes you past more than three dozen stately homes.

Edward Steves Homestead
509 King William St., San Antonio
(210) 227–9160
www.saconservation.org

On a walking or driving tour of King William, you may wonder just what the inside of these mansions is like. Satisfy your curiosity with a tour of the Steves Homestead. Once the home of German immigrant Edward Steves, founder of Steves Lumber Company, today the grand house is owned by the San Antonio Conservation Society.

The home is an example of Victorian French Second Empire style and is furnished with late-nineteenth-century antiques. One unique feature of the property is the River House, a one-story brick building at the rear of the mansion, which contained a natorium—San Antonio's first indoor swimming pool. Today flooring has been laid over the pool, and the building is used as a meeting space for the San Antonio Conservation Society.

Even older than the home is its Carriage House, built a year before the grand residence. This two-story building was later used for storage. The year after the home's completion, servants' quarters were added. Today these serve as the visitor center.

The museum is open daily from 10:00 A.M. to 4:15 P.M.

Guenther House
205 E. Guenther St., San Antonio
(210) 227–1061
www.guentherhouse.com
Free

Built in 1860, this was the home of Carl Hilmar Guenther, founder of Pioneer Flour Mills. With its crystal chandelier, gold-leaf mirrors, and piano from Stuttgart, Germany, the parlor offers a lovely glimpse of the elegance once enjoyed by the Guenther family. The home's library is now a museum, displaying family and mill artifacts such as Dresden china anniversary plates, cookie cutters, and family photos. The San Antonio River Mill Store is housed in the former music room and bedroom, and visitors can purchase stoneware, baking accessories, and gift items here. Finally, the Guenther House Restaurant, decorated in the Art Nouveau style, serves breakfast and lunch Monday through Saturday as well as Sunday brunch (see the Restaurants chapter for details). The museum and River Mill store are open Monday through Saturday 9:00 A.M. to 5:00 P.M., Sunday 8:00 A.M. to 2:00 P.M.

San Antonio Art League Museum
130 King William St., San Antonio
(210) 223–1140
www.saalm.org
Free

The headquarters for the San Antonio Art League is a historic structure built in 1896. Changing exhibits feature various types of art, from members' current works to pieces from previous decades. The museum is open Tuesday through Saturday from 1:00 to 5:00 P.M.

La Villita

La Villita, the "little village," is nestled on the east bank of the River Walk. Although right off a bustling pedestrian area, La Villita has a much different atmosphere, with an emphasis on history and art. Dating back to the days when the Alamo served as a military outpost, La Villita developed as a temporary village of squatters, people without land title. These tradesmen, camp followers, and Spanish soldiers and their families lived in primitive huts.

For years, La Villita remained a temporary settlement until a disastrous flood in 1821. The San Antonio River rose and demolished much of the west bank, but La Villita, with its slightly higher elevation, was spared. Locals began to look at the "little village" as a the place to be on the river, and soon the temporary huts were replaced with more permanent structures of adobe and stone.

La Villita came to historic prominence during the Texas Revolution, when Mexican troopers were defeated after the storming of Bexar. The surrender was signed at the Cos House in the neighborhood (see below). After Texas became a state, La Villita became a neighborhood of recent immigrants. The look of the neighborhood changed from Spanish adobe to European-style limestone blocks.

Within 50 years, though, La Villita hit bottom, reduced to a collection of boarding houses and bathhouses on the river's edge. Water was hauled from the river and sold for a quarter a barrel. The region became a virtual slum. It remained one of the worst areas in the city until 1939. As the city turned its attention to the river, planners realized that La Villita was long due for a renovation. The National Youth Administration and the city began an extensive program of renovation and re-

Shoppers in La Villita will find lots of choices. PHOTO: DAVE G. HOUSER, COURTESY OF THE SAN ANTONIO CONVENTION AND VISITORS BUREAU

creation. Today this is a National Historic District, filled with structures that recall Texas's early days.

The historic buildings now house artisans and craftsmen at work on everything from fine hand-blown glass to woven shawls. You'll find Latin American imports, from tin art to Indian rugs, sold alongside the creations of San Antonio artists. This artists' community nestles between San Antonio's tallest structure and the age-old river. One square block in size, it has retained an air of separateness from the River Walk. Today the area is one of the top shopping districts in the city; it's a place for people to shop for fine souvenirs in a collection of buildings whose styles hark back to the days of Old San Antonio. Most shops are open from 10:00 A.M. to 6:00 P.M. daily.

Cos House
418 Villita St., San Antonio

The Cos House is called by some the birthplace of Texas independence. Here the articles of capitulation were signed in December 9, 1835, relinquishing Mexico's claim to all lands north of the Rio Grande. When General Cos returned to Mexico City and told Santa Anna of the surrender, Santa Anna swore revenge and headed his troops for the Alamo. The home is not open to the public.

Little Church at La Villita
Villita St., San Antonio
(210) 226–3593
Free

The cornerstone of this tiny historic chapel was laid March 2, 1879. First a German Methodist church, the chapel was built in Gothic Revival style, with lancet-shaped casement windows and handcarved pegs made by a Norwegian sailor. Interdenominational services are held Sundays at 11:00 A.M. and 6:00 P.M.,

Haunted San Antonio

Behind a San Antonio home built more than 200 years ago, a night watchman hears the sound of a woman's cries coming from the depths of a sealed well. Elsewhere in the city, a museum's deceased curator still roams his former place of employment. And in an art center, a photographer feels a hand on his shoulder and turns to see a dark shadow in the room with him.

These are just a few examples of the spirited encounters that are said to have occurred in San Antonio and the nearby area. "San Antonio is a very haunted city," says Docia Williams, an author and tour guide who leads groups on night excursions of the city's "occupied" buildings. Williams has interviewed policemen, night watchmen, and residents of private homes throughout the city and searched the library's archives in the process of gathering material for her "Spirits of San Antonio" bus tour and her two ghostly tomes, *Spirits of San Antonio and South Texas* and *Ghosts Along the Texas Coast.*

One of San Antonio's oldest buildings, the Alamo, is also reported to be one of the most haunted. Today's night watchmen have heard unexplained sounds in the old mission, but the hauntings date back to the days of the historic battle. Following the battle, Mexican soldiers were said to have run from the Alamo shouting "diablos" (devils). The reference could have been to their opponents—or to some other presence in the mission.

Another Alamo ghost story concerns the order that was issued to burn the fort following the Battle of San Jacinto. Soldiers entered the old building, but soon fled, refusing to carry out their mission. It is said that when their leader entered the building, he was met by six ghosts holding swords of fire—rumored to be the ghosts of the Spanish priests who built the Alamo.

and the rest of the week it's not uncommon to see a wedding here. The church is open daily 10:00 A.M. to 6:00 P.M.

Monte Vista Historic District

One of San Antonio's oldest neighborhoods, this district was declared public land by King Philip of Spain in 1729. That makes the district's San Pedro Park the country's second-oldest municipal park. Soon the San Pedro Acequia was constructed here by the Canary Islands settlers; this irrigation facility served the city for a century and a half.

In the nineteenth century, the site became a military camp on more than one occasion. In 1846, U.S. soldiers camped here; they were later followed by camels assigned to the region as part of Jefferson Davis's Camel Corps (it didn't work).

Today the neighborhood is a quiet residential district but best known as home of San Pedro Springs Park (see the Parks and Recreation chapter).

Tours

The richest source of tour information is the Visitor Information Center operated by the San Antonio Convention and Visitors Bureau. It is located at 317 Alamo

The priests who haunt the Alamo are in the company of nuns not far away at the Southwest School of Art and Craft, according to Williams. Today a gallery and working studio for many San Antonio craftsmen, the building was once a girls' school run by cloistered nuns. "The only men ever allowed here were the doctor, if someone were very ill, and the parish priest who said the mass on Sunday," says Williams. "No other men were allowed. Now there are all these male teachers and security guards."

"The photography teacher was in the darkroom not too long ago, and he came out and felt a hand on his shoulder kind of shoving him," says the tour guide. "He turned around and there was nothing but a dark shadow. About a month or so later, the same thing happened to him, but this time it was a misty white shadow."

Several San Antonio museums are also rumored to be haunted. The Institute of Texan Cultures is supposedly haunted by the ghost of its former director, a pipe smoker. Williams says late-night employees still report smelling his tobacco smoke. And when night watchmen make their rounds, they often find the doors of the hearse in the Castroville exhibit mysteriously open. They close the hearse doors, make their rounds, and return to find them open once again.

Another allegedly haunted museum is the Jose Navarro house at 228 South Laredo, home of one of the signers of the Texas Declaration of Independence. Located next to the jail, the home is said to have cold spots, rocking chairs that move without human help, and furniture that rearranges itself. Not far away, the Spanish Governor's Palace, built in 1749, is supposedly haunted by the spirit of a former servant in the home. The woman was killed by robbers, and her body was thrown into a well behind the home. Today the well is capped, but night guards still report hearing her moans, says Williams.

Although the itinerary of Docia Williams's "Spirits of San Antonio" tour changes, one thing remains constant: all tours are conducted at night. The reason is simple, says Williams. "No self-respecting ghost would be out in daylight."

For more information on the Spirits of San Antonio tour, contact Docia Williams at (210) 493–2454.

Plaza, directly across from the Alamo. The information center also has brochures, maps, and San Antonio gifts.

The San Antonio Convention and Visitors Bureau also operates a toll-free phone line: (800) 447-3372. Call to order a free visitors packet, get information on convention delegate housing, or to obtain information on specific attractions.

A commercial tourist information center is also located at the Menger Hotel. The Alamo Visitor Center at 216 Alamo Plaza (210-225-8587) provides brochures on area attractions and sells tickets for the IMAX Theatre, San Antonio City Tours, the Texas Trolley, and the riverboat rides. Tours buses and the Texas Trolley also depart from here.

Guided Tours

Gray Line Tours
217 Alamo Plaza, San Antonio
(210) 226–1706, (800) GRAY–LINE
www.grayline.com
$$$$

This coast-to-coast company offers several different San Antonio tours, all in full-size motor coaches with professional guides. The Mission Trail tour (3½ hours) provides a look at the eighteenth-century missions, including the Alamo. The San Antonio Sampler (3½ hours) afternoon tour stops at the lush Japanese Tea Gardens, Fort Sam Houston, the King William Historic District and Steves Homestead

Museum, the Institute of Texan Cultures, and El Mercado. For an all-day look at San Antonio, the Alamo City Grand tour combines the first two tours and includes your choice of an IMAX Theatre show, a visit to the Buckhorn Museum, or a Yanaguana River Cruise. Gray Line tours depart from Alamo Plaza. Pickup service from the downtown hotels is complimentary; reservations are required for pickup service. Gray Line also offers tours of the Texas Hill Country, Austin, San Marcos's Prime Outlet Mall, and Nuevo Laredo, Mexico.

Lone Star Trolley
217 Alamo Plaza, San Antonio
(210) 226–1706, (800) GRAY–LINE
www.grayline.com
$$

Gray Line also operates the Lone Star Trolley, offering a hop-on, hop-off narrated tour. Tickets are valid for two days and stops include Ripley's Believe It or Not, the Alamo, the Hard Rock Cafe, Yanaguana River Cruises, Institute of Texan Cultures, Mission San José, Mission Concepción, King William District, San Fernando Cathedral, Market Square, and the Buckhorn Museum. The trolley tours begin at 10:00 A.M.; the last tour begins at 6:00 P.M.

San Antonio City Tours
Alamo Visitors Center, 216 Alamo Plaza,
San Antonio
(210) 247–0238
$$$$

This company offers visitors several city tours. The full-day tour includes the Alamo, the IMAX Theatre, the Spanish Governor's Palace, a riverboat ride, Market Square/El Mercado, Mission San José, the Japanese Gardens, and Mission Concepción. A half-day tour is offered in the morning and afternoon with stops at the Alamo, Texas Adventure, Market Square, Mission Concepción, and Mission San José.

San Antonio City Tours also offers guided all-day tours to the Texas Hill Country for a look at Fredericksburg and the LBJ Ranch. Another all-day trip travels to Laredo and Nuevo Laredo for a day of shopping.

Tours depart from the Alamo Visitors Center, located next to the Alamo in the Menger Hotel. Pickup service at downtown hotels is complimentary.

"Spirits of San Antonio" Tour
(210) 493–2454

These nighttime ventures take in San Antonio's "haunted" buildings, from the Menger Hotel to the Alamo to the Spanish Governor's Palace. Tours run for groups only, but guide Docia Williams keeps a list of interested individuals and plans a tour when she has 20 participants. See "Haunted San Antonio" in this chapter for the story on local ghosts.

Yanaguana Cruises
315 E. Commerce St., San Antonio
(210) 244–5700
www.sarivercruise.com
$$

These colorful barges are familiar symbols of San Antonio. Yanaguana, which means "refreshing waters," is what the Payaya Indians originally called the San Antonio River; today the company that bears the name offers cruises on the river year-round. The boats are open-air and operate on environmentally friendly compressed gas. Tours are narrated and are a great way to get an overview of the River Walk. You'll find ticket booths at Rivercenter Mall and across the river from the Hilton Palacio del Rio. The company also runs water taxis along the River Walk (see the Getting Here, Getting Around chapter). Charter cruises and dining cruises can also be arranged.

Kidstuff

Amusement Parks

Art Classes and
  Workshops

Bookstores

Camps

Games and Arcades

Historic Sites

Kid-Friendly Festivals

Libraries

Museums

Music

Other Indoor Attractions

Outdoor Attractions

Parks and Playgrounds

Recreation Centers and
  Programs

Sports and Fitness

Theaters

Toy Stores and
  Children's Shops

Water Parks

There's no denying that San Antonio is a city with a youthful atmosphere. With is wide variety of activities, from a world-class zoo to top theme parks, the city attracts families looking for vacation fun.

That youthful atmosphere is also seen in the faces of San Antonio's residents. The median age in San Antonio is just 32.9 years, younger than both the Texas average and the national average. Children are seen at attractions, restaurants, and establishments across town and make up a large part of the population.

An excellent guide to family-friendly San Antonio attractions is the San Antonio Convention and Visitors Bureau's "Just for Kids" brochure. This free brochure, available at the Visitors Information Center at 317 Alamo Plaza, online (www.SanAntonioCVB.com), and by phone (210–207–6748), offers information on attractions across town. "More and more, kids are influencing where a family takes a vacation, and family-oriented travel is becoming increasingly important to the industry," said Carol Morgenthaler, SACVB Visitor Marketing Manager.

Another top source of information on children's activities and attractions is *Our Kids: The Magazine for San Antonio Parents*. This free publication is distributed around town at grocery stores; subscriptions can be purchased for $15 by writing *Our Kids,* 8400 Blanco Road, Suite 201, San Antonio, TX 78216. The magazine also has some information on its Web site, www.parenthoodweb.com. *SA Kids* is another free publication for families. Distributed at many grocery stores and available online at www.primetimenewspapers.com/sakids/, this monthly magazine includes information on special events, arts and recreation, family-friendly movies, and other items of interest to San Antonio–area parents.

Along with the numerous attractions, programs, and activities, both indoors and out, available in this kid-friendly city, we've included many attractions within a short drive of San Antonio. With all that's going on in the Alamo City, there's no reason for kids ever to complain "I'm *bored*" while they're here.

Price-Code Key

The price ratings below are for an adult admission fee during the summer high season. Keep in mind that many attractions offer significant discounts for children, seniors, and military personnel.

$	less than $5
$$	$5–$10
$$$	$11–$20
$$$$	more than $20

Amusement Parks

Kiddie Park
3015 Broadway at Mulberry Ave.,
San Antonio
(210) 824–4351
www.kiddiepark.com
$–$$

Since 1925, children have delighted in this old-fashioned amusement park filled with kid-sized rides. The merry-go-round, carved in 1918, is a longtime favorite and fills the park with festive calliope music. The Little Dipper roller coaster is also popular with small visitors, as is the Ferris wheel, kiddie cars, and the game room. Individual ride prices vary; unlimited-ride passes are available.

Pear Apple County Fair
5820 Northwest Loop 410, San Antonio
(210) 521–9500
$

Local and visiting families who are looking for an afternoon outing often head to Pear Apple County Fair. Spanning 15 acres, this amusement park offers both indoor and outdoor games and rides. Kids can take a turn on the indoor Ferris wheel, ride the train, or bounce around on bumper cars.

Six Flags Fiesta Texas amusement park provides plenty of fun and sun. PHOTO: PARIS PERMENTER & JOHN BIGLEY

There's a go-cart track and two 18-hole miniature golf courses to keep older kids busy and happy. Cost varies by rides, but getting into the park is free.

SeaWorld of Texas
Ellison Dr. and Westover Hills Blvd. off Rte.
151 between Loop 410 and Loop 1604,
San Antonio
(210) 523–3611, (210) 523–3618
www.seaworld.com
$$$$

With its multitude of marine animals, SeaWorld of Texas is a favorite with children. The park also offers many kid-friendly rides, most found at Shamu's Happy Harbor, a play area. This 3-acre playground in the center of the park pulsates with young energy and encourages children to climb and explore. The area includes a large sand box as well as a swinging bridge, net climbing areas, and a square-rigger with water cannons. Here the Banana Cabana Theater present children's plays and musical revues.

Kids' rides range from Pete Penguin's Super Scooters and Penny Penguin's Classic Cars to O. P. Otter's Water Way mini-flume ride and Virgil's Paint Cans teacup ride. Pete's Pinwheel Ferris wheel is always a favorite. Summer visitors also love Lil' Gators Lagoon, a shallow lagoon in Lost Lagoon that encourages plenty of splashing and watery fun.

The park is open March through November; hours vary by season. For additional details, see the Attractions chapter.

Six Flags Fiesta Texas
17000 I–10 W., San Antonio
(210) 697–5050
www.sixflags.com
$$$$

Six Flags Fiesta Texas is justly known for its thrill rides but this popular park also offers plenty of pint-sized rides for younger visitors as well. The Rodeo Rider, a mini version of the park's Scream! ride, takes kids up and down a tower while Daffy's Ducka-neer gives children the chance to ride the waves on a pirate ship. Taz's Tornado features swinging seats, and the Mini Teacups takes kids in circles. The German-themed region of the park, Spassburg, is home to several child-size rides, including Der Pilger Bahnhof (for toddlers), and Der Rollschuhcoaster and Kinder Wagon (both for children at least 36 inches tall). Park hours vary by season. For additional details, see the Attractions chapter.

Art Classes and Workshops

Artworks
N. New Braunfels Ave. in Carousel Court, San Antonio
(210) 826–ARTS
www.artworkstx.com

This art studio was especially designed for children. Starting with early childhood classes, the studio offers art instruction and creative fieldtrips for children. Birthday parties for ages 3 to 12 are also available. The studio is open for general admission Tuesday 4:00 to 7:00 P.M.

Carver Community Cultural Center
226 N. Hackberry, San Antonio
(210) 225–6516

Carver's School of Visual and Performing Arts offers a variety of classes for children and adults. Along with drama and movement, the center offers classes in jazz studies, ceramics, and visual arts.

Jewish Community Center
12500 N.W. Military Hwy., San Antonio
(210) 302–6820

The courses for children ages three and older offered here are open to all residents of San Antonio. In addition to arts and crafts classes, there are sports programs and science classes. Fees vary.

Kids Paint the Town
(210) 545–4209

Artist Sue Telle teaches children's drawing and painting classes at sites around San Antonio. Summer classes are available for children ages 6 to 14 and are scheduled from 9:00 A.M. to noon Monday through Friday.

Northwest Arts and Crafts Group
Michaels' Arts and Craft Center, Ingram Rd., San Antonio
(830) 665–5271, (210) 414–8914

The Michael's craft store is the setting for arts and crafts classes for kids ages 2 to 12. Classes are scheduled throughout the year on the first and the last Wednesday of the month. Parental supervision is required.

San Antonio Museum of Art
200 W. Jones Ave., San Antonio
(210) 978–8100
www.sa-museum.org

Every month this museum features a "Make-n-Take" art class for children ages

4 to 11. The theme of the monthly event varies. The programs are free with paid admission to the museum.

San Antonio Parks and Recreation Mural Project
San Antonio Parks and Recreation Department
www.ci.sat.tx.us/sapar/index.htm
(210) 207–3056

The mural program operated by the Parks and Recreation Department has resulted in murals at several community gardens including the Copernicus, Melendrez, and San Juan Brady Gardens Community Centers. Participants receive certificates of appreciation at the dedication ceremonies.

Southwest School of Art and Craft
300 Augusta St., San Antonio
(210) 224–1848
www.swschool.org

More than 1,600 children enroll in classes at this popular art and craft school every year. One of the favorite programs is the Saturday Morning Discovery (SMD), a free introductory art class scheduled every Saturday morning during the school year. Aimed at children ages 5 to 16, this program has been in operation for more than three decades and has introduced thousands of children to the world of ceramics, drawing, photography, painting, origami, silk-screening, stained glass, and more.

Classes are offered in one-month sessions, and parents are required to remain with their children through the program; often parents have the opportunity to work alongside their child. Advance reservations are required for the program; call (210) 224–1848, ext 321.

The school also sponsors the Mobile Arts Program (MAP), which brings artists into hospitals, public schools, shelters, and community centers. The workshops in drawing, clay sculpture, weaving, architecture, design, and other activities complement classroom instruction; more than 10,000 San Antonio children participate each year. To schedule classes through MAP, teachers should call the Young Artist Programs Director at (210) 224–1848, ext 331.

Bookstores

Barnes and Noble
6065 Loop 410 N.W. at Ingram Mall, San Antonio
(210) 522–1340
18030 U.S. 381 N., San Antonio
(210) 490–0411
321 Loop 410 N.W. at San Pedro Crossing, San Antonio
(210) 342–0008
12635 I–10 W., San Antonio
(210) 561–0205

These extensive bookstores offer story hours with stories, snacks, and crafts. Each store has a specially designated children's area. The free programs vary, but recently the stores have offered a Pajama-rama story time.

Borders Books and Music
255 E. Basse Rd., at Quarry Market, San Antonio
(210) 828–9496
11745 I–10 W., at Huebner Oaks shopping center, San Antonio
(210) 561–0022
www.borders.com

Borders bookstores, each with an extensive children's section, also offer free story times. At the Quarry location, storytimes are scheduled for 7:00 P.M. on Friday nights. The Huebner Oaks location schedules storytimes for 2:00 P.M. on Saturday afternoons.

The Red Balloon
5005 Broadway, San Antonio
(210) 826–5087
www.thetwig.com

This bookstore offers a free story hour every Friday at 10:30 A.M. The children's bookstore also features a variety of special events every month. In the past the store has hosted Diane Gonzales Bertrand, author of the bilingual *The Last Doll/La*

Ultima Muñeca and Paul Epner, author of *Herbert Hilligan and His Magical Lunchbox.* Special appearances by Maisy, Tacky the Penguin, and other costumed characters also give young shoppers the chance to have a photo taken with their favorite story-book friends.

Camps

Camp Fair
HomeCourt America, Callaghan and I–10, San Antonio
(210) 349–6667

This mid-March event is aimed the parents of prospective summer campers. Co-sponsored by *Our Kids* magazine, Home Court America, and the Acadiana Cafe, the fair gives families the opportunity to talk with representatives of many summer-camp programs.

Green Tree Tennis Club
4721 Callaghan Rd., San Antonio
(210) 681–4261

This tennis club sponsors a variety of spring and summer tennis programs for children. From late May through early August, the club offers a tennis camp, with new sessions beginning each week. The camp runs from 10:00 A.M. to 2:00 P.M.; fees are $75 per week. Children learn tennis skills and also have the opportunity to go swimming. During the summer, the Sports Camp here runs from 8:00 A.M. to 5:30 P.M. and includes tennis, swimming, and more activities; the cost is $120 per week. This club also offers a spring-break camp in March.

Kids Sports Network Golf Camps
8206 Roughrider Dr., Suite 104, San Antonio
(210) 654–4707
www.ksnusa.org/camps.htm

Is your child an aspiring Tiger Woods? You just might want to check out this day camp, designed to teach golf to young players ages 7 to 14 of all levels of ability. Participants learn everything from rules and etiquette to keeping score. On the last day of camp, the kids play a partial round of golf to exhibit their new skills.

The week-long camp is held either at San Pedro Golf Center or Alamo Golf Club, depending on the week. All sessions include 15 hours of instruction, a set of five golf clubs, a golf bag, a cap, a polo shirt, a golf rule book, golf balls, and tees. The price of the camp is $145. Each session has a maximum of 40 participants.

Children who attend the San Pedro camps can also sign up for an afternoon of activities at the Downtown YMCA; participants are picked up after the golf camp and taken to the YMCA facility for lunch, a field trip, and swim time. Registration for the YMCA portion of the camp is through the Downtown YMCA; call (210) 246-9600.

The camp also offers scholarships for 60 students; scholarship participants are selected by local nonprofit youth associations.

San Antonio Children's Museum
305 E. Houston St., San Antonio
(210) 212–4453
www.sakids.org/

The museum sponsors two week-long summer camps, each led by museum educators. The camps, held from 9:00 A.M. to noon on weekdays, are aimed at children ages 5 to 12. Themes for the summer camps vary but center around art exploration; previous themes have been "Mask Mania," when participants had the opportunity to learn about cultures around the world as they made masks out of natural and man-made materials, and "Picture Perfect Printing," during which participants produced prints using a variety of objects and foods. At the end of the camp, parents can attend the Campers' Art Exhibit. Cost for the camp is $75 per session ($65 for museum members).

The San Antonio Children's Museum tempts young visitors with all kinds of hands-on exhibits.

PHOTO: PARIS PERMENTER & JOHN BIGLEY

SeaWorld of Texas
Ellison Dr. and Westover Hills Blvd., off Rte. 151 between Loop 410 and Loop 1604, San Antonio
(210) 523–3611, (210) 523–3618
www.seaworld.com

SeaWorld has long been a favorite destination for children, but the popular amusement park also offers many child-specific programs and Camp SeaWorld. This day camp, starting in early June and continuing through early August, is open to kids ages 3 to 14. All SeaWorld programs aim to teach children more about marine animals and about environmental issues.

Most sessions of Camp SeaWorld end with an overnight sleepover at SeaWorld's Sharks/The Coral Reef habitat or the Penguin Encounter habitat.

The park also offers a three-day camp for children ages 3 to 5 to allow young visitors to learn alongside their parents.

Each of the camp curriculums emphasize the interaction between students and their environment. Activities include creating artwork, presenting conservation-oriented skits and songs, touring animal exhibits, and exploring career opportunities in animal-related fields. Camp SeaWorld is accredited by the American Camping Association. Park participants have come from 14 countries and 48 states. Students in grades 6 through 8 can enroll in SeaWorld Expedition Camp, which includes visits to animal habitats throughout the park and two field trips.

Another option is Careers Camp, which allows high school students (grades 9 through 12) to accompany SeaWorld zoological and animal-training staff as they monitor the health of sea lions, weigh killer whales, feed penguins, prepare food for beluga whales, and more. Students must apply for enrollment; application requirements are a high school transcript, a phone interview, a teacher or counselor recommendation, and a 200-word essay.

An advanced Careers Camp for students who have completed Careers Camp is also offered. This camp offers students the chance to apprentice with SeaWorld staff to learn more about marine animals and zoological careers.

Teachers can also take part in the fun, thanks to the Adventure Camp for Teachers. Elementary, middle school, and high school teachers can participate in the camp to obtain continuing education credits; the three-day program helps teachers incorporate environmental and conservation materials into their classroom curriculum.

The cost for the camps varies with the length of the session and the time of year.

Southwest School of Art and Craft
300 Augusta St., San Antonio
(210) 224–1848
www.swschool.org

This school offers one- and two-week art camps for children ages 5 to 17 throughout the summer. Parents can choose from all-day, morning, or afternoon sessions, which run from late May until the first days of August. Classes cover a range of topics such as photography, weaving, painting, drawing, architecture, and more. You'll even find specialized class topics such as cartoon storytelling, the art of Georgia O'Keefe, beading, Egyptian expedition, and clay for teens.

Registration is required for these popular camps. You can register in person or by phone, mail, or fax. Class size is limited and registration is on a first-come, first-served basis. Scholarships based on merit and need are available. To be considered for a Young Artist Programs scholarship, students must submit written recommendations from a classroom teacher or qualified professional and parent or guardian.

The cost of the full-day camps (which include five full days, a supervised lunch hour, and two hours of supervised after-class activities) is $185 for nonmembers. Half-day programs range from $70 to $135 for nonmembers.

Witte Museum
3801 Broadway, San Antonio
(210) 357–1900
www.wittemuseum.org

In the summer months and during holiday and spring-break weeks, the Witte Adventure Club provides plenty of interesting activities for children ages 6 to 11 years of age. Each of the camp sessions is focused on a particular topic such as "Destination: Solar System," "Tepees and Tribal Tales," "Wild World," "The Nuts and Bolts of Chemistry," "Dino Detectives," and "Awesome Ancients."

Both full- and half-day sessions are available. Half-day sessions run from 9:00 A.M. to 12:30 P.M. and 1:30 P.M. to 5:00 P.M.

The cost of the half-day camp is $15 per session for members, $20 for nonmembers; an entire week of half-day sessions is $75 for members, and $100 for nonmembers. Full-day sessions are $40 for members and $55 for nonmembers; by the week, full-day sessions are priced at $180 for members and $210 for nonmembers. A limited number of need-based scholarships are available on a first-come, first-served basis. For information on scholarships, call (210) 357–1850. Reservations are required for all camp sessions; call (210) 357–1910.

YMCA Camp Flaming Arrow
Hunt
(800) 765–YMCA
www.campflamingarrow.org

The YMCA offers one- and two-week residential summer camp sessions for girls and boys ages 6 to 15 at a 280-acre camp. Located between the Hill Country and the Guadalupe River, the ranch is located in the town of Hunt, 90 minutes from San Antonio. Activities include horseback riding, canoeing, archery, swimming, folk arts and crafts, hiking, and more. Campers also learn about the natural world that surrounds them with sessions on the plant and animal life of Texas.

Y.O. Adventure Camp
HC 01, Mountain Home
(830) 640–3220
yoac@ktc.com

The historic Y.O. Ranch, well known

San Antonio Area Wildlife Ranches

From the shade of the century-old tree, the wildebeest yawns and eyes a small herd of springbok, on their way to the watering hole. Nearby, a lanky ostrich saunters across the field, a few wide paces away from a dusty zebra. It's a scene witnessed by a family from the comfort of their vehicle, enjoying a daylong safari—Texas style.

Within a short drive of San Antonio, you'll find several excellent wildlife parks that let families view exotic animals in a natural setting, away from the cages and confinement of a zoo. Here the animals exhibit natural behaviors, relating to fellow herd members, teaching their young, and in other ways acting as they would in the wild.

One of the largest drive-through animal parks in Texas is the Natural Bridge Wildlife Ranch, located next to the caverns of the same name. About half an hour north of San Antonio, the park is located west of I–35 near New Braunfels. This ranch features both native and exotic animals, ranging from some very pushy ostriches to some rather excited zebras. After the drive, enjoy a look around the petting area, which includes some cute critters like pygmy goats, then shop for wildlife-related souvenirs in the gift shop. The park is open daily; for directions and price information, call (210) 438–7400.

East of San Antonio, outside the community of Harwood, near Luling, Noah's Land offers visitors a chance to see some 500 animals. Located 5.5 miles north of I–10, the 400-acre park is divided into 10 sanctuaries, habitats for animals of the plains and the mountains. On your trip through the park, you can see and (sometimes) feed axis

throughout Central and South Texas, hosts an adventure camp for children ages 7 to 16. Especially valuable for city children, the camp lets kids experience life on a 40,000-acre ranch. Campers learn ranch skills and more. One and two-week sessions are offered.

Games and Arcades

GameWorks Studio
255 E. Basse Rd., San Antonio
(210) 930–3500
www.gameworks.com/locations/stu_
sanantonio.html
$

The creation of Sega Enterprises and Universal Studios, this member of the nationally known chain of arcades is a popular choice with kids of all ages. The indoor complex of high-tech, arcade, and video games includes challenges for all skill levels. Sky Pirates VR, a 24-foot interactive video game, gives players the sensation of riding through the sky while battling hot-air balloons. Another longtime favorite at GameWorks is Mr. Bigg VR, which divides groups of players into teams to race the clock while they attempt to free a skyscraper from criminal elements. Many old-fashioned midway games are found in the Big Win Zone. The virtual Max Flight VR2002 Roller Coaster is a real thrill; riders are strapped in to experience 360-degree pitches and rolls while viewing state-of-the-art graphics. Simulators also take would-be car racers to the Indy 500; eight "drivers" can race in simulated cars that move from side to side. Fans of the movie

deer, Corsican sheep, red kangaroos, emus, camels, rhinos, and local favorites like Texas longhorns. A large petting area is home to Angora and pygmy goats, Sicilian donkeys, and more. An aviary contains exotic chickens, peacocks, and pheasants. This park is open daily except Christmas. For more information, call (800) 725–NOAH.

Also north of San Antonio, the community of Johnson City is home to The Exotic Resort, a park that lives up to its name. On 137 acres, unusual species (including many endangered animals) roam across the wooded hill country. In this park you leave the driving to someone else and enjoy a guided ride aboard a safari truck. Professional guides conduct tours of the ranch and provide visitors with information about the animals as you feed the friendly park residents. After the tour, you can see some wildlife up close at the petting zoo. Kids enjoy petting child-sized miniature donkeys, baby deer, llama, baby elk, and even a kangaroo at this special area. For directions, call (210) 868–4357.

If your children enjoy petting zoos, then don't miss the largest one in Texas, located at San Marcos's Wonder World. Just north of San Antonio on I–35, this park is best known for its cave, created by an earthquake about 30 million years ago. There's plenty of action above ground as well, though, at the $7\frac{1}{2}$ acre Texas Wildlife Park. Kids and parents can all hop aboard a miniature train for a ride through the animal enclosure. Along the way, the train stops to allow riders to pet and feed tame white-tailed deer, turkeys, and many exotic species. This park is open March through October; for information call (800) 782–7653, ext. CAVE.

Whichever park you visit, don't forget your camera. And, for best viewing of the animals, try to arrive either early or late in the day. Especially during warm weather months, most animals will retire to the cool shade at midday, so your best chance of seeing active animals is when the park first opens or just before sunset.

will love Jurassic Park—The Lost World, an interactive theater with roller-coaster-type seating that pits guests against the world of dinosaurs. There's a fee for each game.

GameWorks Studio is open Monday through Thursday from 11:00 A.M. to 11:00 P.M., Friday from 11:00 to 1:00 A.M., Saturday from 10:00 to 1:00 A.M., and Sunday from noon to 11:00 P.M.

Jungle Jim's Playland
1311 San Pedro Ave., San Antonio
(210) 490–9595
$–$$

Jungle Jim's is a large franchise of indoor children's entertainment centers in Mexico and the Southwestern United States. They feature child-size rides, a soft playground, and a multitude of games, plus well-trained Jungle Guides to supervise. Visitors can pay for each ride or purchase a general pass.

This playground's indoor setting makes it popular in the summer months as well as on bad weather days.

Kiddie Park
3015 Broadway at Mulberry Ave., San Antonio
(210) 824–4351
www.kiddiepark.com

This San Antonio institution, in operation since 1925, claims to be the oldest children's amusement park in the nation. It features an antique carousel, small roller coaster, and old-fashioned but still kid-pleasing rides such as helicopters and boats. More modern amusements are in the game room. Ticket prices start at 35 cents; unlimited rides are $5.95.

Larzland
U.S. 281, Thousand Oaks exit at Henderson
Pass, San Antonio
(210) 495–1555
$

This family-oriented arcade is filled with both old-fashioned and high-tech games, all played with nickels. The arcade is a popular birthday party site. It's open 3:00 to 9:00 P.M. Thursday, 3:00 to 11:00 P.M. Friday, 11:00 A.M. to 11:00 P.M. Saturday, and 11:00 A.M. to 9:00 P.M. Sunday; closed Monday through Wednesday.

Laser Quest
606 Embassy Oaks, San Antonio
(210) 499–4400
6420 Loop 410 N.W., San Antonio
(210) 520–8555
www.laserquest.com
$$

Laser tag is the name of the game at this high-tech gaming center that adds space-age lasers to the joy of hide and seek. The multilevel gaming area pits players against each other; the idea is to "shoot" other players and remove them from the game. Players can play alone or with friends; the center is also very popular for birthday parties and group gatherings. Reservations are accepted.

Malibu Grand Prix
3330 Cherry Ridge Dr., San Antonio
(210) 341–6664
7702 Briaridge, San Antonio
(210) 341–2500
$–$$

The grand-prix-style tracks are designed so all ages can experience the thrill of driving a mini race car. A video game room, miniature golf course, and electronic batting cage add to the fun. There's a separate fee for each activity. There are two locations in San Antonio.

Historic Sites

Alamo
300 Alamo Plaza, San Antonio
(210) 225–1391
www.thealamo.org
Free

Schoolchildren throughout Texas often see the Alamo on school-sponsored trips, but the historic site makes an excellent destination for family trips as well. The former mission church is a quiet, solemn place where children can learn more about the battle and the Texians and Mexicans who died here. Also part of the complex is the Long Barrack, where a film about the event is shown. The film is of interest to children 10 and over; for younger children, the grounds are a nice place to walk on cool days.

The Alamo offers several educational programs, from teacher in-service programs to an orientation film produced by the History Channel to packets for fourth- and seventh-grade teachers. There's also special teacher information online at www.thealamo.org/teacher_information.htm. Some of the information might also be of interest to parents: how to get the most out of your visit to the Alamo, how to build a model of the Alamo, and the Alamo History Hunt, a fill in the blank form children can complete as they tour the facility.

Recently the Daughters of the Republic of Texas, the caretakers of the Alamo, announced plans to construct a new Education Arbor and Amphitheater on the mission grounds. To be located on the eastern end of the complex, the 78-seat amphitheater will be used for lectures and seminars. For more information on the Alamo, see the Attractions chapter.

Quadrangle at Fort Sam Houston
Grayson St. and N. New Braunfels Ave., San
Antonio
(210) 221–1232

Fort Sam Houston is best known for its extensive military history museum, but to its youngest visitors, the resident deer and peacocks are much more exciting. Many of the deer are so tame that they can be petted and hand-fed. Call for current information regarding visitors to the base.

San Antonio Missions National Historical Park
6701 San José Dr.,
San Antonio (Visitors Center)
(210) 932–1001
www.nps.gov/saan
$ donation

This national park is spread along the Missions Trail, which encompasses four historic missions. Start your self-guided tour at the San José Mission's Visitors Center, where you can pick up a Junior Ranger packet. Geared for children in the second to sixth grades, the packet points out special attractions and activities of interest to children. A 23-minute film shown at Mission San José provides young visitors with a good overview of the purpose and history of the missions. See the Attractions chapter for detailed information on each mission. Be aware that fire ants are a problem in this area and can be very painful for young children. Good walking shoes are important for the irregular floors of the missions as well. The missions are open daily 9:00 A.M. to 5:00 P.M. but are closed Thanksgiving, Christmas, and New Year's Day.

Kid-Friendly Festivals

For schedules, admission fees, and other information about the following events, see the Annual Events and Festivals chapter.

February

San Antonio Stock Show and Rodeo
Freeman Coliseum, 3201 E. Houston St., San Antonio
(210) 225–5851
www.sarodeo.com

The annual Rodeo is definitely a family-friendly event. Along with a Western parade, educational displays, and a carnival midway, families with children also enjoy the rodeo's Family Fair and World of Animals, which gives kids the chance to pet livestock.

March

Remembering the Alamo Weekend
Alamo Plaza, San Antonio
(210) 279–4973, (210) 494–7165
www.artco.org/sa/salha/salha.html

When asked about the Alamo, many children only mention the fateful battle that took place within these walls. However, this former mission and the surrounding area once served as a home for the region's pioneers, both from Mexico and from the United States. This special weekend, always scheduled the Saturday and Sunday nearest March 6 (the anniversary of the fall of the Alamo), takes a look at the life, not the death, of the people of that time period. Costumed actors bring the era to life with demonstrations of spinning, weaving, pioneer medicine, and more.

April

Children's Festival
River Walk, San Antonio
(210) 227–4262
www.thesanantonioriverwalk.com

Adults don't get to have all the fun at Fiesta; this officially sanctioned Fiesta event is especially designed for the youngest partiers. Held along the River Walk and sponsored by the Paseo del Rio Association, this one-day event has plenty of pint-size fun and games. Admission is free.

Peter Rabbit's Great Hill Country Garden Party
Love Creek Orchards, Rte. 16, Medina
(800) 449–0882
www.lovecreekorchards.com

This annual four-day event, held just before Easter, includes a variety of family-friendly activities. There are Easter egg hunts, a hay maze, egg races, a giant bubble tub, and hayrides. Clowns add to the merriment, and children can get cuddly with small livestock. Peter Rabbit's Garden also offers children the chance to grow their own vegetables. You buy the pot, your child decorates it, and they provide the plant and instructions. And, since this is held at an apple orchard, don't forget to sample some apple ice cream or cider. Admission to the event is $3.00 per person.

May

Texas State Arts and Crafts Fair
Schreiner College, Kerrville
(210) 896–5711

This crafts fair is a favorite with adults for its excellent shopping, but it also offers good family fun. There's a special area where children can make their own artwork, pet exotic species, and just play in the sand.

June

Fiesta Noche Del Rio
Arneson River Theatre, San Antonio
(210) 226–4651
www.alamo-kiwanis.org/noche/fiesta.htm

Children enjoy the colorful dances and catchy rhythms of this summer production, staged at the Arneson River Theatre. For nearly four decades, this show has been sponsored by the Alamo Kiwanis Club as a fundraiser for the Children's

Insiders' Tip

On Kids' Day at the Texas Folklife Festival, children 12 and under are admitted free when accompanied by an adult.

Shelter of San Antonio. It celebrates the many cultures of San Antonio through song and dance every Tuesday, Friday, and Saturday night through August.

Texas Folklife Festival
Institute of Texan Cultures, 801 S. Bowie Rd.,
HemisFair Plaza, San Antonio
(210) 458–2390
www.texancultures.utsa.edu

Kids love this summer festival for its crafts exhibits, folk dances, and fun atmosphere. The festival is also an excellent way to introduce children to other cultures (not to mention other cuisines) and to enjoy a fun and educational family weekend.

December

Fiesta de Las Luminarias
Paseo del Rio, San Antonio
(210) 207–8600
www.thesanantonioriverwalk.com

Thousands of luminarias, tiny candles in sand-weighted paper bags, guide visitors to the River Walk during this special Christmas celebration. The candles symbolize the lighting of the way for the Holy Family. For children, a candlelit walk is a magical pre-bedtime treat. This event is sponsored by the Paseo del Rio Association; admission is free.

Holiday River of Lights
Cypress Bend Park, New Braunfels
(830) 608–2100

Children are dazzled by the trail of sparkling lights and animated holiday scenes that make up this winter fantasyland. Located just half an hour north of San Antonio on I–35, this radiant celebration is held on the banks of the Guadalupe River in Cypress Bend Park from mid-November to early January. Turn on the car radio to hear some of your favorite holiday tunes as you wind your way along the shimmering Guadalupe River banks that are aglow with hundreds

Kids experience hands-on learning at the Institute of Texan Cultures. PHOTO: SAN ANTONIO CONVENTION AND VISITORS BUREAU/INFORMEDIA

of thousands of twinkling lights and holiday scenes. Sponsored by the City of New Braunfels, this winter wonderland stretches seven-tenths of a mile.

Las Posadas
Paseo del Rio, San Antonio
(210) 224–6163
www.saconservation.org/posada.html

Costumed boys and girls representing Joseph, Mary, angels, and shepherds lead this beautiful procession along the River Walk. Priests and mariachi players follow the children, singing songs in both English and Spanish. After the procession, kids can enjoy hot chocolate and cookies and take a swing at a piñata at Maverick Plaza in La Villita.

Libraries

In addition to the Central Library (below), San Antonio's library system includes 19 branch libraries throughout the city. The branch libraries all have children's sections and offer special programs for young readers throughout the year. The San Antonio Public Library System also operates Book (Wired), an online program for students in the 8th through 12th grades. Along with research assistance, the program's Web site (www.youthwired.sat.lib.tx.us) offers games, online magazines, and suggestions on teen fiction.

San Antonio Central Library
600 Soledad Plaza, San Antonio
(210) 207–2500
www.sanantonio.gov/library/

Storytime at the "Big Red Library" downtown takes place on the special Children's Floor. There are also puppet shows, arts and crafts classes, and musical activities for kids, all free.

Museums

Buckhorn Saloon and Museum
318 E. Houston St., San Antonio
(210) 247–4000
www.buckhornmuseum.com
$$

This museum displays trophies and wax figures; of greatest interest to children,

Storytellers at the Institute of Texan Cultures make history come alive for young visitors.
PHOTO: SAN ANTONIO CONVENTION AND VISITORS BUREAU/INFORMEDIA

however, is the live entertainment. Although it varies by day, kids can visit the 120-year-old bar for a soda and watch trick roping, gunfighters, or a cowboy poet. The Buckhorn Arcade is also tops with young visitors. The museum is open daily and closed only for Christmas and New Year's. For additional details, see the Attractions chapter.

Institute of Texan Cultures
801 S. Bowie Rd., San Antonio
(210) 458–2300
www.texancultures.utsa.edu
$

Texas was settled by over 30 ethnic groups from around the world, all honored at this museum operated by the University of Texas. Families should start their visit at the Dome Theater; kids can lie back on the floor and watch the show—which highlights the many faces of Texas—overhead. Around the theater are exhibits on groups such as Native Americans, Swedes, and Canary Islanders. The Native American area is always of particular interest to young children; it houses a

Sioux tipi tanned with buffalo brains. Docents are on hand to explain more about the life of the Sioux, and kids can even touch the tools used by these early residents. The historic buildings behind the museum, including a one-room schoolhouse and a frontier fort, are also kid-pleasers. The museum is open Tuesday through Sunday, 9:00 A.M. to 5:00 P.M.; also see the Attractions chapter.

San Antonio Children's Museum
305 E. Houston St., San Antonio
(210) 212–4453
www.hotx.com/cm/FrontDoor.html

Hands-on fun is the theme of this interactive museum. Targeted to children ages 2 to 10, it gives young visitors an opportunity to explore subjects from gardening to global communications. The people and places of San Antonio are represented in displays such as an elevator in the shape of the Tower of the Americas and people puzzles representing historic figures.

This museum also offers many regularly scheduled children's events and classes. The monthly Play with Your Food Day lets children do just that while making such creations as sunflower mosaics, a popcorn bluebonnet, or Texas-shaped cookies.

A new addition to the museum is the Kids Get Mail post office exhibit in the Museum Workshop. Kids can learn about the postal system and about the fun of stamp collecting at the exhibit. During the summer months, the museum schedules FUN shops—mini-workshops held from 11:00 A.M. to noon Tuesday and Thursday through early August. Admission to the workshops is free with museum admission; there's no need to reserve space unless you are bringing more than five children. Parents stay with children during the workshops, which are for kids ages 2 to 12.

The museum is open Monday 9:00 A.M. to noon, Tuesday to Friday 9:00 A.M. to 3:30 P.M., Saturday 9:00 A.M. to 6:00 P.M., and Sunday noon to 4:00 P.M. During the summer months, the museum remains open on weekdays until 5:00 P.M.

Witte Museum of History and Science/ H-E-B Science Treehouse
3801 Broadway, San Antonio
(210) 357–1900
www.wittemuseum.org

This museum has long been a favorite with children because of its interactive exhibits. But for the last several years, families have had more reasons than ever to visit, thanks to the H-E-B Science Treehouse. Built like a genuine tree house, this 15,000-square-foot building spans four levels and is located on the grounds of the museum. Tucked in the trees and sheltered from the sounds of traffic, the Treehouse challenges young visitors with hands-on science exhibits. No matter how energetic the child, this center offers activities that entertain and teach at the same time. Kids can launch a tennis ball two stories in the air, use laser beams to produce music, or lift themselves with pulleys and ropes.

The first and second levels of the Treehouse contain most of the hands-on exhibits. The first floor contains "Move It," a vertical wave ladder made of undulating copper rods; "Flying Forces," a mechanized mobile controlled by joy sticks; and "Suddenly Superhuman," a multigear system that pits six people against one. Discovery Areas help visitors connect the concepts learned in these exhibits with their everyday lives. This floor also includes a museum store and an observation porch overlooking the San Antonio River.

The second level of the Treehouse contains "Eye Spy and Magnify," a high-powered microscope that enables visitors to see inside their own ear; "Magnetic Tug-of-War," a variety of experiments using magnets; "Computer Animation Video," an opportunity for visitors to create unique three-dimensional animation; and the "Internet Surfing Station," with computer terminals offering access to the World Wide Web (special controls protect children from inappropriate material).

The Underground Level of the Treehouse includes an archaeological profile of the site of the Treehouse as well as exhibits on the region's past. One exhibit includes part of a hearth of a campsite dating back 4,000 years. Throughout the year, the museum plans overnight camps as well as live theater performances in this area.

The top level is the Treetop level, overlooking Brackenridge Park. Here children can use telescopes or view exhibits such as "Hang It and Clang It," musical science stations for creating sounds using natural and artificial materials, and "A-Maze Yourself," a large floor maze for visitors to navigate, patterned after a Navajo rug in the Witte's permanent collection.

The grounds are also home to a genuine tree house, which spans two levels. Created by San Antonio sculptor Carlos Cortes, the treehouse is erected on two concrete "oak" trees; the upper level of the tree house offers binoculars for watching area wildlife.

The museum also hosts many special events throughout the year. During the summer months and holiday weeks, the facility sponsors the Witte Adventure Club (see Camps, above). During the spring and fall, the Witte schedules special sleep-ins for visitors age 8 to 12 years. Rates for the overnight camp are $30 per child; the cost includes admission, a movie, a snack, and breakfast.

The museum is open Monday through Saturday 10:00 A.M. to 5:00 P.M. and Tuesday from noon to 5:00 P.M. Admission (to the Witte Museum and the H-E-B Science Treehouse) is $5.95 for adults, $4.95 for seniors 65 years and over, $3.95 for children ages 4 to 11, and free for children 3 and under. The admission fee includes both the Witte Museum and the H-E-B Science Treehouse. For more information about the Witte Museum, see the Attractions chapter.

Music

Babies Make Music Program
Mars Music
25 Northeast Loop 410, San Antonio
(888) 999–MARS
www.marsmusic.com

Would you like to introduce your child to the joy of music at an early—a really early—age? Mars Music has classes that teach children to interact with music for participants as tiny as newborns. The Cricket Chorus, for babies from birth to 18 months, helps children with music interaction. Jumpin' Jamporee, for ages 18 months to 3 years, and Monkey Mambo, for kids ages 3 to 5, take the activity level up a notch with drums, shakers, bells, and other instruments to help children learn to clap, sing, and dance. Classes are for both parents and children. Cost starts at $13 per week and includes use of instruments, a video, and a parent songbook.

Jensen's Yamaha Music School
7218 Blanco Rd., San Antonio
(210) 366–5048

Children ages 4 through 8 are taught according to the Yamaha method at this school, now in operation more than 25 years. Instruction is available in keyboard, singing, rhythm stop, solfège, and music appreciation. Call for a free preview class.

Other Indoor Attractions

IMAX Theater at Rivercenter Mall
849 E. Commerce St. at Rivercenter Mall, San Antonio
(210) 247–4629, (800) 354–4629
www.IMAX-sa.com
$$

"Alamo: The Price of Freedom," the IMAX movie which is the main attraction here, is considered one of the best and historically correct film versions of the famous event. And, it is a pleasure to watch in this state-of-the-art big screen theater Other IMAX releases are also shows periodically. The IMAX also offers 3-D shows on a variety of subjects.

Plaza Wax Museum
301 Alamo Plaza, San Antonio
(210) 224–9299
www.plazatheatreofwax.com
$$$

Located directly across the street from the Alamo, the Plaza Wax Museum has more than 225 lifelike wax figures. For children, the most interesting sections are the Hollywood exhibits, which includes replicas of some present-day actors such as Brad Pitt, and the Heroes of the Lone Star, featuring the historic figures who fought at the Alamo. A note to parents: The Theater of Horrors is especially scary for young (and even not-so-young) children. However, this attraction is accessible only by entering a well-marked door at the bottom of a staircase, so you can easily skip the stairs and bypass the creepy exhibits without even a peek. Of special interest to little ones is the Children's Land of Make Believe, filled with fantasy characters. The theater is open daily Memorial Day through Labor Day, although hours change by season.

The ticket box office closes one hour prior to closing time. Combination tickets with Ripley's Believe it or Not! (below) are available.

Ripley's Believe it or Not!
301 Alamo Plaza, San Antonio
(210) 224–9299
www.plazatheatreofwax.com
$$

Located in the same facility as the Plaza Theatre of Wax just across the street from the Alamo, Ripley's Believe It or Not! is filled with the unusual and odd. Some exhibits in the collection—the torture devices and shrunken heads, for example—may be a little too strange for very young children. Other children will enjoy such unusual exhibits as the Lord's Prayer on a grain of rice. In all, over 500 oddities are housed in the museum. The collection is open daily; hours vary by season.

Scobee Planetarium at San Antonio College
1300 San Pedro Ave., San Antonio
(210) 733–2910
www.accd.edu/sac/ce/scobee/
$

Would-be astronomers will enjoy the presentations projected on the planetarium dome on Friday nights; there are three different shows, at 6:00 P.M., 7:15 P.M., and 8:30 P.M. Children under 6 years of age are not admitted to the two later shows; tots under 4 are not admitted to any shows. The planetarium is named for NASA astronaut Commander Francis R. (Dick) Scobee, former student of San Antonio College, who was killed in the Space Shuttle *Challenger* disaster.

Texas Adventure
307 Alamo Plaza, San Antonio
(210) 227–8224
www.texas-adventure.com
$$

If you're looking for a recounting of the Alamo tale that children can understand, this is a good place to start. Using state-of-the-art technology, this is not just a movie but a 3-D version of the story using animatronics and holographic figures. The half-hour show may be too intense for very young guests, but for schoolage children it is a good look at this historic event. The theater is open daily from 8:30 A.M. to 8:00 P.M.

Outdoor Attractions

Diamond W. Longhorn Ranch Chuckwagon Supper and Dinner Show
18725 Bandera Rd., Helotes
(210) 695–4888
www.wildwestsanantonio.com
$$$$

Located 35 minutes from San Antonio, this ranch gives kids the chance to enjoy a slice of the West as it was during the days of the cattle drives. More than 400,000 Longhorns traveled through this area in the late 1800s and those days are recalled in this family-oriented show. Along with a complete Texas barbecue, guests enjoy a range of Western activities from rope-making to tossing a cow chip. The show includes trick roping, plenty of cowboy songs, and more Western fun.

San Antonio Area Caves

Caverns can be the perfect family activity, especially when the San Antonio summer is getting you down. Within a short drive of San Antonio are seven commercial caves, each offering well-lighted, easy-to-follow trails that every member of the family can enjoy. Here you'll view a quiet world where progress takes place one drop of water at a time.

The following is an overview of the intriguing worlds found under the region's surface, arranged according to their distance from San Antonio (closest to farthest).

Cave tours generally last from 45 minutes to 90 minutes. Good walking shoes are a must for the tours, although the caverns have broad, well-lit trails that even preschoolers can handle. Sweaters are a good idea, too—it's cool underground. Tours generally cost $10 to $12. All the caves are open year-round; call for specific hours.

The small town of Boerne, 22 miles northwest of San Antonio on I-10, is home to Cave Without a Name (210–537–4212). This 50-million-year-old cave is privately owned and, while not as well known as other Hill Country caverns, boasts many beautiful formations. A 45-minute tour takes you through a series of rooms, including one with Texas-size stalagmites. Gravel walkways wind through the cavern.

Nearby Cascade Caverns (210–755–8080), outside of Boerne off I-10, is named for its 90-foot waterfall. Cascade Caverns has welcomed the public since 1932, but it's clear that both man and animals were here much earlier. One of the first visitors, more than 50,000 years ago, was a mastodon whose bones remain in the cave today. Later, ancient Indian tribes held ceremonies within the cave's first room, fearing to venture beyond the reassuring sunlight.

The largest cave in the area is Natural Bridge Caverns, located in San Antonio at exit 175 off I-35 (210–651–6101). Tours take visitors through enormous rooms with names like "The Castle of The White Giants."

The gargantuan halls of limestone were discovered in 1960 by four spelunkers from St. Mary's University. Cave developers later carved passages from room to room, resulting in a comfortable walk through this long cavern. Reminiscent of New Mexico's Carlsbad Caverns, Natural Bridge Caverns takes its name from a rock bridge between two sinkholes, the original entrance to the mouth of the cavern. The sinkholes have been known since the nineteenth century, but there is evidence of much earlier visitors. Bones of a grizzly bear at least 8,000 years old have been discovered, as well as human bones, stone weapons, and other Indian artifacts.

North of San Antonio on I-35 is Wonder Cave (800–782–7653 ext. 228), a cavern where you won't see sparkling cave formations, waterfalls, or auditorium-size rooms. But you will see one very unique attraction: a view of the Balcones Fault from *inside* the fault. The cave was produced during a 3.5 minute earthquake 30 million years ago. That same quake formed the Balcones Fault, an 1,800-mile line separating Texas's western Hill Country from the flat eastern farmland. Within the cave, you'll see boulders lodged in the fissure.

Farther north on I-35 is Georgetown, home of Inner Space (512–863–5545). The cave was discovered in 1963 when road crews building the highway drilled into one of the large rooms. Subsequent drilling and exploration revealed that a major cavern wound below the proposed highway. Remains of Ice Age mastodons, wolves, sabre-toothed tigers, and glyptodons (a kind of prehistoric armadillo) have been discovered, and an 80-foot cavern wall has been decorated with a modern artist's renderings of these ancient creatures.

The granddaddy of all the hill country caves is Longhorn Cavern (512–756–4680), located near Burnet, 123 miles north of San Antonio. The cavern was used by prehistoric people, but its most dramatic events have occurred since the 1800s. Comanches once kidnapped a young woman named Mariel King and brought her back to the cavern. The Indians did not realize they had been followed by three Texas Rangers. When the Indians prepared a campfire, the Rangers fired upon them, grabbed Mariel King, and raced for the entrance. Meanwhile, the surviving Comanches regrouped and began their counterattack, falling upon the Rangers before they reached the cavern entrance. A desperate hand-to-hand battle took place, with the Rangers finally escaping with Mariel King. Ending the story with a fairy-tale flourish, Miss King later married one of her rescuers, Logan Van Deveer, and the couple made their home in Burnet.

Years later, Confederate soldiers used Longhorn Cavern's main room as a munitions factory. Bat guano from the cave was an ingredient in the manufacture of gunpowder. Additional small rooms in the back reaches of the cavern were used as storerooms for the gunpowder. The cave went unused for several decades until the Roaring Twenties. A local businessman opened a dance hall in the largest room of the cave, building a wooden dance floor several feet above the limestone. When it proved successful, he then opened a restaurant in the next room, lowering food through a hole in the cavern ceiling. Next, an area minister decided to take advantage of the cool temperature and built bleachers to accommodate crowds for Sunday services. When the Depression struck, the owners were forced to sell the cave. It was purchased by the state and opened as a state park in 1932.

The Caverns of Sonora (915–387–3105) have been described by some cave experts as the most beautiful in the world. The scenic cavern has two tours, a 45-minute and a 75-minute version, for a look at spectacular stalactites and stalagmites, as well as unusual butterfly-shaped formations. To reach the caverns, just follow I–10 through Junction and past the town of Sonora to RM 1989. They're about 180 miles northwest of San Antonio.

After a tour of some of San Antonio–area caverns, you'll have to agree that this region's beauty reaches far below its surface.

Lightning Ranch
Rte. 16, Pipe Creek
(800) 994–7373
www.lightningranch.com
$$$–$$$$

Located 30 minutes from San Antonio, Lightning Ranch welcomes families for the day or overnight in bed-and-breakfast style guest houses. Kids can help groom a horse, pet barnyard animals, or even hang out in a blacksmith shop. The ranch offers daily guided rides through the Hill Country. The shortest rides are an hour long; half- and full-day rides are also offered. For the half- and full-day rides, the wrangler packs you a saddlebag lunch to enjoy atop one of the area's hills or alongside a flowing creek. Overnight rides can also be arranged; the evening includes a steak dinner prepared outdoors before you stretch out in a tent.

The cost for a one-hour ride is $21 per person; two-hour rides are $50 per person.

Half-day rides (with lunch) are $90 per person; full-day rides (with lunch) are $135. Overnight rides, with meals, are $195 per person. Parents who just want to lead while their small children ride are charged $10 per half-hour. There is a 225-pound weight limit for riders.

Love Creek Orchards
Rte. 16, Medina
FM 2200, Devine
(800) 449–0882
www.lovecreekorchards.com

From April through mid-June, you can pick your own peaches and blackberries at this orchard, with locations in Devine and Medina. Call for ripe reports to find the best time for you and your children to go out and pick some fruit.

Natural Bridge Caverns
26495 Natural Bridge Caverns Rd., exit 175
off I-35, San Antonio
(210) 651–6101
www.naturalbridgecaverns.com
$$

The huge rooms and wide, well-lit walkways of this cavern make it especially popular with families. Most take part in the North Cavern Tour, which runs about 75 minutes. Children enjoy a look at rooms such as Sherwood Forest, named for its many stalagmite formations, and the Hall of the Mountain King, which is over 350 feet in length. Even kids who don't want to visit the cave will enjoy the Natural Bridge Mining Company. A sluice (series of troughs) are seeded with small pieces of amethyst, sapphire, obsidian, topaz, and other stones. For a fee, kids can pan for jewels—and keep anything they find. Hours change seasonally. For additional details, see the Attractions chapter.

Natural Bridge Wildlife Ranch
26515 Natural Bridge Caverns, San Antonio
(830) 438–7400
www.nbwildliferanchtx.com
$$

Want to take your children on an African safari? Here's a chance for an abbreviated version, Texas-style. More than 65 species of exotic animals reside at this, Texas's most-visited safari park. Children especially love the petting zoo at the conclusion of the drive. The park is open daily, although hours change seasonally. For additional details, see the Attractions chapter.

Promised Land Dairy
2016 SH 97 W., Floresville
(830) 216–7182
$–$$

Located southeast of San Antonio outside the community of Floresville, this dairy gives children the opportunity to learn more about life on a real farm. Kids can get close to the animals in the petting barnyard, and tour the dairy farm to see how the Jersey cows are milked. The tour also includes a look at the creamery, where milk is bottled in old-fashioned glass bottles, and ice cream and other dairy products are produced. Hayrides through the surrounding area are offered. If all this activity builds up an appetite, don't worry: the dairy is also home to a restaurant and, predictably enough, an ice-cream shop. The farm also has a nine-hole miniature golf course.

River Walk (Paseo del Rio)
Downtown, San Antonio
(210) 227–4262
Free

The River Walk is an excellent destination for children. Kids enjoy the colorful walk, the shops filled with piñatas and *cascarones* (confetti-filled eggs), and the festive atmosphere. You'll find a handicapped route marked with signs along the River Walk; if you're pushing a stroller, this route will be the easiest to maneuver. For more information see the Attractions chapter.

An inquisitive giraffe takes a peek at his admirers at Natural Bridge Wildlife Ranch. PHOTO: PARIS PERMENTER & JOHN BIGLEY

San Antonio Botanical Gardens and Halsell Conservatory
555 Funston Pl., San Antonio
(210) 207–3255
www.sabot.org/
$

Kids with green thumbs will love the San Antonio Botanical Gardens. These extensive gardens offer plenty of activities for the youngest visitors. One of the most popular programs is the twice-annual Children's Garden. The program accepts children ages 8 through 13 on a first-come, first-served basis. Participants meet every Saturday from 9:00 A.M. to 11:00 A.M. at the garden to learn more about planning, growing, and harvesting vegetables. All supplies are provided by the garden, and the children are assisted by volunteers from the San Antonio Men's Garden Club, Bexar County Master Gardeners, and the staff of the San Antonio Botanical Gardens.

The Children's Garden program has sessions in the fall and spring. Admission to the program is $5 per child, and kids should plan on attending all meetings. (If they have two absences, they may be dropped from the program.) To register, call the garden's office at (210) 207–3270.

Throughout the year, the gardens also host many other child-focused programs. Spout Scouts targets early-childhood educators; it helps teachers provide their students with information about gardening. The Terrarium Program introduces children to the world's many diverse ecosystems thanks to the Lucile Halsell Conservatory; participants learn how to build a terrarium. The Teen Garden program helps teens ages 14 to 19 to understand the economics of gardening as a means to self-sufficiency.

One of the most unique programs sponsored by the San Antonio Botanical Gardens is the Dominguez Community Garden. The program for juvenile offenders and at-risk students aims to teach participants responsibility and the importance of commitment through the process of caring for a garden. This community garden is located at the Fabian Dominguez State Jail and combines the efforts of city, county, and state agencies with the Botanical Society and other agencies from the San Antonio community.

The San Antonio Botanical Gardens also operates a special Web site for children titled Maja's Rainforest! (www.sabot.org/kids/). This site includes all types of kids' activities including connect-the-dots pictures, coloring pages, crossword and word-find puzzles, games, info on weird plants, and even instructions on building your own terrarium.

Throughout the year, the garden schedules numerous classes of special interest to children and families; check the Web site or call the garden for information on upcoming events.

The gardens are open daily except Christmas and New Year's Day. From March through October, the gardens are open 9:00 A.M. to 6:00 P.M.; during the winter months, the hours are 8:00 A.M. to 5:00 P.M. For additional details about the Botanical Gardens, see the Attractions chapter.

San Antonio Zoological Garden and Aquarium
3903 N. St. Mary's St., San Antonio
(210) 734–7183
www.sazoo-aq.org
$$

San Antonio's Zoo is one of the largest in the United States operating on the same site (an old rock quarry) since 1914. Among its 3,500 different animals is an exhibit of endangered whooping cranes; kids will be amazed by their 7-foot wingspans. The zoo runs many educational programs for children. Overnight Camp-Ins at the Zoo, for kids ages 7 and over, include crafts, games and interaction with the animals. The Crawlers and Cruisers program is for parents and children from birth to 2 years; it includes games and encounters with various zoo residents. The Kinderzoo program, for ages 2 to 3 years, is a series of classes that focus on different kinds of critters. Kidszoocation classes, for ages 4 to 10, intro-duce young naturalists to a variety of aspects of the zoo, from the duties of the staff to the world of bats. The zoo is open daily from 9:00 A.M. to 6:00 P.M. in summer; to 5:00 P.M. the rest of the year. For additional information, see the Attractions chapter.

Parks and Playgrounds

Brackenridge Park
2800 N. Broadway, San Antonio
(210) 207–3000

Brackenridge Park is a fine place for a picnic or a stroll, but for visitors it's also a major destination because of the many attractions found there. Families should budget at least half a day, for example, to visit the San Antonio Zoological Garden and Aquarium (see above). Garden lovers, too, will find a wealth of sites to explore. Brackenridge Park is home to the Japanese Tea Gardens (see below), and nearby San Antonio Botanical Gardens and the Halsell Conservatory (see above) display plants from the Lone Star State and from around the globe.

Other children's attractions are sprinkled throughout Brackenridge Park. A miniature railroad, The Brackenridge Eagle (3810 North St. Mary's Street, 210-736-9534) runs 3.5 miles through the park. Every train is a replica of an 1863 C. P. Huntington model. Kids also love the carousel (3910 North St. Mary's Street, 210-734-5401) and the Skyride (3910 North St. Mary's Street, 210-299-8480). Each of these rides has a small admission fee.

For additional information on Brackenridge Park see the Parks and Recreation chapter.

Eisenhower Park
19399 N.W. Military Hwy., San Antonio
(210) 698–1057
$ donation

This park offers the Second Saturday program, which teaches parents and children more about the natural world. Guided hikes and talks focus on the South Texas landscape, birdlife, wildlife, and plants. Reservations are required.

HemisFair Park
Bowie St. at Durango Blvd., San Antonio
(210) 207–8590
Free

HemisFair Park is best known as the home of the Tower of Americas, a soaring symbol of San Antonio. Kids love to survey the scene from 579 feet up. The Tower's one-minute elevator ride is also a hit with young visitors. (For more on the tower, see the Attractions chapter.) Children also love the Downtown All Around Playground, with its extensive playscape and popcorn wagon, and the cooling water gardens.

Japanese Tea Gardens
3800 N. St. Mary's St., San Antonio
(210) 207–3211
Free

One of the city's most beautiful spots, these gardens are built in and around an old rock quarry. There are lots of fun places for kids to explore and for parents to relax and unwind.

Milam Park
Between W. Commerce, W. Houston, and San Saba Sts., San Antonio
(210) 207–7275

Honoring one the heros of the Texas Revolution, this downtown park has several kid-friendly features. A playscape with tunnels and castles is the centerpiece, but children will also love the gazebo.

Friedrich Wilderness Park
Milsa Rd., San Antonio
(210) 698–1057

An unspoiled slice of the Texas Hill Country awaits the family just north of Loop 1604 at Friedrich Wilderness Park. Miles of well-marked hiking trails provide urbanites a rare chance to experience the peace and quiet of the country. If your family chooses, you can arrange for a guide by calling ahead. For more information, see the Parks and Recreation chapter.

Recreation Centers and Programs

San Antonio Parks and Recreation Department
(210) 207–3056
www.ci.sat.tx.us/sapar/index.htm

The San Antonio Parks and Recreation Department offers a variety of programs for youths year-round. Each year, the department sponsors the Summer Youth Recreation Program from early June through late July. More than 60 sites participate in the program, which runs weekdays from 8:30 A.M. to 5:30 P.M. (with community centers open until 9:00 P.M.) The program offers a wide variety of recreational options for kids including arts and crafts, cookouts, basketball and golf clinics, teen pool parties, and field trips.

Throughout the year, children ages 6 to 19 can enroll in the youth membership program. This public-private partnership was developed to encourage youths to participate in positive recreation and activities. Both local and national celebrities help promote the program and stress the importance of positive participation in school, youth programs, career planning, and other aspects of young lives.

The department's Night Owl Program is offered in conjunction with several public and private schools. The program, which runs during the summer months weekdays from 5:00 P.M. to 10:00 P.M. (hours vary at some sites), provides structured activities and supervision for teens. For more on this program, call (210) 207-3000.

Youths from the west side, east side, and downtown neighborhoods are targeted by the Park and Recreation Department's Roving Leader Program. This outreach recreation and referral service features six youth leaders who work in the areas of Alazan-Apache Courts, Victoria Courts, Cassiano Homes, Wheatley Homes, SpringView Apartments, and Sky Harbour. The roving leaders take recreation programs to the areas, bringing activities such as basketball, volleyball, softball, football, and soccer to young residents who may not choose to participate at community centers. At-risk children ages 6 to 19 are targeted by the program. For more information, call (210) 207-3044.

Community centers throughout the city also offer year-around recreational options for local children and teens. Sports such as flag football, volleyball, basketball, and softball are offered along with activities such as arts and crafts, talent shows, and table games. Community centers operated by the Parks and Recreation Department include:

Bode
900 Rigsby Ave., San Antonio
(210) 532–1212

Copernicus
5003 Lord Rd., San Antonio
(210) 648–1072

Cuellar
5626 San Fernando St., San Antonio
(210) 436–0908

Dawson
2500 E. Commerce St., San Antonio
(210) 227–1627

Denver Heights
300 Porter St., San Antonio
(210) 533–5242

Dorie Miller Community Center
2802 Martin Luther King Dr., San Antonio
(210) 333–4650

Frank Garrett Multi-Service Center
1400 Menchaca St., San Antonio
(210) 732–5042

Garza
5627 Seacroft St., San Antonio
(210) 435–6806

Hamilton
10700 Nacogdoches Rd., San Antonio
(210) 654–7749

Harlandale
300 Sussex Ave., San Antonio
(210) 924–8021

Lincoln
2915 E. Commerce St., San Antonio
(210) 271–7741

Lockwood
700 N. Olive St., San Antonio
(210) 271–7748

Meadowcliff
1240 Pinn Rd., San Antonio
(210) 674–0820

Miller's Pond
6075 Pearsall Rd., San Antonio
(210) 623–2900

Melendrez
5906 W. Commerce St., San Antonio
(210) 434–0277

Normoyle
700 Culberson Ave., San Antonio
(210) 924–0770

Palm Heights Center
1201 W. Malone Ave., San Antonio
(210) 922–1034

Ramirez Center
1011 Gillette Blvd., San Antonio
(210) 921–0681

Father Roman Center
11030 Ruidosa, San Antonio
(210) 627–2138

San Juan Brady Gardens Center
2307-S. Calaveras, San Antonio
(210) 225–5410

South San Center
2031 Quintana Rd., San Antonio
(210) 927–1640

Southside Lions Center
3100 Hiawatha St., San Antonio
(210) 532–1502

Tobin
1900 W. Martin St., San Antonio
(210) 225–0941

Ward Center
435 E. Sunshine Dr., San Antonio
(210) 732–2481

Woodard Center
1011 Locke St., San Antonio
(210) 225–5445

Sports and Fitness

For details on youth sport leagues in San Antonio, see the Parks and Recreation chapter.

FitKids
CHRISTUS Santa Rose Outpatient Rehabilitation Center
2701 Babcock Rd., San Antonio
(210) 705–6560

This program features 10-week classes for overweight pre-teens and teenagers. It includes a dietician's evaluation, an individual eating plan, and an individually prepared exercise plan. The sessions also include peer and parental support groups. The cost of the 10-week program is $250.

Kids' Sports Network
8206 Roughrider Dr., San Antonio
(210) 654–4707
www.ksnusa.org

The best resource for information on San Antonio–area children's sports is the Kids' Sports Network. This nonprofit organization acts as a clearinghouse for children's sports information, provides coach training, and conducts special events. The network's website includes extensive listings of sports organizations ranging from flag and tackle football to baseball, volleyball, and soccer.

Theaters

Children's Fine Art Series
Empire Theatre
226 N. St. Mary's St., San Antonio
(210) 340–4060
www.childrensfineartseries.org
$$

Aimed at children age 5 and older, this series features a variety of productions. Recent shows have included *Pippi Longstocking, Franklin's Big Adventure,* and *Are You My Mother?*

Magik Children's Theatre
420 S. Alamo St., HemisFair Park, San Antonio
(210) 227–2751
$$–$$$

San Antonio is the home of a professional repertory theater especially for children and families. Since 1994, this theater has presented favorites such as *When Dinosaurs Rocked the World* and *The Grinch.* One of the troupe's most popular performances was *The Best Christmas Pageant Ever,* which attracted 25,000 people in a five-week run.

The theater produces 11 shows per year and has a cast of 14 full-time actors. More than half the productions are original plays for both elementary-school-age children and teens such as *Phantom of the Alamo.*

Children with an interest in drama can participate in the Magik Children's Theatre classes in acting and stagecraft.

Twenty-five percent of the tickets for each season are distributed through the theater's community assistance program to help disadvantaged children learn about the joy of theater.

Steven Stoli's Backyard Theatre
11838 Wurzbach Rd., San Antonio
(210) 408–0116
www.stolientertainment.com
$$

Award-winning director Steven Stoli produces a variety of shows for children such as *The Princess and the Pea* and *Jack and the Beanstalk* at this 120-seat theater. Shows are held Wednesday, Thursday, and Saturday mornings at 11:00 A.M. For San Antonio area residents, the theater also offers a discounted Backyard Pass for 11 shows.

Children with an interest in acting can also take part in Steven Stoli's week-long acting camp for kids. Limited to 22 students between the ages of 7 and 14 years old, the camp covers techniques for both TV and stage acting. Sessions cover improvisation, theater games, memorization, and more. The final day includes a performance.

Toy Stores and Children's Shops

Gymboree Play and Music
16111 San Pedro Ave. at Galleria Oaks Shopping Center, San Antonio
(210) 490–3710
www.gymboree.com

This unique shop introduces young visitors to the world of music and movement. Parents and children enjoy exploring music together at Gymboree, which sells instruments from around the world.

Labor of Love
Huebner Oaks Shopping Center, I–10 W., San Antonio
(210) 690–9997, (800) 567–1929
www.mommylove.com

Expectant and new mothers find a wealth of items at this maternity and baby store. For pregnant women, the shop features a wide line of career wear and casual wear in sizes that range from petite to XXXL. If you are in need of an elegant outfit but don't want to make a major purchase for a temporary body shape, the store also rents evening dresses. For new mothers, Labor of Love sells nursing clothes and accessories, diaper bags, and baby gifts.

Wild Planet
19 Brees Blvd., Alamo Heights, San Antonio
(210) 828–9399
11600 Bandera Rd. at Loop 1604,
San Antonio
(210) 647–5255
Hwy. 281 and Loop 1604,
San Antonio
(210) 494–1974

With lots of locations in San Antonio, these curriculum-centered stores specialize in developmental toys for all ages.

Zany Brainy
Huebner Oaks Shopping Center, at I–10 W.,
San Antonio
(210) 694–2177

Nonviolent and educational toys are the focus of this toy store. Many items found at this shop are not found in the major chain toy stores or at other retail chains. Also look for books, science and nature items, video- and audio- tapes, crafts, learning games, computer software, and more for toddlers to preteens. The store also has a play area so parents can watch their child interacting with the toy before making the investment. This specialty store also offers a free pre-school story time.

Water Parks

Schlitterbahn
305 W. Austin St., New Braunfels
(830) 625–2351
$$$$

Just up I-35 from San Antonio lies a leader in the world of water parks: Schlitterbahn. This family-oriented park offers water activities for kids of every age, from toddlers to teens.

Schlitterbahn is the sister company of New Braunfels General Store International, a leader in the water feature industry. NBGS was founded in 1984 to manufacture and distribute coated-foam waterpark products that had been developed and used by Schlitterbahn Waterpark. Today NBGS has expanded to include themed play elements in use by waterparks, amusement parks, municipal pools, indoor recreation centers, and even cruise lines.

That trial-and-error process that honed the high-tech features for which NBGS is known today were worked out at Schlitterbahn, a park founded in a way that sounds like a scene straight out of the movies. In the 1970s during a vacation to Walt Disney World, Jeff Henry and his two siblings fell in love with water slides. The youngsters came home and worked with their parents to build four water slides at their riverfront resort in New Braunfels.

Those four slides have grown into the most popular seasonal waterpark in the United States. Today, Schlitterbahn spans 65 acres and features rides and family activities across five themed areas. With two uphill water coasters, nine tube chutes, five giant hot tubs, 17 water slides, a surfing ride, a family wave pool, five swimming pools, five children's playgrounds, water and sand volleyball courts, four gift shops, two restaurants, and 20 refreshment centers all operated by nearly 1,600 seasonal employees, the park truly boasts Texas-size proportions and profits.

Schlitterbahn plays upon local features, both cultural and topographical. Meaning "slippery road" in German, the name Schlitterbahn is a first hint at the German heritage that plays an important role in the community of New Braunfels and indeed in the park itself. The symbol of Schlitterbahn is a 60-foot tall castle, a replica of the guard tower of Solms Castle in Braunfels, Germany. The park's many sections carry on the theme, with names like Kinderlund, Slidenplatz, Das Lagune, and Surfenburg, home of the world's first uphill water coaster. The park also utilizes its natural surroundings, including the Comal River, which serves as the starting and stopping points of a 45-minute tube ride and also supplies 72-degree spring water to the tube chutes.

Floating along at the largest tube park in the world. PHOTO: SCHLITTERBAHN WATERPARK

Schlitterbahn has held the record for many "firsts" in the waterpark world. The park is considered the home of the world's first swim-up refreshment bar, first family wave pool with maximum four foot depth, first continuous wave surfing ride, and first professional competition on a man-made wave. It's also the world's largest tubing park, with over 10,000 inner tubes from which to choose.

The park introduces new and innovative attractions every year. Recent additions include the Torrent, a high-tech ride in the new Blastenhoff section of the park. The Torrent features a 20-foot-wide river in which waves surge at 10-second intervals, taking guests on a wild white-water ride. The waves break onto a 25,000-square-foot sloping beach.

Schlitterbahn is open on weekends in the spring and daily in summer. High-season hours are 10:00 A.M. to 8:00 P.M.

SeaWorld of Texas
Ellison Dr. and Westover Hills Blvd., off Rte.
151 between Loop 410 and Loop 1604,
San Antonio
(210) 523–3611, (210) 523–3618
www.seaworld.com
$$$$

SeaWorld may be best known for its marine life, but the park also offers visitors plenty of chances to get wet. The park's water park, Lost Lagoon, features numerous water rides guaranteed to cool visitors even on the hottest San Antonio days. The Texas Splashdown, the longest and tallest flume ride in the state, takes riders along a half-mile route with plunges from as high as five stories. The Rio Loco (Crazy River), transports six riders on circular rafts down a raging stream under a waterfall. And there's also a Caribbean beach, a three-story funhouse (don't miss the 500-gallon bucket!), and a new five-story tube ride that plunges riders from the top of a slide tower to a splashdown pool. Younger children will find plenty of water features, wave pools, and water slides. In all there are more than a dozen attractions on five acres. SeaWorld of Texas is open daily during the summer months and weekends only during the spring and fall. Call for the current schedule.

Six Flags Fiesta Texas
17000 I–10 W., San Antonio
(210) 697–5050
www.sixflags.com
$$$$

The waterpark at Six Flags Fiesta Texas is a good place to escape the summer heat, with 14 water rides and attractions. Some top offerings include Splash Water Springs, a water pool with a slide, the million-gallon Lone Star Lagoon (the largest wave pool in

Visitors get up-close and personal with some residents of SeaWorld of Texas. PHOTO: TIM THOMPSON, COURTESY OF THE SAN ANTONIO CONVENTION AND VISITORS BUREAU

Good times roll at Six Flags Fiesta Texas.
PHOTO: PARIS PERMENTER & JOHN BIGLEY

Texas), and the Texas Treehouse, a five story treehouse complete with a 1,000-gallon cowboy hat that fills with water. Some of the water park rides have height restrictions.

Park hours vary by season.

Splashtown
3600 N. Pan Am Expressway, San Antonio
(210) 227–1400
www.splashtownsa.com/
$$$$

This waterpark, located along I–35, offers 18 acres of water rides, ranging in speed from lazy river rides to white-knuckle tube rides. In all, the park offers over 50 rides and attractions. The Lone Star Luge sends riders sliding the length of over two football fields while Siesta Del Rio provides a relaxing river ride. Starflight sends riders soaring through total darkness in one of two tubes (and there's a Junior Starflight for young visitors). The park includes a large kiddie area with child-size rides and slides as well as sand volleyball courts and full court basketball on-site. Tubes and lockers are available for rent; the park also has concession stands. The park is open weekends only from mid-May through the end of May then daily until mid-August, returning to a weekend-only schedule until mid-September.

Hours are 11:00 A.M. to 9:00 P.M. Sunday through Thursday, and 11:00 A.M. to 10:00 P.M. Friday and Saturday. Kids can join the Tube Tyler's Kid's Club online for discounts and a free email newsletter about the park.

Annual Events and Festivals

They don't call San Antonio the Fiesta City for nothing. This is one city that parties in style, whatever the reason, whatever the time of year. From bacchanalian gatherings to solemn remembrances, San Antonio knows how to mark an occasion.

Many events here are scheduled for the fall through spring months, San Antonio's most temperate periods. Summer days are downright toasty, so events then are few and far between, compared with other seasons. Winter days can a bit nippy sometimes, but that doesn't slow down the holiday festivities. December is one of the busiest months on the calendar, thanks to the many festivals with religious significance. The River Walk/Paseo del Rio really comes to life at this time of the year, lit by thousands of miniature lights as well as luminarias, candles in sand-filled sacks. The river reflects the thousands of lights, transforming the area into a truly magical spot.

The peak of the festival season is in April, time of Fiesta. This is the granddaddy of San Antonio's festivals, a true Texas-size blowout. Festivities take place all over the city during this period, and traffic can be trying, especially in the downtown area. Hotel space can get tight during this period as well, so make plans early if you plan to attend Fiesta.

Many of San Antonio's celebrations mark special days in Mexican history, such as Cinco de Mayo and Dies y Seis de Septiembre. These cultural festivals, to be enjoyed by everyone, are an excellent window into the Latino heritage of the region and a good way to sample the food, dance, and song that the Hispanic culture has given San Antonio.

Although the following list is extensive, it doesn't include every event hosted in San Antonio; that would be a book in itself. We've listed our favorites and long-time events, ones that consistently take place year after year. The exact dates on which many of these events take place vary from year to year, so the entries listed under each month may not be in chronological order. For a month-by-month listing that's updated frequently, check out the San Antonio Convention and Visitors Bureau Web site at www.sacvb.com. This site includes details and contact information for both one-time and annual events, including festivals to concerts, fund-raisers, and more.

Admission prices are included in these listings but please realize that these can and do change frequently. You'll want to contact the event organizers directly to verify the scheduled date and time of the festival as well as current admission price.

January

Martin Luther King Jr. March and Rally
Citywide, San Antonio
(210) 207–7235
www.ci.sat.tx.us/pio

This annual march is considered the nation's largest honoring Dr. Martin Luther King Jr., the civil rights leader. The event includes free concerts by performers such as the Youth Orchestra of San Antonio. Admission is free.

River Walk Mud Festival
River Walk, San Antonio
(210) 227–4262
www.thesanantonioriverwalk.com

It takes a mighty festive city to turn the

draining and cleaning of a river into a party, but, hey, San Antonio's just that kind of place. Since 1987, this three-day event has elevated mudslinging to an art. The fun begins with the Mud Pie Ball. The peak of the celebration is the election of the Mud King and Mud Queen to preside over the festivities. The King and Queen rise to their positions by collecting the most nickels, money to be used by the Paseo del Rio Association to hold admission-free events along the River Walk throughout the year. The prospective Kings and Queens can obtain nickels any way they choose, and don't think that mud wrestling is out of the question for these campaigners. When the nickels are tallied, the winners enter the "Brown House on Pig Pen-sylvania Avenue" and wear a sand-colored royal robe. Admission to all the festivities is free.

River Walk Arts & Crafts Show
River Walk, San Antonio
(210) 227-4262
www.thesanantonioriverwalk.com

This three-day event is sponsored by the Paseo del Rio Association and showcases the artists of the region. The shady walkways of the River Walk are lined with easels and shelving for the popular event; watercolors, oils, sculpture, and crafts compete with the beauty of the Paseo del Rio itself during this twice-annual show. Admission is free.

Go Western Gala
Freeman Coliseum, 3201 E. Houston St.,
San Antonio
(210) 225-5851

For more than two decades, this annual event has brought the spirit of the West to San Antonio through dance, song, and food. The gala draws many big-name performers; among those who have appeared in the past are Lorrie Morgan and Neal McCoy. Tickets include dinner, drinks, dancing, and more. For an additional fee, attendees can sit in the Golden Corral, a special area directly in front of the stage that is staffed by private waiters; Golden Corral tickets also include valet parking and other extras. Proceeds from this annual event go to the San Antonio Livestock Exposition's Scholarship Fund. The festivities start at 6:30 P.M. and continue through midnight. The gala is for true country music fans: Tickets are $150 per person; tickets for Golden Corral seating are $400 per person.

Cowboy Breakfast
Central Park Mall, San Antonio
(210) 479-3333

This may very well be the world's largest free breakfast. Sponsored by the Cowboy Breakfast Foundation, the event benefits scholarship funds raised through the rental of entertainment stages and vendor tables. And just what is a cowboy breakfast, you ask? In this case, it means a real Texas favorite: scrambled eggs along with tender biscuits beneath plenty of country gravy. Admission is free.

Asian New Year Festival
Institute of Texan Cultures, 801 S. Bowie St.
at HemisFair Plaza, San Antonio
(210) 458-2300
www.texancultures.utsa.edu

The Asian communities of Texas are in the spotlight during this annual celebration of the Asian New Year. Sponsored by the Institute of Texan Cultures, the festival includes dance, music, food, and crafts. The ethnic cuisine served at the festival is a favorite part of the festivities; look for Chinese fried rice, Indian *samosas* (a fried filled snack), Japanese *yakisoba* (a noodle dish), Korean *bulgogi* (marinated beef), and *kim chi* (fermented vegetables), Malaysian/Singaporean beef and chicken satay, Filipino *pancit* rice noodles, Hawaiian/Polynesian almond cookies, and traditional Pakistani foods. The event also includes hands-on activities featuring Asian crafts and traditions such as Chinese calligraphy, brushpainting, paper-cutting, and mahjong; Indian sari-wrapping, rangoli (traditional Indian art), and palm-reading; Japanese calligraphy and origami; Hawaiian/Poly-nesian hula-dancing, tapa cloth–painting, and lei-making; and Vietnamese fortune-telling. Throughout the festival, local groups give demonstrations of yoga, mar-tial arts, tai chi, and more. Admission is $4.00 for adults and teens ages 13 through 64; $2.00 for children 3 to 12 and seniors 65 and older; and free for children 2 and under. Free admission is given to Institute members and visitors wearing traditional Asian costumes.

February

San Antonio Stock Show and Rodeo
Freeman Coliseum, 3201 E. Houston St.,
San Antonio
(210) 225–5851
www.sarodeo.com

Ready, set, rodeo! If you're looking for a taste of a traditional Texas get-together, attend this 16-day show and rodeo at the Joe and Harry Freeman Coliseum. One of San Antonio's largest events, the annual Western festival attracts more than one million attendees every year. Activities include a rodeo, a Western parade, educa-tional displays, a concert series, a carnival midway, and plenty of Western fun.

The event is very family-friendly. The Family Fair is a top stop for parents and kids, with educational displays, entertain-ment of special interest to younger visi-tors, plenty of food, and more. The Hall of Heritage takes visitors back to the days of the Old West. At the World of Agriculture, some of the state's top cooks offer up a taste of their creations; craftspeople also display their wares. A favorite with chil-dren is the World of Animals, where kids and critters can get up close and cuddly. Kids also love the carnival midway, with rides, games of skills, and old-fashioned fun.

More than 1,000 cowboys and cow-girls provide much of the entertainment at the rodeo, which includes competition in the fields of bull riding, calf roping, barrel racing, and other sports sanctioned

> ### Insiders' Tip
> Western wear is the order of the day during the annual Rodeo. Bring your cowboy duds—from Western jeans to 10-gallon hats to pointed-toed boots—for this blowout.

by the Professional Rodeo Cowboy Asso-ciation (PRCA).

The event also features America's largest junior livestock show; teens from across Texas exhibit and sell award-winning cattle, swine, sheep, poultry, and horses. The competition for the title of Grand Champion is fierce.

Entertainment also comes in the form of live music, and that includes all types of Texas sounds, from Tejano to country to rock. Performers change every year, but top-name performers at previous rodeos have included George Jones, Martina McBride, Brooks and Dunn, Loretta Lynn, Toby Keith, Alabama, and other recog-nized names. There's a live performance every night.

Parking is at a premium in the Coli-seum area during Rodeo, but there's a 15-acre paved, lighted, and secured parking lot nearby on Gembler Road. To reach the parking facility, exit Coliseum Road, turn left on Gembler, and proceed to the park-ing area. The free Rodeo Shuttle runs con-tinuously from the parking lot. Cost of parking for the rodeo is $5.00.

Tickets to rodeo competitions are priced at $12.00, $17.00, $20.00, and $22.00; these tickets include ground admission. Ground admission only is $5.00 for adults, $3.00 for seniors, and $2.00 for children under 12.

River Walk Mardi Gras
River Walk, San Antonio
(210) 227–4262
www.thesanantonioriverwalk.com

Sponsored by the Paseo del Rio Association, this pre-Lenten event celebrates Mardi Gras with music, a parade, and more. The fun begins on the Sunday before Lent with a fleet of barges floating down the river in the Bud Light Mardi Gras Parade. Costumed krewes cruise down the river while throngs of onlookers gather along the river banks. Performers keep the parade lively; in previous years, the San Antonio Street Dance and Drum Company, and the San Antonio Iguanas Cheerleaders and Iggy have participated. Later in the week, the festivities continue with the Bud Light Arts and Crafts Show, scheduled for Friday through Sunday. In previous years, free concerts have also been scheduled at the Rivercenter Mall lagoon, featuring local and regional bands performing mariachi, conjunto, and contemporary tunes. Admission to the festival is free.

CineFestival
Guadalupe Cultural Arts Theater,
1300 Guadalupe St., San Antonio
(210) 271–3151
www.guadalupeculturalarts.org

Cinefestival holds the title as the country's largest and oldest Latino film festival. Now in its third decade, the event showcases shorts, features, experimental, documentary, and animated works either by Latinos or about the Latino experience. Admission is $8.00, although some events are free.

March

Remembering the Alamo Weekend
Alamo Plaza, San Antonio
(210) 279–4973, (210) 494–7165
www.artco.org/sa/salha/salha.html

Sponsored by the San Antonio Living History Association, this two-day annual event is scheduled for the Saturday and Sunday nearest March 6, the anniversary of the fall of the Alamo in 1836. The weekend includes education programs and demonstrations about life during the period. Costumed actors help visitors learn more about music of the time as well as food preparation, spinning, weaving, herbal medicine and early medical practices, and warfare. The programs help visitors learn more about the men, women, and children who lived on both sides of the famous conflict between the Texians and the Mexicans. The event also includes an exhibition of Alamo archaeological displays. Admission is free.

Dawn at the Alamo
Alamo Plaza, San Antonio
(210) 279–4973, (210) 494–7165
www.artco.org/sa/salha/salha.html

Members of the San Antonio Living History Association are joined by reenactors from across the country in portraying the armies of the Texian defenders and the Mexican soldiers led by General Santa Anna. The event occurs on March 6, the anniversary of the fall of the Alamo in 1836. The battle is also remembered with quiet solemnity. Thirteen candles are lit to symbolize the 13-day siege of the Alamo; other solemn remembrances include the reading of a reconciliation peace prayer in English and Spanish and the laying of commemorative wreaths. Sponsored by the San Antonio Living History Association, Dawn at the Alamo also includes a flintlock musket volley, with the sounds of the gunfire echoing against the historic walls of the shrine, as well as the reading of eyewitness accounts of the bloody battle. Visitors must get up early for this special event; the one-hour ceremony takes place the hour before dawn. Admission is free.

Wreath Laying Ceremony at the Alamo
Shrine
Alamo, San Antonio
(210) 497–8435

For more than three decades, the Harp and Shamrock Society of Texas has presented a wreath at the Alamo on March 15 to honor the fallen heroes of the battle. Admission is free.

Alamo Irish Festival
La Villita and Arneson River Theatre, San Antonio
(210) 699–8632

Grab your green and head to the river. This three-day festival, held the weekend closest to March 17, celebrates St. Patrick's Day in true Irish-American tradition with music, food, arts and crafts, cultural displays, and dancing. The festival is sponsored by the Harp and Shamrock Society of Texas. The event also includes the city's St. Patrick's Day Street Parade, one of the largest in the Southwest and now in its fourth decade. Admission is free.

St. Patrick's Day River Parade and Pub Crawl
River Walk, San Antonio
(210) 227–4262
www.thesanantonioriverwalk.com

It's not your imagination—on St. Patrick's Day, the San Antonio River *is* a little greener than its usual tint, thanks to the Paseo del Rio Association. The river is actually dyed green for the day and renamed "The River Shannon." On March 17, mariachi music gives way to Irish song and dance in San Antonio, and the River Walk turns into a huge Pub Crawl. The next day, the river hosts a floating parade with Irish dignitaries, pipers and drummers, and the pervasive spirit of the Old Country. Tickets are sold for the Pub Crawl; one fee ($25–$30) buys admission to all pubs on the River Walk. The river parade is free.

April

San Antonio Highland Games
Retama Park, Selma; north of San Antonio, Exit 174A off I-35
(210) 599–4287
www.e-lanresources.com/sahga.html

This three-day event in early April celebrates the spirit of Scotland with Highland games, clan tents, sheep dog demonstrations, a tug-o-war, a shortbread contest, Celtic music, and more. On April 6, a ceremony at the Alamo commemorates Tartan Day with a laying of a wreath at the monument. It's sponsored by the San Antonio Highland Games Association. Admission is $8.00 for adults, $5.00 for children age 6 to 17. Parking is $1.00.

Tejano Music Awards
Alamodome, San Antonio
(210) 222–8862, (800) 500–8470
www.tejanomusicawards.com

This internationally recognized event is considered the Grammy Awards of Tejano Music. Sponsored by the Texas Talent Musicians Association, the awards show is designed to honor the top performers in the field of Tejano music, a Latino music that utilizes accordions and 12-string guitars. The event began in 1980 and today draws more than 40,000 onlookers. Concert seating for the show ranges from $12.50 to $45.50 per person; online reservations can be made at the Tejano Music Awards Web site. The show is also broadcast on radio and television.

Viva Botanica
San Antonio Botanical Gardens, 555 Funston Pl., San Antonio
(210) 829–5100
www.sabot.org

Celebrate spring blossoms at the San Antonio Botanical Gardens during this colorful festival. Sponsored by the San Antonio Botanical Society, the two-day annual event showcases the blooms of San Antonio. You'll have the chance to buy blooming plants if the surrounding greenery inspires you. Along with 33 acres of spring flowers, the festival includes art displays, live entertainment, and food booths. Admission is $5.00 for adults, $1.00 for children, and $4.00 for members of the society.

Fiesta San Antonio
Citywide, San Antonio
(210) 227–5191, (877) SA–FIESTA
www.fiesta-sa.org

While all of San Antonio's annual events and festivals draw a crowd, Fiesta San Antonio is in a league of its own when it comes to popularity. One of Texas's most-attended celebrations, this April blowout draws 3.5 million partygoers every year for more than 150 events, lots of food, and barrels of margaritas. Add to that mix a good dose of Texas pride and the spirit of Old Mexico and you've got a party that draws revelers from across the United States and Mexico.

The 10-day Fiesta dates back to 1891. First a celebration of Texas independence, it later grew to recognize the many diverse cultures that made San Antonio the city it is today. The exact dates of the festival change year to year but the focal point of the event is always April 21, the anniversary of the Battle of San Jacinto, when Texas won its independence from Mexico.

Fiesta's origins may have been serious and solemn but today this event is pure entertainment. Most of the action starts about 10:00 A.M., although the serious fun takes place later in the day—music festivals, colorful parades, and serious grazing through food booths that offer everything from Cajun to Tex-Mex to German specialties. The official partying winds down about midnight each night, but unofficially it continues in the River Walk bars until about 2:00 A.M.

In fact, the River Walk is one of the busiest Fiesta locations, especially from La Mansion del Rio hotel at Navarro Street all the way around the horseshoe-shaped stretch of the river to La Villita historic area.

River parades are among the most unusual aspects of Fiesta. If you're lucky, you can snag a riverside table at one of the crowded restaurants. (But don't just rely on luck; you'll need to arrive plenty early to nab these prime seats as thousands of revelers pack the parade route.)

Three parades bring Texas-size crowds downtown. The Texas Cavalier's River Parade is the first, cruising the river past some 175,000 spectators. The event features more than 40 floats, each bursting with musicians, singers, and celebrities. Later in the week, the Battle of Flowers Parade, with brightly colored floats and the Queen of the Order of the Alamo, draws as many as 375,000 onlookers. Finally, the Fiesta Flambeau parade fills the streets with lighted floats, marching bands, and 400,000 onlookers. For tickets to the parades, call the River Parade Ticket Line (210) 22-RIVER anytime after December 1, or obtain them online at www.texascavaliers.org.

The parades feature the "royalty" of Fiesta. At the Battle of the Flowers, keep an eye out for the Queen and Princesses of the Order of the Alamo. Bedecked in jeweled gowns, the Queen and her court are crowned at Municipal Auditorium earlier during Fiesta; after the parade, the gowns are displayed at North Star Mall.

The biggest Fiesta event is A Night in Old San Antonio, better known by its nickname, NIOSA (n-eye-o-sa). The party, featuring music and food in 15 cultural areas, takes place in La Villita, a restored eighteenth-century village on the River Walk. Dance to live Western, conjunto, oompah, or mariachi music and when you've worked up an appetite stroll over to the food booths selling everything from escargot to German sausages to *antichuchos*, a spicy marinated meat. Tickets for A Night in Old San Antonio are available at

Insiders' Tip

During Fiesta, there's no escape from *cascarones*, dyed eggshells filled with paper confetti and covered with tissue paper. Everyone's a target for these little bombs, sold in many stores.

Colorful cascarones, eggshells filled with confetti, are a symbol of San Antonio's Fiesta.

PHOTO: PARIS PERMENTER & JOHN BIGLEY

the gate or through NIOSA at (210) 226-5188.

After NIOSA, walk to the Mariachi Festival, one of the oldest in the country. Amateurs and pros battle for the spotlight, and the event is filled with all the color and spirit of San Antonio. Admission for some Fiesta events is free.

Children's Festival
River Walk, San Antonio
(210) 227-4262
www.thesanantonioriverwalk.com

Adults don't get to have all the fun at Fiesta; this officially sanctioned Fiesta event is especially designed for the youngest revelers. Held along the River Walk and sponsored by the Paseo del Rio Association, the one-day event offers plenty of pint-size fun and games. Admission is free.

A Taste of New Orleans
Sunken Garden Theater, Brackenridge Park, San Antonio
(210) 475-9887
www.sazainc.com

If you're staying downtown, grab a bus for a ride out to the Sunken Gardens in Brackenridge Park for A Taste of New Orleans. Gumbo, jambalaya, Cajun catfish, boudin, and beignets top the list of offerings, while everything from jazz to salsa to Big Band sounds keep things hopping. This event is sponsored by the San Antonio Zulu Association Commission.

King William Fair
King William Historic District, San Antonio
(210) 271-3247

This one-day festival, an official part of Fiesta San Antonio, showcases the historic neighborhood of King William. Held annually for more than 30 years, the event features the usual fair attractions: arts and crafts, food, and entertainment. Proceeds fund the charity work of the King William Association.

Bowie Street Blues
Institute of Texan Cultures, 801 S. Bowie St. at HemisFair Plaza, San Antonio
(210) 458-2300
www.texancultures.utsa.edu

Now in its second decade, this annual event showcases the blues musicians of Texas. Gates open at 11:30 A.M.; the concert starts at noon and continues to 6:00 P.M. Performers vary from year to year, but previous concerts have featured Tiffany and the Gospel Motions, Neal Black and the Healers, Wild Bill Pitre, Lady Pearl Johnson, and Johnny Nicholas and the Texas All-Stars. This event is officially sanctioned by Fiesta San Antonio. Guests are encouraged to bring lawn chairs or blankets but no ice chests or pets are allowed on the grounds. Admission is $6.00 for adults and $3.00 for children 3 to 12 years old. The fee also includes admission to the Exhibit Floor of the Institute of Texan Cultures.

Walk Across Texas
San Antonio Botanical Garden, 555 Funston Pl., San Antonio
(210) 207–3255
www.sabot.org/

Not too many travelers can say they've walked across Texas, but participants in this officially sanctioned Fiesta event certainly can say they've seen a sampling of all the regions of the Lone Star State. This self-guided walk takes place in the 11-acre native area of the Botanical Garden and includes the piney woods of East Texas, the mesquite stands of South Texas, and the wildflower fields of the Hill Country. Living history groups and docents are positioned along the path to help visitors learn more about how early settlers used natural resources to build their homes. Admission is free.

May

Cinco de Mayo
Market Square, San Antonio
(210) 207–8600

This event celebrates the Battle of Puebla, which won Mexico's independence from France. The battle was waged on May 5, *Cinco de Mayo* in Spanish. The city celebrates with a Cinco de Mayo festival with music, food, arts and crafts exhibits, and other fun. It's sponsored by the Mexican-American Cultural Association. Admission is free.

Classic Cruise Along the Corridor
San Antonio Botanical Gardens, San Antonio
(210) 362–5200

Sponsored by the Alamo Area Council of Governments, this event is a favorite with classic-car buffs. More than 18 classic car clubs participate in this annual drive from San Antonio down the Alamo–La Bahia corridor. Cars depart from the San Antonio Botanical Gardens after a performance by the San Antonio College Brass Ensemble. The drive passes through towns including Seguin, Floresville, Goliad, Poth, Sutherland Springs, Helena, Karnes City, Panna Maria, and others, and features special events in each community. Now in its second decade, the Classic Cruise showcases both vintage cars and motorcycles. Admission is free.

Return of the Chili Queens
514 Market St., Market Square, San Antonio
(210) 207–8600

This is the time to indulge your taste for chili, the spicy concoction created by local women known as "chili queens." To celebrate the state dish, booths are set up every Memorial Day for a three-day tasting sponsored by the El Mercado Merchants Association. The festivities include a chili cook-off sanctioned by the Chili Appreciation Society. The public can sample the tasty concoctions starting at 2:00 P.M.; live music adds to the fun. Admission is free.

Tejano Conjunto Festival en San Antonio
Rosedale Park at Guadalupe Cultural Arts
Center, 1301 Guadalupe St., San Antonio
(210) 271–3151
www.guadalupeculturalarts.org

Take the liveliness of Mexican music, mix in the accordion beat of German music, and you have conjunto, a unique sound born in South Texas. Tejano music adds a newer beat to this old favorite. This festival celebrates conjunto, Tejano, and norteño (Mexican-Latin) music, and it is considered the largest one of its kind in the world. The five-day event features more than 35 hours of live music performed by some 25 artists. Previous performers have included five-time Grammy Award–winner Flaco Jimenez, Esteban Jordan, The Hometown Boys, Los Dos Gilbertos, Mingo Saldivar, Grup Vida, Los Desperados, Jay Perez, Dee, The Garcia Brothers, and Michael Salgado. Special events include inductions into the Conjunto Music Hall of Fame. Admission to the festival is free on Thursday, the opening day. Admission Friday through Sunday is $7.00. A pass sold prior to the festival at the GCAC gift shop at 1300 Guadalupe Street at South Brazos and on opening night includes a color poster and admission to all events for $20.

Kerrville Folk Festival
Quiet Valley Ranch, Texas Hwy. 16, 9 miles
south of Kerrville
(830) 257–3600, (800) 435–8429
www.kerrville-music.com

Starting in late May and continuing into early June, this annual festival is not only one of the largest in the San Antonio area, it is one of the largest in the Lone Star State. The Kerrville Folk Festival features more than 100 songwriters and their bands from Texas, other states, and other countries, too. The festival includes 11 six-hour evening concerts, seven two-hour sundown concerts, 80 arts and crafts booths, and some 30 daytime events. One of Texas's best-loved music gatherings, this extravaganza of song is held 9 miles south of town at the Quiet Valley Ranch.

In previous years, headliners have included Tish Hinojosa, Peter Rowan, David Wilcox, actor Ronny Cox, Guy Clark, Butch Hancock, Riders in the Sky, Jimmy LaFave, Sara Hickman, and Ray Wylie Hubbard. New songwriters are featured at the New Folk Concerts held early in the festival. Previous winners of this prestigious contest include Nanci Griffith, Lyle Lovett, James McMurtry, and Tish Hinojosa. The concert is a casual event, and guests are invited to bring lawn chairs. Ice chests, bottles, cans, or glass containers are not permitted on fair grounds, however. If you want to extend your day trip for a weekend of good music, consider camping at the ranch. There are 20-plus acres, complete with picnic tables, rest rooms, solar-heated showers, and a country store.

Texas State Arts and Crafts Fair
Schreiner College, off Hwy. 27, Kerrville
(210) 896–5711

Scheduled for late May, this event is one of the largest arts and crafts festivals in the state. Just a short drive from San Antonio, the event is held on the grounds of Schriner College in the community of Kerrville. These 16 acres give visitors plenty of room to shop, view the artwork, and enjoy a natural setting that's pure Texas. The event draws more than 200 artists from across the state. No manufactured, mass produced, or molded items are permitted, and the artisans must reside in Texas to participate. The artists are carefully selected so that the fair offers only the best in Texas artwork. The fair also features attractions for its youngest visitors. There's a special area where children can play in sand or make their own artwork, and there's a petting zoo with exotic animals.

June

Fiesta Noche Del Rio
Arneson River Theatre, River Walk,
San Antonio
(210) 226–4651
www.alamo-kiwanis.org/noche/fiesta.htm

You know it's summer when Fiesta Noche Del Rio begins. The Arneson River Theatre has hosted this summer production for nearly four decades. Sponsored by the Alamo Kiwanis Club as a fund-raiser for the Children's Shelter of San Antonio, the show celebrates the many cultures of San Antonio through song and dance every Tuesday, Friday, and Saturday night in June through August. The event includes acts showcasing the music of Spain, Argentina, Mexico, and Texas; there's romantic Latin music, too. Tickets are $10.00 for adults, $5.00 for children age 6 to 14, and $8.00 for seniors.

Texas Folklife Festival
Institute of Texan Cultures, 801 S. Bowie St.,
HemisFair Plaza, San Antonio
(210) 458–2390
www.texancultures.utsa.edu

Formerly held in August, this festival recently moved to June (when temperatures are far more festive). The four-day celebration is one of San Antonio's top

events. Dating back to 1972, it has grown from 2,000 to 70,000 attendees. Held at the Institute of Texan Cultures, the festival carries out the museum's mission—to recognize the contributions of the many cultures that settled Texas—through song, folk dance, game demonstrations, crafts exhibits and demonstrations, and lots of ethnic food. Eleven stages throughout the grounds showcase ethnic song and dance ranging from flamenco dancers to Celtic airs to hula. Advance tickets are $6.00 for adults and teens (13 years and over), and $2.00 for children 6 to 12 years. Advance tickets can be purchased at retail locations and through mail order from the Texas Folklife Festival Office. Tickets at the gate are $8.00 for adults and teens; $2.00 for children 6 to 12 years; and free for children 5 years and under. The festival also sells a special wristband that allows unlimited admission to all events; the price is $20.00. The wristband is nontransferable and must be purchased by late May. For mail-order sales, write Institute of Texan Cultures,

Mexican folkloric dancers liven many special events in San Antonio. PHOTO: AL RENDON, COURTESY OF THE SAN ANTONIO CONVENTION AND VISITORS BUREAU

A Bloomin' Good Time

Grab the car keys in one hand, your camera in the other, and get ready for a bloomin' good time! When the wildflowers are in bloom throughout Central and South Texas, there's no better excuse to hit the roads for a day trip filled with fun, festivities, and flowers. Here's a bouquet of the best getaways during this spring season:

Texas Hill Country Wine Trail. The Hill Country blooms not just with wildflowers but also with vineyards. This trail traces its way through numerous wineries in the region. Wine aficionados should pick up a copy of the "Texas Hill Country Wine Trail" brochure, available from the Fredericksburg Chamber of Commerce and Convention and Visitors Bureau (888–947–3600) or online at www.texaswinetrail.com.

Wildseed Farm, Fredericksburg. The largest family-owned wildflower seed farm in the United States is the site of the annual Wildseed Farms Wildflower Celebration, scheduled for early to mid-April, when the fields are filled with bluebonnets and other Texas wildflowers. You can stroll along a walking trail and even cut your own wildflower bouquet; weekend visitors can also enjoy a taste of local wines and the sound of Texas music. The farm is located 7 miles east of Fredericksburg on U.S. 290. It's open daily from 9:30 A.M. to 6:00 P.M.; admission is free. For information, call (800) 848–0078 or see www.wildseedfarms.com.

Lady Bird Johnson Wildflower Center, Austin. Don't know a primrose from a paintbrush? Or would you like to learn more about how you could incorporate wildflowers into your landscaping? Whatever you know or don't know about wildflowers, if you love beautiful blooms, the Lady Bird Johnson Wildflower Center is the place for you. Located about 85 miles from San Antonio, the only facility in the nation devoted to native plants and flowers offers educational programs as well as plenty of flower-filled walks among its blooming acres. After planting in excess of 2,000 pounds of wildflower seed every fall, the center is a showcase in the spring. During that season, the centerpiece here is the Wildflower Meadow, which explodes with color. And flowers are combined with festivities at the Spring Gardening Festival and Native Plant Sale, scheduled for early April. It's your chance to learn more about native plants and wildflowers and how they can be included in your own garden. Along with demonstrations and lectures, this event includes the sale of native plants from the center's greenhouses. Call (512) 292–4200 or see www.wildflower.org. Admission for nonmembers is $7.00; seniors and children over age 5 pay $5.00.

Kerrville. This Hill Country community, about 60 miles from San Antonio on I–10, is home to the Riverside Nature Center. Located at 150 Francisco Lemos Street, the center is filled with more than 200 varieties of native Texas plants including wildflowers. Drop by the new visitors' center, then take a self-guided walk along the tree trail. While you're in Kerrville, don't miss the Willow City Loop between Fredericksburg and Llano off of Route 16. (North of Fredericksburg on Route 16, take the second Willow City Loop turn to the right; there are three Willow City exits.) This 16-mile loop through unfenced ranch land includes canyon views, bluffs, spectacular wild-flowers, and wildlife. Another popular wildflower drive is Route 16 South out of Kerrville towards Medina. For more on Kerrville, call (800) 221–7958.

Boerne. Check out the wildflowers growing around Boerne, 22 miles northwest of San Antonio on I–10; if you're inspired by all the greenery don't miss the Cibolo Nature Center Plant Sale, scheduled yearly for mid-April. Held at the Kendall County Fairgrounds on Highway 46, the event features native trees, plants, and seeds as well as a kids' activity area. (And when it's time to go, kids will love the mule-driven wagon rides back to the Nature Center.) While you're in Boerne, be sure to visit the Nature Center and the Cibolo Wilderness Trail, where you'll see some of the area's natural habitats, including a reclaimed prairie and marsh. You'll find several walking trails, including a historic farm trail, a prairie trail, a creekside trail, and a marsh loop. The trails wind past native plants and wildflowers as well as birds and animals indigenous to the Hill Country. For more details, call the Greater Boerne Chamber of Commerce at (888) 842–8080.

Corpus Christi. Don't forget the beautiful coastal blooms as you plan your wildflower drives. One of the best places to enjoy the wildflowers is the Corpus Christi Botanical Gardens at 8545 South Staples. This 180-acre park traces the banks of Oso Creek; you can enjoy a walk along the Bird and Butterfly Trail or see the blooms of the plumeria collection or the new hibiscus garden and water garden. As you look around the gardens, you will notice that they're a favorite with winged visitors as well. Spring means bird migration, and the gardens are part of the Greater Texas Coastal Birding Trail. For more information, call (800) 678–6232.

Hotlines. Before you reach for the car keys, spend a few minutes listing to the various hotlines that pinpoint the best sites for flower power. Call the Texas Department of Transportation at (800) 452–9292; along with tourism information, this number offers reports on wildflower sightings throughout the state. Reports are updated weekly with news of spectacular roadside wildflower displays.

---

801 S. Bowie St., San Antonio, TX 78205-3296

Latino Laugh Festival
Rivercenter Comedy Club, 849 E. Commerce St. at Rivercenter Mall, San Antonio
(210) 229–1420
www.hotcomedy.com/rivercenter.htm or www.sitv.com

Since its first year in 1996, this annual festival has grown in popularity and continues to attract bigger, nationally known performers. Co-sponsored by the Rivercenter Comedy Club and SíTV, the event was developed as a way to showcase new comedy talent in the Latino community. The four-day festival includes a variety of English-language comedy acts, including stand-up, sketch comedy, celebrity roasts, and one man/woman shows. The comedians vary by year but previous performers have included Tommy Chong, Cheech Marin, Daisy Fuentes, Edward James Olmos, Maria Conchita Alonso, Jimmy Smits, Hector Elizondo, Erik Estrada, Mario Lopez, Ada Maris, Ricardo Montalban, Liz Torres, and Viki Carr. The event is broadcast as a 13-week series on the Showtime and Comedy Central networks. Tickets for the shows can be purchased at the Rivercenter Comedy Club in Rivercenter

Mall or by calling (210) 229–1420 or (866) 468–7621; online, tickets can be purchased at www.ticketweb.com. Ticket prices range from $10 to $30.

July

Contemporary Art Month
Blue Star Art Space, 116 Blue Star and citywide, San Antonio
(210) 227–6960
www.bluestarartspace.org

For a decade, the work of San Antonio's artists has been recognized in July with exhibits and performances. More than 70 events celebrate the city's performing and visual arts—everything from Latino photography exhibitions to a show featuring one-of-a-kind lamps made by local artists. Events are held at galleries around town and at the Blue Star Art Space. Admission is free.

Fiesta Noche Del Rio
Arneson River Theatre, San Antonio
(210) 226–4651
www.alamo-kiwanis.org/noche/fiesta.htm

This nightly summer festival continues through July; see the June listings for details.

August

Fiesta Noche Del Rio
Arneson River Theatre, San Antonio
(210) 226–4651
www.alamo-kiwanis.org/noche/fiesta.htm

This nightly summer festival continues through August; see the June listings for details.

September

Diez y Seis De Septiembre
Citywide, San Antonio
(800) 447–3372

Diez y Seis De Septiembre (September 16), the anniversary of Mexican independence, is celebrated with festivals and special events at La Villita, the Arneson River Theatre, Market Square, and Guadalupe Plaza. One highlight is the performance by the Guadalupe Dance Company, with new dances and costumes every year.

El Grito Ceremony
Plaza Mexico, HemisFair Park, San Antonio
(210) 227–9145

On September 15, 1810, Father Hidalgo y Costilla gave his *"El Grito"* (Cry for Freedom) speech, which launched Mexico's rebellion against Spain. The reenactment of *El Grito* takes place at the Plaza Mexico in HemisFair Park each September 15, and is followed by plenty of music and dance. Admission is free.

October

Go Rodeo Roundup
Freeman Coliseum, 3201 E. Houston St., San Antonio
(210) 225–5851
www.sarodeo.com

A fund-raiser for the San Antonio Livestock Exposition Scholarship Fund and Junior Livestock Auction, this elegant event is a favorite with country music lovers. The evening function features live music and gourmet dining. Tickets are $75 per person; tables for 10 people can be reserved for $750.

Greek Funstival
St. Sophia Greek Orthodox Church, 2405 N. St. Mary's St., San Antonio
(210) 735–5051, (210) 496–5322

Enjoy Greek food, dances, and music at the St. Sophia Greek Orthodox Church during this three-day fall festival, now in its fourth decade. The event offers guests a taste of such traditional Greek goodies as baklava, dolmades, and souvlaki. You can also purchase imported Greek wines to accompany the homemade food, prepared by the women of the church. Admission is $3.00 for adults; children under 12 are admitted free.

Hispanic folk dancers celebrate Diez y Seis in style. PHOTO: AL RENDON, COURTESY OF THE SAN ANTONIO CONVENTION AND VISITORS BUREAU

International San Antonio Inter-American Bookfair and Literary Festival
Trinity University, 715 Stadium Dr., San Antonio
(210) 271–3151
www.guadalupeculturalarts.org

The works of some 50 international publishers are honored during February with exhibits, readings, and workshops sponsored by the Guadalupe Cultural Arts Center. Considered one of the most important public venues in the country for new Latino and Latina writers, the event features books from the United States and Latin America. Authors at previous bookfairs have included Maya Angelou, Alice Walker, August Wilson, and Elena Poniatowska. Admission to the bookfair is free. Readings by some nationally known writers are by ticket only; admission to these readings is $7.00.

Low and Slow Classic Car Show
Mateo Camargo Park, Hwy. 90 West at Callaghan Rd., San Antonio
(210) 432–1896

Presented by Centro Cultural Aztlan, a promoter of lowrider shows and competitions in Texas, the one-day Low and Slow Classic Car Show attracts hundreds of local and regional competitors who have transformed their factory-built cars into one-of-a-kind machines. There are more than 60 categories of competition, including cars that hop, cars with upholstery, cars with murals, and more. The family-oriented event includes food and drink booths, games for childen, and live music of the 1950s and '60s. The event is held at Camargo Park; to reach the park, travel west on Highway 90 and take the Callaghan Road Exit. The park is across the street from the Nelson Wolf Baseball Stadium. Admission is $6.00, children under 6 are free.

River Art Show
418 Villita St., San Antonio
(210) 226–8752

The River Walk is lined with the work of hundreds of Texas artists during early October. This annual event is sponsored

Holidays in the Hill Country

The Twelve Days of Christmas is fine, but the Hill Country does the holiday up in a Texas-size fashion with a whole month of activities. One of the largest Christmas events in the area is the Texas Hill Country Regional Christmas Lighting Trail, stretching north from San Antonio to encompass many of the communities of this region. Shops, historic sites, courthouses, and churches welcome travelers with a show of spectacular lights and Christmas cheer.

The Christmas Lighting Tour runs from late November through New Year's Day, spreading the holiday spirit with free activities that recall Christmases gone by in historic Hill Country towns. Some activities take place on weekends only; others, especially lighting displays, occur nightly. Grab a coat, the camera, and the kids and jump aboard the sleigh—or at least the minivan—for a look at the dazzling show that awaits just beyond San Antonio's city limits.

Blanco: One of the largest Hill Country light displays is found at the Old Blanco County Courthouse, a historic building aglow with some 100,000 tiny white lights. Blanco, 35 miles north of San Antonio, hosts a month of activities to celebrate the season including the LBJ Heartland Council Holiday Market and the Merry Merchants Market, both with plenty of opportunities for holiday shopping. Later in the month, visitors can take a tour of homes and enjoy a holiday meal then witness the reenactment of Las Posadas at St. Ferdinand's Catholic Church. For more information, call (830) 833–5101.

Bulverde: Start your Hill Country lighting tour in Bulverde, located 9 miles north of Loop 1604 and 1 mile west of U.S. 281. This small town has a lot of Christmas spirit and shows it starting in early December with the Bulverde Senior Holiday Craft Show. The following weekend, the town enjoys a living Nativity scene at St. Paul Lutheran Church and an open house at the Krause House Theater. For more details, call (830) 438–4285 or see www.bulverdechamber.com.

Canyon Lake: It may be a great summertime getaway, but Canyon Lake, 22 miles north of San Antonio, offers plenty of reasons for a holiday visit as well. Early in December, stop by for the Old Fashioned Christmas Lighting. The next week is the lighting of the community Christmas tree, complete with carolers and the arrival of Santa. The annual Canyon Lake Christmas Parade takes place in the town of Sattler, followed by the Parade of Lights on Canyon Lake, with boats sailing at sunset. In mid-December, save room for turkey and all the trimmings at the annual Christmas banquet. For more details, call (800) 528–2104 or see www.canyonlakechamber.com.

Dripping Springs: Tucked between Johnson City and Austin, 76 miles northeast of San Antonio, this community—nicknamed the Gateway to the Hill Country—celebrates Christmas with lots of lights and a contagious holiday spirit. In early December, you'll find two good shopping opportunities here: the Christmas Fair at the Senior Citizens Activity Center, and the Ladies Guild Christmas Bazaar at St. Martin De Porres Catholic Church. When you're done with your shopping, enjoy the Christmas in the Hills Tour of Homes. For more information, call (877) 294–1133.

Fredericksburg: The holiday fun starts at the beginning of December with a lighted Christmas parade on historic Main Street and continues right through the end of the month in this charming community 66 miles northwest of San Antonio. The parade marks the opening of Weihnachten in Fredericksburg, a Christmas market and festival. Designed in the style of an open-air German Christmas market, Weihnachten offers everything from crafts to Christmas beers. There's plenty of holiday fun for the children, too, thanks to the Kinderfest. A real highlight of the season is the Christmas Candlelight Tour, with self-guided tours of 15 historic homes and buildings. The fun continues after Christmas as well. On December 26th, the Pioneer Museum Complex hosts Zweite Weihnachten or Second Christmas. According to this German tradition, the day after the holiday was meant to be shared with friends. For more information, call (888) 997–3600 or see www.fredericksburg-texas.com.

Johnson City: They named it right—Lights Spectacular is downright spectacular, thanks to more than 750,000 lights. At the center of the festivities stands the Blanco County Courthouse, adorned with some 100,000 lights; it's open weekends so visitors can view the Christmas tree and antique toy display. The community, 63 miles north of San Antonio, also has "light art displays," illuminated panels with up to 1,200 lights that portray the 12 days of Christmas. And don't miss the Pedernales Electric Co-op, with over 275,000 shining lights. The free lighting displays take place nightly through New Year's Day but December is also filled with special events including Christmas in the County Carriage Rides, lamplight tours of the LBJ Boyhood home and the Johnson settlement, and the living Nativity scene at the United Methodist Church. Shoppers in the family will want to check out the Blanco County Artists International Art Show, held on the courthouse square. For more information, call (830) 868–7684 or visit www.johnsoncity-texas.com.

Marble Falls: Grab your sunglasses for this display: You're about to see a million tiny lights! The Christmas Walkway of Lights, a virtual tunnel of lights that reflect off the waters of Lake Marble Falls, is one of the most spectacular lighting experiences in the region. More than 125 illuminated sculptures and a tree of over 17,000 lights have attracted visitors from around the world to this celebration, 86 miles north of the Alamo City. For more information, call (800) 759–8178 or visit www.marblefalls.org.

Round Mountain: Located north of Johnson City on U.S. 281, 75 miles north of San Antonio, this small community is big on holiday spirit. Lights outline the area's many historic buildings, including the Round Mountain Stagecoach Inn and Stable, built in 1874, and the recently restored Methodist Church, dating back to 1876. For more information, call (830) 825–3233.

For more information on Christmas in the Hill Country, contact any area chamber of commerce or call the regional office at (830) 997–8515 for a brochure listing all the region's special holiday activities.

by the River Art Group, Inc., a group now in operation for over half a century. If you've visited the Alamo City at other times of the year, you may be familiar with the group's River Walk Group Gallery in historic La Villita (see our Shopping chapter for more details). During the annual October art show, the group expands its coverage to display works not only in La Villita but also along the banks of the River Walk. The event is always scheduled for the first full weekend in October. Admission is free.

November

Wurstfest
Landa Park, New Braunfels
(830) 625–9167, (800) 221–4369
www.wurstfest.com

The month of November starts with a bang—and a bratwurst—at Wurstfest, a celebration of sausage, suds, and song held north of San Antonio in the city of New Braunfels on I-35. Since 1961, Wurstfest has been drawing the attention of merrymakers looking to enjoy the German heritage of this community. Held on the banks of the Comal River in Landa Park, this festival is consistently rated as one of the top events in the United States. An estimated 100,000 visitors from across the nation will participate in this special

festival each year. Get ready to polka to the sounds of accordion tunes and to sample the sausage for which this event is known.

The Wurstfest fun is scattered throughout the community thanks to related special events. The local art league offers a Wurstfest Art Show, highlighting area talent. History buffs can browse the Heritage Exhibit at the New Braunfels Civil Center to see how the first settlers founded this town. And bicyclists can compete in the Tour de Gruene, a scenic 26- and 36-mile recreational bicycle tour that races down River Road through the Gruene Historic District. Tickets for Wurstfest can be obtained by writing Wurstfest Association, P.O. Box 310309, New Braunfels, TX 78131-0309 or by calling the telephone number above.

Late November and December

Caroling in the Caverns
Natural Bridge Caverns, 26495 Natural Bridge Caverns Rd., exit 175 off I–35, San Antonio
(210) 651–6101
www.naturalbridgecaverns.com

Visitors can enjoy the echo of favorite carols in this underground cavern. Reservations are required for this special event.

Christmas Along the Corridor
San Antonio, Goliad, Panna Maria, other communities
(210) 362–5200

Looking for Christmas? Don't search the horizon for a man in a red suit or for eight tiny reindeer. Look for the Pony Express rider. The Alamo–La Bahia corridor, a 90-mile stretch from San Antonio to Goliad, heralds Christmas in true Texas style with an annual Christmas Along the Corridor celebration. This event combines history and Christmas joy in a way that's as unique as the region itself. The festival features Pony Express Christmas Couriers, horseback riders who gallop from

The Alamo is just one place that has beautiful light displays during the holiday season. PHOTO: RICHARD REYNOLDS, COURTESY OF THE SAN ANTONIO CONVENTION AND VISITORS BUREAU

town to town spreading the spirit of Christmas. After an official swearing-in ceremony in late November in front of the Alamo, the 100-plus couriers prepare for their duties in early December.

On the first Saturday in December, the festivities begin in Goliad with the departure of the Pony Express riders from Presidio La Bahia, the oldest fort in the West. From the Presidio, the riders travel to Goliad's Courthouse Square for the reading of a Governor's Proclamation marking the start of the festivities. Following the proclamation, the riders split up along three routes that wind through this historic region and into the city of San Antonio. Like the Pony Express riders of yesteryear, each rider hands off his or her duties to the next rider along the way, so the journey is a team effort.

Riders continue spreading Christmas cheer as they travel to the communities of Runge, Helena, Panna Maria, Cestohowa, Stocksdale, Sutherland Springs, La Vernia,

Kenedy, Karnes City, Hobson, Falls City, Poth, Floresville, Pleasanton, Poteet, and Elmendorf. Many of these communities set up special Pony Express postal cancellation stations. Bring along your Christmas cards for a special cancellation commemorating the festival.

Although the arrival of the Pony Express riders is the most unique element of this celebration, festivities continue throughout the day even after the riders have continued down the road. In Goliad, Santa and Pancho Clauses and the Goliad "reinsteer" delight young visitors, while parents enjoy craft booths, food, live music, and an evening Las Posadas procession from the Courthouse Square to Presidio La Bahia.

Just down the road in Panna Maria, which means "Virgin Mary" in Polish, guests can enjoy walking tours of the historic church, museum, and village. It's appropriate that this historic burg is part of the Christmas corridor festivities, because its very roots date back to a Christmas more than a century ago. After a nine-week voyage from Poland to Galveston, 100 families rented Mexican carts to transport their farm tools and bedding as well as the cross from their parish church. They made the difficult journey to central Texas on foot, finally stopping at the hillside that overlooks the San Antonio River and Cibolo Creek. The day was December 24, 1854, and the pioneers celebrated midnight Mass beneath one of the large hilltop oaks. The site later became Panna Maria.

After a look at the location where those early pioneers built their first church, visitors can shop for locally made crafts or enjoy Polish sausage cooked on site at the Panna Maria Visitors' Center. Evening festivities include a lighting ceremony, evening Mass, and singing of Polish Christmas carols.

Floresville residents and guests celebrate the day with "Christmas in the Country." A Las Posadas procession, Christmas concert, tree lighting, and hayride to view the colorful holiday lights is followed by an evening of holiday foods, the reading of *Cowboys' Night Before Christmas,* and caroling.

The festivities reach their peak with the arrival of more than 100 Pony Express riders in San Antonio. Following an honor guard bearing the six flags of the corridor, the riders gallop through the southeast gates of the Mission San Juan at 4:30 P.M. bearing the Governor's Proclamation. Following the proclamation of the start of the Christmas season, the mission celebrates with period crafts and foods, and Native American dances and music, all representing mission life during the eighteenth century.

Admission to the festivities is free.

Fiesta de Las Luminarias
Paseo del Rio, San Antonio
(210) 207–8600
www.thesanantonioriverwalk.com
Thousands of luminarias, tiny candles in sand-weighted paper bags, guide visitors to the River Walk during this special Christmas celebration. The candles symbolize the lighting of the way for the Holy Family. This event is sponsored by the Paseo del Rio Association; admission is free.

Fiestas Navideñas
Market Square, San Antonio
(210) 227–4262
Every weekend in December, Market Square spreads the holiday spirit with special events such as piñata parties, a blessing of the animals, and, of course, a visit from Pancho Claus.

Hecho-a-Mano
Guadalupe Cultural Arts Theater, 1300 Guadalupe St., San Antonio
(210) 271–3151
www.guadalupeculturalarts.org
This arts and crafts festival, held for three days in late November and early December, showcases the work of local artisans. Only handmade items are allowed at this event, which has been held annually for more than a dozen years. Jewelry, woodwork, furniture, clothing, folk art, toys, ceramics, and more are displayed and sold during the event, which attracts in excess of 10,000 shoppers.

Holiday River of Lights
New Braunfels, north of San Antonio on I–35
(830) 608–2100.
You may be familiar with nearby New Braunfels, just a half-hour drive north of San Antonio, as a popular spring, summer or fall getaway. Shoppers are drawn by its antiques stores and outlet mall; Schlitterbahn attracts crowds from across the nation with its top-notch water rides; and river lovers canoe, raft, and enjoy leisurely floats down the Guadalupe River.

But during December New Braunfels leaves on the lights—Christmas lights, that is—for winter visitors with a grand celebration called the Holiday River of Lights. Considered the first of its kind in the Southwest, this is a trail of sparkling lights and animated holiday scenes that creates a winter fantasyland for seven-tenths of a mile along the banks of the Guadalupe River in Cypress Bend Park.

The Holiday River of Lights flips the "on" switch in mid-November, and the fun continues through early January. Load up the family for a drive through this magical attraction, turn on the car radio to hear some of your favorite holiday tunes, and wind your way along the shimmering Guadalupe River banks that are aglow with hundreds of thousands of twinkling lights and more than 35 holiday scenes silhouetted against the night sky.

Admission is $7.00 for vehicles with up to eight passengers, $15.00 for vehicles with nine to 24 passengers, and $40 for buses. Season passes are available for eight-passenger vehicles for $25. The special holiday display is open from 6:00 to 9:30 P.M. Sunday through Thursday and 6:00 to 10:30 P.M. on Friday and Saturday evenings. The display is located in Cypress Bend Park off Peace Avenue. From San Antonio, travel north on I–35 to exit 189 (Loop 337). Take a left and go approximately a mile and a half to Common Street. Take a left on Common Street and go a half-mile to Peace Avenue. Take a left and drive into the park.

Los Pastores
Mission San José, 6534 San José Dr., San Antonio
(210) 224–6163
www.saconservation.org/pastor.html

The San Antonio Conservation Society and the National Park Service host this Christmas play at Mission San José every season. Usually scheduled for the Saturday following Christmas, Los Pastores (The Shepherds) is considered one of San Antonio's oldest Spanish traditions, dating back more than 250 years. At that time, the play was presented by Franciscan priests at the mission to explain the story of the birth of Christ to the local Indian population. The Franciscans had brought the play with them from Spain, where it originated in the 1500s. It is a story of good versus evil, with masked devils trying to prevent the shepherds from arriving in Bethlehem. Although the story is Spanish, the presentation has some local touches such as the handmade costumes which hark back to Texas traditions. The play itself is a Texas tradition and has been sponsored by the San Antonio Conservation Society since 1947. It remains very much a homegrown effort; the cast consists of members of Our Lady of Guadalupe Catholic Church. Local foods are sold at the performance. Admission is free.

Las Posadas
River Walk, San Antonio
(210) 224–6163
www.saconservation.org/posada.html

This beautiful ceremony, with costumed children leading a procession down the River Walk, dramatizes Joseph and Mary's search for an inn. Sponsored by the San Antonio Conservation Society, the popular holiday event has been delighting both locals and visitors from around the country for four decades. The procession moves along the River Walk, led by costumed boys and girls representing Joseph, Mary, angels, and shepherds. Priests and mariachi players follow the children, singing songs in both English and Spanish. After the procession, guests can stop by Maverick Plaza in La Villita to enjoy hot chocolate and cookies; children can try to break a piñata. Admission is free.

The Arts

Choirs

Dance Troupes

Education

Film

Art Galleries

Museums

Music

Theater Troupes

Venues

The San Antonio arts scene is vibrant and varied. The cultural diversity that makes this city special is reflected in its creative community, which includes Latino artists, Southwestern artists, and representatives from many other genres, who work in both the performing and visual arts in a variety of media.

San Antonio is a patchwork of artistic areas, from the commercial district to the historic King William District. One aspect that has attracted many artists to the city is its attitude toward art. "It offers a 'big sky' attitude where anything is possible," says Alexander Gray, a native New York art administrator who now is a member of the staff of ArtPace, a San Antonio gallery. "Artists support each other and welcome new people to the community. They turn their homes into galleries and invite the public inside to enjoy and learn from their work." ArtPace has received international acclaim for its exhibition of works by artists from around the world.

Blue Star Art Space, San Antonio's arts complex, also brings international talent to South Texas venue. According to Executive Director Carla Stellweg, "since 1985, artists and advocates for contemporary art have used the Blue Star Art Space to spearhead trends in San Antonio."

For those who seek to learn more about art and its creation, the Southwest School of Art and Craft provides instruction in a variety of media. Every year, 2,400 adults and 1,600 children take part in classes taught by local and international artists. Another 10,000 children are taught in special programs in schools, shelters, and community centers. Paula Owen, director of the school, notes that "San Antonio is a fantastic place for artists. There is a new interest in regionalism and San Antonio is a city that catches the imagination. It is different and spirited and it feels as if something is about to happen. Artists feel that energy and welcome the opportunity to learn, exhibit, and interact."

The city's appreciation for art is reflected in many of San Antonio's public buildings. For example, the recent renovation of the Henry B. Gonzales Convention Center included the installation of 16 pieces of public art. Mexican artist Juan O'Gorman created the mosaic mural at the Lila Cockrell Theater for the Performing Arts at the convention center; it tells the story of the region from the days before the conquest to the present day.

At other points in the city, public art also makes an appearance. At the trolley transit center, tile medallions have been designed by quilt artist Ann Adams. The artist also created the mosaic mandala in the sidewalk along the River Walk. At the airport, local artist Bill Fitzgibbons has crafted a gateway of airplane wings and tail sections that links the parking garage and Terminal Two.

San Antonio also has many nonprofit organizations that educate the citizens of the city about the joys of the performing and visual arts. Guadalupe Cultural Arts Center (210–271–3151, www.guadalupeculturalarts.org), located at 1300 Guadalupe Street, was founded in 1980. The largest organization of its kind in the United States, it aims to promote the arts and culture of the Native American, Latino, and Chicano peoples. ¡Arts San

Antonio! (210–226–2891, www.ArtsSanAntonio.com) sponsors performances for the children of the city in an effort to help them develop an appreciation of art. Incorporated as a nonprofit organization in 1992, ¡Arts San Antonio! tries to make the performing arts an accessible avenue of entertainment for everyone in the community.

Choirs

Alamo City Men's Chorale
P.O. Box 120243, San Antonio
(210) 495–SING
www.acmc-texas.org

Since it was founded in 1987 the Alamo City Men's Chorale has sought "to provide quality choral music, performed by gay and gay-friendly voices, that enriches the lives of its audience." Over the past 15 years, it has apparently fulfilled that goal. ACMC performs a range of music, including pop songs, spiritual works, and classics. One critic praised them as "one of the finest men's choruses in the country." At any given time the choir is made up of around 40 individuals. Members must pass an audition process.

Alamo City Men's Chorale has performed across the state and around the country in venues including the Center for the Performing Arts in Tampa, San Jose's Center for the Performing Arts, and the Wortham Center in Houston. It also has appeared with the San Antonio Symphony several times. Over the years, Alamo City Men's Chorale has lost 10 members

Insiders' Tip

To find out what's going on in San Antonio's art realm, pick up a copy of the *San Antonio Current*. The free weekly paper is known for its good coverage of the art scene and its comprehensive art and entertainment listings.

to AIDS. To join the fight against HIV and AIDS, the chorale performs regularly at the annual Procession of Hope, sponsored by the Hispanic AIDS Committee, which, in 1996, presented it with its "Heart of the Community Award." ACMC was honored by the directors of the San Antonio Black Tie Dinner in 1996 "for outstanding service to the lesbian and gay community."

Texas Bach Choir
P.O. Box 90066, San Antonio
(210) 821–5382
www.texasbachchoir.org

The Texas Bach Choir has been performing for San Antonio audiences for more than 25 years. TBC sings a variety of choral arrangements from a range of years and styles, but specializes in the works of composer Johann Sebastian Bach. Each season there is at least one concert devoted solely to his work. Since its founding in 1976, the choir has performed all of Bach's major works for choral choir. The choir is made up of the finest voices in the San Antonio area, who must try out in a competitive audition process.

The Texas Bach Choir has performed in many churches and concert halls throughout the San Antonio area. It has also taken two European concert tours, performing in Central and Eastern Europe. In an effort to educate the community about the beauty of choral music, TBC runs educational programs at San Antonio schools.

Dance Troupes

San Antonio Metropolitan Ballet
2800 N.E. Loop 410, Suite 307, San Antonio
(210) 590–0210
www.sametballet.org

This preprofessional company is aimed at providing entertainment to San Antonio citizens while supplying young dancers with the opportunity to gain experience and broaden their artistic scope. The San Antonio Metropolitan Ballet has been in operation for nearly 20 years and presents two major productions every year, one in spring and one in winter. The company performs modern dance and jazz as well as ballet.

Dancers age 9 and older can participate in the ballet's intensive course in ballet, musical theater styles, jazz, pointe, and modern dance; the classes are usually held during the summer months.

Education

Southwest School of Art and Craft
300 Augusta St., San Antonio
(210) 224–1848
www.swschool.org

The building that now houses the Southwest School of Art and Craft has a history that is almost as interesting as that of the city of San Antonio itself. In the 1840s Bishop Jean-Marie Odin bought 10 acres of land for $1,000 with the intent of starting a girls school in San Antonio. The first group of teachers, Ursuline nuns, were brought to San Antonio from Galveston in 1851, and the school was opened. By 1900, there were 300 students enrolled in the Old Ursuline Academy. In 1965 the school moved to northwest San Antonio; later that year the San Antonio Conservation Society bought the building from the Ursuline Order.

Southwest School of Art and Craft was organized by a group of citizens who felt that there was a void in San Antonio that could be filled by the teaching of handicrafts and art. The 1968 Worlds' Fair in San Antonio provided the opportunity for the school to sponsor a gallery, and enrollment grew quickly. The San Antonio Conservation Society offered the use of the Old Ursuline Academy to the school, and in 1971 the Southwest School of Art and Craft moved into its new quarters. Massive renovation was needed, and the school and the Conservation Society both worked hard to raise money for the restoration, which lasted for 12 years.

Today the school has two campuses: the original Ursuline Campus, and an adjacent Navarro Campus, which was opened in 1998. It offers programs for all age groups, with classes taught by local, regional, and national artists. More than 120 classes and workshops are offered each year, and the annual enrollment is about 2,000 adults and 1,600 children and teenagers.

There are two galleries at the school, which are open to the public from 9:00 A.M. until 5:00 P.M. Monday through Saturday. The Ursuline Hallway Gallery shows works by up-and-coming artists, while the Russell Hill Rogers Gallery on the Navarro Campus displays pieces by more well-known regional, national, and international artists.

Film

CineFestival
Guadalupe Cultural Arts Theater, 1300 Guadalupe St., San Antonio
(210) 271–3151
www.guadalupeculturalarts.org

This February event is the country's largest and oldest Latino film festival. Now in its third decade, Cinefest showcases shorts, features, experimental, documentary and animated works either by Latinos or about the Latino experience. Tickets are $8; some events are free.

San Antonio Film Commission
P.O. Box 2277, San Antonio
(210) 207–6700, (800) 447–3372

The San Antonio Film Commission's purpose is to bring film and video productions to San Antonio. It has lured a number of movie, television, and commercial shoots to the Alamo City. San Antonio has a lot to offer film studios. Within an hour's drive of the city, there are rolling hills, farm land, and arid plains. There are well-preserved historic buildings as well as new buildings downtown that can present a modern look.

For these reasons, San Antonio is becoming a popular movie location. Among the films that have been shot here are *Spy Kids* (2000), *All the Pretty Horses* (1999), and *The Newton Boys* (1997).

Art Galleries

ArtPace
445 N. Main Ave., San Antonio
(210) 212–4900
www.artpace.org

This contemporary arts gallery was founded by Linda Pace, daughter of David Earl Pace of Pace Foods fame (if you've been in San Antonio for long, you've sampled their picante sauce). The gallery opened it doors in January 1995 and quickly attracted attention with its artists-in-residence programs. The 18,000-square-foot facility houses three artists at a time: one international, one national, and one from the San Antonio region. The artists live and work at ArtPace for two months; at the end of that period there is an exhibition of their work.

The gallery is open Wednesday through Sunday from noon to 5:00 P.M. (Thursday until 8:00 P.M.) and also by appointment.

Blue Star Art Space
116 Blue Star, San Antonio
www.bluestarartspace.org

Located directly across from the Pioneer Flour Mill, this collection of former warehouses spans 137,000 square feet and is home to San Antonio's most expansive arts complex, a collection of art galleries, student exhibition space, alternative theater venues, and restaurants. Blue Star was founded by several local artists including Jeffrey Moore, Richard Thompson, Kent Rush, Richard Mogas, Adair Sutherland, and Lewis Tarver; the complex first opened in 1986 with an exhibit featuring the work of local artists. The following years brought more successful shows as well as funding by the City of San Antonio, the National Endowment for the Arts, and the Texas Commission on the Arts.

Within two years of that first exhibit, the complex expanded to include studios and both work and living space for artists. Today shops and galleries here feature a variety of art forms, from folk art to glass objects to jewelry.

Galeria Ortiz
102 Concho St., San Antonio
(210) 225–0731
www.galeriaortiz.com

This distinctive gallery showcases mainly contemporary Southwestern art. Lisa Ortiz moved to San Antonio from New York in 1978. She took over the Dagen-Bela Galeria in 1995, and changed the name to Galeria Ortiz. Up-and-coming artists' work is featured alongside that of internationally recognized artists. Painting, jewelry, and sculpture are displayed and sold.

Greenhouse Gallery of Fine Art
2218 Breezewood Dr., San Antonio
(800) 453–8991
www.greenhousegallery.com

This gallery is one of the most respected in the United States. It features works by many nationally and internationally known artists, including oil paintings and bronze sculptures by some of the 21st-century art world's biggest stars. The Greenhouse Gallery is closed Sunday and Monday.

Museums

McNay Art Museum
6000 N. New Braunfels Ave., San Antonio
(210) 824–5368
www.mcnayart.org

Works by famous artists such as Picasso, Matisse, O'Keeffe, and Cézanne are featured in this art museum, which is housed in the home of the late Marion Koogler McNay, heiress to an oil fortune and an artist herself. Built in the 1920s, the Spanish Mediterranean–style 24-room house

The museum's education department provides educational programs for 42,000 local school children, teachers, and other adults each year. From October through May, "Sunday Highlights Tours" of the expansive museum are offered each week. Art historians and museum curators give presentations about the exhibits as part of the "Gallery Talks on Exhibitions" program. Lectures by visiting curators, artists, and scholars are presented on selected Sundays.

Also on select Sundays, local musicians and actors perform at McNay's Leeper Auditorium. Family Days allow parents and children to enjoy art in a fun atmosphere; check the McNay calendar for specific dates. On the last Sunday of each month, a storyteller entertains the kids (and parents) or conducts a workshop.

The McNay Art Museum Library is open to visitors who wish to use its collection for research and reference. The library is open Tuesday through Friday from 10:00 A.M. until 4:45 P.M. The library is closed on most holidays and the entire month of December.

The museum store is located on the first floor of the museum. It sells art books, posters and souvenirs.

McNay Art Museum is closed Mondays as well as New Year's Day, July 4th, Thanksgiving, and Christmas. There is no admission fee except for special exhibitions and events.

The McNay Art Museum houses a fine collection of French Impressionist works. PHOTO: TOM BECKER, COURTESY OF THE SAN ANTONIO CONVENTION AND VISITORS BUREAU

was converted to a museum after Mrs. McNay's death in 1950. She left her art collection, home, and endowment "for the advancement and enjoyment of modern art." The collection numbers over 13,000 prints, drawings, and sculptures and is considered among the finest in the Southwest United States. The museum also features a 30,000-volume research library, an auditorium, and a museum store.

San Antonio Museum of Art
200 W. Jones Ave., San Antonio
(210) 978–8100
www.sa-museum.org

The San Antonio Museum of Art is one of the largest museums in the Southwest, and the building that houses it is as unique as the museum itself. It's the former Lone Star Brewery, and even today the building maintains a factory-like atmosphere with bright, airy spaces, skywalks, and even glass elevators.

The museum has a permanent collection of ancient glass and pottery as well as artifacts from around the world. It is especially noted for its ancient Egyptian, Greek, and Roman antiquities; Asian art; and American works.

But the latest pride of the museum is the Nelson A. Rockefeller Center for Latin American Art, considered the finest collection of Latin American art in the Americas. Opened in late 1998, this three-story, 30,000-square-foot center, designed by San Antonio's Overland Partners, is a repository of all types of Latin American art. Located on the east side of the museum, it features an introductory gallery with computer stations that help visitors learn more about the art history and culture of the region. Exhibits portray the long history of Latin American art starting with the Pre-Classic Period in 2000 B.C. and continuing through the Magical Realism Movement of recent decades.

The San Antonio Museum of Art is an icon of culture in San Antonio. PHOTO: AL RENDON, COURTESY OF THE SAN ANTONIO CONVENTION AND VISITORS BUREAU

Indeed, education is an important aspect of the center's mission. "We want this to be a state-of-the-art installation because we feel like this center is going to be a nationwide resource for people who are interested in Latin American culture," said Tracy Baker-White, the museum's curator of education. The center plans special events and educational programs throughout the year.

The museum is open Tuesday from 10:00 A.M. to 9:00 P.M.; Wednesday through Saturday from 10:00 A.M. to 5:00 P.M.; and Sunday from noon to 5:00 P.M. Admission is $5.00 for adults, $4.00 for seniors and college students with I.D., $1.75 for children ages 4 to 11. Admission is free every Tuesday from 3:00 to 9:00 P.M.

Music

Lyric Opera of San Antonio
1500 S. Zarzamora St. #219, San Antonio
(210) 532–5100
www.lyricoperasa.com

Local businessman Mark A. Richter founded the Lyric Opera of San Antonio in 1997 with the stated mission "to produce fully staged opera in an evolving fashion, starting with modest budgets, increasing its production and musical values with each opera until the level of grand opera is achieved." The company has grown at such a rate that only three years later the opera's production of "Madame Butterfly" was budgeted at $70,000. It produces full operas in a 1,000-seat auditorium with a 30-piece orchestra and professional costumes. A night at the opera is a popular outing for San Antonio locals and visitors alike.

Before 1997, there had been an absence of live opera in San Antonio for 15 years, since the San Antonio Symphony stopped producing operas. The Lyric Opera hopes to bring a love of the art to a generation raised in a San Antonio without opera. For people looking to perform professionally in opera, the Lyric Opera of San Antonio formed The Lyric Studio, which trains young singers under the age of 32 at the university level and allows them to appear in actual opera productions.

San Antonio Symphony
222 E. Houston St., #200, San Antonio
(210) 554–1010
www.sasymphony.org

Under the direction of Christopher Wilkins, the San Antonio Symphony performs in the beautiful Majestic Theatre in downtown San Antonio. Composed of 76 professional musicians, the symphony performs a 39-week season every year. The San Antonio Mastersingers is the symphony's chorus, made up of 120 volunteers from the San Antonio area. The symphony is a highly competitive organization; as many as 600 candidates from all around the globe compete for every opening through an anonymous audition process.

The Symphony's Young People's Concert Series, started in 1945, has taught generations of San Antonio youngsters about the joys of music. The series of four concerts is very affordable and is aimed at children in grades 4 and 5.

Theater Troupes

Jump Start Performance Company
108 Blue Star, San Antonio
(210) 227–5867

Found in the arty Blue Star complex (see "Venues," below), Jump Start Performance Company presents enjoyable shows of contemporary theater. Jump Start is committed to bringing artists together, despite ethnicity or other differences. The non-profit company produces works by its members, and features local and international artists in a guest artist series. It also offers classes and workshops.

Jump Start presents some of San Antonio's most innovative theater work.

Magik Children's Theatre
420 S. Alamo St., San Antonio
(210) 227–2751

Currently performing in HemisFair Park at Beethoven Hall, this troupe aims to

provide an enjoyable theatergoing experience for audience members of all ages. More than 150,000 people attend a performance by the group every year. Magik Children's Theatre is committed to bringing affordable yet quality productions to the stage; a quarter of the tickets each season are distributed to disadvantaged children. Many of the plays performed are chosen from local school reading lists, but in the evenings, classical productions are staged for adults.

Offstage, Inc.
3702 Big Meadows St., San Antonio
(210) 690–8454

Offstage, Inc. claims to be "the second-oldest constantly producing company in San Antonio." Dan H. Laurence and Wayne K. Elkins, Jr., founded the experimental theater company in 1972, and its first production took place during Christmastime of the same year. Since that time, Offstage, Inc. has continued to push the social, political, and creative limits through original works and new interpretations of theatrical classics. During the U.S.-Cuban embargo, the company staged Cuban playwright José Trinana's *The Criminals*. Its production of *Romeo and Juliet* depicted Verona as a circus, with the Capulets as aerialists and the Montagues as ground dwellers.

The company does not have its own theater, but moves from venue to venue. George Orwell's *Animal Farm* was staged at the San Antonio Zoo with the guest train transporting the audience from the gates. The company's innovative ideas have not gone unnoticed in the San Antonio community. One critic has called Offstage

"One of the two or three truly vital stage production groups in the city. More challenging and endearing with each outing." Another declares that "Offstage has evolved to the point of being San Antonio's only reliable experimental theatre."

Venues

Alamo Street Restaurant and Theatre
1150 S. Alamo St., San Antonio
(210) 271–7791

The building that houses the Alamo Street Theatre was erected in 1912 and was a Methodist church until 1968. In 1976, the building was bought by Bill and Marcie Larsen, who converted the lower level into a restaurant and put a stage in the former chapel. The building now is listed on the National Register of Historic Places.

Most evenings, two shows are presented. The lower Green Room Dinner Theatre presents original mysteries, dramas, and comedies while patrons enjoy a delicious buffet dinner. The upper theater hosts more traditional productions.

Insiders' Tip

If you're attending a show at the Alamo Street Theater and think that you see the figure of a young boy making mischief around the theater's kitchen, it might be Eddie, one of the many resident ghosts seen from time to time in the building. The theater puts on a show several times a year called *In The Company of Ghosts,* based on stories about Eddie and the building's other supposed specters.

Reservations are required. Note that shows can change without prior notice.

Arneson River Theater
River Walk, San Antonio
(210) 227–4262 (Paseo del Rio Association)

This unique theater was erected in 1939, designed by River Walk architect Robert Hugman and built by the WPA. When you are on the River Walk, have a seat on the grass-covered steps and enjoy a look. In this open-air format, the river, not a curtain, separates performers from the audience. Some of San Antonio's top events take place here, including Fiesta Noche del Rio, a summer show that has been in operation nearly four decades (see our Annual Events and Festivals chapter for more information).

Carver Community Cultural Center
226 N. Hackberry St., San Antonio
(210) 225–6516

In the past, when it was known as the Library Auditorium, this historic structure hosted Ella Fitzgerald, Duke Ellington, Nat King Cole, Paul Robeson, and many other nationally known performers. Later rescued from demolition and reopened in 1977 as the Carver Cultural Community Center, it continues to stage a wide range of shows. In recent years, the auditorium has featured the Dance Theatre of Harlem, a performance of Gershwin's *Porgy and Bess,* and a concert by the Muddy Waters Tribute Band.

Majestic Performing Arts Center
226 E. Houston St., San Antonio
(210) 226–3333

One of San Antonio's most famous theaters, the Majestic was built in 1928 by John Eberson as a vaudeville and movie palace. This proud building holds the title as the nation's oldest city-built playhouse. The Majestic is now home to the San Antonio Symphony as well as touring Broadway shows and traveling concerts. Parking for the theater is on Houston Street and costs about $5.

The Majestic blends baroque, Spanish, Mission, and Greek and Roman traditions into its own flamboyant style. PHOTO: PARIS PERMENTER & JOHN BIGLEY

San Pedro Playhouse
800 E. Ashby Pl., San Antonio
(210) 733-7258
The exterior of the San Pedro Playhouse is a reproduction of an old market house, making the building truly one of a kind.

The structure was built in 1929 and has two stages, the main stage and the cellar theater. Usually musicals are shown on the main stage, while the downstairs theater is reserved for dramas. This is a great place to see an informal show staged by local actors.

Parks and Recreation

Whether your interests lie in golf, biking, swimming, or just plain enjoying the outdoors, you're in luck in the Alamo City. San Antonio is filled with park and recreation facilities of all types, sprinkled from downtown to the city's outer reaches. Within the city's boundaries, you'll find park land maintained by the city, county, state, and even national government. And still more parks are just a short distance away. Many of the local parks and recreation facilities are free; others have a small admission fee.

In all, the San Antonio Parks and Recreation Department operates 160 city-owned parks and recreational facilities, which includes swimming pools, gyms, many municipal golf courses, and more. The list also includes some of the city's top attractions: the River Walk, the Tower of the Americas, La Villita, the Spanish Governor's Palace, Market Square, the Botanical Gardens and Conservatory. In all, the Parks and Recreation Department oversees and maintains more than 7,300 acres of park land throughout the region. For more on city parks, call (210) 207–PARK or see www.ci.sat.tx.us/sapar.

You can reserve facilities at city-and county-owned parks by calling (210) 207–PARK, (210) 207–3120, or (210) 207–3121. Reservation specialists at these numbers can assist you with reserving facilities for a group picnic, birthday party, reunion, or other group function. (Fees vary by facility.) You can also make reservations in person at the reservation office at 531 Brackenridge Avenue; the office in located in Brackenridge Park across from Joske Pavilion and is open 8:00 A.M. to 6:00 P.M., Monday through Friday.

Along with city parks, this region is rich with state parks, facilities that offer visitors the chance to enjoy ecological or historic attractions. Several are located right around the city; others are found within a short drive that's well worth the time.

Finally, San Antonio is also home to a national park, the San Antonio Missions National Historical Park. Although the Alamo is often thought of as the prime mission in the city, San Antonio boasts a mission trail with several historic facilities that give visitors a better feeling of mission life. San Antonio Missions National Historical Park is covered in the Attractions chapter.

Whether you plan to visit a city, state, or national park, be sure to keep San Antonio's environment in mind. Temperatures during the summer months can be very high. Morning visits are best from June through September. Parks in the surrounding area that feature water recreation are very popular during the summer months, so expect crowds, especially on weekends and holidays.

Also, please remember that the parks are natural settings, filled with nature's creatures, some of which bite and sting. Central and South Texas are home to several poisonous snakes including rattlesnakes, copperheads, water moccasins, and coral snakes. While these are typically shy creatures and would prefer to flee rather than bite, be wary when hiking. Bites are fairly rare but if you are bitten, seek medical attention immediately. The region is also home to several nasty crawly creatures such as scorpions and fire ants. Mosquitoes can be the most annoying insect during warm-weather months; pack repellent to enjoy your trip.

This chapter is divided into two sections: parks and recreation. The parks section focuses on all types of parks in and around San Antonio. The recreation section is divided into recreation activities you can enjoy in the region, from bicycling and bowling to swimming and tennis.

Parks

Admission to parks is free unless otherwise noted.

City Parks

Brackenridge Park
2800 N. Broadway, San Antonio
(210) 207–3000, (210) 207–8590 (park rangers)

Located two miles north of downtown, this is the granddaddy of San Antonio's parks; if you have time for only one park visit, this is the one. The sprawling 343-acre facility is home to the San Antonio Zoological Garden and Aquarium (3903 North St. Mary's Street, 210–734–7183), widely considered one of the best zoos in the nation. Housed in a former rock quarry, the zoo spans 25 acres and holds the distinction of being the only zoo in the country to exhibit the endangered whooping crane. For more on the zoo see the Attractions chapter.

The park also has many other special features, including a miniature railroad (3810 North St. Mary's Street, 210–736–9534) that runs 3.5 miles through the park. The train is a replica of an 1863 C. P. Huntington steam locomotive. Kids also love the carousel (3910 North St. Mary's Street, 210–734–5401), which is part of the adjacent Kiddie Park (see the Kidstuff chapter). Your best view of the park is from aboard the Skyride (3910 North St. Mary's Street, 210–299–8480). Catch a ride on the bubble-shaped cars near the zoo entrance.

Brackenridge Park also has plenty of shady picnic areas, swings and slides, and green space in which to play. One of the park's most beautiful areas is the Japanese Tea Gardens (3800 North St. Mary's Street, 210–299–3000). San Antonio's semitropical climate encourages the lush flowers, climbing vines, and tall palms found inside this quiet, serene place. The ponds, with beautiful rock bridges and walkways, are home to numerous koi (large goldfish). For more information on the gardens, see the Attractions chapter.

The history of this swath of land dates back far earlier than its days as a park. Archaeologists have unearthed proof that this region has been visited by human beings for more than 11,000 years. More recently, the Spanish settlers in the region used the river here to feed their *acequias* (aqueducts) used for irrigation. One of these aqueducts, the Upper Labor *acequia*, can still be seen at the zoo.

This region remained largely uninhabited, however, until the mid-nineteenth century. After the Civil War, the local rock quarry enjoyed a booming business, thanks to the discovery that its limestone could be used to manufacture cement.

In 1866, George W. Brackenridge came to San Antonio from Austin; he and his mother later began to purchase riverfront property. A few decades later, Brackenridge developed a waterworks system to supply the city with artesian spring water. Eventually, he donated nearly 200 acres to the city for use as a public park. Brackenridge Park was born.

Development of the park began almost immediately. A zoo was built, incorporating old quarry walls and an old tannery site. Later, a public golf course was added, designed by A. W. Tillinghast of Philadelphia. This was the state's first public golf course. In 1917, work began on the Japanese Tea Gardens, also in the abandoned quarry. Prison laborers created the lush gardens, and local residents donated the plants. The Witte Museum was built on the northeast edge of the park in 1926, and during the Great

Depression several public works projects were completed in the park. Today Brackenridge Park remains much as it was 50 years ago.

Comanche Lookout Park
15551 Nacogdoches Rd., San Antonio
(210) 207–PARK

This 96-acre park is indeed a lookout; it is home to the fourth-highest point in Bexar County. Perched at an elevation of 1,340 feet (that's nosebleed territory for South Texas), the lookout was first used by Apache and Comanche Indians searching for game. It was later acquired by Mirabeau B. Lamar, the second president of the Republic of Texas. Lamar's land was passed down through his family who eventually sold it to German immigrants for farming. It was finally purchased by the city in 1994. The view includes miles of native trees such as Mexican buckeye, chinaberry, mesquite, huisache, and ash juniper.

Dawson Park
2500 E. Commerce St., San Antonio
(210) 227–1627

This neighborhood park, first named East End Park, was later named in honor of aviator Charles A. Lindbergh. In 1986, at the urging of local citizens, the park was renamed for another aviator, Robert A. Dawson. The first licensed African-American pilot was a graduate of the local Phyllis Wheatley High School. The aviation pioneer trained as an Army Air Corps flying cadet during World War II and was later killed in an air crash. Today the park is a favorite getaway for neighborhood residents

Eisenhower Park
19399 N.W. Military Dr., San Antonio

Once part of Camp Bullis, this park was opened to the public in 1988 and is now a favorite with birders. Dotted with juniper and oak, the rocky park is home to many native birds including the black-crested titmouse and the ladder-backed wood-

Insiders' Tip
The San Antonio Parks and Recreation Department maintains an online calendar of events, including special activities at area facilities. See www.ci.sat.tx.us/sapar.

pecker. Many deer, raccoon, rabbits, and armadillos also live here. There are 5 miles of hiking trails; the Cedar Flats Trail leads to the park's highest point. A lookout tower offers good views of the surrounding countryside.

Special programs sponsored by the Parks and Recreation Department and the Bexar County Audubon Society are offered on the second Saturday of the month from May through August.

Camping is permitted in the park by reservation, and pets on a leash are allowed. Eisenhower Park is open from dawn to dusk; no admission fee is charged.

Friedrich Wilderness Park
21395 Milsa St., San Antonio
(210) 698–1057
www.fofriedrichpark.org

Nature lovers flock to Friedrich Wilderness Park for its birding opportunities and its hiking trails. Located near Six Flags Fiesta Texas, across I–10 from the Dominion Golf Course, it is the city's only nature preserve. The 232-acre park offers more than 5 miles of hiking trails, including the Forest Ridge Trail, an excellent trail that is wheelchair accessible. The park is known not only in Texas but also internationally for its birding opportunities. It is shaded by thick juniper trees that provide nesting sites to the golden-cheeked warbler and the black-capped vireo, both endangered species. The park is also home to many other forms of wildlife including whitetail deer, raccoons, rabbits, squirrels, and

Beautiful Halsell Conservatory has world-class plant exhibits. PHOTO: PARIS PERMENTER & JOHN BIGLEY

more. Guided hikes are scheduled for the first Saturday of each month; a $2.00 donation is requested, and reservations are required.

Pets are not allowed in this nature reserve; also prohibited are fires, camping, hunting, and smoking on the trails. Hikers must stick to marked trails.

Nature lovers can take part in the park's Master Naturalists Program. Participants take part in a 40-hour program at Friedrich Park to learn more about local ecology, native plants, site maintenance, and more. After completion of the course, they give 40 hours or more in volunteer work. For more on the program, call the park number or see the Web site. The park is open 8:00 A.M. to 8:00 P.M. April through September; it closes at 5:00 P.M. the rest of the year.

Monterrey Park
5909 W. Commerce St., San Antonio
(210) 432–2727

Established in 1962, this park is named for San Antonio's sister city in Mexico. Especially popular for its recreational facilities, the park offers a community center, a swimming pool, picnic sites, a football field, a soccer field, basketball and tennis courts, and more.

Riverside Park
100 McDonald, San Antonio
(210) 207–PARK

This was once a privately owned park and a popular picnic grounds. Formerly located at the end of a streetcar line, it was a favorite getaway for San Antonians. In the late nineteenth century, the park was used as a training grounds for the Rough Riders, Teddy Roosevelt's troops gathered for the Spanish-American War.

For years, the park was overshadowed by Brackenridge Park. In 1927, the city purchased additional land and added a nine-hole golf course; today the course boasts 27 holes and the park has reclaimed its place as a good getaway on a weekend afternoon.

San Pedro Springs Park
1315 San Pedro Ave., San Antonio
(210) 207–8480

This is the city's oldest designated park and in fact is one of the oldest in the country. (Only Boston Common predates it.) This land was first reserved for public use by the Spanish government in the eighteenth century, although history shows that the site has been used by humans for more than 12,000 years.

The natural springs on the site were first named San Pedro Springs in 1709 and soon thereafter the first permanent settlement in the area was founded nearby. The Spanish later constructed an *acequia* to carry water from the springs into town.

The cool springs and shady surrounding trees drew many visitors and in 1852 the city established a reserve around the site. Soon pavilions were constructed to sell food and drink. In 1856 the U.S. Army decided to stable camels here as part of an experimental camel corp. A few years later, Sam Houston spoke at a rally here; later the park was used as a site for holding prisoners during the Civil War.

Sadly, the springs began to dwindle when artesian wells were drilled for city use. The park was renovated in 1899, however, and again began to attract visitors. It was again renovated a century later and in 1979 it was added to the National Register of Historic Places.

San Antonio Botanical Gardens and Halsell Conservatory
555 Funston Pl., San Antonio
(210) 821–5115
Roses, herbs, a garden for the blind, and native plants are all found within these lovely 38-acre gardens. The centerpiece here is the Lucile Halsell Conservatory, a 90,000-square foot architectural masterpiece designed by Emilio Ambasz, formerly curator of design at New York's Museum of Modern Art. Opened in 1988, the Halsell Conservatory departs from the house-shape of typical conservatories, relying instead on conical and triangular roof shapes. To take advantage of the cooling effect of the earth during hot Texas summers, the greenhouse is built 16 feet underground. Separate structures showcase palm trees from around the world, desert plants, and tropical foliage. For more on the conservatory see "A Texas Oasis" elsewhere in this chapter.

Travis Park
Travis and Pecan Sts., San Antonio
(210) 207–8480
This third-oldest park in the country, this small downtown greenspace is across from the St. Anthony Hotel. It frequently hosts outdoor concerts, and it's a popular place with downtown employees, who like to take a picnic lunch and enjoy a little quiet time here.

Walker Ranch Historic Landmark Park
12603 West Ave., San Antonio
(210) 207–PARK
Opened in May 1999, San Antonio's newest park is the Walker Ranch Historic

A cool oasis in the midst of San Antonio, the Botanical Gardens invite you to learn as you walk.
PHOTO: BOB MAXHAM, COURTESY OF THE SAN ANTONIO CONVENTION AND VISITORS BUREAU

Landmark Park, located on the city's northwest side. This park may be new, but the site was used by hunter-gatherers 8,000 years ago. Later the park site was part of the Monte Galvan, a ranch that supplied the Mission San Antonio de Valero, better known as the Alamo.

The long-standing popularity of the site is due to its location near the confluence of Panther Springs Creek and Salado Creek. Today it offers hiking, an exercise trail, a pavilion, and information stations. The park is open daily from 6:00 A.M. to 10:00 P.M.

State Parks Near San Antonio

The year was 1923. Texans were enamored with the automobile, eagerly looking to weekends for a chance to cruise along paved roads and enjoy the scenic byways of the state.

Governor Pat Neff recognized the need to set aside parcels of land along those roads to be enjoyed by all the citizens of the state and by visitors and worked to ensure the passage of the state parks bill. And so the Texas state parks system was born.

Today Texas boasts an extensive state park system. When it comes to state parks, San Antonio residents and visitors have only one problem: selecting from a long list of excellent facilities. Here's a look at parks you can enjoy as a day trip or a weekend getaway. (The one state park located in San Antonio itself, Casa Navarro State Historical Park, is covered in the Attractions chapter.)

The National Museum of the Pacific War
Fredericksburg, 66 miles north of San Antonio via I–10 and U.S. 87
(830) 997-4379

Formerly known as the Admiral Nimitz Center, this expansive museum attracts visitors from around the globe. This fascinating museum consists of the Admiral Nimitz Museum, the George Bush Gallery, the Center for Pacific War Studies, a Japanese Garden of Peace, the Memorial Wall, the Pacific Combat Zone, and the Plaza of the Presidents. Presently the museum is undergoing an expansion and the renovation of the original Nimitz Hotel building, once operated by the grandfather of Fredericksburg's most famous son, Admiral Chester Nimitz. The World War II Commander-in-Chief of the Pacific (CinCPac) commanded 2.5 million troops from the time he assumed command 18 days after the attack on Pearl Harbor until the Japanese surrendered.

Behind the museum lies the Garden of Peace, a gift from the people of Japan. Follow the signs from the Garden of Peace for one block to the Pacific History Walk. This takes you past a collection of military artifacts including a "fat man" Nagasaki-type atomic bomb case, a Japanese tank, and a restored barge like the one used by Nimitz. Admission is $5.

Blanco State Park, Blanco
35 miles north of San Antonio via U.S. 281
(830) 833-4333

Located along the Blanco River, this park dates back to the days of the Depression when the Civilian Conservation Corps built two stone dams here as well as a group pavilion, stone picnic tables, and an arched bridge. Admission is $3.

Bastrop State Park, Bastrop
97 miles northeast of San Antonio via I-35 and TX 21
(512) 321-2101

Beautiful piney woods are the main draw at this park, the fourth-busiest state park in Texas. Facilities include a golf course, campsites, hiking trails, and a 10-acre fishing lake. The 1930s-built stone and cedar cabins featuring fireplaces, bathrooms, and kitchen facilities are very popular and should be booked well in advance. Naturalists appreciate the site for its unique ecology and for an endangered species: the Houston toad. During the toad's breeding season from January through March, guided night tours are available to learn more about this special park resident. Admission is $3.

Enchanted Rock State Natural Area
84 miles north of San Antonio via I-10, U.S. 87
(915) 247-3903

This state park features the largest stone formation in the West. Nationally this 640-acre granite outcropping takes second place only to Georgia's Stone Mountain.

People of all ages in reasonably good physical condition can enjoy a climb up Enchanted Rock. The walk takes about an hour, and hikers are rewarded with a magnificent view of the Hill Country. Those interested in technical rock climbing can practice their skills here as well; rock climbers must check in at park headquarters.

Consider planning your visit to Enchanted Rock on non-peak weekends because there is a limit on the number of cars allowed in the park. Admission is $5.

Guadalupe River State Park
47 miles northwest of San Antonio via I-10, Rte. 46
(830) 438-2656

The star of this park is the clear, cold Guadalupe River. This park stretches along four miles of river banks and offers visitors the chance to enjoy the scenic beauty of the Texas Hill Country. On Saturday mornings, take an interpretive tour of the Honey Creek State Natural Area to learn more about the plants and animals of the region. Admission is $4.

Landmark Inn State Historic Park
20 miles west of San Antonio via U.S. 90
(830) 931-2133

This historic Landmark Inn and museum was first a home and general store before becoming the Vance Hotel. Robert E. Lee and Bigfoot Wallace, a famous Texas Ranger, were said to have stayed here on the banks of the Medina River. Today this park offers overnight accommodations at the inn as well as activities for the day visitor. A museum contains displays illustrating Henri Castro's early efforts to recruit settlers to this region as well as exhibits covering early Castroville life. On the river, visitors can swim, fish, or canoe.

Guest rooms contain antique furnishings but no televisions or telephones. All

A Texas Oasis

It was a Texas-size problem: How do you keep delicate greenhouse plants from roasting in the heat of the summer? The typical greenhouse, with its glass walls and ceiling, would only intensify the extreme temperatures typically of this sunny state.

But the San Antonio Botanical Society came up with a Texas-size answer: the Lucile Halsell Conservatory. This unique 90,000-square-foot conservatory, which opened in 1988, is an important feature of the San Antonio Botanical Gardens. Located 16 feet underground, the building uses the cooling effects of the earth to help maintain a stable temperature even on the hottest of days.

And the plants are lovin' it. With a 99 percent survival rate for its exotic plant species, the Halsell Conservatory is alive with buds and blooms.

This 90,000-square-foot conservatory is an architectural masterpiece, designed by Emilio Ambasz, former curator of design at New York's Museum of Modern Art. Ambasz created a new type of conservatory, choosing a form that's as functional as it is eye-catching.

Instead of a typical box-shaped conservatory, the Halsell Conservatory consists of seven tall glass spires that surround a center courtyard. The glass and steel cones, which give the conservatory a futuristic look, rise to the height of a five-story building.

Visitors enter the conservatory via a ramp that feeds into the first exhibit area, actually a concrete passageway containing the Alpine Room. This glassed-in exhibit (the only nonaccessible one in the conservatory) contains delicate alpine fauna such as the popular eidelweiss and the alpine sunflower. This may look like an ordinary exhibit, but it's definitely high-tech. The lighting in the Alpine Room is artificial to simulate daylight at various latitudes. From here visitors continue the gradual descent to the breathtaking Exhibit Hall. This circular garden, with its ever-changing display of color, features seasonal floral exhibits, from Easter lilies to fall mums. To facilitate display changes, the plants are kept in their pots and buried in a bed of sand.

The Exhibit Hall is your first look at one of the glass structures that provide controlled light to the delicate plants. Here, as in the other conservatory rooms, temperature and humidity are read automatically, and the data is fed into a central computer that controls the very different environments of the conservatory's six areas. Specially constructed "shades" are found in each area, and when told by the computer to limit light, they automatically stretch over the glazed areas to diminish the sunshine entering the room.

As you leave the Exhibit Hall, there's a stunning view of the main section of the conservatory, which lies before you. Unlike the Exhibit Hall, this large area is not protected by glass, only by the coolness of the surrounding earth. The courtyard's focal point is a lagoon-shaped pool crisscrossed with walkways and stepping stones. Various plants and flowers fill the courtyard and even the aquamarine water is decorated with a scattering of lily pads and lotus.

Take any route you want through the conservatory at this point: you're in for a treat no matter which direction you choose.

To the right lies the Desert Room, one of the most extreme environments found in the Conservatory. Feel the blast of warm air as you enter the glass doors of the Desert Pavilion. At 94 degrees, the temperature's hot enough for the cacti. Like tall sentinels throwing their arms up in surrender, the giant saguaros stand watch over the bizarre plants of the pavilion. The cacti come in shapes from pencil to barrel, with names as colorful as chocolate drop, strawberry, and rainbow. Don't miss the Queen Agave Cactus from Mexico. It's hard to miss—each spine is more than four inches long!

Be ready for a complete change of climate as you continue through the conservatory into the Gretchen Northrup Tropical Conservatory. Suddenly you're dropped into the world of the jungle, missing only the slither of some snake or the raucous call of an exotic bird. The room is filled with greenery, ranging from the Scarlet Plume from Mexico to Bolivia's Red Powderpuff. You'll find plants from as far away as India and Cambodia in the humid tropical room as well.

Exotic blossoms are a special treat, filling the room with their heady fragrance and a burst of color among the greenery. Look for orchids, hibiscus, and bromeliads scattered throughout the display, and pause for a moment at the small waterfall and reflection pool in the center of the room.

After the dense tropical room, head for the airy Palm House—a five-story structure that dominates the conservatory. The wide, 110-foot base of the Palm House is planted with palms and cycads from the New World, including Florida's Royal Palm, the Saw Palmetto from the Southeast United States, Peaberry Palm from the Florida Keys, and Cuba's Queen Palm.

The Palm House is built in a spiral design, so you'll ascend to the higher levels by means of a winding sidewalk, passing more New World Palms on you way to the Old World Palms of the upper area. These include Africa's Queen Sage, South Africa's White-bird of Paradise, and exotic palms from New Guinea, Thailand, and Madagascar.

The Palm House offers the best view of the unusual roof structure that makes the Halsell Conservatory so special. As you ascend to the upper level, look overhead at the steel supports and the glazing that combine to create a graceful conical tower to house the tall trees.

When you reach the top of the Palm House, step outside for a bird's-eye view of the conservatory. From this vantage point, it's easy to see what's hidden at the front entrance: the fact that the conservatory, the whole half-acre of it, is truly underground. Off in the distance you can see the skyscrapers of downtown San Antonio and the towers of Trinity University.

You'll take a staircase back down to the Orangerie, where exotic fruit trees produce a bounty of guavas, cherries, limes, and oranges. Look for unusual trees such as coffee, breadfruit, chocolate, allspice, and miracle fruit along the narrow walkway.

The Orangerie ends in perhaps the most popular room of the conservatory—the greenery-filled Fern Room. Open the doors and step into the humidity-laden air where the ferns thrive, climbing the simulated rock walls to reach to the sky. Many visitors believe the walls are limestone, but simulated rock was used to provide a germ-free, clean environment.

The focal point of this room is a double-tier waterfall that fills the air with the sound of falling water. A large pond planted with lilies lies at the foot of the waterfall. Enjoy a cool (but damp!) walk behind the waterfall as you circle the crowded room. Exotic plants such as Bear's Foot Fern from Malaysia, climbing fern from China, and Tailflower from Tropical America grow alongside giant elephant ears and Hawaiian fern trees in this, the lushest of the conservatory's environments.

Given its inexpensive admission fees ($4.00 for adults, $2.00 for seniors and military, $1.00 for children), the Lucile Halsell Conservatory is one of Central Texas's best bargains. After all, where else could you travel from the chilly world of the Swiss Alps to the starkness of the Mojave Desert to the humid Amazon jungle in just one afternoon?

rooms are nonsmoking and include air conditioning; some rooms offer private baths. Admission to the park is $1.

Lyndon B. Johnson State Historical Park
77 miles northwest of San Antonio via U.S. 281 and U.S. 290
(830) 644–2252

During Johnson's life, the ranch was closed to all but official visitors. In hopes of catching a glimpse of the president, travelers often stopped along RR 1, located across the river from the "Texas White House," the nickname for the Johnsons' home. Today the park draws visitors from around the world who come for a look at the history behind the Hill Country, the presidency of LBJ, and a working Texas ranch.

A Visitors Center presents displays on LBJ's life; nearby, historic cabins offer a look back at early Texas living. Guided tours of the LBJ Ranch, operated by the National Park Service, stop at the one-room Junction School where Johnson began his education, slow down for a photo of the Texas White House then continue past the president's airstrip and cattle barns. Other stops include a look at the reconstructed birthplace home as well as the family cemetery where the former president is buried. The Sauer-Beckman Living Historical Farm, two 1918 farm homes, are furnished in period style and manned by costumed interpreters who garden, tend livestock, and perform chores. Children can have a great time petting the farm animals.

Although the park does not have overnight facilities, there are two picnic areas and hiking trails for day use. Admission is free.

Palmetto State Park
63 miles northeast of San Antonio via I–10, U.S. 183
(830) 672–3266

Along the banks of the San Marcos River, Palmetto State Park is a topographical anomaly amidst gently rolling farm and ranchland. According to scientists, the river shifted course thousands of years ago, leaving a huge deposit of silt. This sediment absorbed rain and groundwater, nurturing a marshy swamp estimated to be over 18,000 years old. Now the swamp is filled with tropical dwarf palmettos as well as moss-draped trees, four-foot-tall irises, and many bird species. Nature trails wind throughout the area. The park has full hookups and tent sites. There's also picnicking, but during the warmer months bring along mosquito repellent. Admission is $2.

Recreation

Baseball

Baseball SA
750 Merida St., San Antonio
(210) 889–5332
www.baseballsa.com

Based at Gunn Park Complex, this non-profit corporation runs youth baseball leagues for the city's best young players. There are leagues for eight different age groups; players ages 9 to 16 who are not already on a team must try out for team placement.

Little League District 19
(210) 496–2359
www.salittleleague.org/

District 19 encompasses northern San Antonio as well as the northern portions of Bexar County. Operated by a volunteer crew, the organization is composed of 14 programs covering various portions of the region. Player registration is held in mid-January.

Little League District 20
(210) 674–2973
www.littleleague.org/

Covering the southern portion of the city and Bexar County, District 20 is a volunteer organization. Registration for teams is held in mid-January.

Basketball

San Antonio Parks and Recreation Department
(210) 207–3127, or 207–3109
www.ci.sat.tx.us/sapar

You may not be San Antonio Spurs material, but if you enjoy a little hoops, consider participating in the adult men's basketball leagues. Games are played weekdays at San Fernando Gym, 319 West Travis Street, and at Woodlawn Gym, 1103 Cincinnati Avenue.

Bowling

Bowling is booming in San Antonio, with more than 15,000 league bowlers in the city spread among 500-plus leagues. The city is home to two dozen bowling centers, both commercial and military.

The city is well known to dedicated bowlers as the home of Columbia Industries, one of the largest manufacturers of bowling balls, now distributed to more than 30 countries.

Astro Bowling Center
3203 Harry Wurzbach Rd., San Antonio
(210) 824–6348

This mega-center features 44 lanes, perfect for high-demand Friday and Saturday nights. If your scoring skills are a little rusty, don't worry: the center offers computerized scoring. The center also has a restaurant, a lounge, and a pro shop. Senior and youth discounts are available.

San Antonio Bowling Association
226 Hall Park Dr., San Antonio
(210) 657–7070
home.att.net/~SAN-ANTONIO-BOWLING/

This club is sanctioned by the ABC/WIBC and is the best place in the city if you're serious about bowling. In the last few years, the association's Tournament Club has paid out over $100,000 in prize money to area bowlers.

Cycling/Mountain Biking

B and J Bicycle Shop
8800 Broadway, San Antonio
(210) 826–0177

This shop on Broadway rents bicycles by the hour, day, week, or even longer. To rent, you have to be at least 18 years old and have a valid driver's license or military ID. All riders must wear helmets. Hourly rentals range from $8.00 to $15.00 depending on the bike. Daily rentals run from $25.00 to $45.00, and weekly rentals go from $63.00 to $115.00.

San Antonio Wheelmen
(210) 826–5015

San Antonio's local bicycling club, the Wheelmen, has been in existence more than two decades and has a membership list of some 700 residents. The club plans evening rides as well as weekend rides through the Hill Country and along the Mission Trail. Throughout the year, several bicycling activities are scheduled, including October's Fall Century, a 100-mile ride with an overnight stop, and the Easter Hill Country Ride.

VIA Metropolitan Transit
(210) 362–2020
www.viainfo.net

Take your bike for a ride, literally, aboard one of the VIA buses. Recently VIA installed 460 bike racks on all its vehicles except the downtown streetcars, making it easier than ever for bicyclists to take their wheels out to the less-traveled reaches of the city for an excursion to the neighboring Hill Country. The quarter-million-dollar project to install the bike racks was paid for by the Federal Surface Transportation Program, with matching funds by VIA. The company is also looking at the possibility of bike lockers.

Dance

San Antonio Parks and Recreation Department
Youth Dance Classes
(210) 207–3115
www.ci.sat.tx.us/sapar

During the summer months, free dance classes are offered to local children ages 5 to 19 in all types of dance: ballet, Spanish, Mexican folkloric, jazz, hip-hop, ballroom, and more. The program also sponsors performing groups including Fandango, a troupe of young dancers who display their skills in Flamenco and Mexican Folklorico dancing. Young residents ages 12 to 19 are welcome to audition for the troupe, which has performed in Germany, Mexico, and regularly at San Antonio's Arneson River Theatre. The Parks and Recreation Department troupe is Texas Starlite, which specializes in clogging, tap, jazz, and ballet. During the summer months, the performers, ages 12 to 19 years, perform regularly at the Arneson River Theatre.

Fitness Centers

Downtown YMCA
903 N. St. Mary's St., San Antonio
(210) 246–9600

This is one of seven YMCA branches in San Antonio. A $2 million renovation to the downtown YMCA has improved much of the equipment and has made the facility more accessible to handicapped members.

Golf

San Antonio is a golfer's paradise, with numerous courses in and around the Alamo City. All but a handful are open to the public; some are municipal courses owned and operated by the city and some are privately-owned courses that are open to anyone. All share the same golf-friendly weather, which allows year-round play, and most offer views of San Antonio's scenic beauty. Green fees, including cart rentals, range from $20 to the $100 neighborhood, with $45 being about average. Average green fee for municipal courses is $30; private courses, $80.

Municipal Golf Courses

Brackenridge Park Golf Course
2315 Avenue B, San Antonio
(210) 226–5612

This course, designed by Philadelphia's A. W. Tillinghast (who also designed Inverness, Baltusrol, and Winged Foot), holds the distinction as the oldest 18-hole public course in the state. Opened in 1916, the course was designed to utilize the river and the many tall oak and pecan trees of the park, especially on the front nine. The par 72 course first hosted the Texas Open in 1922 and today is listed in the Texas Registry of Historic Sites, the Texas Golf Hall of Fame, and the Texas Open Hall of Honor.

Cedar Creek Golf Course
8250 Vista Colina, San Antonio
(210) 695–5050

This course is often named the best municipal golf course in South Texas. Nestled in the scenic Hill Country, the demanding 18-hole par 72 layout incorporates limestone hillsides, creeks, and several waterfalls.

Mission del Lago Golf Course
1250 Mission Grande, San Antonio
(210) 627–2522

This 18-hole par 72 course spans 7,004 yards, much of it fairly flat. The course has 124 bunkers as well as water features on 10 of its holes.

Olmos Basin Golf Course
7022 N. McCullough Ave., San Antonio
(210) 826–4041

This course has hosted the Men's City Championship 27 times and remains one of the city's most popular municipal courses. The 18-hole par 72 course has many par 3 holes and straightforward holes.

Riverside Golf Course
203 McDonald, San Antonio
(210) 533–8371

Located in Riverside Park, this course began as a nine-hole course; today it offers 27 holes: a par 3 course and a full-size, 18-hole par 72 championship course. The course's biggest challenge is on the seventh hole, where trees block the right side of the fairway.

Willow Springs Golf Course
202 Coliseum Rd., San Antonio
(210) 226–6721

This course dates back to 1923 and through the years many famous players have completed here, including Ben Hogan, Sam Snead, and Byron Nelson. The 18-hole par 72 long course has many tough par 4 holes as well as the city's longest hole: The second hole is a par 5 and spans 663 yards.

Private Golf Courses

These privately owned courses are all open to the public.

Canyon Springs Golf Club
24400 Canyon Springs Golf Rd., San Antonio
(210) 497–1770

This 18-hole par 72 course, located north of San Antonio in the Hill Country, is known for its wide fairways as well as its bunkers and natural hazards. On the 10th hole, golfers tee off on the cliff top. The club also has a driving range, practice greens, and a pro shop.

Canyon Springs Golf Club was nominated by Golf Digest *and* Golf Magazine *as "America's Best New Public Golf Course" in 1998.* PHOTO: STEVE MOORE, COURTESY OF THE SAN ANTONIO CONVENTION AND VISITORS BUREAU

Hyatt Hill Country Resort
9800 Hyatt Resort Dr., San Antonio
(210) 647–1234

Designed by Arthur Hills, this championship course utilizes native cacti, oaks, and a beautiful setting. The 18-hole, par 72 course has a double green on the 9th and 18th holes. Other facilities include a restaurant and bar housed in a ranch-style clubhouse, a driving range, a practice green, and a pro shop.

La Cantera Golf Club
Westin La Cantera Resort
16641 La Cantera Pkwy., San Antonio
(210) 558–GOLF, (800) 4–GOLFUS

This course, designed by Jay Morrish and Tom Weiskopf, utilizes the walls of a former limestone quarry as well as acres of live oak trees to challenge golfers. The 18-hole, par 72 course is the site of The Westin Texas Open at La Cantera, Texas's oldest golf tournament and part of the PGA Tour; the tournament is held each fall. Among the unusual features here is the tee shot from an 80-foot quarry wall looking right out at Fiesta Texas's Rattler roller coaster. The club includes a driving range, practice green, restaurant, and golf academy.

Pecan Valley Golf Club
4700 Pecan Valley Dr., San Antonio
(210) 333–9018, (800) 336–3418

This 18-hole, par 71 course has been rated one of the top 50 public courses in America by *Golf Digest* magazine. Its assets include oak-lined fairways and beautiful greens. This was the site of the 50th PGA Championship in 1968; the course was also selected by the USGA as the site of the 2001 U.S. Amateur Public Links Championship. Pecan Valley's original architect was J. Press Maxwell, although recently the course underwent a $5.5-million renovation under the direction of architect Bob Cupp. The club includes a restaurant, pro shop, driving range, and practice green; if you get thirsty, there's even a beverage cart that makes the rounds.

The Quarry Golf Club
444 E. Basse Rd., San Antonio
(210) 824–4500
www.quarrygolf.com

Designed by Keith Foster, this links-style 18-hole, par 71 course is yet another example of San Antonio's creative reuse of limestone quarries. The back nine of this beautiful course are set in a century-old quarry pit; the front nine are tucked in rolling grasslands. Tee times are accepted up to 30 days in advance. The Quarry also has a clubhouse and a pro shop.

Silverhorn Golf Club
1100 W. Bitters Rd., San Antonio
(210) 545–5300

This course is San Antonio's newest, located about 20 minutes from downtown. Designed by Randy Heckenkemper with input from PGA pros Scott Verplank and Willie Wood, the course utilizes 262 acres of wooded land. Operated by American Golf Corporation, the 18-hole par 72 course accepts tee times up to seven days in advance. The club also includes a pro shop and a driving range.

Tapatio Springs Resort and Conference Center
Johns Rd. W., Boerne
(800) 999–3299
www.tapatio.com/

This course boasts 27 holes, the first 18 designed by Billy Johnston. The additional nine holes give golfers three options: "The Lakes," "The Valley," and "The Ridge;" the latter is the most challenging of the three. For the past decade, this course consistently has been named one of the top 10 resort courses in Texas by the *Dallas Morning News*.

Woodlake Golf and Country Club
6500 Woodlake Pkwy., San Antonio
(210) 661–6124

This course holds the distinction of being the site of the PGA Tour's Texas Open for five years; it's where Ben Crenshaw earned his first PGA victory in 1973. Designed by

La Cantera golf course hosts the PGA Texas Open. PHOTO: TIM THOMPSON, COURTESY OF THE SAN ANTONIO CONVENTION AND VISITORS BUREAU

Desmond Muirhead, the 18-hole, par 72 course has a driving range, pro shop, bar and grill, two practice greens, and a club pro.

Area Golf Courses

These courses are all within a 50-mile drive of San Antonio.

The Bandit
6019 FM 725, New Braunfels
(830) 609–4665, (888) 923–7846

This Keith Foster Signature Course, located just north of San Antonio in the community of New Braunfels, is a lot of fun. The 18-hole, 6,928-yard, par 72 layout features elevation changes as well as beautiful greens.

Canyon Lake Golf Club
405 Watts La., Canyon Lake
(830) 899–3301

This 18-hole par 72 course features Canyon Lake as a backdrop; you might also spot white-tailed deer while you play.

The 6,500-yard, 72 par course is known for its tight fairways.

Chapparal Golf Course
300 Chaparral Dr., Seguin
(830) 303–0669

This 7,008-yard course is dotted with more than 700 ash trees as well as tall pecans and oaks. The 18-hole course is par 72.

Flying L Golf Course
Hwy. 173 S. and Wharton Dock Rd., Bandera
(800) 646–5407

Located northwest of San Antonio, this 18-hole, par 72 course is located at the Flying L Resort. The par 72 layout has a slope rating of 123 and can be enjoyed by players of all abilities.

Las Palomas Country Club
120 Las Palomas Dr., La Vernia
(830) 217–4653

This links-style layout takes advantage of low, rolling hills. The 18-hole course has a rating of 72.5 and a slope rating of 122.

Driving Ranges

Alamo Country Club
9700 Rochelle Rd., San Antonio
(210) 696–4000

This range is both covered and lighted. On-site extras include a pro shop, concessions, and professional instruction. The range is open from 7:30 A.M. to 10:00 P.M. daily.

Blossom Golf Center
13800 Jones Maltsberger Rd., San Antonio
(210) 494–0002

This driving range offers private instruction as well as clinics. Greens are dedicated to putting, pitching, and chipping. The range is open Monday through Saturday from 8:00 A.M. to 9:00 P.M., and Sunday from 8:00 A.M. to 8:00 P.M.

Eagle Quest at Panther Springs
16900 Blanco Rd., San Antonio
(210) 492–7888

Weekly putting contests are sponsored by this range, which also offers a pro shop, club rental, club repair, professional lessons, and clinics. In addition to the driving range, the complex includes both a putting and a chipping green as well as a sand trap; the facility is lighted. During the months when daylight saving time is observed, the range is open daily from 8:00 A.M. to 10:00 P.M.; the rest of the year the hours are 9:00 A.M. to 8:00 P.M.

Eagle Quest Precision Golf Center
450 Ira Lee Rd., San Antonio
(210) 822–9412

This center includes a pro shop, PGA club fitting, club repair, rentals, golf clinics, private lessons, and more. The lighted facility offers a driving range, a putting green, a chipping green, and a sand trap. Weekly putting contests are sponsored. From February through October, the range is open daily from 8:00 A.M. to 10:00 P.M.; from November through February, the range is open 9:00 A.M. to 9:00 P.M.

Polo Field Driving and Practice Range
915 E. Mulberry, San Antonio
(210) 736–9592

This driving range offers separate greens for putting and chipping, and a sand trap for valuable practice. It's open daily from sunrise to sunset.

Rolling Oaks Golf Center
5550 Mountain Vista Dr., San Antonio
(210) 655–4653

This range includes target greens, putting and chipping greens, and sand traps along with professional lessons, a pro shop, and club repair. The facility is open daily from 8:30 A.M. to 10:00 P.M.

San Pedro Driving Range and Par 3
6102 San Pedro Ave., San Antonio
(210) 349–5113

This large range can accommodate up to 50 players. Along with a night-illuminated driving range that spans 350 yards, the facility includes two practice greens for putting and chipping and a nine-hole, par 3 course. Lessons are available. The facility is open daily from 7:30 A.M. to 10:00 P.M.

Hockey

Crystal Ice Palace Ice Arena
12332 I–10 W. at DeZavala, San Antonio
(210) 696–0006, (888) 423–7529
www.iceplay.com

The Crystal Ice Palace offers hockey lessons and also is home to The River City Hockey League. The league offers several levels of play for kids age 4 through high school.

Running/Walking

San Antonio has many great trails to run or walk on. Some of the most popular are found at McAllister Park, Alamo Heights, and Mission Park.

Scuba Diving

Oceans Window Tropical Divers
12241 San Pedro Way, San Antonio
(210) 490–3483, (888) 696–3483
www.tropicaldivers.com

This PADI 5-Star facility offers scuba lessons for all levels of divers. The facility has two classrooms as well as an 85,000-gallon indoor heated pool. In operation in South Texas since 1985, Oceans Window has classes for ages 5 through 9, ages 10 to 15, age 15 and up, and age 18 and professional level. The facility also offers a SASY (Supplied Air Snorkeling for Youth) program, an excellent way for young divers to get the feel for scuba diving without complicated instruction. Adult versions of SASY allow older participants to have an easy introduction to scuba diving.

Trident Dive Center
2110 West Ave., San Antonio
(210) 734–7442
www.tridentdiving.com

Now in operation more than four decades, Trident Dive Center offers a variety of guided dives to Cozumel as well as dive instruction programs. The facility also offers several dive equipment service and inspection programs.

Skating

Crystal Ice Palace Ice Arena
12332 I–10 W. at DeZavala, San Antonio
(210) 696–0006, (888) 423–7529
www.iceplay.com

No matter what the season, it's cool at the Ice Palace. That year-around ice makes this a popular stop for all levels of skaters. Public ice-skating sessions are offered Wednesday through Sunday; the cost is $8.36 for adults, $7.01 for children age 12 and under, and $7.54 for military personnel and seniors (prices include skate rental and tax). The facility also offers both figure skating and hockey classes for all ages.

The Rollercade
223 Recoleta Rd., San Antonio
(210) 826–6361
6807 Bandera Rd., San Antonio
(210) 684–8900
2351 Goliad Rd., San Antonio
(210) 337–6200
8901 Fourwinds, San Antonio
(210) 653–5333

These family-owned roller-skating rinks have been keeping San Antonians rolling for more than 40 years. Each has a wooden skating surface and state-of-the-art music and lighting systems. Lessons are available from professional instructors for all ages. These rinks are especially popular for birthday parties; call about public skating hours. Admission is $5.00 to $8.00, depending on the day and time.

Soccer

Soccer League
San Antonio Parks and Recreation Department
(210) 207–3056
www.ci.sat.tx.us/sapar/index.htm

The Parks and Recreation Department offers a spring soccer league for boys and girls ages 6 to 14. Some 2,000 players participate.

Softball

San Antonio Parks and Recreation Department
(210) 821–3110, (210) 207–3109, or
(210) 207–3127
www.ci.sat.tx.us/sapar

The Parks and Recreation Department sponsors several softball leagues: adult slow pitch (men's, women's, and co-ed), adult fast pitch (men only), and girls' fast pitch (ages 10 and under, 12 and under, 14 and under, 16 and under, and 18 and under). Games are played on weekdays; admission to games is 25 cents for adults and free for children ages 12 and under. Both fall/winter and spring/summer leagues are offered. To register, check with Parks and Recreation. Games are held at the following locations:

Alva Jo Fischer Softball Complex
10700 Nacogdoches Rd., San Antonio
(210) 646–9604

Gunn Sports Club
2100 Wetmore Rd., San Antonio
(210) 545–2700

Kennedy Complex
3101 Roselawn Rd., San Antonio
(210) 434–4324

Koger Stokes Complex
611 W. Myrtle St., San Antonio
(210) 735–0823

Rusty Lyons Complex
6300 McCollough Ave., San Antonio
(210) 826–4834

Tony "Skipper" Martinez Complex
3610 N. St. Mary's St., San Antonio
(210) 735–4879

Lambert Beach Softball Field
4000 N. St. Mary's St., San Antonio
(210) 828–6623

Swimming

Indoor Pools

Palo Alto Pool
1400 W. Villaret Blvd., San Antonio
(210) 921–5234

Located in the southwest section of San Antonio at Palo Alto College, this pool is frequently used for competitive events in the fields of water polo, swimming, diving, synchronized swimming, and pentathlon. The City of San Antonio co-owns this excellent facility and in summer the pool at times is open to the general public. Both open swimming and lap swimming are available, although the schedule varies due to classes and swim meets.

San Antonio Natorium
1430 W. Durango Blvd., San Antonio
(210) 226–8541

This indoor pool is open daily and offers lap swimming, learn-to-swim programs, senior swims, and more. Adult lap swimming is generally scheduled from 11:00 A.M. to noon; admission is $1.50. The general public can swim from noon to 7:45 P.M. for $1.50; children ages 16 and under are admitted for 50 cents.

Outdoor Pools

The San Antonio Parks and Recreation Department (210-207-PARK, www.ci.sat. tx.us/sapar) oversees 21 outdoor pools, most of which are only open from late May until early August. Pool hours are typically 1:00 P.M. to 7:00 P.M. daily (Woodlawn is open 2:00 P.M. to 8:00 P.M. seven days a week).

Nine regional pools remain open through August until Labor Day weekend. These are Cassiano, Dellview, Elmendorf, Fairchild, Kennedy, Normoyle, Roosevelt, Southside Lions, and Woodlawn pools.

Admission fees at these city pools is 25 cents for children 6 and under; 50 cents for children 7 to 12 years old; and 75 cents for visitors age 13 and older.

The outdoor pools operated by the Parks and Recreation Department are:

Cassiano
114 S. Zarzamora St. and Cassiano Park,
San Antonio
(210) 434–7482

Concepcion
600 E. Theo Ave. and Concepcion Park,
San Antonio
(210) 532–3473

Cuellar
503 S.W. 36th St. and Cuellar Park,
San Antonio
(210) 434–8028

Dellview
500 Basswood Dr. and Dellview Park,
San Antonio
(210) 349–0570

Elmendorf
4400 W. Commerce St. and Elmendorf Park,
San Antonio
(210) 434–7380

Fairchild
1214 E. Crockett St., San Antonio
(210) 226–6722

Garza
5800 Hemphill Dr., San Antonio
(210) 434–8122

Joe Ward
435 E. Sunshine Dr., San Antonio
(210) 732–7350

Kennedy
3299 S.W. 28th St. and Emerson,
San Antonio
(210) 436–7009

Kingsborough
350 Felps St., San Antonio
(210) 924–6761

Lincoln
2803 E. Commerce St. and Lincoln Park,
San Antonio
(210) 224–7590

Monterrey
5919 W. Commerce St. and Monterrey Park,
San Antonio
(210) 432–2727

Normoyle
700 Culberson Ave. and Normoyle Park,
San Antonio
(210) 923–2442

New Territories
9023 Bowen Dr., San Antonio
(210) 681–2929

Roosevelt
500 Lonestar Blvd. and Roosevelt,
San Antonio
(210) 532–6091

San Pedro
2200 N. Flores and San Pedro Park,
San Antonio
(210) 732–5992

Southcross
819 W. Southcross Blvd. and Flores Park,
San Antonio
(210) 927–2001

Southside Lions
900 Hiawatha St. and Springfellow Park,
San Antonio
(210) 532–2027

Sunset Hills
103 Chesswood Dr., San Antonio
(210) 435–4011

Westwood
7601 W. Military Dr., San Antonio
(210) 673–3382

Woodlawn
1100 Cincinnati Ave. and Woodlawn Park,
San Antonio
(210) 732–5789

Swimming lessons

Oceans Window Tropical Divers
12241 San Pedro Way, San Antonio
(210) 490–3483, (888) 696–3483
www.tropicaldivers.com

SwimQuest, Inc. offers swim instruction at the Ocean Window facility for all ages from six months to adults. All lessons are offered in small groups in an indoor heated pool and can be geared to all levels of swimmers. Children are divided by age; private lessons are also available.

San Antonio Parks and Recreation Department
(210) 207–3113
www.ci.sat.tx.us/sapar

All outdoor city pools (see list above) offer four sessions of swimming classes in the summer months. Each session runs for two weeks on a Monday through Thursday schedule. Sessions are $15. To register for a class, call the Parks and Recreation Department or your nearest pool.

Tennis

Public Courts

More than 140 tennis courts throughout the city are managed by the Parks and Recreation Department. The largest facility in town is the McFarlin Tennis Center at San Pedro Park, where reservations are required for court use. Other tennis courts are available on a first-come, first-served basis without charge. For more on San Antonio tennis, contact the San Antonio Tennis Association at (210) 735–3069.

McFarlin Tennis Center
1503 San Pedro Ave., San Antonio
(210) 732–1223

San Antonio's premier tennis facility is McFarlin Tennis Center. The U.S. Tennis Association has recognized this site as one of the best public facilities in the country. The center was designed in 1974 and offers 22 lighted hard tennis courts as well as a pro shop. The facility offers lessons and clinics as well as leagues for adult play. The San Antonio Tennis Association sponsors tournaments at the center throughout the year.

San Antonio Parks and Recreation Department
(210) 207–PARK
www.ci.sat.tx.us/sapar

The San Antonio Parks and Recreation Department also operates tennis courts throughout the city at the following parks:

Arnold
1011 Gillette Rd., San Antonio

Benavides
1500 Saltillo St., San Antonio

Brackenridge
3500 N. St. Mary's, San Antonio

Camargo
5500 Castroville Rd., San Antonio

Colins Gardens
601 S. Park, San Antonio

Copernicus
5003 Lord Rd., San Antonio

Cuellar
5626 San Fernando St., San Antonio

Dafoste
210 Dafoste Ave., San Antonio

Dawson
2500 E. Commerce St., San Antonio

Escobar
1400 S. Zarzamora St., San Antonio

Flores
743 Flores St., San Antonio

Forge
1900 W. Pyron Ave., San Antonio

Garza
5627 Seacroft St., San Antonio

Highland
900 Rigsby Ave., San Antonio

J Street
800 J St., San Antonio

Kennedy
3101 Roselawn Rd., San Antonio

Lady Bird Johnson
10700 Nacogdoches Rd., San Antonio

Las Palmas
503 Castroville Rd., San Antonio

Martinez
200 Merida St., San Antonio

Martin Luther King
3503 M. L. King Dr., San Antonio

Monterrey
5906 W. Commerce St., San Antonio

New Territories
9023 Bowen Dr., San Antonio

Normoyle
800 Culberson Ave., San Antonio

Oakhaven
16400 Parkstone Blvd., San Antonio

Palm Heights
1201 Palo Alto Rd., San Antonio

Palo Alto
1500 Palo Alto Rd., San Antonio

Pittman Sullivan
1100 Iowa St., San Antonio

Rosedale
303 Dartmouth St., San Antonio

Royalgate
5900 Windy Hill Dr., San Antonio

San Juan Brady
2307 S. Calaveras, San Antonio

Southside Lions
900 Hiawatha St., San Antonio

Tejeda
500 Division Ave., San Antonio

Villa Coronado
10420 Renova St., San Antonio

West End
1400 Menchaca St., San Antonio

Windsor
2300 Ingleside Dr., San Antonio

Volleyball

Fatso's Sports Garden
1704 Bandera Rd., San Antonio
(210) 432–0121
This popular sports bar is best known as a place to kick back and enjoy happy hour while watching big-screen TV sports. However, for those looking for more active diversions, Fatso's has six sand volleyball courts. The bar hosts leagues nightly and offers the courts for rental.

Gunn Sports Club
12001 Wetmore Rd., San Antonio
(210) 545–2700
This sports club offers San Antonio's largest number of volleyball courts, both sand and clay varieties. Call ahead—these courts are frequently used for league play.

Spectator Sports

Basketball
Baseball
Football
Golf Tournaments
Ice Hockey
Rodeo
Running/Marathons
Thoroughbred Racing

Spectator sports in San Antonio can be divided into two eras—before 1973 and after 1973. Before 1973, it was a toss-up as to whether the biggest game in town was college football or minor-league baseball. In 1973, the San Antonio Spurs moved to town, bringing the unmistakable aura of big-time sports to the Alamo City. That year began a series of developments, each of which solidified the city's infatuation with the professional basketball team: In 1976 the Spurs became part of the National Basketball Association; in 1993 the Alamodome opened as the Spurs' home court. The peak of Spurs worship occurred in 1999, when the team won its first NBA championship. Indirectly, other sports besides basketball have benefited from the Spurs' popularity, too. Let's face it, San Antonians just love their sports.

Basketball

San Antonio Spurs
Alamodome
100 Montana St., San Antonio
(210) 554-7700
SBC Center
Houston and Callaghan Rds., San Antonio
(210) 554-7799
www.nba.com/spurs/

It's hard to overestimate the impact that the Spurs have had in San Antonio. Particularly since 1976, when the team joined the NBA, fan interest has been very high. In the beginning, the focus was on George Gervin, the sweet-shooting guard who led the team for nine seasons, beginning in 1973 when he won a spot on the All-Rookie team of the American Basketball Association. When the Spurs hit the big time in 1976, the "Iceman," as Gervin was affectionately known, continued his winning ways, earning NBA All-Star honors for nine consecutive seasons. He was the NBA's scoring leader in 1978, 1979, 1980, and 1982, and still holds the NBA record for the most points scored in a single quarter—33 points. He also holds numerous team records—most points scored, most free throws made, most field goals made, to name a few. His No. 44 jersey was retired by the Spurs after he left the NBA in 1986. Today Gervin remains one of only three such Spurs players to be so honored. In 1995, he became one of four charter members of the San Antonio Sports Hall of Fame.

Spur mania rules in San Antonio!
PHOTO: PARIS PERMENTER & JOHN BIGLEY

236

The Alamodome was the home court of the San Antonio Spurs. PHOTO: BOB MAXHAM, COURTESY OF THE SAN ANTONIO CONVENTION AND VISITORS BUREAU

Despite the Iceman's heroics, which led the Spurs to five division titles, the thrill of winning it all eluded the team and their loyal fans until the 1999 season. Inspired by longtime center David Robinson and Tim Duncan, the Spurs put together a sterling season, which they topped off by winning the World Championship series. It was San Antonio's first major sport championship, and the city reacted with predictable adulation. Although the Spurs haven't won another championship since 1999, they remain among the NBA's elite teams and are still the hottest ticket in town.

The Spurs have played in the Alamodome since the 1993–94 season. In fact, their first home game in the Alamodome set an NBA record for attendance—some 36,523 fans attended. In recent seasons, the Spurs have drawn nearly one million fans per year to their home court. Although the team will move into a new structure for the 2002–03 season, the Alamodome has served them well. The $186-million multipurpose dome was built with flexibility in mind, and in addition to Spurs games has hosted conventions, business conferences and trade shows, concerts and performances, and other sporting events such as NCAA football's Sylvania Alamo Bowl and several National Football League pre-season games. It has a striking facade with a cable-suspension roof and can be configured to best accommodate whatever event is in progress. It is located in downtown San Antonio, near the Henry B. Gonzales Convention Center and the River Walk area.

The Spurs' new home, the SBC Center, located near Freeman Coliseum a few miles north of downtown, promises to raise the excitement level at Spurs games. It offers a more intimate viewing environment—all the seats are much closer to the action on the court. A facility built with fans, particularly NBA fans, in mind, it will include the

Fan Fiesta area featuring video games and a Tex-Mex–styled courtyard with food kiosks, picnic tables, and plenty of shade. With the new venue and the recent contract signings of stars Tim Duncan and David Robinson, the future looks like smooth ridin' for the Spurs.

Spurs' tickets are easy to get—but buy early. You can charge by phone at (210) 224–9600 or buy online at www.tickemaster. com. Tickets cost from $10 to $60.

Season tickets for Spurs games range from $675 to a whopping $18,000 for floor seats. To buy season tickets, call (210) 554–7799 on weekdays or visit www.nba.com/spurs.

Baseball

San Antonio Missions
Wolff Stadium
5757 Hwy. 90 W., San Antonio
(210) 675–7275
www.samissions.com

As members of the Texas League, the Missions have been around in one form or another for more than 100 years. Until 2001, the team had been the AA affiliate of the Los Angeles Dodgers of the National League. Currently, it is part of the Seattle Mariners organization. The team has a proud past, winning championships in 1897, 1908, 1933, 1950, 1961, 1964, and 1997. A host of Missions players went on to become major league stars, among them Brooks Robinson, Joe Morgan, Pedro Martinez, Mike Piazza, Orel Hershiser, and Fernando Valenzuela. Before Municipal Stadium (since renamed for longtime Mission patron and former city mayor, Nelson W. Wolff) opened in 1994, the Missions played for 26 seasons at V.J. Keefe Stadium on the campus of St. Mary's University. Longtime fans of the Missions wax nostalgic about attending night games there. Wolff Stadium is located west of the downtown area, on U.S. Highway 90 at Callaghan Road; it seats 6,300 (with an additional 3,000 more on the grass beyond the outfield walls) and also boasts 14 skyboxes. One unique aspect of the park is the presence of two bell towers, which mirror a feature of long-gone Mission Field, where the team played between 1947 and 1968.

Games at Wolff Stadium usually begin at 7:05 P.M., Monday through Saturday. Sunday games usually begin at 6:05 P.M. However, you may want to check game times by calling the number above. Advance or same-day tickets can be purchased at the ticket window on the first-base side of the stadium. Tickets can be purchased for any future home game through the fifth inning. For additional information call (210) 675–PARK. Advance tickets may also be purchased by calling Ticketmaster or visiting its Web site at ticketmaster.com. Tickets cost $4.50 to $8.00.

Smoking is not allowed inside the stadium but is permitted on the concourse area and on the left field berm. A spacious parking lot can accommodate up to 2,600 vehicles; additional parking is located at Mateo Camargo Park. Wheelchair-accessible seating is available in sections 100, 101, 102, 113, 114, 115, 116, 209, 210, and on the concourse. Wolff Stadium hosts numerous food and drink concessions.

Football

College Football

Trinity University Tigers
Trinity University
715 Stadium Dr., San Antonio
(210) 999-8447
www.trinity.edu/athletics/

The Tigers play NCAA Division III football in the Southern Collegiate Athletic Conference. They have enjoyed considerable success, earning SCAC Championships in 1993, 1994, 1995, 1996, 1997, 1998, 1999, and 2000, and are led by the winningest coach in Trinity University history, Steve Mohr. Home games are played at Trinity's on-campus stadium and are well-attended by parents, students, and other avid football fans. The games feature lots of team spirit and pretty good football, too. Admission to games is free.

Pro Football

San Antonio Thunder
South San Antonio Stadium
2515 Bobcat La., San Antonio
(201) 313-6606

When San Antonio businessman/dealmaker-par-excellence Red McCombs, former owner of the Spurs, bought the Minnesota Vikings a few seasons ago, many fans thought it would only be a matter of time before the NFL powerhouse was calling the Alamodome home. So far, that hasn't happened, so football fans must content themselves with lesser football venues. At present, there is minor-league football in town: the AAA-class Thunder is a member of the North American Football League and plays a schedule of games beginning in late July. Home games take place at South San Antonio Stadium. Most games begin at 7:00 P.M. To get to the stadium, drive south on I-35, take the Palo Alto Road exit, then go north on Palo Alto Road past the first traffic light,

Insiders' Tip

The San Antonio Sports Hall of Fame, located in the Alamodome, honors sports legends such as Cliff Gustafson, Rita Crockett, Pat Knight, Red McCombs, Joe Williams, and others. It's open to the public on Thursdays and Fridays.

then turn right on Bobcat Lane. The stadium is on the right-hand side of Bobcat Lane. Tickets, which cost about $5.00, can be bought at the gate. For season tickets and general information call (201) 313-6606.

Golf Tournaments

Westin Texas Open
La Cantera Golf Club
Hwy. 10 and Loop 1604, San Antonio
(210) 341-0823
www.golfweb.com/tournaments/r041

The Westin Texas Open (informally known as the Texas Open) has been a part of the Professional Golfers' Association tour for nearly 80 years, making it the fourth-oldest pro golf competition in the United States. Now held at the elegant La Cantera Golf Club, the event is more popular than ever. The 2001 WTO boasted a total purse of $3 million. The tournament typically draws large numbers of spectators, so advance tickets are a good idea. Individual or package tickets are sold through Ticketmaster (and ticketmaster.com).

La Cantera is one of San Antonio's newest and largest resorts. Located northeast of San Antonio, it's part of the huge La Cantera planned community, which will eventually feature residential, business, and recreational areas. La Cantera's original course, now named The Resort Course, was designed by Tom Weiskopf and Jay Morrish, a design team that has produced some of the top courses in the country. The Resort Course was laid out around an old stone quarry (La Cantera is "the quarry" in Spanish) and features native flora and fauna to ensure that golfers remember that they are playing in the heart of Texas. It is not unusual to spot a native wild turkey on the fairways. In 1998, La Cantera was designated an Audubon wildlife sanctuary, a rare honor for a golf course, due to its strong commitment to preserving the natural resources of the area. A second La Cantera course, designed by golfing legend Arnold Palmer, opened in 2000.

Ice Hockey

San Antonio Iguanas
Freeman Coliseum
3201 E. Houston St., San Antonio
(210) 227–4449
www.sa-iguanas.com

Come on now, ice hockey in San Antonio? Well, they laughed at the Wright Brothers, and probably at Bill Gates, too! When the Central Hockey League came to town in the early 1990s, there were doubtless a few snickers of disbelief at first. But now, after a few successful seasons in the league's Western Conference, the Iguanas have become a permanent, and popular, part of San Antonio's sports scene. The team plays at Freeman Coliseum, a venerable edifice seating 9,500 and located a few miles northeast of downtown. Over the years, the Coliseum has hosted all types of events, from the annual San Antonio Livestock Show and Rodeo to concerts starring everyone from Elvis to Menudo. In 1993, a chiller unit was installed, making it possible to turn the central section of concrete floor into an ice rink. The next year, the Iguanas began their first season.

To get to Freeman Coliseum from the downtown area, take I–35 north to Coliseum Drive, turn south on Coliseum, then take a right on Houston Street. Tickets for Iguanas games can be purchased from the Coliseum box office by calling (210) 224-1374, from the Iguanas ticket line at (210) 227-4449, or from Ticketmaster at (210) 224-9600 or www.ticketmaster.com. Single-game tickets can be purchased after 5:00 P.M. on the day preceding the match. If you'll be in town for a while, discounted six- and nine-packs of tickets are available. Tickets for individual matches range from $9.50 for a corner seat to $16.50 for an up-close-and-personal view from behind the ringside glass. The Iguanas season runs from mid-October through March; play-offs are scheduled for April. Games. During the 2000–01 season, the Iguanas made the Western Conference playoffs but were eliminated after a tough 1-0 loss, removing them from the running for the Miron Cup.

Games are fast-moving, the athletes are talented, and the crowd creates an intense excitement. And after all, where else can you sit in air-conditioned comfort and watch a team with *four* team colors (purple, orange, black, and white)?

Rodeo

San Antonio Livestock Show and Rodeo
Freeman Coliseum
3201 E. Houston St., San Antonio
(210) 225–0612
www.SARodeo.com

If you are in town around mid-February you can take in some real down-and-dirty sports action, Texas-style. No, it's not championship wrestling, it's the San Antonio Livestock Show and Rodeo. This annual event is one of San Antonio's biggest happenings, drawing more than one million attendees every year. Activities include a rodeo, a Western parade, educational displays, a concert series, a carnival midway, and plenty of Western fun. Some 1,000 cowboys and cowgirls provide much of the entertainment at the rodeo, which includes competition in the fields of bull riding, calf roping, barrel racing, and other Western sports sanctioned by the Professional Rodeo Cowboy

Association (PRCA). Top country-and-western and Tejano entertainers are also featured. For the Livestock Show, cattle, sheep, swine, and horses are exhibited, judged, and sold. Competition for the Grand Champion animal in each division is intense, and the stakes are high.

The Rodeo is also home to the largest junior livestock show in the country. Cattle, sheep, poultry, swine, and horses are exhibited by hard-working teenagers from across the state, all hoping that their animal will be awarded the title of Grand Champion.

The Rodeo also boasts exhibits such as the Hall of Heritage, a look at the days of the Old West, and the World of Agriculture, showcasing the creations of some of the state's best cooks. Children instinctively head for the World of Animals, with its petting zoo, and the Carnival Midway, filled with old-fashioned games and rides.

Parking is at a premium in the Coliseum area during Rodeo, but the event offers a 15-acre paved, lighted, and secured parking lot a block away on Gembler Road. To reach the parking facility, exit at Coliseum Road, turn left on Gembler, and proceed to the parking area. From the parking lot, you may take the free SBC Rodeo Shuttle; the shuttle runs continuously. Cost of parking for the rodeo is $5.00.

Tickets to Rodeo competitions are $12, $17, $20, and $22, and include admission to the grounds. Ground admission only is $5.00 for adults, $3.00 for seniors, and $2.00 for children under 12.

Running/Marathons

San Antonio Marathon
San Antonio YMCA
1123 Navarro St., San Antonio
(210) 246–9622
www.samarathon.org

San Antonio's YMCA hosts the annual San Antonio Marathon each fall. The race follows a course from the Alamodome to Fort Sam Houston, through several city parks including Brackenridge Park, and ends at HemisFair Plaza. An added bonus for both runners and spectators is that the race course winds through several historic areas of the city. Previous races have had as many as 1,500 participants competing for cash prizes. The race attracts runners from around the nation and from other countries as well. Since the course is basically flat, it offers runners a chance to set a good pace and provides onlookers with unlimited vantage points within the city parks. Related events include a relay race, a 5-K Challenge, a 5-K Fitness Walk, a Kid's Klassic race, and an exposition held on the grounds of Fort Sam Houston.

Thoroughbred Racing

Retama Park
1 Retama Pkwy., Selma
(210) 651–7000
www.retamapark.com

Between August and October, the thoroughbred racing season at Retama Park offers the thrill of live horse racing and the chance to win big at the betting window. Opened in 1995, Retama is located a few miles northeast of downtown, just off I–35. It's a handsome, impressive structure with comfortable seating for up to 20,000 spectators among several levels, including outside and enclosed-seating areas. The

And they're off! Retama Park offers the excitement of thoroughbred racing. PHOTO: SAN ANTONIO CONVENTION AND VISITORS BUREAU, COURTESY OF RETAMA PARK

lower level includes good views of the action on the track as well as a food court. The grandstand level also has a food court as well as a large off-track simulcasting area where fans may watch and wager on races being run elsewhere in the United States. The clubhouse level is fully enclosed and air-conditioned and offers several dining options including the Terrace Dining Room, the Sports Bar, and the members-only Player's Club. Up one floor, the Press Box level is the site of the luxurious Turf and Field Club as well suites for race announcers and judges and, as the name indicates, the racing press.

Races are generally held Thursdays through Sundays in August, and Wednesdays through Saturdays in September and October. Although the live racing season is limited, the park is open every day for simulcast viewing and wagering. Retama

is also the venue for a variety of concerts and other special events. Post time is 5:30 P.M. on Sundays, and 6:45 P.M. the rest of the week. Gates open daily at 10:30 A.M.

Retama tries hard to be a family-friendly facility where parents will feel good about taking their kids for an evening's entertainment. Several special-event nights are scheduled during each racing season, often offering discounted prices on food and drink and activities such as pony rides and face painting for the children. The park does manage to project a more-or-less wholesome atmosphere, at least when there's live racing. It is quite a spectacle to see several thousand pounds of muscular animal churning around the turns and to sense the excitement of the horses and their riders. Even without the wagering, Retama can be a good bet for a fun outing.

Day Trips

North of San Antonio

Northwest of San Antonio

East of San Antonio

West of San Antonio

Mention "Texas" and some travelers might picture the Texas of the movies: miles of rugged, uncivilized land where outlines of cattle and lonely windmills stretch above the horizon. For others, the land near the Louisiana border might come to mind, a region of tall pine forests and bountiful lakes. Some might see the high-tech cities bustling with world-class attractions, shop-'til-you-drop opportunities, and a pulsating nightlife.

And they'd all be right. For years, Texas has promoted itself as the "land of contrasts." Rolling hills, rugged deserts, verdant forests, and sandy beaches are all found within its borders. For city slickers, everything from the culture of Dallas to the cowboy fun of Fort Worth, from the South-of-the-Border style of El Paso to the youthful exuberance of Austin, awaits within a few hours of San Antonio.

Nature lovers find plenty of fun as well, thanks to the rolling hills and fish-filled lakes of central Texas's Hill Country, and the beautiful beaches of the Texas coast.

All of the following destinations are within a two-hour drive of the Alamo City.

North of San Antonio

Austin

Maybe it's the college-student population that tops 50,000. Maybe it's the music industry that has made this city a haven for fans and performers alike. Or maybe it's just geography—the city has a downtown lake and is perched at the edge of a second lake, a rambling Hill Country one that offers everything from sunbathing to windsurfing.

Whatever the reason, there's one thing for certain: Austin is a town that doesn't want to grow up. Like a perpetual teenager, the capital city of Texas—83 miles north of San Antonio via I–35—is brash, sassy, and sometimes just downright silly.

The city is home to both high-tech industry and countless state officials, but residents use any excuse to toss off the ties and three-piece suits. They don elaborate costumes for an annual party in Pease Park to celebrate (believe it or not) the birthday of Eeyore, the pal of Winnie the Pooh. But those costumes are just a dress rehearsal for the Halloween party that's considered one of the nation's largest, complete with 20,000 to 70,000 merrymakers.

This carefree attitude is just one of the reasons that Austin is a great day-trip destination from the Alamo City. Less than a two-hour drive from San Antonio, the Texas capital offers visitors plenty of ways to spend their time: historic sites, museums, water sports on the lake, other outdoor activities, good restaurants, and a lively nightlife. There's even a spa and, in summer, the chance to see hundreds of bats fill the sky at sunset.

As the state capital, Austin is steeped in history. When Mirabeau B. Lamar, the president-elect of the Texas Republic, set out to hunt buffalo in the fall of 1838, he returned home with a much greater catch than a prize buffalo: a home for the new state capital. Lamar fell in love with a tiny settlement surrounded by rolling hills and fed by cool springs. Within the ensuing year, the government arrived and construction of the Capitol building began. Austin was on its way to becoming a city.

Today Austin is a city of 465,622, and it continues to prosper and grow. High-tech industries have migrated to the area, making this Texas's answer to Silicon Valley. But this big city still has a small-town atmosphere that makes it attractive to residents and visitors alike. Even Hollywood has taken notice of Austin—it's not uncommon these days to see film crews blocking off an oak-lined street.

Downtown, the Colorado River slices through the heart of the city. Once an unpredictable waterway, the Colorado has now been tamed into a series of lakes, including two within the Austin city limits. The 22-mile-long Lake Austin begins at the foot of the Hill Country and flows through the western part of the city into Town Lake, a narrow stretch of water that meanders for five miles though the center of downtown Austin. Several hotels overlook the beautifully planted greenbelts that line the lake shores.

Visitors who enjoy natural beauty and outdoor activities join locals along the shores of Town Lake, in the clear waters of Barton Springs swimming hole, or at Zilker Park, a favorite with joggers, picnickers, swimmers, soccer teams, and kite flyers. The park also features Japanese gardens, a rose garden, and a nature center. Chuy's, a restaurant at the entrance to Zilker Park, is a good place to stop for lunch. With its funky Elvis paintings on velvet and decor that includes everything from hubcaps to plastic dinosaurs, it's a fun example of Austin style and offers a menu of Tex-Mex delights. Beyond the borders of Austin lies nearby Lake Travis; in summer it's a great place to boat, swim, or just enjoy a sunny day.

A sightseeing excursion through Austin should start at the State Capital (11th St. and Congress Ave., 512-463-0063), truly a building of Texas-size proportions. Taller than its national counterpart, the pink granite structure is filled with history and legend; there are exhibits on the building and the state, and guided tours are available. A block south of the Capitol stands the Governor's Mansion (1010 Colorado St., 512-463-5516), the grand building that Texas governors have called home for more than 130 years. A free morning tour of the public rooms is offered Monday through Thursday, but call first because the mansion is sometimes closed for official events.

The most famous resident of the Texas Hill Country did not live in Austin, but he is remembered at the city's LBJ Presidential Library (2313 Red River St., 512-916-5137). This grand facility houses more than 35 million historic documents, films, and exhibits on Johnson's life and career. There's even a reproduction of the White House Oval Office.

LBJ's first lady was the powerhouse behind the Lady Bird Johnson National

The Texas Capitol stands taller than the nation's capitol building. PHOTO: PARIS PERMENTER & JOHN BIGLEY

The Austin Steam Train offers scenic views of the Texas Hill Country. PHOTO: PARIS PERMENTER & JOHN BIGLEY

Wildflower Center (4801 LaCrosse Ave., 512–292–4200), located on the south side of town. This unique institution is the only one in the nation devoted to the conservation and promotion of native plants and flowers. Bring your camera for self-guided tours of the blooming grounds.

Visitors from San Antonio will have seen the Alamo and heard the story of the predawn battle that fueled the fire for Texas independence. But while San Antonio is the site of that famous shrine, Austin now boasts a world-class museum that takes a closer look at the Alamo and the history of Texas. The Bob Bullock Texas State History Museum (Congress Ave. and Martin Luther King Blvd., 512–936–8746, www.storyoftexas.com), opened in 2001, is a showcase for the history of the Lone Star State from early European exploration to recent times. There are three floors exhibits, including the multimedia Texas Spirit Theater, the only one of its kind in Texas, and an IMAX Theatre that can show both 2-D and 3-D movies.

The second floor of the museum is focused on the Alamo. In the Revolution Theater, built to resemble the Alamo the day after the battle, a video told from the point of view of military leader Juan Seguin takes visitors back to the fateful day. Just outside the theater, a display showcases a letter written from within the Alamo's walls by William B. Travis urging the independence fighters to send more troops.

Another popular area attraction, located on the outskirts of Austin, is a historic steam railroad. Operated by the Austin Steam Train Association (512–477–8468, www.atcrr.com), this historic train, built in 1916, offers several routes. From fall through spring, the Hill Country Flyer travels from Cedar Park to Burnet every weekend. During the summer months, there are two routes from which to choose: the Bertram Flyer, winding from Cedar Park to Bertram every Saturday, and the River City Flyer, a Sunday trip that travels from downtown through the

Lower Colorado River Authority Parks

When it comes to parks, San Antonians have only one problem: selecting from a long list of excellent facilities located a short drive of the Alamo City. Many of these parks are part of a conservation and reclamation district that generates and transmits electricity produced by the powerful Colorado River. As such they are overseen by the Lower Colorado River Authority (LCRA). The LCRA also manages the waters of the river and assists riverside and lakeside communities with their economic development.But most people think of the parks when they hear of the LCRA. Scattered from the shores of Lake Buchanan, down through the rest of the Highland Lakes, and along the riverbanks of the Colorado River all the way to Matagorda County on the Gulf coast, these reservoirs offer vacationers a great place to relax.

The LCRA dates back to 1934, when it was created by the Texas Legislature to control the waters of the mighty Colorado River, which originates in northwest Texas. For years the river wrecked havoc on the ranches and towns that lined its banks. During the wet season, the river turned into a malevolent monster, threatening homes and businesses as it quickly rose from its banks. Through hot summer months, it was undependable as a water source for the farmers and ranchers of the area, diminishing to a trickle at spots during severe droughts.

To control the river, six dams were constructed; in the process the LCRA bought up thousands of acres along the riverway. In 1971, the Texas Legislature gave approval for those lands to become public parks. For two decades, the parks offered minimal services. It wasn't until 1991 that the LCRA began to pour resources into the development of these lands. Since that time, $12.3 million has been invested, along with $9 million from other sources such as the Texas Parks and Wildlife Department.

The result? A wealth of parks to appeal to families, hikers, scuba divers, birders, anglers, campers, and others. Canoeists and kayakers have especially benefited from LCRA's projects southeast of Austin to the Gulf.

Today the parks fall into several categories, each financed by electric and water revenues rather than tax money. Developed parks provide visitors with all the necessary facilities: rest rooms, showers, campsites, RV sites, playgrounds, and hiking trails. Recreation areas offer a more back-to-nature experience with only minimal facilities such as paved roads, hiking trails, fire rings, and compost toilets. LCRA Research Centers are sites with particular educational value. The LCRA also operates numerous parks in conjunction with Travis County, popular sites including Pace Bend, Mansfield Dam, Hippie Hollow and Bob Wentz/Windy Point. (For more information on these Travis County parks, call 512–473–9437.)

LCRA's parks begin along the shores of Lake Buchanan, in the upper reaches of the Highland Lakes. Contained by one of the largest multiple-arch dams in the world, Buchanan covers 23,000 acres—more than 30 miles in length and 8 miles in width. Here travelers can select from numerous recreation areas to enjoy summer fun from boating and swimming to quieter pursuits such as bird watching and hiking.

Small fishing and resort communities are found along Buchanan's shoreline, but miles of land are untouched by development. The land bordering this lake is the wildest of any on the Highland Lakes chain. Lucky boaters often see wild goats and javalina venturing down for a drink, as well as white-tailed deer, especially in the early morning and late-evening hours. From November through March, many American bald eagles live in the tallest trees along the banks. Surprisingly, the eagles are very tolerant of boats and one chartered boat tour takes visitors right up to the spectacular birds. At other times of the year, expect to see great blue herons wading in the shallows or perched atop stumps, eyeing passersby. The lake is also an angler's paradise, filled with striped bass, white bass, black bass, perch, yellow catfish, and crappie.

Many of those anglers are familiar with one of the most popular sites along Lake Buchanan: Black Rock Park (northwest of Burnet, 123 miles north of San Antonio). This location has just completed a major renovation, with improvements that include new campsites and rest rooms. Anglers can try their luck with either bank or boat fishing. Boats can launch without charge from the ramp at neighboring Llano County Park.

This park is also a favorite destination among birders. The northeast side of the lake offers one of the best opportunities to spot the American bald eagle from November through March. Other species often sighted include great blue herons, kingfishers, double-crested cormorants, roadrunners, osprey, red-breasted mergansers, common loons, horned grebes, and Bonaparte's gulls.

If you'd like to extend your stay at Black Rock, the park has 30 campsites, each with a table and grill. Campsites can fill up on busy weekends and they are offered on a first-come, first-served basis.

Birders also flock to another nearby park: Canyon of the Eagles Nature Park (north side of Lake Buchanan, 137 miles north of San Antonio). Named for the American bald eagles that nest in this wilderness area, this park offers back-to-nature activities such as bird watching from an observation platform to canoeing along quiet waters.

Another top LCRA park is Shaffer Bend Recreation Area (north side of Lake Travis, 95 miles north of San Antonio). This free park is one of the largest on Lake Travis, covering 523 acres. Shaffer is a favorite with day-trippers and campers looking for an undeveloped site that offers good lake views, plenty of wildlife, and various kinds of vegetation. The recreation area, located between Marble Falls and Lago Vista on the lake's north shore, is dotted with hills lined with dense cedar. From these peaks, you can enjoy good lake views at several points along the park road. The hills gradually give way to savannah shaded by oaks and pecan trees. Here you can also see the guayacan, a plant not usually seen east of Del Rio. A mile-long swimming area offers a chance to cool off after hiking.

While Shaffer offers undeveloped fun, downstream on Lake Bastrop two LCRA parks offer visitors more facilities. North Shore (north side of Lake Bastrop, 100 miles northeast of San Antonio) has campsites, RV sites, group pavilions, a two-lane boat ramp, a fishing pier, playgrounds, trails, and more. Extensive renovations on the South Shore Park (south side of Lake Bastrop, 99 miles from San Antonio) have also been completed. The park was totally renovated by the Texas Parks and Wildlife Department at the cost of $1.6 million. The LCRA leases both shoreline parks to Texas Parks and Wildlife and to meet the increased visitor numbers at these parks the agency revitalized the visitor facilities. Today the South Shore Park includes 38 recreational vehicle sites with water and electricity, paved parking and roads, more than 3 miles of hiking trails, a new bathhouse, a new pavilion, and improvements to the pier, boat dock and boat ramp. A day-use facility offers picnic tables, grills, a playground, a swim area, and volleyball nets.

For more information on LCRA parks, call (800) 776–5272 or check out the Web site at www.lcra.org.

historic neighborhoods of East and Central Austin.

When the sun sets on summer days in Austin, attention turns to the Congress Avenue bridge, location of the country's largest urban colony of Mexican free-tailed bats. The bats make their nightly exodus after sunset to feed on insects in the hill country.

Austin has plenty to keep visitors amused after the sun goes down. If it's nightlife you're seeking, you may want to stay in town overnight. Many of the city's clubs are found along downtown's Sixth Street, an entertainment district that's sometimes compared to New Orleans's Bourbon Street. But here blues, rather than jazz, is king. The area offers several lunch and dinner options as well, from the pricy steaks of Dan McKlusky's (301 E. Sixth St., 512–473–8924) to inexpensive Reuben sandwiches at Katz's Deli and Bar (618 W. Sixth St., 512–476–3354).

An increasingly popular nighttime destination is Austin's Warehouse District. This area, extending from Second to Sixth Streets and east-west from Congress Avenue to Shoal Creek, was once lined with dilapidated warehouses. Just over a decade ago, however, things started to change. Quiet evening venues moved into the area, soon joined by highbrow restaurants. But a 1993 change in Texas law that paved the way for brewpubs really changed the face of this district. Today several brew pubs are joined by nearby cof-

feehouses, fine restaurants, and plenty of places like the Austin Music Hall that showcase homegrown musical talent. Popular restaurants like Mezzaluna draw evening crowds.

Another reason to consider an overnight in Austin is Lake Austin Spa Resort (1705 South Quinlan Park Rd., 512–372–7300). Recently ranked one of the "Top 10 Destination Spas in North America" by the readers of Conde Nast Traveler, this resort rejuvenates guests with its spa treatments, healthy cuisine, and tranquil setting, providing a vacation for mind, body, and spirit.

For more information, contact the Austin Convention and Visitors Bureau at (800) 926-ACVB, see www.austin360. com/acvb, or stop by the downtown Visitor Information Center at 201 East Second Street.

Georgetown

Located 113 miles north of San Antonio on I-35, Georgetown has all the ingredients of small-town Texas in one neat package. Start with a small Texas county seat. Add a sprinkling of cultural attractions, a pinch of recreational sites, a dash of locally owned businesses, and a heaping helping of restored historic buildings. What do you have? The perfect day-trip destination from San Antonio.

Although it is the seat of the second-fastest-growing county in the nation, Georgetown continues to hang on to its cozy charm. It's still the kind of place where folks can walk around the square and be welcomed by a smile and a friendly nod. Now celebrating over a century and a half of small town life, Georgetown has found the secret to its survival in one important ingredient: preservation.

The community's small-town foundations date back to July 4, 1848, when Georgetown was founded on a 10-acre site donated by George Washington Glasscock Sr. and his partner, Thomas B. Huling. For years the sleepy town stirred to life only when the cotton or grain harvest came in from the fields. After the Civil War, however, the railroad sliced through those fertile fields. About the same time, the cattle industry rode in and the oldest university in the state relocated to this central Texas town. Georgetown was on the map and before long the streets were busy with the sound of construction. Local limestone was quarried to create elegant downtown buildings. In 1911, a Classic Revival–style courthouse took its place in the square.

Eventually Georgetown stepped out of the limelight, overshadowed by its big-city neighbor to the south, Austin. Stores closed, shopping habits changed, and downtown Georgetown became just a place to pick up necessities between trips to Austin.

No more. Today shoppers stroll the Georgetown's square, just as their predecessors did more than a century ago, looking for local bounty picked fresh from the fields. Fruits and vegetables glisten in the afternoon sunshine at the Farmer's Market, held on the square on a weekly basis during harvest season. The square is also a place to stroll cobbled sidewalks and visit the many small boutiques.

From 1982 to 1986, Georgetown participated in the Main Street project, renovating and rejuvenating historic structures to bring back the look of the 1890s. With the help of the National Trust for Historic Preservation, more than $8 million were invested in this project.

The investment paid off in both appearance of the downtown and its appreciation not only by the residents of Georgetown but by the nation. In 1997 Georgetown was selected as one of five national winners of the Great American Main Street Award. Co-sponsored by the National Trust for Historic Preservation's National Main Street Center, the award recognizes communities that have grasped the reins of preservation and guided their towns to stronger economic positions. Today that future is looking bright for residents who own and operate downtown businesses. For travelers, the square holds special appeal because of its many specialty shops.

The square really comes alive during seasonal special events, when visitors and residents saunter these streets for a little shopping and a lot of socializing. MayFair on the Square begins with traditional Maypole dance. Later, more than 150 artisans from the area sell their wares and demonstrate their artistic techniques. When all that shopping works up an appetite, food booths feature local ethnic cuisines — from fajitas to German sausage.

Beyond the square, the small town spirit continues, even as big-city recognitions have turned the spotlight on this community and its longtime institutions. East of downtown stands Southwestern University, the oldest college in Texas, and now also one of the most recognized.

Opportunities for visitors lie in every direction. North of the courthouse square, San Gabriel Park has served for centuries as a gathering site. Native Americans camped on the verdant grounds, pioneers met here, and early Georgetown residents congregated on the river banks for parades and meetings, including one event that featured speaker Sam Houston.

Today, park lovers enjoy shady picnics on the oak- and pecan-dotted grounds. Children romp on the playscape while fishermen try their luck from the grassy river banks. Crystal-clear springs bubble up at three sites on the park grounds, and often you can watch these little "salt and pepper" springs spewing up chilly spring waters.

West of the park at Blue Hole, where river waters reflect limestone cliffs, a revitalization project has made this beautiful spot again a place to be appreciated by residents and visitors. At Blue Hole, walkers and joggers hurry along the wide paths that wind beside waters as green as fresh spring leaves. At this deep-water swimming hole on the South San Gabriel, teens take daredevil plunges off the sheer cliffs into the watery depths and on quiet mornings anglers try their luck with just the sound of an occasional cardinal singing its friendly song in the distance.

Upstream, the North San Gabriel River has been controlled to create Lake Georgetown, a 1,310-acre lake popular with fishermen, boaters, water skiers, and swimmers. A favorite getaway with nature lovers is the 17-mile Good Water Trail, named in honor of the Tonkawa, a people who made the region near the San Gabriel River their home. Known for their flint arrowheads and tools, these Native Americans called this region takatchue pouetsu or "land of good water."

The trail is marked by mileposts as it snakes its way along the lake, passing through several historical points of interest. One such spot is Russell Crossing, later known as the Second Bootys Crossing, located near milepost one. In the late 1860s, Frank Russell resided at this crossing, and his rock house served as a postal substation. From saddlebags, mail was distributed to the local residents. Between mileposts two and three, hikers can see Crockett Gardens, a natural spring. A flour mill was operated here in 1855, and a few decades later the first strawberries in Williamson Country were grown in truck gardens at this site. Today the remains of the springhouse and corrals can still be seen.

Besides man-made attractions, hikers are also surrounded by natural beauty. White-tailed deer, coyote, skunk, raccoon, ringtail cat, armadillo and opossum thrive in this area. From February to August, the region is home to the endangered golden-cheeked warbler, a small bird that nests in older juniper trees.

Visitors can drive south on I-35 to reach Georgetown's subterranean attraction: Inner Space Cavern (west of I-35 at exit 259, 512–863–5545), discovered during road construction. The highway was built as planned, and soon afterward the cavern was developed for commercial use. It remains one of the most accessible caverns in the state due to its roadside location. Guests enter the cavern on a cog-railroad car, descending from the visitors center to a well-lit, easy-to-follow trail.

More than 80,000 years of dripping water carved Inner Space Cavern from the limestone. Today, visitors view discoveries such as the remains of Ice Age mastodons, wolves, sabre-toothed tigers, and glyptodons (a kind of prehistoric armadillo) as well as delicate cave formations on their walk through the cool cave.

Just across the highway lies another popular visitor attraction: the Candle Factory (I-35 north at exit 259, 512–863–6025). No matter what the season, it feels like Christmas at the factory. The large operation makes and sells to the public hundreds of styles of candles in an assortment of colors, scents, and sizes, from tiny votive candles to hand-painted candles, arrangements, and ceramic candleholders. On most days, shoppers can watch workers producing the candles, dipping tapers in the traditional manner.

Doing things the old fashioned way is just part of everyday life in Georgetown. A century and a half after the city's founders settled these banks of the San Gabriel River, Georgetown wouldn't have it any other way.

Contact the Georgetown Convention and Visitors Bureau (800–GEO–TOWN) for brochures on attractions, lodging, shopping, and special events. In town, stop by the Georgetown History and Visitor Information Center on the square at 101 West Seventh Street (512–863–5598) for information and assistance.

San Marcos

Ready to shop 'til you drop? Then set your compass north toward the community of San Marcos. Located 50 miles north of San Antonio on I-35, this city offers the largest outlet malls in Texas as well as plenty of hometown relaxation, outdoor recreation, and fun-loving festivals.

San Marcos's most popular shopping stops are located alongside I-35 at exit 200. This is the location of the Prime Outlets, an open-air mall that features more than 125 factory-direct shops. Luggage, shoes, leather goods, outdoor gear, china, kitchen goods, and other specialty items are sold. Along with stores, shoppers find plenty of special features: a food court, children's playground, free stroller use, wheelchair loans, and tourist information. The mall recently launched Super Senior Tuesdays, with special discounts for senior citizens.

Next door to Prime Outlets lies the expansive Tanger Factory Outlet Center (800-4-TANGER). Here you can shop for name-brand goods ranging from housewares and footwear to home furnishings and fine perfumes. And shoppers, don't miss downtown San Marcos, where you'll find many specialty shops selling everything from cigars to collectibles along the square.

Every doll and toy collector should make their first stop at the Millie Seaton Collection of Dolls and Toys (1104 W. Hopkins, 512-396-1944). For 30 years, Millie Seaton has collected dolls from around the world. The number of dolls grew and grew—until finally the avid collector bought a three-story Victorian home just to house the 4,000 dolls! Tours are by appointment only.

If you're a history buff, don't miss the Calaboose African American History Museum (Martin Luther King Dr. and Fredericksburg St., 512-353-0124; open by appointment). Housed in the first jail in Hays County, the building became known as the Calaboose. Later it served as a USO Center for African-American servicemen during World War II. Today the historic structure preserves the history of African-Americans in San Marcos from the nineteenth century to the present.

Another not-to-be-missed stop is the historic downtown. Take time to stroll through this scenic district, which has been transformed into a shopping and dining area. Here visitors can see the work of Texas artists, dine on Texas cuisine, and/or drink Texas beer or wines.

Recently San Marcos was recognized by the Texas Historical Commission and the National Trust for Historic Preserva-

tion as one of 39 National Main Street cities in Texas. San Marcos has been participating in the Main Street program since 1984, and during that time the program has helped garner the public and private reinvestment of more than $29 million in the city.

Save time for a look at the natural attractions that have given this town the nickname "San Marcos, A Texas Natural." Many of these attractions lie on the banks of the San Marcos River, an area that is considered by many to be the oldest continually inhabited area in North America.

The river is a popular swimming and snorkeling destination in the summer months, but year-round it is home to the Aquarena Center (I-35 at Aquarena Springs exit, 512-245-7575), a family park that features glass-bottom boat rides, an endangered species exhibit, the San Xaiver Spanish Mission, historic homes from San Marcos's earliest days, and plenty of educational fun. Admission to the park, which is operated by Southwest Texas State University, is free; there are fees for glass-bottom boat rides and group tours.

Nearby, Wonder World (I-35 at Wonder World Dr., 877-492-4654) offers a look at San Marcos's natural attractions both above and below the ground. Guided tours last nearly two hours and cover the entire park, including the 7.5-acre Texas Wildlife Park, Texas's largest petting zoo. But the highlight of the tour is Wonder Cave, created during a three-and-a-half-minute earthquake 30 million years ago. It was the same earthquake that produced the Balcones Fault, an 1,800-mile line separating the western Hill Country from the flat eastern farmland. At the end of the cave tour, visitors take the elevator ride to the top of the 110-foot Tejas Tower, which offers a spectacular view of the Balcones Fault and the contrasting terrain it produced.

For more information, call the San Marcos Convention and Visitors Bureau at (888) 200-5620 or see www.sanmarcos-texas.com.

Gruene

The pronunciation of Gruene is one of those things that sets a real Texan apart from visitors and newcomers. To sound like a local, just say "Green."

This former ghost town now booms with live music, outdoor recreation, and shopping. Gruene is a neighborhood of New Braunfels, located north of San Antonio along I-35. To get here, take I-35 to exit 191 (Canyon Lake/FM 306 exit), go west 1.5 miles and turn left at the first traffic light (Hunter Road), continuing for a half mile into Gruene.

Tucked under tall live oaks near the banks of the Guadalupe River, the Gruene of today is a "shop-'til-you-drop" kind of town, filled with antique stores and boutiques, alfresco restaurants, and historic buildings. The hamlet is quiet on weekdays, but on Friday afternoons the streets fill with shoppers, river rafters and tubers, and city folks looking for a small town weekend escape.

Gruene's days have not always been so prosperous. The town was founded in the 1870s by H. D. Gruene at a time when cotton was king. With its swinging dance hall and busy cotton gin, prosperity reigned until the boll weevil arrived in Texas, with the Great Depression right on its heels. Gruene's foreman hanged himself from the water tower, and H. D.'s plans for the town withered like the cotton in the fields. Gruene became a ghost town.

A century after its founding, investors began restoring Gruene's historic buildings, and little by little, businesses began moving into the once-deserted structures. Gruene eventually was placed on the National Register of Historic Places. Today all the downtown structures are filled with thriving establishments that range from restaurants to a potter to a general store. The commercial area of Gruene is a T-shape formed by Gruene and Hunter Roads.

The heart of the community remains Gruene Hall, the oldest dance hall in the Lone Star State. Since 1878, this joint has reverberated to the sounds of Texas music; crowds still line up to listen to all types of music, from gospel to country.

Nearby, the Gruene General Store brings back memories of Gruene's heyday as a cotton center. This was the town's first mercantile store, built in 1878 to serve the families that worked on the cotton farms. It also served as a stagecoach stop and a post office. Instead of farm implements and dry goods, however, this modern general store now sells cookbooks, fudge, Texas-themed clothing, and sodas from an old-fashioned fountain.

As the population of Gruene rose, so did the need for merchandise, and in 1904 the original general store moved to a new brick building. This was once the biggest store in Comal County, selling everything from lamp oil to caskets. Today the Gruene Antique Company fills this huge building with the wares of numerous vendors.

Located on the banks of the Guadalupe River, the Grist Mill Restaurant is housed in the ruins of a 100-year old cotton gin. In the early days, an explosion blew a hole in the side of the building that today serves fried chicken, chicken-fried steak, and other Texas favorites.

The Guadalupe River also fuels Gruene's most popular summer activities: river rafting and tubing. Several operators take visitors of all abilities—from families to daredevils—to one of the drop-off points on the Guadalupe. From there, you can drift beneath the tall cypress trees for hours.

Although there's always plenty going on in town, Gruene really springs to life during Market Days, the third weekend of every month. This arts and crafts festival attracts more than 100 vendors from across the state along with shoppers from Central and South Texas who come to look for everything from handmade furniture to hot sauces.

For more information on Gruene Hall's scheduled performers, see www.gruenehall.com or call (830) 629-5077. For information on Gruene, call (830) 606-1601.

To Market, To Market

The small communities surrounding San Antonio have always offered travelers plenty of reasons to visit for the day: charming restaurants, important historic sites, beautiful natural surroundings, the list goes on and on. But one weekend out of every month, many of these small towns tempt day-trippers with another fun activity: market day.

Just as in the days of the old-fashioned farmers' markets when townspeople came to buy and barter, today's markets are a place to come and socialize, to spend a few hours with local townspeople, and to enjoy a relaxing shopping atmosphere with a wide variety of goods. Unlike the markets of a century ago, however, the markets of today offer one-of-a-kind crafts, artwork, gourmet gift foods, and other specialty items.

Nearly every month, the community of Gruene, once an independent community but today part of the town of New Braunfels, holds market days. Tucked under tall live oaks near the banks of the Guadalupe River, Gruene is always a shoppers' town. But on the third weekend of every month from February through November, Gruene really springs to life. Its Market Days are arts and crafts festivals that attract more than 100 vendors from across the state as well as shoppers from Central and South Texas. A Christmas market takes place on the first weekend in December. For more information, call the Gruene Information Center at (830) 629–5077.

The small town of Wimberley is another Hill Country community that's known for its excellent shopping. With only 7,200 residents, the town boasts dozens of specialty stores, art galleries and studios, and accommodations ranging from river resorts to historic bed-and-breakfasts. Wimberley holds its Market Days on the first Saturday of every month from April through December. More than 400 vendors sell antiques, collectibles, and arts and crafts during these events. For more information, call the Wimberley Chamber of Commerce at (512) 847–2201.

North of San Antonio on U.S. 281, the community of Johnson City, best known as the hometown of President Lyndon Baines Johnson, hosts Market Days on the third weekend of the month from April through September. Look for antiques, crafts, collectibles, and food booths during this downtown event. And, even if you can't visit during the market, this historic town offers excellent shopping anytime and many bed-and-breakfast guest houses to extend your day trip for a luxurious weekend. For more information, call the Johnson City Visitors Center at (830) 868–7684.

New Braunfels

Located 33 miles north of San Antonio on I-35, New Braunfels combines a full menu of day-trip attractions with a rich history. Over a century and a half ago, the German Prince Carl of Solms, Braunfels, and a group of German settlers founded the city of New Braunfels, naming it for their homeland. Afraid of attack, the prince donned an iron vest, wearing it everywhere even in the sweltering summer heat.

After 11 months in Texas, Prince Solms returned to Germany to marry Sophie, a woman he had hoped would return to Texas with him. Sophie had no interest in coming to this frontier land, however, so the prince remained in Germany, leaving

New Braunfels in the hands of its German settlers.

Today you'll find that this community has never forgotten those German roots. It says Wilkommen throughout the fall and winter months, with plenty of festivals and fun for the whole family. While the city is a popular summer attraction thanks to its Texas-size Schlitterbahn water park, the cooler months also mean plenty of outdoor fun—both above and below the ground.

Drive out to Texas's largest cave, Natural Bridge Caverns (RR3009, southwest of New Braunfels, 830-651-6101, www.naturalbridgecaverns.com), for a look at what lies beneath the Hill Country. Natural Bridge is a limestone cave, formed by underground waters. It's a showcase of glittery stalactites and stalagmites, with huge flowstones and rooms larger than football fields.

Just next door, animals are the star attractions at Natural Bridge Wildlife Ranch (RR3009 next to Natural Bridge Caverns, 830-438-7400, www.nbwildlife ranchtx.com). Texas's most visited safari park (and the state's oldest) was established on the family's century-old ranch and now boasts species from around the globe. More than 500 animals roam these fields. You'll receive a bucket of food when you arrive, and the animals come right up to the car to greet their guests. Don't miss the expanded rhinoceros facility, a specially designed building to help rhinos endure the chilly winter days.

No trip to New Braunfels should overlook the historical side of this Hill Country town. Stop by the Sophienburg Museum (401 West Coll St., 830-629-1572) for a look at the early days of this German settlement. You'll see exhibits on founder Prince Solms at the Sophienburg, named for his bride.

The history of downtown New Braunfels is drawing the attention of many visitors, thanks to the Main Street Project and the Downtown Association of New Braunfels. Colorful plantings, a renovated fountain, old-fashioned lamp posts, benches, and the rehabilitation of many of the downtown buildings has brought renewed focus on this section of town. You'll even find walking-tour brochures available, highlighting stops in the downtown region.

One downtown stop not to be missed is the newly renamed New Braunfels Museum of Art (199 Main Plaza, 830-625-5636), formerly the Hummel Museum. The facility still showcases the world's largest collection of Hummel figurines on public display, but today you'll find a broader focus on folk art, crafts, music and decorative arts of the South and West.

Those decorative and folk arts hold a special place in New Braunfels, which is nicknamed the "Antique Capital of Texas." With dozens of shops, this community is a shopper's dream. In addition to the downtown area, there are shops along I-35 and in neighboring Gruene. Art lovers find plenty of temptation at the local small galleries, and bargain hunters flock to New Braunfels Marketplace (I-35 at exits 187 and 189, 830-620-6806), with outlet shops that draw busloads of shoppers from as far as Dallas and Houston.

So that visitors don't literally shop 'til they drop, the city is home to many varied restaurants. Oma's Haus (541 Rte. 46 S., 830-625-3280) serves moderately priced German dishes as well as Texas favorites; New Braunfels Smokehouse (Rte. 46 and U.S. 81, 830-625-2416) specializes in barbecued sausage.

All these attractions and more make New Braunfels a special place to visit any time of year, but in November this town really starts to oompah. Special events held in November and December promise weekend after weekend of getaway fun. The biggest blowout is Wurstfest, a 10-day "Salute to Sausage" in early November. One of the top German celebrations in the nation, Wurstfest celebrates with sausage, strudel, suds, and plenty of song.

But the fun doesn't end with Wurstfest. Festtage (Holidays) in New Braunfels includes a myriad of special events including Weihnachtsmarkt, a German Christmas shopping market, and the Christmas Showcase of Arts and Crafts, scheduled for late November.

New Braunfels is a good destination year-round, whether your interests are shopping or spelunking. And, unlike Prince Solms, you can leave your iron vest at home. You'll find the locals are very friendly.

For more information on New Braunfels attractions, call the New Braunfels Chamber of Commerce at (800) 572-2626.

Northwest of San Antonio

Enchanted Rock State Natural Area

Enchanted Rock looms over the Texas hillside like a massive bald mountain, an enormous dome of pink granite that rises 325 feet above the small stream flowing at its base. Covering over a square mile, the formation is second in size only to Georgia's Stone Mountain.

Located northwest of San Antonio near Fredericksburg, in the heart of the Hill Country, Enchanted Rock can be reached via U.S. 281 (to Johnson City) and U.S. 290 (west to Fredericksburg). In Fredericksburg, follow Route 965 for 18 miles to this unique geological formation.

Over the years, rumors about the rock have been plentiful: it glows in the dark, human sacrifices were held on its smooth granite surface, it moans at night, it hides veins of gold and diamonds, and it is haunted. Everything about the rock, from its name to its legends, is enchanted.

The land here is covered with live oaks, sharp rock formations and steep hills that jut from the land. No hills in the area compare to this granite monolith, though, which catches the attention of travelers even miles away. Today, the park is a favorite playground for rock climbers, backpackers, and even sedentary tourists who don't mind a lung-expanding walk up the dome for a look at mile after mile of rural Texas.

The story of Enchanted Rock dates back over a billion years, when underground upheavals created the rock. When it was first formed, the giant dome was covered by dirt. The actual face of the rock appeared on the scene about 600 million years ago, when erosion removed all the sediment and left the bald mountain exposed.

Over the years, the rock has been heated and cooled so many times that giant cracks have been left in the surface, giving the appearance of giant sheets of rock that look like they're ready to flake off and slide down the mountain. This heating and cooling process continues every day, and it's said to be accountable for the noises that come from the rock in the dark, cool hours of the night.

Native Americans believed that those creaking sounds came from a less worldly source. A legend told of a young Indian woman who was brought to the apex of the stone by her father, an ambitious chieftain. Eager to win the favor of his

> ## Insiders' Tip
> The best times to visit Enchanted Rock are spring and fall, when temperatures are moderate and visibility is high.

gods, he sacrificed his daughter. Too late he learned that the offering was condemned. As punishment, the gods commanded his unhappy spirit to wander forever the surface of Enchanted Rock.

Not all the tales of Enchanted Rock are fiction, however. Near the summit, a bronze plaque recounts the escape of Texas Ranger Captain Jack Hays from the Comache in 1841. Surprised and cut off from his companions, Hays fled up the rock and hid in one of the cracks that cover its surface, pursued by the angry Comache, who were convinced that Hays had violated the sanctity of their sacred mountain. The ranger managed to avoid capture and, thanks to his superior weapons, killed so many Comanche that the rest quickly abandoned the chase when Hays' companions arrived on the scene.

Today the face of Enchanted Rock is little changed from those pioneer days. Although at first glance the granite appears to be barren of any plant life, scattered shallow pools of rainwater grow wild onion and lichen, and several small trees grow near the summit.

Wildlife is also found here. The collared lizard, a green, yellow, and red iguana cousin with a black-and-white collar, calls Enchanted Rock home. Many species of birds circle the rock, and most days you'll be able to see buzzards, miles away, circling a potential meal. Keep an eye out for mockingbirds, as well as hawks, doves and bobwhites.

The entire park is of interest to biologists, botanists and geologists who now know that Enchanted Rock is composed of granite. Years ago, however, speculators had different ideas about the rock. The promise of precious metals and gems lured the earliest Europeans to the vicinity of Enchanted Rock. The Spanish began organizing explorations of the area in 1753 after hearing reports of "a red mountain." Small samples of silver bearing ore were sent back to San Antonio for analysis, but the silver was found to be of inferior quality. Rumors of vast gold and silver treasures hoarded by the Indians continued to attract the Spaniards' attention. By the time settlers from the United States arrived in Texas, the folklore concerning Enchanted Rock dictated that the entire rock was a giant gold nugget. Later, Texas pioneer Stephen F. Austin said that experiments had proven that the hill was made of pure iron.

See the granite for yourself with a walk up the dome. Bring your best walking shoes for the trek. Except when wet or icy, it is a fairly easy climb, though, and the view is worth the effort. Experienced climbers can also scale the smaller formations located adjacent to the main dome. These bare rocks are steep and dotted with boulders and crevices, and their ascent requires special equipment.

If you'd like to extend your stay at the park, tent camping and primitive backpack camping is available. For more information on Enchanted Rock, call (915) 247-3903.

Comfort

Located 39 miles northwest of San Antonio on I-10, Comfort is a community with strong German roots and ties to earlier generations. Settlers were first planning to name the town gemuetlichkeit, meaning peace, serenity, comfort and happiness. Fortunately, they settled on the easier-to-pronounce name of Comfort.

That name still perfectly describes the atmosphere of this Hill Country community. The streets here are as busy today as they were a century ago, when customers would come in to the local establishments for kerosene, oil, and washboards. The only difference is that many of these historic structures now house antique shops, restaurants, and bed-and-breakfast inns instead of the feed, dry goods, and grocery stores of a century past. The downtown historic district boasts numerous buildings, and one of Texas's oldest general stores, the Ingenhuett Store, is still open for business, featuring a collection of historic photos of Comfort's early days.

Just down the street from the general store, the Ingenhuett family once owned the Ingenhuett-Faust Hotel. Today that historic buildings is the Comfort Common (818 High St., 830–995–3030), a combination bed-and-breakfast inn and antiques cooperative. Travelers watch small-town life from rocking chairs on the wide porches of the two-story inn. Day-trippers can shop for antiques in the hotel and in several outbuildings located in the shady back yard.

At one time, however, things were far from comfortable here. This town suffered a massacre of many of its citizens, an event called "the blackest day in the history of the Civil War." Comfort was first settled in 1854 by German immigrants who were followers of the "Freethinker" philosophy. These settlers felt an intense loyalty to their new country and its commitment to democracy and freedom of religion. When the Civil War broke out and Texas began to talk of seceding from the Union, the German immigrants strongly opposed secession, because of their feeling of allegiance to their adopted country and because they were against the institution of slavery. Some of the German farmers openly backed the Union government, an act that the Confederates considered treasonous. To make matters worse, the local residents of Comfort formed the Union Loyal League to protect themselves from Indian and outlaw attacks. A nervous Confederacy felt that the group might be a serious threat to their government.

Finally, martial law was declared, and the Texas Rangers were sent to order all males over 16 years old to take an oath of allegiance to the Confederacy. When many refused, farms and homes were burned, and some dissidents were lynched. Some accounts say as many as 150 citizens were killed. With these mounting troubles and threats to their families, a group of Comfort men decided to leave Texas and head to Mexico to wait out the war. A band of 60 left on August 1, 1862. They did not know that the Confederates had been told of their move by an informant. The Unionists were followed to the banks of the Nueces River before the attack began. When it was over, 19 Comfort citizens had been killed in battle. Nine others were captured, but they were later executed by the leader of the Confederates.

On October 18, eight other Unionists were killed while crossing the Rio Grande near the Devil's River. The bodies of these farmers and those killed on the Nueces River were left unburied until the end of the war. It was three years later when the remains were returned and buried in a mass grave in Comfort. The next year, on August 10, 1866, the first monument in Texas was erected at the gravesite to remember this grim battle. The Treue der Union or True to the Union Monument was a simple obelisk, inscribed with the name of the men who were killed. Outside of National Cemeteries, this remains the only monument to the Union erected in a state south of the Mason-Dixon line. The Treue der Union Monument is located on High Street, between Third and Fourth Streets.

For more information on Comfort's many historic attractions, contact the Comfort Chamber of Commerce at (830) 995–3131.

Fredericksburg

What's your idea of a vacation? An international trip to explore new cultures, music, and cuisines? A shopping excursion to seek out one-of-a-kind items? A romantic getaway, tucked in historic lodging, just you and yours? Or a fiesta, a chance to kick up your heels and enjoy a few carefree days?

In Fredericksburg, you'll have the chance to fulfill any of those vacation fantasies. This Hill Country community, located 66 miles northwest of San Antonio on U.S. 290, has something for everyone. To reach Fredericksburg, travel north on U.S. 281 through Blanco to Johnson City; turn west in Johnson City on U.S. 290 and continue to Fredericksburg.

There are several outstanding wineries in the Fredericksburg area, including

Grape Creek Vineyard (U.S. 290, 4 miles west of Stonewall or 10 miles east of Fredericksburg, 830–644–2710, www.grapecreek.com), Fredericksburg Winery (247 W. Main, 830–990–8747), Chisholm Trail Winery (2367 Usener Rd., 9 miles west of Fredericksburg on U.S. 290, 830–990–CORK, www.chisolmtrailwinery.com), and Becker Vineyards (10 miles east of Fredericksburg, off U.S. Hwy 290 on Jenschke Lane, 830–644–2681, www.becker vineyards.com). Wine aficionados should pick up a copy of the "Texas Hill Country Wine Trail" brochure, available from the Fredericksburg Chamber of Commerce and Convention and Visitors Bureau or online at www.texaswinetrail.com. The trail showcases 16 wineries throughout the region.

Or do you feel that fine art and sculpture might be more your style? You're in luck: Fredericksburg is home to many excellent galleries that represent nationally and internationally known talents. Whistle Pik Galleries (104 N. Elk, 830–990–8151), Fredericksburg Art Gallery (314 E. Main St., 830–990–2707), Beckendorf Gallery (519 E. Main St.), and many others offer shoppers unique opportunities to purchase original works of art.

This community is also a prime destination for day-trippers looking for antiques, gifts, books, and crafts. The shops along Fredericksburg's Main Street and nearby side streets offer travelers myriad shopping opportunities, no matter what their tastes. One-of-a-kind gifts can be found at shops like the Fredericksburg Herb Farm (402 Whitney St., 830–997–8615) and the Wildseed Farms Market Center (425 Wildflower Hills, east of town on U.S. 281, 800–848–0078, www.wildseed farms.com).

History buffs also find plenty of attractions in the town and its environs. For a look at early Fredericksburg, visit the Pioneer Museum Complex at 309 West Main Street. This collection of historic houses includes a 1849 pioneer log home and store, the old First Methodist Church, and a smokehouse and log cabin. Also on the premises you'll see a typical nineteenth-century "Sunday house." These houses catered to farmers and their families who would travel long distances to do business in town, often staying the weekend.

Have another look at Fredericksburg's rich history at the Vereins Kirche Museum at Market Square on Main Street. You can't miss this attraction: it's housed in an

Is that a steamboat on Fredericksburg's Main Street? Nope, it's the National Museum of the Pacific War, honoring the town's favorite son, Admiral Chester A. Nimitz. PHOTO: PARIS PERMENTER & JOHN BIGLEY

exact replica of an octagonal structure erected in 1847. The museum is sometimes called the Coffee Mill (or Die Kaffe-Muehle) Church because of its unusual shape. Exhibits here explore Fredericksburg's German heritage; there are also Indian artifacts from archaeological digs.

More about the town's early history can be learned at Fort Martin Scott Historic Site, located 2 miles east of town on U.S. 290. Established in 1848, this was the first frontier military fort in Texas. Today the original stockade, a guardhouse, and a visitors center with displays on local Indians are open to visitors; historic re-enactments keep the history lesson lively.

More recent military history is explored at the National Museum of the Pacific War (formerly the Admiral Nimitz State Historical Park) at 340 East Main Street (830-997-4379). Admiral Chester Nimitz, World War II Commander-in-Chief of the Pacific (CinCPac), was Fredericksburg's most famous resident. He commanded 2.5 million troops from the time he assumed command 18 days after the attack on Pearl Harbor until the Japanese surrendered.

The Nimitz name was well known here even years earlier. Having spent time in the merchant marines, Captain Charles H. Nimitz, the admiral's grandfather, decided to build a hotel here, adding a structure resembling a ship's bridge to the front of his establishment. Built in 1852, the Nimitz Steamboat Hotel today houses a three-story museum honoring Admiral Nimitz and Fredericksburg's early residents. The latest addition to the museum is the George Bush Gallery, showcasing the wartime service of the former president.

For a look at the life and times of another former president, drive west on U.S. 290 from Fredericksburg to Stonewall, site of the Lyndon B. Johnson National and State Historic Parks (830-644-2252, www.nps.gov/lyjo/). These combined parks span approximately 700 acres. The visitors center offers displays on LBJ's life, which include mementos of President Johnson's boyhood years. Guided National Park Ser-

vice bus tours depart for a look at the working ranch with an optional stop at a living history farm, operated like a 1918 farm, furnished in period style, and manned by costumed interpreters.

Just a short drive farther west on U.S. 290 is Johnson City, home to the LBJ National Historic Park (Ninth St. between Avenues F and G, 830-868-7128). The visitors center showcases the life and history of Lyndon Johnson and his ancestors and the role the family played in the Hill Country. Adjacent to the center lies the Johnson Settlement for a look at 1860s cabins that once belonged to LBJ's cattle-driving grandfather. Nearby the LBJ Boyhood Home is still furnished with the Johnsons' belongings and can be seen on guided tours. Admission is free.

If you want to extend your day trip into a weekend visit, Fredericksburg is the capital city of Texas bed-and-breakfast inns. More than 300 B&B accommodations are located in Gillespie County in everything from Sunday houses to local farmhouses to residences just off Main Street.

For more information on Fredericksburg, call the Convention and Visitors Bureau at (888) 997-3600.

Castroville

Imagine a place where the nineteenth and twentieth centuries join together, treating visitors to modern conveniences and comforts in an Old World atmosphere. Add to this a gazpacho of cultures, a blend of French, German, English and Spanish with a heavy dose of Alsatian heritage.

What you have is Castroville, located only 20 miles west of San Antonio on U.S. 90 West. This town, nicknamed "The Little Alsace of Texas," may be near the Alamo City, but in terms of mood and atmosphere it is in another world. The community was founded by Frenchman Henri Castro, who contracted with the Republic of Texas to bring settlers from Europe. These pioneers came from the

LBJ's boyhood home is preserved for visitors in rural Johnson City. PHOTO: PARIS PERMENTER & JOHN BIGLEY

French province of Alsace in 1844, bringing with them the Alsatian language, a Germanic dialect. Today only the oldest residents of Castroville carry on the mother tongue.

Traditional Alsatian houses sport European-style, nonsymmetrical, steeply sloping roofs. To have a look at this distinctive architecture, take a self-guided tour of Old Castroville. Pick up a free map from the Castroville Chamber of Commerce (802 London St.). This town boasts 97 historic homes and buildings, including Henri Castro's homestead, a 1910 meat market, an 1854 gristmill, and homes dating back to the earliest pioneers. The entire section known as Old Castroville is now a National Historic District.

But perhaps the best way to absorb the atmosphere of Castroville is with a stay in one of its bed-and-breakfast inns. The most famous is the inexpensive Landmark Inn (402 E. Florence St., 830–931–2133), operated by the Texas Parks and Wildlife Department. This inn was first a home and general store before becoming the Vance Hotel. Robert E. Lee and Bigfoot

Wallace, the famous Texas Ranger, were said to have stayed at the hotel that was renamed the Landmark Inn during World War II.

Today's guests select from historic rooms decorated with antique furnishings. The absence of telephones and televisions helps transport visitors back to the time when visitors to the hotel enjoyed a welcome rest from the stagecoaches traveling the Old San Antonio El Paso Road.

Even if you don't have the pleasure of staying overnight in one of the historic rooms, stop by the inn for a look at the museum, with displays illustrating Henri Castro's early efforts to recruit settlers, as well as exhibits covering early Castroville life. You can also enjoy a self-guided tour of the beautifully manicured inn grounds and have a look at the 1850s grist mill and dam and the old bathhouse.

With Castroville's rich history, it's not surprising that the community is a magnet for antiques dealers. Fifteen antiques shops dot the downtown area. Park and walk historic streets with names such as Paris, London, Madrid, and Petersburg, where you'll find shops offering furniture, glassware, china, pottery, and collectibles of all kinds.

Castroville's cuisine also reflects its varied history. La Normandie Restaurant (1302 Fiorella St., 830-538-3070) boasts an elegant French menu; Haby's Alsatian Bakery (207 U.S. 290 E., 830-931-2118) offers inexpensive Alsatian and German baked goods.

Castroville hosts many special events through the year. Every September, 75 antique dealers from around the country come to town for an antique show. On the second Saturday of the month from March through December, Castroville hosts Market Trail Days, a shopping extravaganza with everything from arts and crafts to antiques to food.

Whether you come to shop, tour, or dine, the local residents have one bit of Alsatian advice: "Kum Sah Castroville" or "Come See Castroville!"

For more information on Castroville, call the Castroville Chamber of Commerce at (800) 778-6775.

Wimberley

Looking for more shopping and outdoor fun? Just north of San Antonio, the community of Wimberley offers something for everyone. This day trip begins with a 35-mile drive north on U.S. 281 to just south of the town of Blanco. Turn east on Route 32 and continue to Route 12, your turnoff for Wimberley. Bring along your camera for the drive that's often cited as one of the most scenic in the Lone Star State: the Devil's Backbone. It stretches along Route 32 from the little community of Fischer to the intersection with Route 12. There aren't any steep climbs or stomach-churning lookouts; a high ridge of hills provides a gentle drive with excellent views along the way. At the end of the Devil's Backbone, Route 32 intersects with Route 12, and the road drops from the steep ridge to a fertile valley where the Blanco River and the town of Wimberley are nestled.

The small town of Wimberley boasts dozens of specialty stores, art galleries and studios, and accommodations ranging from river resorts to historic bed-and-breakfasts. The busiest time to visit is the first Saturday of the month, from April through December. This is Market Day, when hundreds of vendors set up to sell antiques, collectibles, and arts and crafts. Even if you can't visit on Market Day, you'll find plenty of potential purchases at the shops on the square and surrounding area.

Many spring visitors come to enjoy the town's two water sources: the Blanco River and clear, chilly Cypress Creek. Both are filled with inner-tubers and swimmers during hot summer months. During the spring, the waterways provide a temporary home for campers and vacationers who stay in resorts and cabins along the shady water's edge.

Family travelers especially appreciate Wimberley's popular Pioneer Town (7-A Ranch Resort, 512-847-2517), located one mile west of Route 12 on County Road 178. Visitors can see a medicine show, tour a general store museum, or spend some time at the town jail in this Wild West village. Stop by the free General Store Museum for a look at the items used by early settlers, from shot loaders to bath tubs. You might feel like a time traveler as you leave the highway for roads lined with hitching posts and return to the early days of this region.

For more information, call the Wimberley Chamber of Commerce at (512) 847-2201.

Boerne

Boerne is located 22 miles northwest of San Antonio on I-10. Boerne (pronounced "Bernie") was founded in 1847 by German immigrants, members of the same group who settled nearby New Braunfels. They named the town for author Ludwig Borne, whose writings inspired many settlers to leave Germany for the New World.

During the 1880s, Boerne became known as a health spot, and vacationers came by railroad to soak in mineral water spas and enjoy the clean country air. Although no mineral spas remain today, Boerne still offers a quiet country atmosphere and plenty of attractions to fill a day trip.

For many of those day-trippers, Boerne means shopping, especially for antiques. Many of the antiques you'll see reflect the German heritage that is so strong in this region.

Many of those shops are found along Main Plaza, the site of many of the town's historic structures. The perfect spot for a weekend getaway is Ye Kendall Inn (128 W. Blanco St., 800–364–2138). Located on the main plaza, this historic inn dates back to 1859; today's guests find all the modern comforts in historic rooms filled with period antiques. If you can't make this a weekend getaway, budget some time to stop by the inn's village of shops and its Limestone Grille (128 W. Blanco St., Main Plaza), an eclectic restaurant featuring Southwestern, Cajun, Northern Italian and classic French influences. Next door, the Coffee Cafe serves coffees from around the globe as well as breakfast and lunch.

In summer the Main Plaza hosts Abendkonzerte, concerts performed by the Boerne Village Band. For nearly 140 years this German band (the oldest continuously active German band in the country and the oldest in the world outside of Munich) has entertained residents and visitors with their Old World sound.

Outdoor lovers will be thrilled with Boerne's many natural attractions, located both above and below ground. Cave Without a Name (325 Kreutzberg Rd., 830–537–4212, www.cavewithoutaname. com) is a 50-million-year-old cavern with many beautiful formations. A 45-minute tour takes you through a series of rooms, including one with Texas-size stalagmites. Natural attractions are found aboveground as well. Cibolo Nature Center (Boerne City Park, Rte. 46 at Cibolo Creek, 830–249–4616) preserves some of the nat-ural habitat of this area with a reclaimed prairie and reclaimed marsh. You'll find several walking trails, including a one-mile historic farm trail, a quarter-mile prairie trail, and a half-mile marsh loop. These areas are filled with native plants as well as birds and animals native to the Hill Country. Look for great horned owl, opossum, white-tailed deer, and cottontail rabbits.

Outdoor lovers will also find plenty of fun at the Guadalupe River State Park (Park Road 31, 830–438–2656), located 13 miles east of Boerne on Route 46. Swim in the cool waters of the Guadalupe River or try to spot wildlife, which ranges from coyotes to the endangered Golden-Checked Warbler. You can turn your day trip into a weekend excursion by camping here (both tent and RV camping sites are available).

In the mood for something a little more luxurious? How about the 46-room Guadalupe River Ranch (800–460–2005, www.guadaluperiverranch.com)? This 377-acre resort is perched on a bluff overlooking a bend in the Guadalupe River. Guests can spend a day adventuring in the hill country then come back to the rustic elegance of the ranch for a gourmet dinner or to unwind in the luxurious spa.

If golf's your game, head over to Tapatio Springs Golf Resort and Conference Center (800–999–3299, www.tapatio. com), located 22 miles northwest of San Antonio. This hotel is home to one of the nation's best resort courses, with 27 holes of championship golf.

History buffs will also find plenty of activity in Boerne. On Saturday and Sunday afternoons, tour the Kuhlmann-King Historical House and the Graham Building (Main St. and Blanco Rd., 830–249–2030). The home was built by a local businessman in 1885 for his German bride, and today it is staffed by volunteer docents who provide weekend tours. Next door, the Graham Building, an 1880s office building, is today a museum and store with exhibits on local history.

Farming was important to the history of this community, and its contribution is remembered at the Agricultural Heritage Center (Rte. 46, 1 mile from Main St., 830-249-8000). This museum features farm and ranch tools used by pioneers in the late nineteenth and early twentieth centuries, including a working steam-operated blacksmith shop. Six acres surrounding the museum are dotted with hand-drawn plows, wagons, early tractors and woodworking tools.

For more information on Boerne attractions, give the Chamber of Commerce a call at (888) 842-8080 or see www.boerne.org.

Kerrville

From Boerne, continue north on I-10 then turn west on Route for another 19 miles. With its surrounding hills and the clear waters of the Guadalupe River, Kerrville is an outdoor lover's paradise, especially during the spring months. Make time for a visit to the Kerrville-Schreiner State Park, which offers seven miles of hiking trails, as well as fishing and swimming in the Guadalupe River. If you'd like to extend your day trip, screened shelters and campsites are also available. You can learn more about the flora and fauna of the Hill Country with a stop at the Riverside Nature Center. This informative center includes walking paths, a wildflower meadow, butterfly gardens, and gardens featuring native grasses, trees, and flowers.

Those rolling hills have also been the inspiration for many artists, so it's not surprising that Kerrville is home to many internationally recognized artists. For a look at world-class Western art, make a visit to the Cowboy Artists of America Museum (1550 Bandera Hwy./Rte. 173, 830-896-2553, www.caamuseum.com). This hilltop museum features Western-themed paintings and sculpture by members of the Cowboy Artists of America.

Kerrville's appreciation for the arts continues in its revitalized downtown, where antiques shops and art galleries offer excellent shopping. The high quality of the artwork available in Kerrville attests to the community's status as a magnet for artists from across the Southwest.

Whatever type of art you're looking for, you'll find it at one of the festivals for which Kerrville is known throughout the state. The Texas State Arts and Crafts Fair, scheduled for late May, draws more than 200 artists from across the state. No manufactured, mass-produced, or molded items are permitted, and all the artisans must reside in Texas to participate.

Mark your calendar for the annual Kerrville Folk Festival, held from late May through early June. This Texas-size festival features songwriters and their bands from Texas as well as numerous other states. One of Texas's best-loved music gatherings, this extravaganza of song is held 9 miles south of town at the Quiet Valley Ranch.

The ranches that surround Kerrville are as much an attraction as the city itself. One of the best known is the Y.O. Ranch (800-YO-RANCH, www.yoranch.com). This famous ranch once spanned over 600,000 acres, covering a distance of 80 miles. Today the Schreiner family still owns the ranch, located in nearby Mountain Home. You can visit and tour the ranch for a look at its Texas Longhorns and many exotic species.

Every May, the Y.O. Ranch hosts the annual Y.O. Ranch Texas Longhorn Trail Drive, your opportunity to drive a herd of

Insiders' Tip

The early summer Kerrville Folk Festival is a favorite with campers who stake out their space on the ranch to enjoy a few days of live music.

Longhorns, cook over a campfire, and camp out like a cowboy. The trail drive is always scheduled for three days in late May, starting with an 1880's costume party, dinner and dance on Friday. On Saturday, participants ride horseback (or in a covered wagon) and herd the Longhorns through the ranch. That night, guests enjoy steak cooked over a campfire, then curl up beneath a blanket of stars. Reservations are required for this popular event.

For more about Kerrville's many attractions, call the Kerrville Convention and Visitors Bureau at (800) 221-7958 or see www.kerrvilletx.com.

East of San Antonio

Seguin

Many Texas towns boast nicknames, but Seguin, located 36 miles east of San Antonio on either U.S. 90 or I-10, must hold the title for most unusual monikers: "The Mother of Concrete Cities" and, later, the "Athens of Texas." In the nineteenth century, a chemist in this town, located east of San Antonio, held several concrete production patents, and his invention was used to construct more than 90 area buildings.

Today many of those early buildings still greet visitors to this community on the banks of the Guadalupe River. Seguin (pronounced "se-GEEN") was named for Lieutenant Colonel Juan Seguin, a hero of the Texas Revolution.

Seguin is a shady place that combines historic attractions with the natural beauty of its surroundings. Don't miss Starcke Park, the perfect spot for a picnic beneath towering pecan, oak, and cypress trees. Those pecan trees cover not just the park but the yards of most downtown residences, and several local pecan houses sell the nut by the pound. The town even calls itself the home of the "World's Largest Pecan," a statue located on the courthouse lawn at Court Street.

There are plenty of special reasons to make a day trip to this city of 19,000 residents. History and architecture buffs should plan a visit to Sebastopol State Historical Park (704 Zorn St., 830-379-4833), one of the best examples of the early use of concrete in the Southwest. Sebastopol, once a private home, was constructed of concrete with a plaster overlay. Today it is open for tours and contains exhibits illustrating the construction of this historic building and its restoration in 1988.

Other historic sites in Seguin are familiar to readers of the best-selling novel *True Women,* an epic tale than combines frontier heroism with love, murder, and war. Readers can pick up a free brochure at the Seguin-Guadalupe County Chamber of Commerce office at 427 North Austin Street to trace the path of this novel and visit the locations where the book's exciting events, from the Wild West Show to the saving of the horses from the flood, took place. Sites such as Courthouse Square, the King Cemetery, the Juan Seguin Gravesite, and the former Magnolia Hotel, one of the first structures that used concrete, are marked along the trail.

For other visitors, it's not the historic but the new attractions which make a day trip to Seguin special. Youngsters love Buffalo Roam, a drive-through animal park located on I-10 at exit 617. Here more than 40 kinds on animals, including buffalo, camels, zebras, antelopes, gazelles, and many exotic species roam the ranch, eager for a handout from travelers. Unlike many drive-through wildlife parks, Buffalo Roam (830-372-4747) has chosen to leave the natural vegetation—the mesquite trees, cactus, and oak. Although removal might have aided spotting of the animals, the unaltered setting gives visitors the chance to see the animals in a more natural habitat, with behaviors closer to what might be witnessed in the wild. Along the ride, Buffalo Roam provides an audiotape discussing the animals. After the drive, the Fun Farm Petting Pen offers young visitors the chance to get close to the smaller residents of the ranch and hand-feed the animals.

Another popular spot for families is the Wave Pool, located in Starcke Park East. In this 14,000-square-foot pool, youngsters can cool off under the Mushroom Shower or splash in the simulated waves. Nearby, the $100,000 Kids Kingdom Playscape makes an excellent stop for energetic young travelers as well.

For more information on Seguin, call (800) 580-PECAN.

West of San Antonio

Laredo

Silver and serapes. Pottery and piñatas. For a getaway that combines shopping with historic and cultural fun, it's time to make a run for the border. Laredo and its sister city, Nuevo Laredo, have enough shops, street vendors and markets to satisfy any souvenir hunter. And when it's time to take a break from the buying, you'll find plenty of attractions to turn your shopping excursion into a day or weekend of fun.

You might start your shopping in downtown Laredo, with its dozens of shops in the San Agustin and Mercado Historic Districts. This area has often been called America's largest urban outlet mall. Near the international bridge, wholesalers along Zaragoza Street entice shoppers with goods ranging from electronics to clothing and shoes to jewelry. Linger in perfume shops where you can purchase the world's famous fragrances at prices far lower than you might expect.

But, as enticing as the Laredo stores can be, the charms of its sister city act as a magnet for the dedicated shopper. Nuevo Laredo boasts an amazing procession of shops along its avenues. Here the air fills with the scent of roasted ears of corn sold from steaming carts, the sunlight glints off a jumble of silver-plated necklaces on a vendor's arm, a tablecloth salesman flaunts his wares like a bullfighter's cape.

Crossing the border is simple. Most travelers walk across the international bridge (parking is available on the Texas side near the bridge) and stroll to the tourist district, a convenience not found in any other border city.

In Nuevo Laredo, shopping runs the gamut of prices, from a dollar for trinkets such as yarn bracelets sold by street vendors to thousands of dollars for fine jewelry at top of the line shops. A memento of the border doesn't have to be confined to a stuffed armadillo or a bargain bottle of tequila; your selection is limited only by your pocketbook.

The main shopping district is along Avenida Guerrero, located just steps across the International Bridge. This street is also the home of Nuevo Laredo's top shopping destination: the New Market or Nuevo Mercado. The block-long, open-air market fills with shoppers daily. Two stories contain over 100 small shops selling everything from jewelry to serapes to onyx chess sets.

The shopping that ties these two cities are just a hint at the long history these communities share. Although the famed river separates the sister cities, little else divides the communities of Laredo and Nuevo Laredo. Originally, only a single city—Laredo—occupied the north bank of the Rio Grande. Founded by an officer of the Spanish army in 1755, it was one of the first settlements in the region. Following the Mexican War in the early 1840s, some families who wished to protect their divided land holdings made the decision to leave. Some family members remained in Laredo and others headed across the newly drawn border to found Nuevo Laredo, literally New Laredo.

Today, the Republic of the Rio Grande Museum (1003 Zaragoza St., 956-727-3480) traces the history of this movement. This unique museum, a must for history buffs, utilizes a historic structure. Constructed in the 1830s as a home, the building later served as the Capitol of the Republic of the Rio Grande, a country formed when Northern Mexico seceded from Mexico in 1839. The new state existed until 1841. Today the museum contains guns, saddles, and household belongings from the short-lived Republic.

Beyond the city streets lies a whole other side to Laredo—a place filled with desert wildlife, walking trails, fish-filled lakes and more. The Brush Country offers plenty of winter activities for travelers, regardless of their interest. Birders find more than 300 species on record in the Brush Country, including several rare species such as the white-collared seed eater, the red-billed pigeon, and the gray-crowned yellowthroat. Some popular sightings include the long-billed dowitcher, the purple martin, and the green kingfisher.

More interested in marine life? Anglers find plenty of challenge at Lake Casa Blanca, located 5 miles east of the city off U.S. 59 on Loop 20. This manmade lake is filled with black bass as well as blue and yellow catfish. The lake is also popular for boating, sailing, and picnicking. Not far from the lake lies the Casa Blanca Lake Golf Course, an 18-hole challenge that you can play year-round.

Whether you're in search of historic sites, exuberant festivals or non-stop shopping, one thing's for certain: Laredo is the place to make a little history of your own.

Contact the Laredo Convention and Visitors Bureau, (800) 361-3360, or see the official Web site, www.visitlaredo.com, for information on hotels, shopping, and dining.

Weekend Getaways

South of San Antonio
West of San Antonio
East of San Antonio

In addition to the many day-trip options from San Antonio, there are several destinations within range of the city that make for perfect weekend getaways. Many of these getaways lie to the south and west of San Antonio. When you head in those directions, you quickly move from the busy metropolis to the sparsely populated brushland and coastal plains. A trip to the Coastal Bend can combine the fun of a beach weekend with other back-to-nature activities like camping, birding, fishing, or hiking.

To turn your excursion into a "two nation vacation," don't forget the border towns. Along the U.S.–Mexico border, numerous weekend getaways allow travelers to enjoy an easy trip into Mexico. From the cities of the Rio Grande Valley to the sister cities of Laredo and Nuevo Laredo to ecotourism attractions of Del Rio and Ciudad Acuña, you'll find plenty of south-of-the-border charm with north-of-the-border conveniences.

South of San Antonio

Corpus Christi

One of America's 10 busiest ports, there's always something happening in this lively bayside town. To reach Corpus Christi from San Antonio, follow I-37 south for 145 miles.

The heart of Corpus Christi is Shoreline Drive, which boasts proud palms and spectacular views of the bay. Shoreline Drive's northern stretch is its most active, especially near the piers. Each of these piers bustles with life—whether in the predawn hours when the shrimp boats head out for their day's work or at midnight when night cruises offer anglers a chance at that trophy catch.

Attractions throughout Corpus Christi are offering travelers more reasons than ever before to plan a visit. Just over the Harbor Bridge, the U.S.S. *Lexington* Museum on the Bay (2914 N. Shoreline Blvd., 361-888-4873, www.usslexington.com) is now home to the Joe Jessel Mega Theater. This state-of-the-art theater has a three-story giant screen and is capable of showing IMAX productions. While you're at the ship, known as the most decorated aircraft carrier in U.S. Naval history, save time to take part in one of five self-guided tour routes. Wear good walking shoes for your tour of the *Lexington*, as you will climb the stairs that sailors once raced up and down during wartime half a century ago. Visitors can follow routes to the flight deck and bridge, the captain's quarters, the sick bay and engine room, and the hangar deck as well as other areas. Step into the flight simulator if you'd like to feel what it's like to be on a bomber planes making an attack and then coming in for a landing on the carrier.

If you feel like you recognize the U.S.S. *Lexington*, you very well might—the gray ship is somewhat of a star. If you saw the recent film *Pearl Harbor,* you saw the *Lexington;* the carrier has also appeared in the movie *Midway* as well as on the TV series *JAG.*

Corpus Christi is a port city with lots of marine activities. PHOTO: PARIS PERMENTER & JOHN BIGLEY

Next door to the *Lexington* lies the Texas State Aquarium (2710 Shoreline Dr., 800–477–GULF, www.texasstateaquarium. org), which showcases the aquatic animals and habitats indigenous to the Gulf of Mexico. Considered Corpus Christi's most popular tourist attraction, the aquarium has welcomed more than five million visitors since it opened in 1990. Its tanks are filled with nurse sharks, amberjack, beautiful coral gardens, moray eels, tarpon, rays, and more. The aquarium hosts several daily programs to help visitors gain a deeper understanding of these marine creatures. Three times a day, visitors can touch a small shark or a stingray, while several times daily guests can watch scuba divers to learn more about coral reefs and their inhabitants. Outdoors, young visitors enjoy touch tanks filled with small sharks and rays; the Otter Space, where playful river otters amuse visitors with their antics; and the Octopus' Garden, a marine-inspired playground dominated by a 20-foot tall purple octopus.

Another top family attraction is the Museum of Science and History and The Ships of Columbus (1900 North Chaparral, 361–886–4492). Recently the Ships of Columbus reopened, allowing visitors to step aboard life-sized replicas of the *Pinta* and the *Santa Maria*. The adjacent museum offers displays to fascinate all ages, covering everything from dinosaurs to Spanish shipwrecks. Don't miss the "Seeds of Change" exhibit, designed by the Smithsonian's National Museum of Natural History for the 500th anniversary of the European discovery of America.

And no visit to the coast would be complete without a look at America's longest national seashore: Padre Island. The drive to the island takes you past several excellent seafood restaurants and seaside accommodations. Several parks offer fun for all members of the family. Padre Island National Seashore is open year-round for beachcombing, fishing, and swimming, and also has a visitors center with exhibits on the region. Surfers will find wave action created by a surf pier at the J.P. Luby Surf Park on Highway 361, while campers can enjoy covered picnic areas and overnight hookups at Padre Balli Park on Park Road 22.

Weekend visitors to Corpus Christi find a full range of dining and accommodations options. Seafood, often caught that morning, is the specialty of many restaurants such as the moderately priced Water Street Seafood Company (309 N. Water St., 361-881-9448) and Landry's Dockside (People's St. T-Head, 361-882-6666). Accommodations in Corpus Christi include the Omni Bayfront (900 N. Shoreline Blvd., 800-843-6664), Omni Marina (707 N. Shoreline Blvd., 800-843-6664), and the Holiday Inn Emerald Beach (1102 S. Shoreline Blvd., 361-883-5731), the only hotel in downtown Corpus Christi with its one beach.

For more information, call the Corpus Christi Convention and Visitors Department at (800) 678-6232.

Rockport

Rockport is considered a bird-watching paradise, with over 500 species on record. For a weekend of communing with nature, take I-37 south from San Antonio

Insiders' Tip

When traveling across the U.S.-Mexico border, be sure to bring identification for your return trip to the United States. U.S. citizens do not need a passport to travel to Mexico.

for 145 miles to Corpus Christi. Continue across the Harbor Bridge and follow U.S. 181 north to Rte. 35 to Aransas Pass. In Aransas Pass, continue on Rte. 35 for 11 miles to Rockport.

Rockport's annual Hummer/Bird Celebration, scheduled for mid-September, features both fun and educational activities, from boat trips to butterfly feeding, although the real star of the show is the hummingbird, who stops here in a final feeding frenzy before the nonstop migration across the Gulf of Mexico.

If you visit Rockport during the winter months, the attention turns to the rare whooping crane, the five-foot-tall bird who make its home at the nearby Aransas National Wildlife Refuge (45 minutes northeast of Rockport, 361-286-3559). These statuesque birds, with a seven-foot wingspan, once numbered below 20 and were placed on the endangered species list. Today, their numbers have increased considerably, and naturalists excitedly make a head count every year, always on the lookout for a new chick.

After a day of bird watching, Rockport offers many activities to give you a break from the binoculars. Rockport Beach Park boasts more than a mile of sandy beach, with swimming, boating, fishing, and water sports. History buffs will also find plenty of activities in Rockport and nearby Fulton. The Fulton Mansion State Historic Structure (three miles south of Rockport off Rte. 35 at the corner of Henderson St. and Fulton Beach, 361-729-0386), completely refurbished by the Texas Parks and Wildlife Department, was somewhat of a futuristic home when first built in 1876. The house included central forced-air heating, and a central cast-iron furnace in the basement provided heat through a series of flues to false, decorative fireplaces in the main rooms. Hot and cold running water was achieved with a tank located in the tower attic. A gas plant located at the back of the house provided fuel for gas chandeliers.

Rockport and the Texas Coastal Bend attract bird lovers from around the world. PHOTO: PARIS PERMENTER & JOHN BIGLEY

For a look at even earlier coastal history, stop by the Texas Maritime Museum (1202 Navigation Circle, 361–729–1271), which traces maritime history from the Spanish shipwrecks off the Gulf Coast to the offshore oil industry. Nearby, the Rockport Center for the Arts serves as a showcase for regional artists.

Many of Rockport's accommodations are fishing cottages and furnished condominiums such as Key Allegro Rentals (1798 Bayshore Dr., 361–729–2333) and Kontiki Beach Motel and Condominiums (Fulton Beach Rd., 800–242–3407). Although many people use the kitchen facilities to cook meals, Rockport is also home to a wide selection of restaurants, among them the casual Boiling Pot (Fulton Beach Rd., 361–729–6972), which serves spicy seafood on paper-covered tables.

For more information, call the Rockport-Fulton Area Chamber of Commerce at (800) 242-0071.

Port Aransas

Not far from Rockport, lies Port Aransas—just "Port A" to most Texans—perched on the northern tip of Mustang Island. To reach Port Aransas, take I–37 south from San Antonio for 145 miles to Corpus Christi. Continue across the Harbor Bridge and follow U.S. 181 north to Rte. 35 to Aransas Pass. Follow Rte. 361 from Aransas Pass across the Redfish Bay Causeway to Harbor Island and Port Aransas.

One of the area's top attractions is Mustang Island State Park, the perfect place for a beach campout. The park offers a mile and a half of beach camping, and many visitors like to go horseback riding along the island's beaches.

Another popular activity is spending an afternoon out on the Gulf on deep-sea fishing cruise. Large tour boats, taking as many as 100 passengers, provide bait and tackle. Serious anglers looking for big game fish such as marlin and shark should book charter excursions for personalized service.

For a chance to see dolphins, stop by the Roberts Point Park on Highway 361. Dolphins often chase the ferries as they make their way across the ship channel. If you'd like to learn more about marine life, stop by the small aquarium at the University of Texas Marine Science Institute (Ship Channel, 361-749-6729); admission is free.

Another good way to see the local wildlife is a nature cruise aboard *The Duke* (Woody's Boat Basin, 361-749-5252). Travelers can take a two-hour nature tour to watch dolphins and birds. Families enjoy the dolphin watch, a tour scheduled throughout the day. Other cruises departing from Woody's include a sunset cruise and a sightseeing tour with a look at the U.S. Naval Station (home of the largest U.S. mine-sweeping fleet), the Lydia Ann Lighthouse, and the intracoastal waterway.

This city is also home to the Port Aransas Birding Center (Ross Ave., off Cut Off Rd.), part of the Great Texas Coastal Birding Trail. The center is landscaped with plants to attract migrating hummingbirds and also harbors a six-foot alligator and a family of nutria, members of the rodent family who nest in fallen reeds.

Port Aransas offers numerous lodging places—everything from resorts to condominium complexes to mom-and-pop motels that cater to visiting anglers. A longtime favorite has been the Tarpon Inn (200 East Cotter St., 800-365-6784), which dates back to 1923. Many families enjoy the conveniences of condominium complexes such as the Dunes Condominiums (1000 Lantana, 800-288-DUNE), which offers kitchenettes as well as resort amenities such as a pool and tennis.

For more information, call the Port Aransas Tourist and Convention Bureau at (800) 45-COAST.

Kingsville

King Ranch is almost synonymous with the Texas ranching industry, and today it welcomes visitors from around the world to the community of Kingsville, 39 miles south of Corpus Christi on U.S. 77. Larger than the state of Rhode Island, the King Ranch sprawls across 825,000 acres. The ranch has long been known for its role in the American ranching industry and is still a worldwide leader. Here the Santa Gertrudis and King Ranch Santa Cruz breeds of cattle were developed, as was the first registered American quarter horse.

For vacationers, the King Ranch (Highway 141 West, 361-592-8055) is an important ecotourism destination, thanks to its population of migratory birds. The green jay has been named the bird of Kingsville, and more than 350 bird species such as pygmy owls and common paurauque are spotted on different areas of the ranch. In addition to excellent birding, the King Ranch has nature trails that offer glimpses at white-tailed deer, javelinas, coyotes, and other animals native to this region, which was first known as the Wild Horse Desert.

Vacationers can enjoy a one-and-a-half hour tour of the ranch aboard air-conditioned buses. The drive around the ranch includes a look at Longhorns, horses, and the many breeds of cattle that made this ranch famous.

One of the most popular annual events at the ranch is the Ranch Hand Breakfast, scheduled for the Saturday before Thanksgiving. More than 7,000 visitors show up for a real ranch breakfast.

Beyond the ranch in the town of Kingsville, the King legacy is also apparent. The King Ranch Museum (405 North Sixth St., 361-595-1881) provides visitors with a look at the history of the ranch, including a stunning photographic essay of life on King Ranch in the 1940s. There's also a collection of saddles, antique carriages, and antique cars.

Kingsville is home to the Conner Museum (Santa Gertrudis St., 361-593-2810) on the campus of Texas A & I University. Highlighting the natural and social history of South Texas, the museum includes exhibits on ranching, South Texas ecosystems, and area fossil and minerals.

Many Kingsville visitors make the journey a day trip from their home base in Corpus Christi or on Padre Island; others opt to stay at one of the city's motels such as the Holiday Inn Kingsville (3430 S. Hwy. 77, 361-595-5753).

For more information on area activities, contact the Kingsville Convention and Visitors Bureau at (800) 333-5032.

West of San Antonio

Del Rio

Whether you define a nature getaway as a weekend of camping, birding, houseboating, fishing, waterskiing, or exploring, there's one Texas destination that has it all: Del Rio, located 152 miles west of San Antonio via U.S. 90.

The city that's known as "the best of the border" certainly lives up to that title when it comes to outdoor fun. Perched at the edge of the Chihuahuan desert, Del Rio is an oasis lush with vegetation thanks to the San Felipe Springs, artesian wells that gush more than 90 million gallons of water each day.

While the town offers a full getaway's worth of activities—everything from the Val Verde Winery to the Whitehead Memorial Museum (1308 S. Main St., 830-774-7568)—many of Del Rio's natural attractions are located beyond the city's borders. Three rivers, including the Rio Grande, form Lake Amistad. Amistad, derived from the Spanish word for friendship, was a joint project between Mexico and the United States. Today it's a vacationer's delight, offering water sports of all varieties and plenty of great fishing. Anglers try for black bass, crappie, catfish,

and striper, and professional guides are available to help lead the way to a great fishing spot.

The best way to see the lake is aboard a boat, and the most luxurious ride is aboard a houseboat. With innumerable coves tucked inside sheer canyon walls, houseboaters can find seclusion as well as some beautiful, spring-fed swimming holes. Several operators rent houseboats that include all the comforts of home, from separate bedrooms to fully-equipped kitchens—some boats even include a hot tub on deck! You'll also find fishing boats, powerboats, and personal watercraft for rent if you'd like to explore the lake on something smaller.

If you'd rather let someone else take the wheel, guided boat tours journey into the far reaches of the Pecos and Devil's Rivers for a look at prehistoric Indian pictographs painted on the canyon walls. Call the Chamber of Commerce for more information on guided tours to these picturesque areas.

About 45 miles northwest of Del Rio lies Seminole Canyon State Historical Park (U.S. 90, 9 miles past the town of Comstock, 915-292-4464). This is a stop archaeology buffs shouldn't miss, and a perfect getaway for bird enthusiasts as well. More than 300 bird species have been recorded in the Del Rio area, so bring your binoculars and birding guide for this getaway.

Seminole Canyon is home to a mystery that has never been solved. Delicate pictographs were drawn on canyon walls by ancient Indians about 8,500 years ago. The paintings in the caves and on canyon walls represent animals, Native Americans, and supernatural shamans, but their meaning is still unknown.

Archaeologists believe the early residents of Seminole Canyon were hunter-gatherers. Hunting was limited to deer and rabbits, and instead the residents survived as foragers, living on sotol, prickly pear, and lechugilla. The culture that made its home in this canyon produced the artwork now seen on guided tours. At

10:00 A.M. and 3:00 P.M., Wednesday through Sunday, take a ranger-led walk to the Fate Bell Shelter. This rock overhang boasts ochre, black and white paintings that are the oldest rock art in North America. One painting, known as "The Three Shamans," portrays three figures, one with antlers atop his head.

This park has some quiet camp sites located high above the canyon. They offer a spectacular view of the Chihuahuan Desert, dotted with cactus. If you'd rather have a roof over your head than a tent canvas, you'll find a variety of accommodations in Del Rio, ranging from bed-and-breakfast inns like Villa del Rio (123 Hudson St., 830–768–1100) to full-service motels such as the Ramada Inn (2101 Avenue F, 800–272–6232).

For more information on Del Rio area attractions, call the Del Rio Chamber of Commerce at (800) 889–8149 or see www.drchamber.com.

South Padre Island

The livin' is definitely easy on South Padre Island—whether it's summer or not. Whether a good weekend getaway to you means gulls or gambling, shops or surf, this island destination has got it all.

South Padre is an easy drive from the Alamo City. Travel I–37 south toward Corpus Christi. Just 15 miles before reaching Corpus Christi, turn south on U.S. 77 and continue to Kingsville. In Kingsville, head south on U.S. 77 for 75 miles to Harlingen. From Harlingen, continue south on U.S. 77 for 12 miles to the intersection with Route 100; turn east on Route 100 and continue to Port Isabel and across the causeway to South Padre Island. Air service to South Padre Island is also available from San Antonio through several communities in South Texas. Harlingen's Valley International Airport, a 45-minute drive from the island, and the Brownsville-South Padre Island International Airport, a 30-minute drive, offers numerous flights.

South Padre Island offers beach fun for all ages.
PHOTO: PARIS PERMENTER & JOHN BIGLEY

South Padre stretches for 34 miles, hugging the Texas coastline and serving as a protective barrier against Gulf storms. At its widest point, the island is just a half-mile across, providing all its hotel rooms with an unbeatable view.

Your visit to Texas's southernmost island begins with a drive over the Queen Isabella Causeway, the longest bridge in the state. It spans 2.5 miles, starting at the base of the Port Isabel Lighthouse. In Port Isabel, you'll find plenty of opportunities to fish or just enjoy the catch of the day at one of the excellent seafood restaurants.

For some visitors, the chance to enjoy miles of pristine beach is reason enough to journey to South Padre. Miles of toasted sand invite travelers to enjoy horseback riding, sailboarding, surfing, sandcastle building, or just wave-hopping in the surf.

But there are plenty of activities to keep travelers busy in and out of the water. Try your luck at fishing, one of the most popular activities both in bay and Gulf waters. For little over the price of a movie ticket, you can go out on a cruise and have a chance at any one of the species that populate these waters: whiting, drum, flounder, trout, wahoo, and even sailfish.

Everyone thinks of South Padre as a magnet for college students looking for a spring break party, but few know that the island is a classroom for students at the University of Texas Coastal Studies Laboratory. Research here focuses on coastal ecosystems, including a study of the sea turtles and dolphins that live in the area. You can stop by the lab Sunday through Friday for a look at aquariums filled with marine life.

Regardless of your interests, you'll spend part of your visit along Padre Boulevard, the main street in town. This road is lined with restaurants, shell shops, and tourist facilities that can make your trip easier and more fun. Park your car and catch a ride on "The Wave," a motorized trolley that stops at attractions along the way.

For more information, call the South Padre Convention and Visitors Bureau at (800) OKPADRE or stop by the Visitors Center at 600 Padre Boulevard.

Rio Grande Valley

While you are at South Padre Island, don't miss the treasures of the Rio Grande Valley. Here, among miles of citrus groves and coastal flats filled with birds from throughout North America, you'll find many attractions. Have a look at the Web site of the Rio Grande Valley Chamber of Commerce, www.valleychamber.com, for a look at the region's many activities and events.

Most South Padre visitors spend at least part of their trip enjoying an excursion to Brownsville, Matamoros, and other communities of the Rio Grande Valley. The southernmost city in Texas, Brownsville features one of the top 10 zoos in the country, a must-see for families. The Gladys Porter Zoo is home to about 2,000 animals, most contained by waterways rather than fences.

From Brownsville, it's a quick five-minute walk across the International Bridge to Matamoros, Mexico. Follow Route 48 downtown to the convention center and park at the free municipal lot. After crossing the bridge, it's a short taxi ride to the mercado. Here you can bargain for silver jewelry, leather goods, glassware, blankets, serapes, Baja jackets, and onyx creations.

Harlingen is a top destination in the Valley and makes a good central point from which to enjoy a look at all of the southern tip of Texas. The rich history of this region is traced at the Rio Grande Valley Museum in Harlingen. This attraction includes a traditional museum as well as historic buildings: the Harlingen Hospital, the restored home of Harlingen's founder, and a stagecoach inn. For more history in this area, be sure to pick up a copy of Harlingen's new Heritage Trail brochure. It details historic churches, theaters, and homes throughout the city.

West of Harlingen, McAllen also offers activities both in the city and in Mexico. Home to more than 100,00 residents, McAllen is located just 8 miles from the Mexican city of Reynosa, a favorite with families looking for a chance to shop at a traditional mercado. Several hotels offer van service to the International Bridge or you can drive to Hidalgo and park for the day on the Texas side for just a couple of dollars.

McAllen is also a favorite with weekend travelers looking to spend some time enjoying nature and the great outdoors. Birding is especially popular. About 16 miles southeast of the city, the Santa Ana National Wildlife Refuge challenges birders with many rare species. Interpretive tram rides are available during winter months. Every April, McAllen holds the Annual Texas Tropics Nature Festival. This event celebrates the bountiful bird and wildlife of the region with field trips, guest speakers, seminars and more.

For more information on Brownsville, call (956) 546-3721; on Harlingen, call (800) 531-7346); and on McAllen, call (800) 250-2591).

East of San Antonio

Houston

Sometimes a getaway means big-city fun and in Texas that means Houston, the nation's fourth largest city. Houston is a sprawling mix of cultures, and it offers plenty of sight-seeing, family attractions, shopping, and nightlife. To reach Houston, follow I-10 east of San Antonio, a drive of 200 miles.

For families, one of the top attractions is Six Flags Houston AstroWorld/WaterWorld. It has 10 roller-coasters—including the "Texas Cyclone," rated one of the best in the world—as well as numerous live shows. Bugs Bunny's Enchanted Kingdom is a hit with the youngest visitors.

The arts play a major role in Houston. One of the most noteworthy sights is the Museum of Fine Arts at 1001 Bissonnet. Founded in 1900, this was the first municipal art museum in Texas. Among its permanent collections are the Strauss Collection of Renaissance and Eighteenth-Century Art, the Glassell Collection of African Gold, and the Beck Collection of Impressionist and Post-Impressionist Art. On the museum grounds is the Bayou Bend Collection and Gardens.

Art buffs also won't want to miss The Menil Collection at 1515 Sul Ross (between Mandell and Montrose). More than 15,000 pieces of art are displayed here. Check out the collection of African tribal art, as well as the modern art. The Menil Collection also has one of the largest Surrealist collections in the world.

Located in walking distance of other attractions in the Houston Museum District, the Contemporary Arts Museum, 5216 Montrose, is set in a striking metal building that's a local landmark. A tight focus on art of the past 40 years allows the CAM to explore its specialty in great detail. Changing exhibits ensure that the galleries remain fresh and provocative.

The beauty displayed in the city's many art museums is a stark contrast to one of its most solemn sights: the Holocaust Museum Houston at 5401 Caroline Street. Houston residents who suffered through the Holocaust are remembered here, along with the victims throughout the world. At The Ethel and Al Herzstein Theater, the film Voices is a sobering account of the Holocaust told by Houston residents who witnessed it. The museum's Josef and Edith Micberg Gallery features artwork inspired by the Holocaust, and the Eric Alexander Garden of Hope remembers the children who died in the Holocaust. Some parts of this museum might be too intense for young children.

One museum that's appropriate for children of all ages is the Houston Museum of Natural Science at 1 Hermann Circle Drive. In addition to the expected hands-on, kid-friendly exhibitions, this extremely popular museum has a number of specialty collections that shouldn't be missed. The Cullen Hall of Gems and Minerals is a vast and unique attraction, more impressive because of its skillful lighting. The Strake Hall display of seashells is similarly stunning. Favorites with children are the Fondren Discovery Place and the Challenger Learning Center. And all visitors are delighted by the Cockrell Butterfly Center, where free-flying butterflies are spotted along the walkways.

Wildlife of all sizes and shapes is found at the Houston Zoological Gardens at 1513 North MacGregor Way. Houston's 55-acre zoo is home to more than 5,000 animals. The sea lion training exhibit is very popular with visitors as is the vampire bat feeding. The zoo is one of the most visited in the entire Southwest.

Space Center Houston, located near the community of Clear Lake about 20 minutes south of Houston, is another popular local attraction. Starting with a mock-up of the space shuttle, the center is filled with hands-on displays. The $70-million facility is usually filled to bursting with children engaging in hands-on learning. Video exhibits let kids try their hands at piloting a shuttle or driving a lunar rover.

The real technology lies in the far less flashy Johnson Space Center. Visitors have their choice of three tram tours for a behind-the-scenes look at the training facilities and control center. The Mission Control Center tour is, by far, the most popular; wait times can exceed one hour.

It's sea, not space, travel that's the focus of Battleship *Texas* State Historical Park, located 21 miles from downtown Houston on Route 225. One of the state's top historic attractions, the USS *Texas* fought in both World Wars and was renovated by money raised by the schoolchildren of Texas. The largest part of the park is aboard the massive battleship, which has been restored and is open for self-guided tours.

Directly across from the Battleship *Texas* stands the San Jacinto Battleground State Historical Park. Here the Battle of San Jacinto was fought, winning Texas its freedom from Mexico. Although some of its exhibits are dated and old-fashioned, the museum does have an extensive collection on the Texas Revolution, the Republic of Texas, and the early days of statehood.

For more on Houston, call (800) 365-7575.

Galveston

When you're ready for a weekend at the beach, drive 50 miles southeast of Houston to the resort community of Galveston, a place known for fun in the sun. Any time of year there's always something to do in this coastal community.

Shoppers find numerous antiques shops along Post Office Street, a shopping district that runs from 20th to 25th Streets. Along with restaurants and specialty shops, Post Office Street is also home to The Grand 1894 Opera House, which once hosted performers such as Sarah Bernhardt, John Philip Sousa, and Anna Pavlova. It has has been restored to its turn-of-the-century grandeur.

After a morning at Post Office Street, stroll over to The Strand, just three blocks away. In the late nineteenth century, The Strand was the city's business district. It's a block away from the busy seaport, where shippers unloaded merchandise from around the world and took on a cargo of Texas cotton. Bankers and traders filled the buildings of the Strand, so it was known as the "Wall Street of the Southwest."

Today trolleys clang along the historic streets, transporting visitors along a district filled with specialty shops and restaurants housed in one of the nation's largest collections of Victorian commercial architecture. The district is also home to the Elissa, a restored 1877 tall ship that's open for self-guided tours. The ship is housed at the Texas Seaport Museum, which has displays on Galveston's shipping history as well as a database with information about more than 133,000 immigrants who entered the United States through Galveston. Thousands of immigrants made their way through the port, earning it the name "little Ellis Island."

Eventually Galveston went on to become the richest city in the state and home of many Texas firsts: post office, naval base, grocery store, insurance company, jewelry store, private bank, gas lights, hospital, cotton exchange, electric lights, telephone, golf course, real estate firm, and more.

Galveston's thriving economy took a downswing on September 8, 1900, with the arrival of one of the worst storms in U.S. history. Known as the Great Storm, the hurricane killed more than 6,000 residents and destroyed one-third of the city. To prevent future damage by storm surges, the city constructed a 7-mile seawall and raised the level of the island. Near the Texas Seaport Museum, you can watch a documentary film on the Great Storm and its aftermath.

While the storm took many of the island's oldest buildings, others were spared and still welcome guests. One of the most famous is The Bishop's Palace, located at 1402 Broadway. Built as a private home by a local railroad founder, the home is built of Texas granite and is open for guided tours. Among its unique features are fireplaces and mantels from around the world.

Galveston also has plenty of modern-day attractions, and one of the best is Moody Gardens. Save an entire day for this Texas-size attraction, now even larger with the opening of the Aquarium Pyramid, a 130,000-square-foot structure that houses 1.5 million gallons of water and more than 10,000 marine animals, The aquarium features North Pacific, Caribbean, Tropical Pacific, and Edge of the Antarctic displays with true-to-life habitats. Moody Gardens' first major attraction was the Rainforest Pyramid, where more than 1,700 exotic plants, fish, birds, and insects from the world's rainforests live. The complex is also home to the nation's first 3-D IMAX theater. The Discovery Pyramid showcases the work of NASA through space habitats, exhibits, and interactive displays. The Discovery Pyramid also features the IMAX Ridefilm Theater with a 180-degree wraparound screen. Other attractions at Moody Gardens include Palm Beach, constructed using sand shipped in from Florida, and The Colonel, a re-created paddlewheeler.

Moody Gardens is just steps from the Moody Gardens Hotel, one of many reasons to turn a day trip into a weekend excursion. Throughout the island, January brings lower room rates and the chance to enjoy a relaxed atmosphere. Along Seawall Boulevard, one of the top properties is the San Luis Resort and Conference Center, a 22-acre complex consisting of the San Luis Hotel, the Hilton Resort Beachfront Galveston Island, the San Luis Condominiums, the Sealy Mansion, and five restaurants. The resort will soon offer a spa and fitness center, the perfect way to warm up and relax on a winter day.

If you're in the mood for a more historic hotel, look to one of Galveston's grande dames. The Hotel Galvez, known as the "Queen of the Gulf," recently underwent an extensive renovation. On The Strand, the Tremont House is a favorite for guests looking for European-style luxury just steps from the shopping and entertainment district.

Many of Galveston's hotels and resorts are located in walking distance of its excellent restaurants. Fresh Gulf seafood is the specialty at many restaurants—shrimp, oysters, and fresh fish prepared in a variety of ways fill the menus.

For more information on Galveston, call the Convention and Visitors Bureau at (888) GAL–ISLE.

Neighborhoods and Real Estate

Neighborhoods

San Antonio has long been known for its multicultural diversity, drawing residents from numerous nations. Once a part of Mexico, this city in its early days welcomed new citizens from countries from as far away as the Canary Islands, Lebanon, and Germany.

When people of those groups arrived in San Antonio, many settled in neighborhoods with those who shared their language and customs. Many of those early neighborhoods still exist today. Some still boast the structures built during their early years; others are still populated by descendants of the immigrants who settled the Alamo City.

One of the earliest neighborhoods in San Antonio grew up on the land surrounding the San Antonio de Valero, the Alamo. Settled by Spanish missionaries, this territory soon gave rise to the King William District, built on mission land that was sold at a public auction. Settled in the 1840s by German immigrants, many of them merchants, this region became known as "Sauerkraut Bend" to San Antonio residents outside the neigh-

borhood. For years, this was considered the most cosmopolitan neighborhood in the city with tree-lined streets, beautiful mansions, and homes built as investments by the wealthy merchants.

King William eventually fell into disrepair and remained run-down until downtown living was again in vogue. In 1967, King William was designated the first Historic Neighborhood District in Texas thanks to the many nineteenth-century mansions and structures here that had been restored to their original grandeur. Today the district is again one of San Antonio's most desirable addresses, either for a permanent home or for a temporary residence in one of the neighborhood's elegant bed and breakfast inns.

Beyond King William's boundaries northeast of downtown, another historic section of town is known as Government Hill. This area of the city is the site of Fort Sam Houston, home to military personnel from around the world who come to train at this center for military combat medicine. Around the fort stand numerous historic buildings; 27 percent of the structures in this area have been designated historic.

Just west of Government Hill stands the neighborhood of Tobin Hill, a favorite with college students and faculty from the University of the Incarnate Word, Trinity University, and San Antonio College. Located at St. Mary's and Josephine Streets, this district is lively with restaurants, theaters, and a diversity of cultures. The neighborhood is home to St. Sophia Greek Orthodox Church, Our Lady of Sorrows, and numerous other houses of wor-

Insiders' Tip

To connect your heat and electrical service, you'll need to call the City Public Service office at (210) 225-2541.

ship that have served neighborhood residents for generations. The district is also the site of Brackenridge Park. Lately the homes in this neighborhood have undergone extensive renovation.

Another revitalized neighborhood is Monticello, once considered a rural cousin to San Antonio, with numerous dairy and goat farms. Development came in the 1920s with a crop of architecturally diverse homes in styles including Colonial, Monterey, French Revival, Tudor, Art Deco, and Mediterranean. Also architecturally noteworthy are the public buildings in this neighborhood; the centerpiece of the district is Thomas Jefferson High School, built in 1929 at a cost of $1.2 million. The building is a miniature version of Spain's Alhambra and was featured on the cover of *Life* and *National Geographic* magazines.

West of downtown lies Prospect Hill. Originally populated primarily by German immigrants, it later became primarily Hispanic. Comedienne Carol Burnett, actress Carol Channing, and former San Antonio mayor and HUD secretary Henry Cisneros grew up here. Prospect Hill remained a middle-class neighborhood until nearby Kelly Air Force Base declined; today it is home to only a few of the young families that once resided in the area to be close to the base. However, the neighborhood is now experiencing a revitalization of sorts.

East of downtown lies Ellis Alley, one of the first San Antonio neighborhoods to be settled by African-American residents following the Civil War. The area was long home to many African-American–owned newspapers, nightclubs, restaurants, and other businesses. Located east of the Alamodome, the neighborhood's centerpiece is the 1902 Sunset Depot; the train station is now a collection of nightclubs. One historic structure that retains its original use is St. Paul United Methodist Church, established in 1866. This is the oldest African-American church in San Antonio.

Within San Antonio's boundaries also lie several neighborhoods that are officially separate municipalities. One of

these neighborhood/cities is Alamo Heights, located on Broadway. This beautiful, wealthy community was originally a project of the Alamo Heights Land and Improvement Company of Texas. Starting in 1890 with a private waterworks, a few streets, and some parks, the developers waited for growth, but it failed to come due to the neighborhood's distance from downtown. The company failed and the development was later taken over by more successful companies, which by 1922 had the benefit of the automobile to bring residents to this neighborhood. Today Alamo Heights has its own independent school district and is also home to the University of the Incarnate Word.

Another historic neighborhood/city is Olmos Park, located southeast of Alamo Heights. The city was incorporated in the 1940s, when it had a population of 1,822 residents, a number that nearly doubled by the 1950s. Today the number of Olmos Park residents is lower than it was during that peak period. The residential neighborhood's property values remain high, however; the average price for a single-family dwelling is $216,128.

On the east side of San Antonio near Randolph Air Force Base stands Universal City, a community that primarily serves the base. Property values remain modest here, with single-family houses averaging $78,600.

In all, 22 incorporated cities including San Antonio lie within Bexar County, which covers 1,248 square miles. Each incorporated city has its own tax rate. For example, Olmos Park residents pay $.59618 per $100 in property value, for city taxes and school taxes, while Universal City citizens pay $2.12 per $100. San Antonio residents pay $2.78 per $100 in property value in taxes.

San Antonio's housing market has remained strong even during difficult economic times.

PHOTO: PARIS PERMENTER & JOHN BIGLEY

Real Estate

The San Antonio real estate picture has been excellent in recent years, thanks to corporate relocations. Some of that growth can be attributed to the city's relatively low cost of living. According to the latest Runzheimer Index of Selected High-Tech Cities, which uses a rating of 100 as the median cost of living, San Antonio ranked 90.9 compared to 106 for Atlanta, 111.9 for Chicago, 113.9 for Los Angeles, and 141.9 for San Francisco.

Home prices in San Antonio also compare very favorably with other cities across the nation. A $155,396 home in San Antonio would sell for $163,150 in Memphis, $207,570 in Phoenix, $232,888 in Denver, and $289,331 in San Diego according to the Association of Applied Community Researchers (ACCRA). The median price of a new home in San Antonio is $116,400. Homes are on the market for an average of 100 days. Of course, these fig-

ures are subject to change, particularly in light of the economic downturn that began in 2001.

The Northwest section of the city is hottest these days, grabbing 32 percent of the market. This area is defined by the Northside Independent School District. North Central San Antonio is also popular; here new home sales average $200,000. Sales in this area account for nearly 20 percent of new home sales in the city. Another top area is the Northeast, claiming almost 22 percent of the real estate market.

San Antonio is also home to many new subdivisions. In the north-central portion of town, these include Canyon Rim, Champions Ridge, Champion Springs, Mesa Verde, Mesa Vista, and Mountain Lodge. Many of these areas south of Loop 1604 are gated communities.

In the northwest portion of town near the Medical Center, new subdivisions include Chase Oaks and the Retreat at

Oak Hills inside Loop 1604. Outside Loop 1604, new areas include Bridgewood, Canyon Park Estates, Fossil Springs Ranch, Helotes Park Terrace, and Retablo Ranch. Some of these communities are gated.

In the northeast section of the city, several new subdivisions are being constructed outside Loop 1604 including Encino Mesa, Encino Ranch, Encino Rio, Evans Ranch, Fossil Creek, Redland Heights, Remington Heights, The Terraces of Encino, and Verde Mountain Estates. Inside the Loop, real estate buyers find new houses at subdivisions such as Redland Estates and Stafford Heights South.

On the west side of the city, new subdivisions are being constructed near the theme parks and the Air Force bases; these include Caracol Creek, El Sendero of Westlakes, Lindsey Place, Park Place, Retreat at Oak Hills, Sunset, and the Reserve of Westover Hills.

East of the city, subdivisions near Randolph Air Force Base include Arroyo Verde, Trails of Deer Creek, and Oak Trail Estates.

Real estate also is strong in the multi-family market. On average, the city has a 94.63 percent occupancy level for apartments and multi-family dwellings. Rents have risen about 4.5 percent in the past five years but still remain lower than rents in many other Texas cities. The average rental rate for an apartment in San Antonio is $592.53 a month. The city's highest rental rates are found in the Alamo Heights area, where an average rental is $760.50 per month.

To break it down by size, the average rent for a one-bedroom apartment is $585 per month. A two-bedroom apartment rents for an average of $695 per month, while the average rent for a three-bedroom apartment is $850 per month.

Real Estate Agencies

Best Homes GMAC Real Estate
11845 W. I–10, Suite 401,
San Antonio
(210) 694–4234, (800) 780–4103
10223 McAllister Fwy., San Antonio
(210) 490–2200, (800) 375–9680

The San Antonio Chamber of Commerce office provides information on local real estate.
PHOTO: PARIS PERMENTER & JOHN BIGLEY

Insiders' Tip

The San Antonio Chamber of Commerce maintains an online membership directory of real estate agencies at www.sachamber.org.

7510 Culebra Rd., San Antonio
(210) 523–1300, (800) 375–9797
3393 Thousand Oaks Dr., San Antonio
(210) 494–1300, (800) 375–9723
www.besthomesgmac.com

A member of the San Antonio Chamber of Commerce since 1992, this extensive agency has listings throughout the region in a variety of price ranges. Many properties are listed online on the company's Web site. Best Homes GMAC Real Estate can also prepare a customized relocation packet for prospective home buyers.

Bradfield Properties
11306 Sir Winston St., San Antonio
(210) 340–6500
www.bradfieldproperties.com

Owned by Joyce and Boyd Bradfield, this agency has been a member of the San Antonio Chamber of Commerce since 1979. Bradfield Properties is a network of eight area offices with 200 agents specializing in residential, commercial, property management, and relocation. The agency is affiliated with CENDANT Real Estate Network, the largest relocation-service provider in North America, Mexico, and Europe. Bradfield has a full-time relocation staff and offers numerous relocation services including a weekly television show that lets viewers preview local homes, personalized tours, employment information, temporary housing assistance, and more. The agency maintains a special toll-free number dedicated to relocation: (800) 594–8894.

Phyllis Browning Company
6101 Broadway, San Antonio
(210) 824–7878, (800) 266–0676
www.phyllisbrowning.com/

This company is the exclusive local affiliate of Christie's Great Estates. With a variety of listings in many price ranges, the online Web site for this company permits potential purchasers to shop by price, neighborhood, or even particular aspects of a home such as the number of bedrooms, square footage, or acreage.

Larry Campbell—Jack Biegger, Inc., Realtors
7121 Bandera Rd., San Antonio
(210) 520–3543
www.larry-campbell.com

This Realtor offers a variety of residential listings. The company Web site includes many features of interest to those new to San Antonio including school information, real estate news, and more. Prospective buyers can sign up to receive free email notice of new realty listings.

Guy Chipman Company Realtors
18503 Sigma Rd., Suite 200, San Antonio
(210) 483–7000
www.guy-chipman.com

A member of the Chamber of Commerce since 1959 and serving San Antonio since 1946, this company of Realtors has extensive listings for both the San Antonio and the Boerne areas. The agency also has an extensive relocation program. Prior to arrival in San Antonio, prospective buyers receive an information packet with information on homes, cultural events, school test scores, and more; a videotape of the company's *Sunday Showcase of Homes* TV show; a list of Web addresses for San Antonio; and an assortment of children's activities. The company can also provide information on employment opportunities for spouses, public and private education, special education, child care, elder care, community activities, and other matters of interest to new residents.

Kuper Realty Corporation
6606 N. New Braunfels Ave., San Antonio
(210) 822–8602
www.kuperrealty.com

A member of the San Antonio Chamber of Commerce since 1971, this Realtor was founded as a commercial brokerage and residential development firm, expanding in 1979 to include residential brokerage, farm and ranch brokerage, and relocation divisions. The company, which has more than 75 associates, is the exclusive representative for Sotheby's International Realty for Central and South Texas. The agency offers free relocation packets and materials for those interested in moving to the city.

Norma Pearson Realtor
16350 Blanco Rd., Suite 110, San Antonio
(210) 493–3030, (800) 650–3745
www.normapearson.com

In business since 1978, this agency offers many services for those relocating to the city including a pre-visit telephone call, a relocation and video package, private or public school information, hotel and car rental reservation, and country club orientations and complimentary golf passes.

Prudential, Don Johnson Company Realtors
16845 Blanco Rd., Suite 101, San Antonio
(210) 493–1766
www.realsa.com

Both residential and commercial real estate are handled by this firm, which has been a member of the San Antonio Chamber of Commerce since 1973. The company Web site also includes Veterans

Administration properties of special interest to military personnel and retirees.

Re/Max Associates 2000
16635 Huebner Rd., San Antonio
(210) 408–2000, (888) 209–2001
www.dianecraig.net/

A member of the San Antonio Chamber of Commerce since 1997, this company is led by Diane Craig, with nearly two decades of real-estate experience. The company features a variety of property types; its Web site offers access to more than 700,000 Re/Max listings around the country.

J. J. Rodriguez ERA Troy Realtor
16664 San Pedro Ave., San Antonio
(210) 494–1985, (800) 695–1994
www.jjrodriguez.com

This native San Antonian Realtor is also a licensed loan officer and can assist purchasers with obtaining a mortgage. The company Web site includes a mortgage center as well as information on schools and the community.

Education and Child Care

Higher Education

Public Schools

Private Schools and
Academies

Child-Care Centers

San Antonio's educational heritage is as old as the city itself. A mission-based educational system was used by the founding Spanish as a necessary first step in colonizing the New World. Their plan called for Spanish missionaries to convert enough native people to establish Spanish Christianity in the region. Thus schools for the native inhabitants were of supreme importance, as education was the means to win the hearts and minds of the indigenous peoples.

The friars who were first in charge of these missions schools were Franciscans from the competing colleges of Zacatecas and Queretaro in Mexico. The College of Santa Cruz in Quertaro was the first Catholic college in the New World and was founded in 1683, primarily to oversee the establishment of other missions in Spain's New World colonies. The College of Nuestra Senora de Guadalupe de Zacatecas was established in 1707 in Northern Mexico and oversaw the Texas missions, including those at Bexar, through the late 1700s. Father Gaspar José de Solís, who presided as master of the Zacatecas college, made a journey to visit the Texas missions of the school in 1767–68, and his travel journal of the trip has proven to be an important source of information about Texas and Bexar at the time.

The first attempt to found a traditional school for San Antonio's settlers' sons in 1798 did not succeed, as there was little support for it. The boys it attempted to teach were mainly occupied, as was the town as a whole, with the more basic activities of survival on the frontier. In 1803, a future signer of the Texas Declaration of Independence, Jose Francisco Ruiz, was appointed schoolmaster, but his school did not last long either.

Considering the city's strong Catholic heritage, it is no surprise that the city's first true educational institution, the Ursuline Academy for girls, was founded in 1851 by seven Ursuline nuns. The sisters, led by Sister St. Marie Trouard, moved to San Antonio from New Orleans and Galveston and established a girl's boarding school on the San Antonio River at Augusta Street. There the Academy stayed until 1965, when new facilities were constructed on the city's northwest side. Ursuline Academy is still owned by the Ursuline order, although a board now oversees its operation. Its former campus, designed by San Antonio architect Francois Giraud, is now the site of the Southwest School of Art and Craft. The original buildings are architecturally signficant for the pise de terre technique that Giraud and another architect, Jules Poinsard, employed in their construction. This method uses local materials, rock, straw, and clay that are compressed by hand. The buildings, restored by the SSAC, are now listed on the National Register of Historic Places.

Modern-day San Antonio now boasts five fully accredited universities, an extensive community college system, 10 public school districts, several private schools and academies, and numerous preschools and child-care centers.

Higher Education

Our Lady of the Lake University
411 Southwest 24th St., San Antonio
(210) 434–6711
www.ollousa.edu

Another Catholic institution of higher education, Our Lady of the Lake was founded as a private school for girls in 1895. It was chartered by the state in 1919, and was opened to both men and women in 1969. The university's Old Main building, completed in 1895, has long been admired for its Victorian Gothic architecture, as has the Gothic Chapel (1923), designed by Leo M. J. Dielmann, which features stairs of Italian marble and stained-glass windows.

Current enrollment of the university is 3,300 students. Our Lady of the Lake awards bachelor's degrees in some 56 areas of study and master's degrees in 30; it also offers a doctorate in counseling psychology. It receives accolades for two of its programs, the Worden School of Social Work and the Harry Jersig Center for Communication Disorders. Its popular Weekend College program offers degrees in several areas.

St. Mary's University
1 Camino Santa Maria, San Antonio
(210) 436–3327
www.stmarytx.edu

This university traces its roots to St. Mary's Institute, established in San Antonio in 1852 by brothers of the Society of Mary. Recognized by the State of Texas in 1897, the institution, renamed St. Mary's College, grew rapidly after the turn of the century. It eventually was divided into three major schools: arts, sciences, and business. In 1927, it began operating as St. Mary's University.

St. Mary's University now has an enrollment of 4,000 students and includes five schools: the School of Humanities and Social Sciences; the School of Science, Engineering, and Technology; the School of Business and Administration; the School of Law; and the Graduate School. In addition to bachelor's degrees, master's degrees and doctorate degrees are also offered in some fields. St. Mary's is San Antonio's only law school.

Trinity University
715 Stadium Dr., San Antonio
(210) 999–7011
www.trinity.edu

Although Trinity traces its roots in Texas to three small Presbyterian institutions founded before the Civil War (making it one of the oldest universities in the state), the university itself was moved to San Antonio from Waxahachie in 1942 and to its present site in 1945. The striking campus skyline with its familiar bell tower can be seen from many areas of town. Architects O'Neil Ford and Bartlett Cocke designed the campus buildings using the revolutionary Youtz-Slick system of construction, which uses prefinished concrete floor slabs.

No longer a religious institution, Trinity now describes itself as a "professionally oriented liberal arts university." Its current student body of 2,500 consists mostly of undergraduate students. The university prides itself on its dedicated, distinguished faculty, its bright students, and its small class size.

University of Texas at San Antonio
6900 N.W. Loop 1604 West (Main Campus),
San Antonio
(210) 458–4011
www.utsa.edu

Part of the huge state University system, UTSA was established in 1973 and now

---

Insiders' Tip
Applications to many San Antonio universities are due the fall before a prospective student's freshman year.

---

has an enrollment of nearly 20,000 students. It offers bachelor's, master's, and doctoral degrees in some 90 areas of study. The main campus is located on the northwest side of the city; a smaller downtown campus was opened in 1997.

University of Texas Health Science Center
7703 Floyd Curl Dr., San Antonio
(210) 567–7000
www.uthscsa.edu

Another institution of higher learning located on San Antonio's northwest side, the University of Texas Health Science Center serves the city and South Texas. In addition to its main campus, it has campuses in Laredo and the Rio Grande Valley. More than 3,000 students a year train at the center, which is affiliated with more than 100 hospitals, clinics, and healthcare facilities in South Texas.

University of the Incarnate Word
4301 Broadway, San Antonio
(210) 829–6000
www.uiw.edu

In 1884, San Antonio's first hospital, Santa Rosa Hospital, was founded by the Sisters of Charity of the Incarnate Word, a French order. The same order also founded a school on land bought from the Colonel George W. Brackinridge family.

The university now has more than 3,000 students, many of whom are attracted by the strong nursing program here. The university offers degrees in some 50 different subject areas. Its Adult Degree Completion Program is designed to make it easier for students to complete unfinished college degrees. Its other unique degree programs include Music Therapy and Sports Management.

Community Colleges

The Alamo Community College District (210-208-8000) has four separate campuses:

Northwest Vista College
210 W. Sheridan St., Building C, San Antonio
(210) 208–8001

This campus specializes in health-related training and serves the city's northwest area.

Palo Alto College
1400 Villaret St., San Antonio
(210) 921–5000
www.accd.edu/pac

This campus, which opened in 1985, serves San Antonio's south side with courses in agribusiness, food science, veterinary science, and environmental technology.

St. Phillips College
1801 Martin Luther King Dr., San Antonio
(210) 531–3200
www.accd.edu/spc

St. Phillips College dates back to 1898, when it was founded as a Episcopal girl's school in La Villita. Now part of the Alamo Community College District, it offers courses on a variety of technical specialties via a nationally known program in computer-assisted instruction. The campus is located on the east side of downtown San Antonio.

San Antonio College
1300 San Pedro Ave., San Antonio
(210) 733–2000
www.accd.edu/sac

With an enrollment of more than 20,000, SAC is the largest institution in the city's community college system. It has both an Arts and Sciences division and a Technical Education division and offers classes both day and night.

Public Schools

Ten school districts serve the city of San Antonio, including several that serve only students who reside on the many military bases located in San Antonio. Each district has an elected board and a superintend-

The San Antonio Independent School District is composed of public schools throughout the region, including this high school. PHOTO: PARIS PERMENTER & JOHN BIGLEY

ent, who is appointed. Each child must attend school in the district where his or her family resides. To enter first grade, a child must be 6 years old on or before September 1. Kindergarten is optional. Buses are provided to transport children to and from school, but do not cross district boundaries. Some schools, such as magnet schools or specialized schools, accept students from other districts.

San Antonio's public school districts have a total of 209 elementary schools, 55 middle schools, five junior high schools, two junior high/senior high schools, and 35 high schools. There are also one childhood center, 10 special schools, two alternative centers, four academies, one career-education center, one competency high school, and four magnet schools. All districts combined have a total enrollment of 236,626 students.

Several local districts are noteworthy for their size or their academic excellence. Northside Independent School District is the fifth-largest school district in Texas. North East Independent School District has been praised by several local publications as being a superior school district. East Central High School in the East Central district achieved "Recognized School" status with the Texas Education Agency due to its low dropout rates, high student test scores, and high attendance numbers. Collier Elementary in Harlandale ISD has been placed among the top 1 percent of elementary schools in the country by the U.S. Department of Education.

To enroll your child in a San Antonio public school, contact your local school district. When you take your child to register, make sure that you bring your child's birth certificate, immunization records, and proof of residence.

School Districts

Alamo Heights Independent School District
7101 Broadway, San Antonio
(210) 824-2483
www.ahisd.net

In 1909 a two-room schoolhouse was built in a rural community, the area that is now known as Alamo Heights. The Alamo Heights Independent School District was officially created in 1923, with a total of 300 students.

In 1938, the athletic stadium was constructed by the Work Projects Administration, part of President Franklin D. Roosevelt's New Deal program to help pull the United States out of the Great Depression. After World War II, the community of Alamo Heights became a suburb of San Antonio. The district almost doubled in size in the few years following the war, thanks to the baby boom. The building that is today Alamo Heights High School was finished in 1950, but not before housing a number of different schools. Today's Alamo Heights Independent School District covers 9.4 square miles; contains two elementary schools, one junior high school, and one high school; and enrolls 3,600 students. The neighborhoods that are served by this school district are Alamo Heights, Terrell Hills, and Olmos Park.

East Central Independent School District
7173 FM 1628, San Antonio
(210) 649-2951
www.ecisd.net

Serving more than 7,000 students, East Central Independent School District has one middle school, four elementary schools, two intermediate schools, and an early childhood development center. East Central is affiliated with the East Central School Foundation Incorporated, a nonprofit organization that raises money to help promote public education programs in the district. Funds raised by the foundation go to computer software and equipment in the schools, alternative education programs, library materials, college scholarships for district students, and other programs that benefit the schools and students. ECISD also runs a Parents In Touch program; parents are invited to attend lectures and workshops on subjects such as parent-child communication, step-parenting, sibling rivalry, and stress.

East Central High School has received "Recognized School" status by the Texas Education Agency, which acknowledges the school's low dropout rates, good testing scores, and high attendance.

Edgewood Independent School District
5358 W. Commerce St., San Antonio
(210) 433-2361
www.edgewood-sa.k12.tx.us

With 15,000 students, Edgewood Independent School District is made up of 15 elementary schools, Wrenn Junior High, John F. Kennedy High School, Memorial High School, and a unique Math and Science Academy. Students from district high schools can apply to take advanced math and science courses at the academy, in place of these classes at their regular campus. The Math & Science Academy opened in the fall semester of 1994 with

Insiders' Tip
The San Antonio Independent School District requires a school uniform: khaki trousers, shorts, skirts, skorts, or jumpers along with white long- or short-sleeved blouses or collared shirts. Alternate school-approved shirts in the school colors are also allowed. No manufacturers' logos or brand names can be visible on the garments.

fewer than 100 students; today, 250 students are enrolled for at least one class.

Fort Sam Houston Independent School District
1902 Winans Rd., Fort Sam Houston, San Antonio
(210) 368–8700
www.fshtx.army.mil

Created in 1951, this school district serves the area around Fort Sam Houston Army Post in the northeast portion of the city. The student body includes 1,500 military dependents who live on the post and Camp Bullis. The school district is composed of one elementary school and Robert G. Cole Junior-Senior High School, with 460 students.

Harlandale Independent School District
102 Genevieve St., San Antonio
(210) 921–4300
www.harlandale.k12.tx.us

There are 15 elementary schools, four middle schools, two high schools, and four alternative learning centers in the Harlandale Independent School District, which serves 15,000 students. The Harlandale district's Collier Elementary has been awarded Blue Ribbon status by the U.S. Department of Education. This distinction, shared with only 264 other schools in the nation, places Collier Elementary among the top 1 percent of elementary schools in the United States. The honor recognizes Collier's superior teaching and student performance, high curriculum standards, safe environment, and strong community involvement. Harlandale ISD is affiliated with the Harlandale Education Foundation, whose aim is to ensure that every Harlandale district graduate receive at least $1,000 in financial aid for higher education at any type of institution.

Lackland Independent School District
2460 Kenly, Building 8265, Lackland Air Force Base, San Antonio
(210) 357–5002
www.lackland.af.mil/homepage/

Created in 1953, this school district serves Lackland Air Force Base and the children who live on the base. The district averages 930 students.

North East Independent School District
8961 Tesoro Dr., San Antonio
(210) 804–7000
www.northeast.isd.tenet.edu

North East Independent School District encompasses 144 square miles of the San Antonio area. A total of 50,000 students attend 35 elementary schools, 10 middle schools, and six high schools. North East School District has been praised as "one of the city's public-school gems" by the *San Antonio Express-News*. It has also been placed among the top 100 school districts in the country by *Money Magazine*.

Northside Independent School District
5900 Evers Rd., San Antonio
(210) 647–2100
www.nisd.net

Nearly 64,000 students attend schools in the Northside Independent School District, whose boundaries encompass 355 square miles of the San Antonio area. If the enrollment count seems high to you, you're right. Northside is the fifth-largest independent school district in Texas. Of those students, 53 percent are of Hispanic origin and 38.1 percent are Caucasians. The area is growing at an astounding rate. The district has grown by 2 percent per year since 1990, and more than 12,000 students have enrolled in the schools since that year. The growth rate is so astounding that in the recent past, nine new schools have been constructed in the district, and seven other schools recently have been approved for construction.

Randolph Field Independent School District
Randolph Air Force Base, San Antonio
(210) 357–2300
www.lackland.af.mil/homepage/

This public school district serves 1,000 students, the children of military personnel living on Randolph Air Force Base. Randolph Field ISD is composed of one elementary school and one school that serves middle- and high-school students.

San Antonio Independent School District
141 Lavaca St., San Antonio
(210) 299–5500
www.saisd.net

Established in 1899, San Antonio Independent School District is the seventh-largest school district in Texas. SAISD encompasses 79 square miles, and serves 56,000 students. San Antonio ISD students come from the city and also the cities of Olmos Park and Balcones Heights and other parts of Bexar County. There are 95 schools in the district: 65 elementary schools, 17 middle schools, eight high schools, and five alternative schools. The ethnic makeup of San Antonio Independent School District's student body is as diverse as the city of San Antonio itself: 85.3 percent are of Hispanic origin, 10 percent are African-American, and 4.4 percent are Caucasian. Less than 1 percent of the students are Asian or Pacific Islanders or American Indian. SAISD offers its students the chance to attend magnet schools at the middle school and high school levels. There are nine on the high school level and three for middle schoolers. Each magnet school focuses on a particular area of study such as science engineering, and technology; fine arts; multilingual studies; or American Heritage.

South San Antonio Independent School District
2515 Bobcat La., San Antonio
(210) 977–7000
www.southsanisd.net

The South San Antonio Independent School District has five high schools, three middle schools, and 10 elementary schools, and serves 11,000 students. This district offers many specialized programs, including an English as a Second Language (ESL) program, a Gifted and Talented program, and a Special Education program. South San Antonio ISD also has departments for students with dyslexia and for those who are deaf.

Southside Independent School District
1610 Martinez Losoya Rd., San Antonio
(210) 626–0600
www.southside.k12.tx.us

With 3,000 students, this district includes one primary school, one elementary school, an intermediate school, a middle school, and a high school. There is also an alternative education placement center. Special programs offered at Southside I.S.D. include English as a Second Language (ESL), a Gifted and Talented program, ROTC, and Special Education.

Southwest Independent School District
11914 Dragon La., San Antonio
(210) 622–3488
www.southwest.k12.tx.us

Southwest Independent School District contains nine elementary schools, four junior high schools, and one high school. The district covers a mixture of urban, suburban, and rural areas in southwestern Bexar County and educates 8,000 students.

Private Schools and Academies

Catholic Schools of San Antonio
Archdiocese of San Antonio
2718 W. Woodlawn Ave., San Antonio
(210) 734–2620, ext. 232
www.sacatholicschools.org

Given San Antonio's strong ties to the Catholic Church, it's not surprising that the city and the surrounding areas are home to numerous Catholic schools. The Archdiocese of San Antonio runs 39 elementary and eight secondary schools. The elementary schools are located within the city of San Antonio as well as in nearby communities of Castroville, Converse, Del Rio, Floresville, Fredericksburg, Kerrville, New Braunfels, Seguin, Selma, and Uvalde; the secondary schools are all located in San Antonio. All of the schools are accredited through the Texas Catholic Conference Education Department.

St. Anthony Catholic High School
3200 McCullough Ave., San Antonio
(210) 832–5600
www.sachs.org

St. Anthony is a Catholic college-prep high school for boys in grades 9 through 12. The school's philosophy is "to provide a quality education, within a framework of morals and values, while providing service to others." St. Anthony was founded in 1903 by the Oblates of Mary Immaculate, and was incorporated as part of the University of the Incarnate Word in 1995. The students are encouraged to not only focus on their academic studies, but also on athletics, community service, and religion.

St. Mary's Hall
9401 Starcrest Dr., San Antonio
(210) 483–9100

For more than 120 years, this coeducational independent school, affiliated with the American Montessori Society, has offered both boarding school and day school programs. Admission to the school is limited and selective, so the school recommends an early application. The day program covers preschool through grade 12; the boarding school program is for grades eight through 12. The school offers a variety of special programs including visual and performing arts and athletics as well as a standard curriculum.

San Antonio Academy
117 E. French Pl., San Antonio
(210) 733–7331
www.sa-academy.org

San Antonio Academy accepts boys from pre-kindergarten through the eighth grade. The interdenominational school aims to teach students values like integrity, character, and spirituality, while providing a challenging curriculum. Classes at San Antonio Academy are small: There are 325 students and 34 full-time teachers, which means a 10-to-1 student-to-teacher ratio. For the last 10 years, the SAT scores of students at San Antonio Academy have been in the top 3 percent nationwide.

Child-Care Centers

Child-care centers can be a great help to families with working parents. Many San Antonio day-care centers offer field trips, meals, and activities that are both fun and educational. There are many child-care businesses in the San Antonio area, and we've only been able to list a few in this book. Parents can consult the San Antonio Yellow Pages to find the complete listing of centers in the city.

We also strongly encourage parents to personally inspect the child-care centers they are interested in and to interview the centers' personnel. There are also several child-care referral services in San Antonio (usually free) that will help parents in the process of selecting day care for their children. The Children Resources Division (210–246–5276) at 1222 North Main Avenue, and the Family Service Association of San Antonio (210–225–0276), which has several locations around San Antonio, can recommend child-care services in San Antonio.

Addie's Playhouse
5455 Prue Rd., San Antonio
(210) 691–0064

Addie's Playhouse offers after-school care as well as day care. Infants through children up to age 12 are accepted here. Children have access to computers and can even learn skills like gardening. Addie's Playhouse has a country atmosphere, and the playground is shaded—a plus, given the intense San Antonio sun.

Bright Kids Day Care/Learning Center
4230 Clear Springs, San Antonio
(210) 655–9225

Bright Kids has day-care, pre-kindergarten, and after-school programs. The facility provides transportation from Serna and Clear Spring Elementary Schools. Kids may participate in classes in computers, music, and piano. There is an on-site playground for more active pursuits. Bright Kids is open weekdays from 6:30 A.M. until 6:30 P.M.

Buttons-N-Bows
9035 Huebner Rd., San Antonio
(210) 690–6093

Buttons-N-Bows has been in business for more than 25 years. This day-care and after-school program accepts infants through age 12. It aims to provide a Christian education to children attending both the day-care and after-school programs. The center is open from 6:30 A.M. until 6:30 P.M., and will pick up children at their schools.

Castle Hills Learning Center and Day Care
8030 Blanco Rd., San Antonio
(210) 342–9810
2769 Nacogdoches, San Antonio
(210) 826–5650

Kids who attend Castle Hills' day-care and before- and after-school programs have access to computers and enjoy an on-site pool, dance and music experiences, and year-round field trips. Transportation is provided to and from area schools. Every room at Castle Hills is monitored by video. Infants through 12-year-olds are accepted.

Children's World Learning Centers
14230 Cross Canyon Rd., San Antonio
(210) 490–0187
11814 Parliament Dr., San Antonio
(210) 349–3568
8680 Guilbeau Rd., San Antonio
(210) 522–0629
8031 Culebra Rd., San Antonio
(210) 681–8030
8003 Midcrown Dr., San Antonio
(210) 653–4990
13030 Nacogdoches Rd., San Antonio
(210) 653–5991
8110 Lone Shadow, San Antonio
(210) 659–0364
www.childrensworld.com

Children's World offers educational programs that are also fun for kids. Full and part-time day-care and after-school programs are available, and there is van service to and from area schools for kids. These centers aim to help kids use their creativity and enhance self-esteem.

Childtime Children's Center
5965 Babcock Rd., San Antonio
(210) 641–7002
1107 W. Bitters Rd., San Antonio

(210) 496–3779
14907 Nacogdoches Rd., San Antonio
(210) 654–1624
9302 Timber Path, San Antonio
(210) 681–3056
www.childtime.com

Parents are always welcome at these centers, now in business more than 25 years. Every location has a different approach to learning. Full-time and part-time child care is available. Childtime offers before- and after-school supervision for kids who attend elementary schools as well as preschool programs.

Country Home Learning Center
13315 Northwest Military Hwy., San Antonio
(210) 492–3731
104 Galleria Fair, off Hwy. 281, San Antonio
(210) 496–6718
6750 Poss Rd., off Bandera Hwy., San Antonio
(210) 680–2997
14966 Spring Farm Rd., San Antonio
(210) 654–7311
11909 Toepperwein Rd., San Antonio
(210) 650–3115
8155 Fredericksburg Rd., San Antonio
(210) 692–7205

These centers provide infants to 12-year-olds with unique day-care and after-school programs. Children who attend have the opportunity to learn dance, gymnastics, Spanish, computer literacy, music and to ride horses. The classes here are very small, so each child receives individual attention. Kids have access to a library, gymnasium, and Montessori centers.

Educare Child Care Inc.
1550 Bandera Rd., San Antonio
(210) 435–1244
3838 West Ave., San Antonio
(210) 979–9219
5431 Ingram Rd., San Antonio
(210) 435–5123
536 E. Courtland Pl., San Antonio
(210) 735–9572
4201 S. Presa St., San Antonio
(210) 534–2911

6037 Thunder Rd., San Antonio
(210) 521–9039

Educare Child Care Centers are open year-round, so parents don't have to adjust their schedules in the summer. Children from infant until 12 years are accepted in the day-care and after-school programs. After-school pickup is available. These facilities are conveniently open from 6:30 A.M. until 6:00 P.M.

KinderCare
6237 Evers Rd., San Antonio
(210) 684–0878
8980 Guilbeau Rd., San Antonio
(210) 680–4077
15170 Judson Rd., San Antonio
(210) 655–8775
7330 Marbach Rd., San Antonio
(210) 673–1210
2711 Mossrock Dr., San Antonio
(210) 341–1447
1127 Patricia Dr., San Antonio
(210) 342–1218
7030 Ray Bon Dr., San Antonio
(210) 656–6391
4503 Thousand Oaks Dr., San Antonio
(210) 653–9364
8787 Timber Path, San Antonio
(210) 680–2825
11501 Toepperwein Rd., San Antonio
(210) 653–8255
www.kindercare.com

These centers offer both day-care and after-school programs. Kids attending KinderCare after school can be transported to and from schools in the area.

> ## Insiders' Tip
> Carefully investigate any child-care facility that you're considering. After your planned visit, make an unscheduled visit for a closer inspection.

The Kinderletters preschool program helps kids start reading at an early age. Most locations of KinderCare accept children from 6 weeks to 12 years, although some do not accept infants. All participants are served meals and snacks that are good for them.

La Petite Academy
318 W. Sunset Rd., San Antonio
(210) 824–1200
6634 Springtime Dr., San Antonio
(210) 690–1136
6865 Beech Trail Dr., San Antonio
(210) 661–9718
700 Rayburn Dr., San Antonio
(210) 924–5377
8796 Marbach Rd., San Antonio
(210) 674–1323
www.lapetite.com

Full-day and half-day care and before- and after-school programs are offered at La Petite. For kids who attend school, transportation to and from school is available. Summer programs are also offered. Ages vary by location, as do opening and closing hours. La Petite Academy has more than 15 locations in the San Antonio area; check the San Antonio Yellow Pages for a complete list.

Luv-N-Care
16081 Henderson Pass, San Antonio
(210) 496–0789
6509 Grissom Rd., San Antonio
(210) 681–4228
10918 Wurzbach Rd., San Antonio
(210) 696–5677

These centers accept children from birth to age 12. Full- and part-time day care and before- and after-school programs are offered. Luv-N-Care also offers a summer camp program and a private kindergarten program. There is a swimming pool at each location, and extracurricular activities include piano, computer literacy, gymnastics, and dancing.

A Place For Kids Christian Learning Center
6011 Grissom Rd., San Antonio
(210) 680–5474

Infants through preschool kids are welcome at this center, which offers Christian learning programs. Small classes ensure that every child gets individual attention. Instruction in areas as diverse as computers and gymnastics is provided. Full summer programs are available. A Place For Kids is open from 6:30 A.M. until 6:30 P.M.

Tutor Time Child Care/Learning Centers
Parkwood Pl., San Antonio
(210) 499–1419
www.tutortime.com

Tutor Time is an after-school program that helps kids advance in school. Kids can use a computer lab, participate in educational programs such as Tutor Time Phonics Express, and complete workbook assignments designed to help them get a head start in learning. There is a summer camp program, too. Tutor Time has a special security system and closed-circuit monitoring.

Health Care
and Wellness

Emergency Services

Hospitals

Public Health Care

Referral Agencies

Resources

Specialized Health-
Care Programs

San Antonio's medical industry ranks among the best in Texas and in the Southwest, offering world-class training and treatment facilities. In fact, the industry serves as one of San Antonio's largest moneymakers, joining the booming tourism business and the steady military world as the city's top industries. A payroll topping $3 billion keeps many San Antonians employed while more than $10 billion is added to the region's local economy thanks to the medical business.

On the treatment end, San Antonio attracts patients from across the United States as well as Mexico. And more than 40 countries regularly send physicians, dentists, and others in the medical field to the city for training. Over 65 percent of the Air Force's medical specialists and 85 percent of its dentists received training at Wilford Hall Medical Center at Lackland Air Force Base.

The area's largest health facility is the South Texas Medical Center. Located in the northwest portion of the city, this center spans over 900 acres and is home to 11 major hospitals as well as almost 80 clinics. The center is composed of the Audie Murphy Branch of the South Texas Veterans Health Care System, Christus Santa Rosa Medical Center, the Methodist Ambulatory Surgery Hospital, Methodist Hospital, Methodist Specialty and Transplant Hospital, Methodist Children's Hospital of South Texas, St. Luke's Baptist Hospital, University Hospital, and Warm Springs Rehabilitation Hospital. In all, the center treats nearly 4.5 million outpatients and nearly 100,000 inpatients per year. Although the center is already extensive, plans call for an increase in facilities with a $257-million expansion on 300 undeveloped acres.

The University of Texas Health Science Center at San Antonio is the core of the Medical Center, housing five professional medical schools covering both patient care and research. The schools award more than 50 degrees and professional certificates including Doctor of Medicine, Doctor of Dental Surgery, and Doctor of Philosophy in Nursing. The dental school has frequently been cited as one of the country's best.

The center is also noted for its excellent cancer care and research facilities. The Cancer Therapy and Research Center, along with the UT Health Science Center, make up the San Antonio Cancer Institute or SACI. Designated a Comprehensive Cancer Center by the National Cancer Institute, the facility is noted for both its outpatient services and its research in the areas of breast cancer, cancer prevention, and molecular genetics.

Through the years, the South Texas Medical Center's resources have grown dramatically. In 1970, the center had an annual budget of $32 million with just over 3,000 employees; three decades later, the annual budget was over $2 billion and staff had increased to nearly 26,000.

San Antonio's military medical facilities also draw worldwide attention. Brooke Army Medical Center at Fort Sam Houston is considered one of the top burn hospitals in the world; the center also serves as a trauma center and a cancer center. Wilford Hall Medical Center is the largest medical facility of the U.S. Air Force. In addition to medical and dental education, this facility provides a quarter of San Antonio's emergency medical care.

Emergency Services

All the local public hospitals are equipped with emergency rooms. Major medical services can also be obtained there. For information on treatment facilities throughout the city, contact the Bexar County Medical Society, (210) 301–4368.

Hospitals

Baptist Medical Center
111 Dallas St., San Antonio
(210) 297–7000
www.baptisthealthsystem.org/bmc.asp

This 654-bed hospital is located right off the River Walk and offers services in surgery, obstetrics, pediatrics, intensive care, emergency service, renal dialysis, and other fields. The hospital also has a complete cardiac care unit, the first in San Antonio to offer dedicated facilities for heart disease treatment. The Baptist Medical Center is also connected by a walkway to the Baptist Cancer Center, the only hospital-based facility in South Texas with radiation therapy, high-dose brachytherapy, and hyperthermia therapy in one location. The center is the focal point of the Baptist Health System, considered one of the leading medical providers in South Texas. The health-care system dates back to 1902 and the construction of the Physicians' and Surgeons'

> ### Insiders' Tip
>
> San Antonio has been a major center for military medicine since the first hospital was built at Fort Sam Houston in the late 1870s. Several of San Antonio's military bases have medical museums (see the Military chapter for details).

Hospital on Dallas Street. The next year, the P & S School of Nursing welcomed its first class of 16 nursing students. Today the health-care system has grown to include five not-for-profit acute-care hospitals as well as a wellness and fitness center, community health and wellness programs, ambulatory surgery centers, and air medical transport.

Brooke Army Medical Center
Fort Sam Houston, San Antonio
(210) 916–4141

This military center is housed in a new 1.5-million-square-foot facility located at Fort Sam Houston. The hospital is best known for its burn treatment and research but it also provides primary care to more than 600,000 military personnel, both active duty and retired. The center also serves as a trauma center and a cancer research facility, conducting numerous research projects and anticancer drug trials.

CHRISTUS Santa Rosa Children's Hospital
519 W. Houston, San Antonio
(210) 704–2011
www.christussantarosa.org/
childrenshospital.html

San Antonio's first dedicated children's hospital now serves more than 90,000 children per year through its inpatient, outpatient, and emergency-care facilities. Following a recent $2.2 million renovation, on-site units include a pediatric rehabilitation unit, a children's cancer and blood-disorders center, and a pediatric hospice suite designed to help families of terminally ill children live in a home-like setting. In conjunction with the San Antonio Independent School District, the hospital also has an on-site classroom. Instruction is free and can include traditional classroom teaching or bedside instruction.

CHRISTUS Santa Rosa Hospital
519 W. Houston St., San Antonio
(210) 704–2011

This facility was San Antonio's first private

hospital, founded in 1869 by the Sisters of Charity of the Incarnate Word. Today the downtown hospital boasts some 400 beds and serves as a general acute-care facility. Recently the hospital has been undergoing a $75-million renovation.

Methodist Ambulatory Surgery Hospital Northwest
9150 Huebner Rd., San Antonio
(210) 691–8000
mas.sahealth.com/

This 37-bed facility specializes in inpatient and day surgery. Along with 10 operating rooms, the hospital also has one cystoscopy suite; all the hospital's staff is specially trained in surgery and post-operative care.

Methodist Hospital
7700 Floyd Curl Dr., San Antonio
(210) 575–4000
mh.sahealth.com/

Methodist Hospital is San Antonio's largest private hospital; it is the largest provider of medical care for the rural areas of South Texas and is known for its care of international patients from Mexico. The facility opened in 1963 and today offers 672 beds. The centerpiece of the Methodist Health Care System, the hospital has several specialty areas including bone-marrow transplants, oncology, cardiology, orthopedics, and women's services, thanks to a newly expanded Women's Pavilion. Another unique facility is its Gamma Knife Center, opened in 1998. The first of its kind in South Texas, the center specializes in noninvasive radiological treatment of brain tumors and neurological disorders. Several critical-care facilities offer specialized coronary care, neurological critical care, surgical intensive care, and more. More than 2,000 physicians staff the facility.

Methodist Specialty and Transplant Hospital
8026 Floyd Curl Dr., San Antonio
(210) 575–8110
msth.sahealth.com

This 382-bed facility has received wide-

Much of San Antonio's vast medical center lies on the city's northwest side. PHOTO: PARIS PERMENTER & JOHN BIGLEY

spread attention for its transplant facilities including heart/lung, kidney, kidney/pancreas, and others. The hospital also performs laparoscopic surgery in dedicated surgical suites. A special section is staffed by specialized nurses trained in working with victims of sexual assault. It also offers psychiatric and chemical-dependence programs, an inpatient hospice, and long-term acute care. The Methodist Cancer Center is also located within this hospital and offers specialized care for patients with all types of cancers.

Methodist Children's Hospital of South Texas
7700 Floyd Curl Dr., San Antonio
(210) 575–4000
mch.sahealth.com

Child health care is the focal point of this specialized hospital staffed by board-certified pediatric physicians and other pediatric-health-care professionals. The hospital has San Antonio's largest private neonatal intensive-care unit with 46 beds; other facilities include a dedicated children's imaging service, seven pediatric operating suites, and specialized outpatient pediatric clinics for diseases such as cystic fibrosis, brain tumors, bone-marrow transplant, and others. The facility also has an emergency room just for children. Children's rooms at the hospital are decorated in a homey, kid-friendly style; there's even a two-story tree house and a play area in the lobby. The hospital's Call-a-Nurse for Children phone line (210–22–NURSE) operates 24 hours per day, seven days a week, and provides free advice, in English or Spanish, from pediatric nurses about nonemergency questions.

Metropolitan Methodist Hospital
1310 McCullough Ave., San Antonio
(210) 208–2200
metro.sahealth.com

This downtown hospital, just two blocks north of I–35, serves as an acute-care facility. The 278-bed hospital has a complete maternity ward with prenatal testing; the facility also offers general medical and surgical care in areas including cardiology, orthopedics, rehabilitation, neurosurgery, and diagnostic imaging.

Audie L. Murphy Memorial Veterans Hospital
7400 Merton Minter St., San Antonio
(210) 617–5300

This facility provides patient care, including geriatric care in its federally funded Geriatric Research, Education, and Clinic Center. The hospital is also home to one of the world's largest fungus-identification and -testing labs.

North Central Baptist Hospital
520 Madison Oak Dr., San Antonio
(210) 297–4000
www.baptisthealthsystem.org/NCBH.asp

This 126-bed hospital offers 24-hour emergency services for both adults and children. The facility is also the home of the Baptist Regional Children's Center, with special child-friendly programs to help ease young patients' fears about surgery and medical treatments. The facility also has family-oriented maternity services, including postpartum rooms with Hill Country views. The hospital also offers many outpatient services, with separate outpatient registration, waiting, and recovery areas.

Northeast Baptist Hospital
8811 Village Dr., San Antonio
(210) 297–1000

This 291-bed hospital is designed for general acute care, with special facilities for cardiac care, women's health issues, neonatal care including a newborn intensive care service, pediatric medicine, cancer care, and 24-hour emergency care. The hospital is one of the largest ambulatory care centers in San Antonio.

Northeast Methodist Hospital
12412 Judson Rd., San Antonio
(210) 650–4949
nemh.sahealth.com/

Founded in 1985, this hospital now offers 117 beds to serve the needs of northeast San Antonio. The hospital offers cardiovascular services, including an open-heart surgery and cardiac catherization facility. Also here: the Breast Care Center, a 24-hour emergency department, imaging services, and mental-health care.

Southeast Baptist Hospital
4124 E. Southcross Blvd., San Antonio
(210) 297–3000

This 181-bed hospital is considered an international center for small-incision surgery. This was San Antonio's first hospital to offer ercutaneous laparoscopic laser cholecystectomy for gallbladder removal; the hospital also has received accolades for small-incision surgery in other areas, such as hernia repair. In addition Southeast Baptist offers 24-hour emergency care, sports medicine, an outpatient surgery center, and an imaging center.

St. Luke's Baptist Hospital
7930 Floyd Curl Dr., San Antonio
(210) 297–5000

Part of the South Texas Medical Center, this 291-bed facility offers specialized care in many fields including cardiology, colorectal surgery, orthopedics, neuroradiology, gynecology, plastic surgery, and microsurgery. The hospital also offers 24-hour emergency care as well as physical therapy, occupational therapy, and speech therapy. The St. Luke's Behavioral Health Center treats older adults with mental and emotional problems.

Warm Springs Rehabilitation Hospital
5101 Medical Dr., San Antonio
(210) 616–0100, (800) 741–6321
www.warmsprings.org

The original Warm Springs hospital is located east of San Antonio near Gonzales, where natural thermal springs are found near Palmetto State Park. Discov-

ered in 1909, the warm springs gave rise to a system of hospitals and outpatient facilities that now includes this hospital in San Antonio. The facility offers occupational, physical, and speech therapy as well as rehabilitation programs for amputation, brain injuries, major joint and orthopedic problems, pulmonary problems, spinal cord injury, stroke, and more. The facility also houses specialty services and programs in the fields of aquatic therapy, behavioral medicine, hyperbaric medicine, and wound care, among others.

Wilford Hall Medical Center
Lackland Air Force Base, San Antonio
(210) 292–7100

The largest medical center operated by the U.S. Air Force, this facility serves as a primary-care facility, a trauma center, and an educational facility for physicians and dentists. More than 65 percent of the physicians in the U.S. Air Force are trained at this facility, along with 85 percent of the force's dental specialists. Research projects are also conducted here in the areas of hyperbaric procedures, hypobaric procedures, bone-marrow transplant, and organ transplant.

Public Health Care

Public health assistance is provided through the San Antonio Metropolitan Health District at 332 West Commerce Street (210-207-8780, www.samhd.org). This governmental agency promotes health care throughout Bexar County in areas including disease control, family health services, environmental health, and dental health. The district operates many public health clinics that offer a variety of services. Some offer walk-in immunizations, sexually transmitted disease diagnosis and treatment, substance-abuse treatment, administration of the Women's, Infants, and Children's Nutrition Program (WIC), and HIV testing and counseling. Not all services are available at all locations. Public clinics include:

> ## Insiders' Tip
> San Antonio's South Texas Medical Center employs more than 26,000 health-care workers.

Buena Vista Clinic
2315 Buena Vista St., San Antonio
(210) 225–0213

Callaghan Clinic
4412 Callaghan Rd., San Antonio
(210) 436–5042

Dorie Miller Center
2802 Martin Luther King Dr., San Antonio
(210) 333–6432

Eastside Branch
210 N. Rio Grande St., San Antonio
(210) 224–7981

Fredericksburg Clinic
3600 Fredericksburg Rd., San Antonio
(210) 738–3486

Immunization Center
345 W. Commerce St., San Antonio
(210) 207–8894

Isom Road Clinic
722C Isom Rd., San Antonio
(210) 342–1434

Kenwood Clinic
302 Dora St., San Antonio
(210) 736–1536

Las Palmas Public Health Center
911 Castroville Rd., San Antonio
(210) 435–9771

Marbach Clinic
7452 Military Dr., San Antonio
(210) 645–4480

Old Highway 90 Clinic
911 Old Hwy. 90, San Antonio
(210) 433–3279

Pecan Valley Clinic
802 Pecan Valley Dr., San Antonio
(210) 337–7511

Rittiman Clinic
1013 Rittiman Rd., San Antonio
(210) 804–2096

Ryan White Dental Clinic
818 E. Grayson St., San Antonio
(210) 224–8950

San Pedro Branch
910 San Pedro Ave., San Antonio
(210) 207–2437

Southeast Clinic
3630 Southeast Military Dr., San Antonio
(210) 337–5132

South Flores Clinic
7902 S. Flores St., San Antonio
(210) 924–2552

Thousand Oaks Clinic
4342 Thousand Oaks Dr., San Antonio
(210) 655–8208

Tuberculosis Clinic
814 McCullough Ave., San Antonio
(210) 207–8823

West End Multi Service Center
1226 Northwest 18th St., San Antonio
(210) 734–0945

Zarzamora Clinic
4503 S. Zarzamora St., San Antonio
(210) 921–6500

Referral Agencies

Bexar County Medical Society
202 W. French Pl., San Antonio
(210) 734–6691

Need a doctor? If you're new in town and you don't know where to start, give this number a call for a referral in the specialty you seek.

San Antonio District Dental Society
202 W. French Pl., San Antonio
(210) 732–1264

Like the medical society housed at the same address, this referral agency help match patients and doctors, in this case, dentists. The agency can help you find a dentist that meets your needs, whether that means one at a convenient location or one with a particular medical specialization.

Resources

United Way of San Antono and Bexar County
700 S. Alamo St., San Antonio
(210) 352–7000
www.unitedwaysatx.org/

This agency publishes *The Community Assistance Directory,* which lists nonprofit health, welfare, recreational, and educational resources for the community. You can obtain a copy of this publication by calling the office or ordering it by mail.

Specialized Health-Care Programs

AIDS/HIV Care

The following facilities offer a wide range of services, including medical and dental care and referrals, psychiatric counseling and support groups, education and prevention programs, HIV testing, assistance with applications for governmental aid, legal assistance, referrals for rental and utility assistance, meals, and food pantries. Not every clinic offers all these services; call for details.

Alamo Area Resource Center
800 Lexington Ave., San Antonio
(210) 222–2437

BEAT AIDS
707 Dawson St., San Antonio
(210) 212–2266

Center for Health Care Services—Crisis Center
711 E. Josephine St., San Antonio
(210) 225–5481

Centro Del Barrio—Laurel Heights Clinic
2608 N. Main Ave., San Antonio
(210) 738–8215

Ella Austin Health Center
1920 Burnet St., San Antonio
(210) 224–2112

Gay and Lesbian Community Center
3126 N. St. Mary's St., San Antonio
(210) 732–4300
www.stic.net/users/glccsa

Hope, Actlon, Care
126 E. Grayson, San Antonio
(210) 224–7330

House of Hope
1436 E. Highland Blvd., San Antonio
(210) 534–3741

Immunosuppression Clinic, University Health Center, Downtown
527 N. Leona St., San Antonio
(210) 358–3710

Interim Health Care
8299 Fredericksburg Rd., San Antonio
(210) 614–8299

Mujeres Project
904 Nolan, San Antonio
(210) 222–9417

Providence Home
2650 Castroville Rd., San Antonio
(210) 434–2111

Ryan White Dental Clinic
818 E. Grayson St., San Antonio
(210) 224–8950

Insiders' Tip

Students attending Texas schools are required to have a number of immunizations; for a complete chart of the required shots, see the Texas Department of Health Web site, www.tdh.state.tx.us.

San Antonio AIDS Foundation
818 E. Grayson St., San Antonio
(210) 225–4715

San Antonio Metropolitan Health District—
Supportive Services
910 San Pedro Ave., San Antonio
(210) 207–2437

South Texas AIDS Center for Families and
Children
7271 Wurzbach Rd., San Antonio
(210) 567–7400

Texas Department of Health
Public Health Region 8
7210 W. Olmos Dr., San Antonio
(210) 821–5522
www.tdh.state.tx.us

Wellness Connection
1424 Fredricksburg Rd., San Antonio
(210) 732–3111

Mental Health

Center for Health Care Services
3031 I–10 West, San Antonio
(210) 731–1300

This agency operates four mental-health programs covering substance abuse, mental retardation, mental health, and residential programs. Referrals are made on weekdays; for emergency referrals, call the Crisis Stabilization Unit at (210) 226-9241.

Mental Health Association
901 Northeast Loop 410, Suite 704, San Antonio
(210) 826–2288

This nonprofit association works as a referral agency to promote better mental health for San Antonio residents. The group can match callers with one or more of the 500 support groups, self-help groups, and mental health services throughout the city.

Poison Center

South Texas Poison Center
(800) POISON–1, (800) 764–7661
www.uthscsa.edu/surgery/poisoncenter/
index.html

Questions about poison control? Call the South Texas Poison Center for information on poisoning prevention and treatment for poisoning victims. The phone is answered daily around the clock and assistance can be received in English, Spanish, or TDD for hearing-impaired callers. Interpreters are available for other languages.

Therapeutic Programs

Therapeutic Recreation Program
San Antonio Parks and Recreation Program
Copernicus Community Center
5003 Lord Rd., San Antonio

Lackland Terrace Community Center
7902 Westshire Dr., San Antonio

Garrett Community Center
1226 Northwest 18th St., San Antonio
(210) 207–3048

San Antonio residents with disabilities can enjoy a variety of activities through this program, operated Monday through Friday from 8:00 A.M. to 3:30 P.M. Basketball, bowling, dancing, hiking, swimming, and low-impact exercise classes are offered, as are arts and crafts, table games, gardening, and local outings using a van service. The program also schedules special events such as dances and festivals for people with disabilities and their families. To participate in the therapeutic recreation program, applications must be made to the program and participants must have their own transportation. Programs are held at three community centers (see above).

Retirement

Senior Resources

Senior Centers

Support Groups

Lifetime Learning

Community Activities

Employment
   Opportunities

Volunteer
   Opportunities

Transportation

Housing

Publications

Thanks to the many military employees who come through San Antonio during their years of duty, the Alamo City is a favorite retirement destination with former military personnel and their families. With its high standard of living, favorable cost of living when compared with many other cities its size, and good climate, San Antonio is considered one of Texas's top retirement spots. The San Antonio Chamber of Commerce estimates that retirees make up about 15 percent of the city's population. Many are active participants in the city's art scene, ecotourism, volunteerism, and employment worlds.

Many of San Antonio's retired residents live in the northwest portion of the city, at the entrance to the Hill Country. The northwest communities of Bandera and Kerrville are especially popular with active retirees who enjoy a small-town atmosphere. North of Austin, and about 90 minutes from San Antonio, Sun City Georgetown offers an extensive retirement community akin to Arizona and Florida's Sun City facilities.

Senior Resources

American Association of Retired Persons
Central Park Mall
622 Northwest Loop 410
(210) 348–8684
www.aarp.com/

The American Association of Retired Persons (AARP) has 16 chapters in the San Antonio area. The association also has an information center at Central Park Mall (see above). The center is open 10:00 A.M. to 6:00 P.M. Monday through Friday and 10:00 A.M. to 2:00 P.M. on Saturday. Staffed by volunteers, this center can provide information about AARP, which offers members (who are age 50 and over) information on legislative issues, health, money, volunteerism, and more.

City of San Antonio Elderly and Disabled Services
700 S. Zarzamora, Suite 205, San Antonio
(210) 207–7172
www.ci.sat.tx.us

This department offers five services: a comprehensive nutrition program, supportive services for the elderly, a city homemaker program, a client-managed program, and a personal-attendant services program. Funded by the City of San Antonio General Fund, the Alamo Area Council of Governments, the Texas Department of Human Resources, and the Texas Rehabilitation Commission, the agency works to better the lives of elderly and disabled persons in Bexar County.

The Comprehensive Nutrition Program is available to citizens age 60 and older. Meals are served in a group setting to offer participants the opportunity to socialize. The program also offers transportation, recreation, health screenings, shopping assistance, and health and welfare counseling.

The Supportive Services for the Elderly Program offers door-to-door transportation for citizens age 60 and older to medical appointments, Social Security offices, food-stamp offices, and legal appointments as well as to the grocery store and bank. The service is free.

The Client-Managed Program provides assistance to adults who are permanently disabled. Along with personal care, the program offers meal preparation, home management, grocery shopping, companionship, and more. The Personal-Attendant Service is similar, but is designed for disabled persons who are employed. The City Homemaker Program assists elderly citizens at home and also provides in-home attendant care.

Community Care Services to Aged and Disabled (CCAD)
Texas Department of Human Services
11307 Roszell St., San Antonio
(210) 619–8001
www.dhs.state.tx.us

This service provides home-delivered meals to elderly San Antonians as well as primary home care. The agency runs out-of-the-home programs such as day activities and health services.

Social Security Administration
Downtown: 727 E. Durango, San Antonio
Northwest: 8020 Alamo Downs Parkway, San Antonio
South: 4100 S. New Braunfels, San Antonio
(800) 772–1213
www.ssa.gov

The Social Security Administration has several offices in San Antonio to assist residents with applying for benefits. The easiest way is to call the national toll-free number above (avoid Mondays: they're the busiest calling days).

Senior Centers

San Antonio is home to numerous senior centers that sponsor a host of programs—social activities, health screenings, transportation, meals, and even trips. Call the individual centers for details on hours (many are open weekdays only) and services.

Activity Center for Frail and Elderly (Centro del Barrio)
317 King St., San Antonio
(210) 924–0588

Bethel Senior Center
227 S. Acme Rd., San Antonio
(210) 433–3599

Casa Helotes Senior Center
12070 Leslie Rd., Helotes
(210) 695–8510

Chandler Estate in Laurel Heights Senior Activity Center
137 W. French Pl., San Antonio
(210) 737–5195

Christ the King Senior Center
2610 Perez St., San Antonio
(210) 434–3027

Claude Black Community Center
2805 E. Commerce St., San Antonio
(210) 226–8561

Comanche Park #2 Senior Center
2600 Rigsby, Navajo Building, San Antonio
(210) 333–0414

Commander's House
647 S. Main Ave., San Antonio
(210) 224–1684

Ella Austin Community Center
1023 N. Pine St., San Antonio
(210) 224–2351

El Carmen Senior Center
18555 Leal Rd., San Antonio
(210) 626–2485

First Presbyterian Senior Center
404 N. Alamo St., San Antonio
(210) 226–0215

Good Samaritan Center
1600 Saltillo St., San Antonio
(210) 434–5531

Retirees can enjoy all of San Antonio's attractions, such as the Spanish Governor's Palace.
PHOTO: AL RENDON, COURTESY OF THE SAN ANTONIO CONVENTION AND VISITORS BUREAU

Granada Homes
311 S. St. Mary's St., San Antonio
(210) 225–2645

Greater Randolph Area Senior Program
250 Donalan, Converse
(210) 658–3575

Harlandale Senior Center
115 W. Southcross Blvd., San Antonio
(210) 924–4771

Holy Family Senior Center
152 Florencia, San Antonio
(210) 433–4265

Holy Rosary Senior Center
159 Camino Santa Maria, San Antonio
(210) 434–4628

Holy Spirit Episcopal Senior Center
6676 UTSA Blvd., San Antonio
(210) 699–6460

HOPE
512 W. Elmira St., San Antonio
(210) 352–2010

Jardin de St. James
420 Nunes St., San Antonio
(210) 532–9239

Jewish Community Center
12500 Northwest Military Hwy., San Antonio
(210) 302–6820

Jefferson Area Co-Op
201 Meredith Dr., San Antonio
(210) 734–5016

Kenwood Community Center
305 Dora St., San Antonio
(210) 732–1718

Kirby Senior Center
3211 Allen Sheppard Dr., San Antonio
(210) 666–5124

Leon Valley Community Center
6427 Evers Rd., San Antonio
(210) 522–9966

Lions Field Adult and Senior Center
2809 Broadway, San Antonio
(210) 826–9041

Madonna Neighborhood Center
1906 Castroville Rd., San Antonio
(210) 432–2374

Meals on Wheels
4306 Northwest Loop 410, San Antonio
(210) 735–5115

Mission San Jose Senior Center
6712 E. Pyron Ave., San Antonio
(210) 923–8681

New Mount Pleasant Baptist Senior Center
1639 Hays St., San Antonio
(210) 225–7907

Northeast Senior Center
2930 E. Bitters Rd., San Antonio
(210) 832–9387

Northeast San Antonio Senior Center
10635 I-35 N., San Antonio
(210) 967–6372

Northwood Presbyterian Senior Center
518 Pike St., San Antonio
(210) 821–6800

Our Lady of Angels Senior Center
1224 Stonewall St., San Antonio
(210) 923–6270

Our Lady of Guadalupe Church Senior Center
1321 El Paso St., San Antonio
(210) 222–1762

Our Lady of Sorrows Senior Center
3107 N. St. Mary's St., San Antonio
(210) 733–1247

Palacio del Sol Senior Center
400 N. Frio St., San Antonio
(210) 224–0442

Presa Community Center
3721 S. Presa St., San Antonio
(210) 532–5295

Rolling Oaks Baptist Church
6401 Wenzel Rd., San Antonio
(210) 590–4177

Sacred Heart Senior Center
2123 W. Commerce St., San Antonio
(210) 226–3536

St. Agnes Senior Center
804 Ruiz St., San Antonio
(210) 223–1603

St. Alphonsus Senior Center
1200 S. Rosillo St., San Antonio
(210) 432–8311

St. Bonaventure Senior Center
1918 Palo Alto Rd., San Antonio
(210) 923–0899

Insiders' Tip

Retirees who bring pets to San Antonio will need licenses for both dogs and cats. If your pet already has a current vaccination certificate, bring it by the Animal Control Facility at 201 Tuleta Drive (210-737-1442). If the animal's shots are not current, veterinarians can provide a license upon vaccination. San Antonio also has a leash law. All dogs must either be in a fenced yard or on a leash.

St. Gregory Senior Center
720 Beryl St., San Antonio
(210) 349–9893

St. Henry's Catholic Church Senior Center
1619 S. Flores St., San Antonio
(210) 924–4771

St. Jude's Senior Center
130 S. San Augustine Ave., San Antonio
(210) 432–8814

St. Mary Magdalen's Senior Center
1701 Alametos, San Antonio
(210) 735–3700

St. Matthew's Catholic Church Senior Center
10703 Wurzbach Rd., San Antonio
(210) 691–8947

St. Paul Senior Center
1201 Donaldson Ave., San Antonio
(210) 736–6279

St. Stephen's Senior Center
2127 S. Zarzamora St., San Antonio
(210) 224–1934

St. Timothy Senior Center
1515 Saltillo St., San Antonio
(210) 432–4477

St. Lawrence Senior Center
236 Petaluma Blvd., San Antonio
(210) 924–4401

St. Vincent de Paul Senior Center
4222 Southwest Loop 410, San Antonio
(210) 670–1800

Salvation Army Peacock Center
615 Peacock St., San Antonio
(210) 733–0665

San Juan de los Lagos Senior Center
3231 El Paso St., San Antonio
(210) 434–6361

Senior Opportunity Services of Texas
4139 E. Houston St., San Antonio
(210) 337–6925

Insiders' Tip

New San Antonio residents register to vote with the Bexar County Elections Department, 203 West Nueva Street, (210-978-0362). There's a 30-day waiting period after registration before you can vote in a San Antonio election.

Southeast Community Outreach for Older People (SCOOP)
1602 Goliad Rd., San Antonio
(210) 359–6678

South San Antonio YWCA Senior Center
503 Lovett Ave., San Antonio
(210) 924–4691

Walnut Manor
3822 West Ave., San Antonio
(210) 349–1076

West End Park Senior Center
1226 Northwest 18th St., San Antonio
(210) 737–1054

Support Groups

Alzheimer's Association of South Central Texas
7400 Louis Pasteur Dr., Suite 200, San Antonio
(210) 822–6449, (800) 523–2007
www.sctx-alzheimers.org

This association serves people in Central and South Texas who have Alzheimer's or who have a family member with the disease. Founded in 1981 by the wife of an Alzheimer's victim, the association serves as a support group and an information center. It hosts annual fund-raising walks and golf tournaments.

Caring for Your Aging Parent
Trinity Baptist Counseling Center
319 E. Mulberry Ave., San Antonio
(210) 733–6201

This support group is designed for those who care for one or more aging parent. The group meets on the first Tuesday of every month at the counseling center, which is in the Monte Vista neighborhood.

Grief Support Group
Trinity Baptist Counseling Center
319 E. Mulberry Ave., San Antonio
(210) 733–6201

This support group meets every Thursday, offering assistance to those who have lost a spouse or significant other to death.

Widowed Persons Service
(210) 738–8141

Sponsored by the American Association of Retired Persons (AARP), this nonprofit group provides support services to both men and women who have lost a spouse or significant other to death.

Lifetime Learning

Northside Independent School District
6632 Bandera Rd., San Antonio
(210) 522–8100
www.nisd.net/comedww/

This large school system offers a variety of leisure-learning classes. Seniors new to computers or wishing to expand their computer skills can sign up for a variety of computer and Internet classes. Many classes in cooking, health, language, law, sewing, hobbies, and gardening are also offered.

North East Independent School District
10333 Broadway, San Antonio
(210) 657–8866
www.northeast.isd.tenet.edu/

Community classes offered through this school district run the gamut from "Fun with Physics" to foreign languages to bluegrass banjo. Self-defense, oil-painting, birding, and drama workshops are other popular programs.

Community Activities

San Antonio Parks and Recreation Department Senior Programming
Commander's House
645 S. Main, San Antonio
(210) 224–1684
www.ci.sat.tx.us/sapar

Seniors age 50 and over can participate in community activities through the San Antonio Parks and Recreation Department. A range of activities are held at the Commander's House, a historic facility built in 1883 as the living quarters for the Commanding Officer of the Texas Arsenal. Classes here range from painting to guitar to ballroom dancing. Defensive-driving classes are offered on the last Monday and Tuesday of every month. The facility also sponsors free blood-pressure checks once a month. For a minimal charge, participants at the center can purchase lunch every Tuesday, Wednesday, and Thursday.

San Antonio Parks and Recreation Department Senior Programming
Lion's Field Adult and Senior Citizens Center
2809 Broadway, San Antonio
(210) 826–9041

Seniors can sign up for a variety of classes at this seniors' center; programs include ceramics, bridge, painting, exercise, and more. The Woodlawn Camera Club and the San Antonio Historic Association hold their regular meetings here as well. The center also operates a boutique featuring items made by center participants; the boutique is operated with volunteer help Monday through Friday. The center runs special events throughout the year, including an annual Christmas Arts and Crafts sale.

Employment Opportunities

Goodwill Industries of San Antonio
(210) 222–1294
www.goodwillsa.org

Goodwill, known as "the place that puts people to work," helps San Antonio seniors find employment through its Senior Employment Service and Older Worker Program.

Volunteer Opportunities

Bexar County Retired Senior Volunteer Program (RSVP)
1405 N. Main Ave., Suite 223, San Antonio
(210) 222–0301
www.seniorcorps.org

Seniors looking for volunteer opportunities find plenty of options through the Retired Senior Volunteer Program or RSVP.

San Antonio Parks and Recreation Department
(210) 207–8452
www.ci.sat.tx.us/sapar

The Parks and Recreation Department offers a variety of volunteer opportunities: working with people with special needs, assisting participants in recreational education programs, working with others at community centers, and participating in park cleanups. Citizens can also help ensure the safety of the local parks by becoming a San Antonio Park Ranger. For information on this volunteer park watch program, call (210) 207–8529.

United Way of San Antonio and Bexar County
700 S. Alamo St., San Antonio
(210) 352–7000
www.unitedwaysatx.org/

The Volunteer Center at United Way of San Antonio and Bexar County offers participants a variety of opportunities, depending on their desires and their previous experience. The job bank (as well as the United Way Web site) lists volunteer openings ranging from marketing assistants to clerical help to youth assistance.

Transportation

VIA Metropolitan Transit Service
(210) 362–2020
www.viainfo.net

San Antonio and Bexar County's public transportation system offers a wide range of buses that crisscross the region. Seniors age 62 and over receive discount rides: 35 cents per limited-stop bus ride and 75 cents for express bus fare. Off-peak discounts for senior citizens and persons with disabilities are available weekdays from 9:00 A.M. to 3:00 P.M. and all day weekends; these fares are for fixed routes only.

There are ramps on some VIA buses; most have floors at curb level. VIA also operates VIAtrans for residents with disabilities and their personal care attendants. Application for use of this minivan service has to be made to (210) 362–2140; applications are also available online at www.viainfo.net/accessible_services/apps.html. Once admitted to the program, riders can schedule rides on VIAtrans; reservations must be made at least 24 hours but not more than 12 days before a trip. The fee for VIAtrans rides is $1.25 per one-way trip. If you travel outside the VIAtrans service area, there is an additional charge of $4.00 each way. (The VIAtrans service area is inside I–410.) No fare is charged for personal-care attendants but companions pay the $1.00 base fare and $4.00 surcharge, if applicable.

Housing

Alzheimer's Care

Arden Courts
15290 Huebner Rd., San Antonio
(210) 408–9100

Completely devoted to the care of people with Alzheimer's, this assisted-living facility is designed for residents in the early or middle stages of the disease. The facility is staffed 24 hours a day and offers home-style meals and several small residential buildings that consist of 16 studio units with a bedroom and bath and shared living rooms, dining rooms, and kitchens. Arden Courts includes crafts rooms, indoor walking paths, secured outdoor courtyards, a health center, and a beauty and barber shop. The all-inclusive fee includes three meals daily, wellness and exercise programs, and more; there are no entrance fees or security deposits.

Assisted Living

The Beacon House
8005 Chambers Rd., San Antonio
(210) 375–1445
www.thebeaconhouse.net

This assisted-living facility is located in the countryside and offers a full range of services, including 24-hour assistance,

personal care assistance, and supervision of medications.

Brighton Gardens by Marriott—San Antonio
855 E. Basse Rd., San Antonio
(210) 930–1040
www.marriottseniorliving.com

Located in the Alamo Heights area, this assisted-living facility offers private suites and three meals daily. The centrally located property provides scheduled transportation and weekly housekeeping, and has staff members on call around the clock.

Chandler Assisted Living
1510 Howard St., San Antonio
(210) 737–5200
www.morningsidemin.org

This church-related organization has provided senior health care for more than four decades and has assisted-living facilities as well as retirement-living, health-care, and home-care programs. The assisted-living facility offers residential suites for residents who do not require nursing care. This property also offers restaurant-style dining, a library, washers and dryers, housekeeping service, basic cable television service, social activities, transportation, and 24-hour emergency response.

Esplanade Gardens
10790 Toepperwein Rd., San Antonio
(210) 566–7600

This privately owned facility is located near Northeast Methodist Hospital. Three meals daily are provided along with housekeeping, transportation, medication administration, activities, cable television, and more. The staff includes certified nursing aides and LVNs. Residents are welcome to have small pets.

The Grand Court I
5034 Newforest Dr., San Antonio
(210) 680–3649
www.grandcourtlifestyles.com

These assisted-living apartments include full kitchens, although dining is also available three times daily. Residents can take advantage of scheduled transportation, weekly housekeeping, outings, and activities.

The Inn at Los Patios Personal Care Center
8700 Post Oak La., San Antonio
(210) 829–7357
www.theinnatlospatios.com

This facility, located in northwest San Antonio, offers residents three meals per day as well as assistance with daily chores and personal care. The complex includes 30 apartments and offers residents activities and trips planned by a full-time activities director.

Kingsley Place
Oakwell Farms, 3360 Oakwell Court,
San Antonio
(210) 820–8744
The Medical Center, 9000 Floyd Curl Drive,
San Antonio
(210) 697–0772
www.senr.com

These are two 80-suite assisted-living complexes for residents who need help with some basic tasks, from transportation to bathing to meals. Residents are welcome to have small pets.

The Meadows Retirement Community
730 Babcock Rd., San Antonio
(210) 734–1155
www.morningsidemin.org

The community is for independent seniors who are seeking additional help with some daily chores. Services include meals, transportation, housekeeping, and 24-hour emergency response.

Merrill Gardens
9203 Cinnamon Hill, San Antonio
(210) 641–5046, (800) 889–5510
www.merrillgardens.com

This facility offers 82 units for independent seniors who might need occasional assistance. The facility offers emergency call systems in each apartment; respite care is also available. Residents receive a 60-day guaran-

> **Insiders' Tip**
>
> All Texas drivers must have liability insurance. You'll need to show proof of liability insurance to obtain a Texas driver's license, to register a car, or to get an inspection sticker for your vehicle.

tee of a full refund if they are not completely satisfied with their new home. Merrill Gardens has additional locations north of San Antonio in Round Rock and San Marcos.

Regent at Hamilton House
5331 Hamilton Wolfe Rd., San Antonio
(210) 641–7200
www.regentassistedliving.com

Located near the South Texas Medical Center, this 92-apartment complex offers assisted-living services. On-site staff are available around the clock, and three meals are served daily. Scheduled transportation, housekeeping, laundry, and other services are also provided. One- and two-bedroom apartments are available; pets are welcomed.

The Waterford at Huebner
8551 Huebner Rd., San Antonio
(210) 656–7052

This 120-unit facility offers studio, one-, and two-bedroom apartments on a month-to-month rental basis. Daily meals are served and residents also can take advantage of recreational programs, 24-hour staffing, scheduled transportation, and weekly housekeeping. On-site facilities include a beauty and barber shop, a library, and a billiards room.

Publications

Ageless Times
(210) 453–3300

Distributed at more than 400 locations across the city, this free monthly has news and features of interest to seniors. With a circulation of 30,000, it is San Antonio's leading publication for retirees.

New Lifestyles
(800) 869–9549
www.newlifestyles.com

Published twice a year, this free guide to senior housing covers senior apartments, continuing-care retirement communities, retirement communities, assisted-living facilities, Alzheimer's care facilities, nursing and rehabilitation centers, home-care agencies, hospice-care agencies, and adult day-care centers.

San Antonio Retirement Guide
(210) 229–2104, (210) 229–2105
www.sachamber.org/pubretire.htm

Published twice a year by the San Antonio Chamber of Commerce, this helpful guide provides an overview of retirement communities and senior resources and activities throughout the Alamo City. The guide can be purchased online or by calling the Chamber office directly.

Media

Visitors to San Antonio who want to learn about the city should probably begin with something simple: turning on their radio or TV, or reading a newspaper. The local media offer the quickest way to really get a feel for the Alamo City. Pick up a copy of the *San Antonio Express-News* or one of the smaller newspapers that focus on events and news in a particular area of town. Or tune in to a local TV or radio news program. In addition to helping visitors decide where to go and what to do, these media outlets offer great insight into how citizens of San Antonio conduct their day-to-day lives.

Newspapers and Magazines

Dailies

San Antonio Express-News
400 Third St., San Antonio
(210) 250–3000
www.expressnews.com

In September, 1865, only a few months after the end of the Civil War, August Siemering and H. Pollmar published the first issue of the weekly *San Antonio Express*. Daily papers began to be published in December of 1866, with a subscription rate of $16 a year. Today this is San Antonio's main daily newspaper. The *San Antonio Express-News* covers weather, local events, business, and sports in addition to local and national news. Pick up a Friday issue for all of the information about what's happening in the Alamo City during the upcoming weekend.

Other Newspapers and Magazines

Daily Commercial Recorder
17400 Judson Rd., San Antonio
(210) 453–3300
www.primetimenewspapers.com/dcr

This newspaper is published weekdays (except legal holidays). *Commercial Recorder* is a great source of public notices and public records taken from Bexar County Courts, including court transactions, liens, and bankruptcies. The paper also publishes such business information as the granting of beer and wine permits, building permits, and sales tax permits. Copies of *Daily Commercial Recorder* are available at several locations around the Bexar County Courthouse. Readers may also subscribe to the paper for $150 a year or $55 per quarter.

Fiesta Magazine
P.O. Box 2171, San Antonio
(210) 250–3000

Published by the *San Antonio Express-News,* this monthly magazine is aimed at visitors to the Alamo City. Articles cover local

Insiders' Tip

When you arrive in town, locate a copy of the free *San Antonio Current* newspaper for up-to-the-minute listings of the arts and entertainment scene.

food, events, and daytrips within the region.

La Prensa de San Antonio
318 S. Flores St., San Antonio
(210) 242–7900
www.laprensa.com

La Prensa de San Antonio is San Antonio's only bilingual newspaper. Published in both Spanish and English, it comes out every Wednesday and Sunday. *La Prensa* covers local and national news, business, entertainment, and sports. You can also check out *La Prensa*'s Web site, which offers access to the paper's archives.

Prime Time Newspapers
17400 Judson Rd., San Antonio
(210) 453–3300

This newspaper corporation publishes many specialty newspapers and magazines in the San Antonio area. In addition to *The Daily Commercial Recorder* (see above), Prime Time Newspapers publishes *Que Pasa San Antonio,* a bimonthly magazine that focuses on San Antonio's tourist and meeting/convention markets and covers what to do and see in the Alamo City. The corporation also publishes the *Ageless Times,* San Antonio's leading retirement publication. This free monthly paper carries articles of interest to senior citizens in San Antonio. *S. A. Kids,* another monthly publication, has articles for kids and parents on such issues at health, education, sports, movies, and area events area that are suitable for San Antonio's youngest citizens. Prime Time Newspapers also publishes San Antonio's weekly community papers, which cover specific areas of the city. These include the *Bulverde Community News, Southside Reporter, North San Antonio Times,* and *Northside Reporter.*

San Antonio Business Journal
70 N.E. Loop 410, San Antonio
(210) 341–3202
sanantonio.bcentral.com/sanantonio/index.html

As you might expect, the *San Antonio Business Journal* is a great place to find information on the San Antonio business scene. And much of the information in the print version of this weekly is also found on the *Journal*'s Web site. The Web site also allows readers to access nearly 40 other business papers. The online Web archive includes *Journal* articles from as far back as 1996.

San Antonio Current
1500 N. St. Mary's St., San Antonio
(210) 227–0044
www.sacurrent.com

The *Current* is San Antonio's free alternative newspaper, published weekly and distributed all over town. It covers the hipper element of the city and is particularly strong on local entertainment news. It often offers a different slant on local politics, and its classifieds can also make for interesting reading.

Radio Stations

If you like Tejano and Conjunto music, then you'll love San Antonio radio. Due to its extensive cultural diversity and major Mexican influences, San Antonio's radio stations are filled with sounds from South of the Border. Tejano music can be found feature the radio dials in the San Antonio area. In fact, the Tejano sound is so popular in San Antonio, that there are several clubs around the city that feature music with a Latin beat. (See the Nightlife chapter for more information.) But whatever your taste in music, you're bound to find a local station that plays your favorite tunes.

Radio DJs are also a good source of inside information in San Antonio. Many have been working in San Antonio radio for more than a decade and know a great deal about local clubs, restaurants, and news. Change the frequency on the car radio often to get a variety of spins on the local scene.

Christian

KSLR AM 630
9601 McAllister Fwy., San Antonio
(210) 344–8481
www.kslr.com

This station offers inspirational Christian talk radio. The lineup is varied, and every hour brings a new topic and host. On Monday through Friday, tune in for "Truth for Life" with Alister Begg at 8:30 A.M., "Truths that Transform" with D. James Kennedy at 11:30 A.M., "Take A Stand," a live talk show with Adam McManus at 3:00 P.M., and "The Bible Answer Man" at 6:00 P.M. The lineup and times are different on the weekends.

KYFS FM 90.9
9330 Corporate Dr., Suite 808, Selma
(210) 651–9093

Owned by the Bible Broadcasting Network of Charlotte, North Carolina, this 100,000-watt station covers San Antonio and surrounding South Texas with gospel-based programming around the clock. Highlights of the KYFS broadcast day include scripture readings at 4:00 P.M. and a "Good News" newscast on the hour; Sunday School and sermons are broadcast on Sunday mornings.

Country

KCYY FM 100
8122 Datapoint Dr., Suite 500, San Antonio
(210) 615–5400, (210) 470–5299 (request line)
www.y100fm.com

If you've come to Texas for country music, then tune in to Y100 FM. And if you're looking for music news, then log on to the station's website, which has the latest entertainment headlines, listings for events in the San Antonio area, and local and national news and weather. The morning show runs from 5:30 A.M. until 10:00 A.M. It features disc jockeys Kris Winston and Alyce Ian, who have been working together in radio for 18 years, 15 of those in San Antonio. Their on-air chemistry makes the show a local favorite.

KJ97 FM 97
6222 N.W. I–10, San Antonio
(210) 736–9700, (800) 373–9700, (210) 470–KJ97 (request line)
www.kj97.com

KJ97 broadcasts Texas's favorite country music. Tune in to hear the latest country hits as well as the chart-toppers of yesteryears. The KJ97 Web site is a good source of country-music news, events listings, contests, upcoming album information, and more.

Public Radio

KPAC FM 88.3
8401 Datapoint Dr., San Antonio
(210) 614–8977
www.tpr.org

KPAC has been San Antonio's classical music source on FM since 1982, broadcasting musical programming 24 hours each day. Weekend highlights include "Saturday Afternoon at the Opera," at

Insiders' Tip

San Antonio's current weather information is available 24 hours a day on National Weather Service radio station WXK67, at 162.5 mgz. If your regular AM radio cannot pick up the signal (it broadcasts at only 1000 watts) you can purchase special weather alert radios at retailers such as Radio Shack.

noon on Saturdays, and the popular "Listener's Choice," at 7:00 P.M. on Saturdays. Programs for children and broadcasts of early music recordings are also scheduled.

KSTX FM 89.1
8401 Datapoint Dr., San Antonio
(210) 614–8977
www.tpr.org

KSTX, KPAC's sister station, has a talk radio format, with most of its weekday programming produced by National Public Radio, including the popular news magazine "All Things Considered," which airs at 3:00 P.M. Tune in to KSTX on Saturdays to hear live broadcasts of "A Prairie Home Companion" at 5:00 P.M. and the local "Riverwalk, Live From the Landing," which features the Jim Cullum Jazz Band broadcasting from Jim Cullum's The Landing at the Hyatt, on San Antonio's Riverwalk.

Retro

KSMG FM 105.3
8930 Fourwinds Dr., San Antonio
(210) 646–0105, (800) 366–KSMG,
(210) 470–KSMG (request line)
www.magic105.com

Magic 105.3's Retro Lunch Café is one of the best reasons to listen to this station. At noon Monday through Friday, the station plays all 1980s music from the most popular artists of the decade. From The Police to Flock of Seagulls, this station plays all the favorites. If you still want more, tune in for Awesome '80s Night at 7:00 P.M. every weeknight, and Awesome '80s Weekends, which are every weekend. Needless to say, this station loves the Eighties, as does much of the San Antonio listening audience.

Insiders' Tip
To get your Dr. Laura fix, tune to WOAI, AM 1200.

Rock

KISS FM 99.5
8930 Four Winds Dr., Suite 500, San Antonio
(210) 646–0105,
(210) 470-KISS (request line)
www.kissrocks.com

This rock radio station has many extra features to entice listeners to stay tuned. The Kiss Concert Line (210-871-6120), keeps listeners up to date on current music events in San Antonio, including national tours. "The Nooner" is an all-request lunch hour. At 5:00 P.M., listeners enjoy "5 O'Clock Rock Blocks" on their drive home after work. Wrestling fans should tune in on Sundays between 10:00 P.M. and midnight to hear interviews with some of today's most popular wrestlers. If you're looking for something to do at night, then listen Monday through Saturday at 7:20 P.M. and 9:20 P.M. for a listing of what's happening in San Antonio.

KZEP FM 104.5
427 Ninth St., San Antonio
(210) 226–6444, (210) 470–5104
www.kzep.com

Tune in to KZEP for the greatest hits in classic rock music. The station also runs several contests, with prizes ranging from radio station collectables to concert tickets. The station Web site has information on station DJs, rock news, and radio station contests.

Talk

KTSA AM 550
4050 Eisenhauer Rd., San Antonio
(210) 528–5500, (210) 599–5555 (talk show call-in line)
www.ktsa.com

This radio station began in 1922 as WCAR. Its name was changed to KTSA in 1927 when it was bought by Alamo Broadcast Company, and the company has changed hands several times since then. One of the highlights of KTSA history was a live interview with Orson Welles and H.G. Wells in 1939, one year after Orson Welles' broadcast of the author's "War of the Worlds." In 1956, new owners introduced a "Top 40" format at KTSA, and in 1982 KTSA was the country's first AM station to broadcast in stereo. The station changed to all-talk radio in 1991, and has used that format since.

WOAI AM 1200
6222 N.W. I–10, San Antonio
(210) 737–1200
www.woai.com

This station has talk radio about a range of subjects, including the popular Rush Limbaugh program at 11:00 A.M. WOAI also has live broadcasts of the San Antonio Spurs basketball games.

Tejano

KLEY-FM 94.1
7800 West I–10, Suite 330, San Antonio
(210) 340–1234,
(210) 470–5539 (request line)

This 50,000-watt station featuring Tejano and Latin tunes of today and yesterday has been on the air since July of 1997. Weekday mornings from 6:00 A.M. until 10:00 A.M., the morning show keeps listeners laughing and toes tapping while the morning show hosts Alondra (a Mexican pop star of the 1980s and '90s) and her partner, Ever, supply news, trivia games, listener calls, and lots of music. From 10:00 A.M. until 3:00 P.M., Rick Maxx gets listeners through the workday, while Luis "The Bird" Rodriguez takes over from 3:00 P.M. until 7:00 P.M. for the drive home. From 7:00 P.M. until midnight, Alex Cruz delights listeners with his upbeat personality.

KXTN 107.5
1777 N.E. Loop 410 Ste. 400, San Antonio
(210) 829–1075

This station keeps listeners entertained with past and present Tejano hits the whole day through. From 7:00 P.M. until midnight, KXTN's "Jukebox" features requests from listeners, and at 8:00 P.M. the "Top Eight at Eight" countdown showcases the eight most-requested songs in San Antonio.

Urban

KSJL FM 96.1
6222 N.W. I–10, San Antonio
(210) 736–9700, (800) 227–7685 (request line)
www.ksjl.com

KSJL is San Antonio's station for contemporary urban music. Through the work day, "The Touch" mixes urban adult contemporary music with urban oldies dating from the 1950s. From 6:00 P.M. until 11:00 P.M., the "Love Zone" features requests of romantic music from San Antonio listeners. On Sundays from 5:00 A.M. until noon, Sunday Inspirations features music by top gospel artists, then from noon until 9:00 P.M., "Solid Gold Sunday" offers classic soul sounds from the Sixties to the present.

Television Stations

KABB Channel 11
4335 N.W. Loop 410, San Antonio
(210) 366–1129
www.kabb.com

KABB-TV began in December of 1987 as an independent station that was not affiliated with a national network. The station began its popular KABB-TV Kids Fair in 1993, which attracted the Alamo City Heat (a pop band formed by members of the San Antonio Police Department) and the Die Wurst Players from Fiesta Texas. Proceeds went to the San Antonio D.A.R.E. program, which encourages children to stay off drugs. Kids Fair became so popular that it had to move to the Alamodome in 1994 to accommodate the large crowds. In 1995, KABB affiliated with the FOX Network. Tours are available of the KABB Studios on Mondays and Wednesdays from 4:00 P.M. until 5:00 P.M., with a limit of 12 persons; call for reservations. KABB is planning to broadcast a digital signal from a new channel by mid-2002.

KENS 5 Channel 5
5400 Fredericksburg Rd., San Antonio
(210) 366–5000
www.kens-tv.com

In 1950, George Stores formed the San Antonio Television Company, making San Antonio's KEYL the 99th TV station in the United States. KEYL was changed to KENS 5 in 1955. KENS news anchors Chris Marrou and Albert Flores are San Antonio's longest-running news team; Marrou is a native San Antonian with 25 years at Eyewitness News. The most advanced weather technology in Southern Texas is owned and operated by KENS 5, including Super Doppler, the most powerful radar of its kind in the San Antonio area. The station is also known for its in-depth coverage of San Antonio sports.

KLRN Channel 9
501 Broadway, San Antonio
(210) 270–9000
www.klrn.org

PBS's San Antonio station KLRN provides daily programming that focuses on education for all ages. Through the day, most programs are aimed at preschool to grade-school children. In the evening, educational shows like Frontline and Nova are aired. KLRN-TV began broadcasting in 1962 and served both San Antonio and Austin through a transmitter in New Braunfels until 1984. At that time, a second transmitter was installed in San Antonio, finally giving San Antonio its own public television coverage. Today, broadcasting from its 36,000-square-foot studio, KLRN offers local, regional, and national public broadcast shows.

KMOL Channel 4
1031 Navarro St., San Antonio
(210) 226–4444
www.kmol.com

KMOL is San Antonio's NBC affiliate. KMOL's programming includes such popular NBC shows as ER, Frasier, and The West Wing. KMOL is also home to a local daytime entertainment program called 4 San Antonio Living, which offers news, weather, entertainment headlines, education reports, and health updates. With live on-site broadcasts from around the city, "Living" host Tanji Patton delves into the many aspects of San Antonio and gives viewers a real feel for the city.

KSAT Channel 12
1408 N. St. Marys St., San Antonio
(210) 351–1200
www.clickonsa.com

This ABC affiliate station hit the airwaves in February of 1957 as KONO TV, broadcasting the inauguration of President Eisenhower. When purchased in 1969, the station became KSAT Channel 12. The station has changed hands several times since 1969, and today is owned by Post-Newsweek, which bought KSAT in 1994.

KRRT Channel 35
4335 N.W. Loop 410, San Antonio
(210) 366–1129
www.krrt.com

Channel 35 is KRRT, San Antonio's WB Station. In addition to the national WB shows, this station runs episodes of classic TV favorites such as M*A*S*H, The Cosby Show, and Home Improvement. KRRT

San Antonio is served by numerous television and radio stations. PHOTO: PARIS PERMENTER & JOHN BIGLEY

also produces its own shows. One of the most unique and helpful of these is *Focus on South Texas,* which covers a variety of topics relevant to South Texas, including events such as Kerrville's Annual Wine and Music Festival and interviews with representatives from area businesses. *Focus on South Texas* is particularly helpful for new residents and visitors who are trying to get a feel for what San Antonio and Southern Texas are really like.

KVDA Channel 60
6234 San Pedro Ave., San Antonio
(210) 340–8860
www.kvda.com
This Spanish-language station is an affiliate of the UPN network, Telemundo. The station transmits within a 60-mile radius of its San Antonio transmitter.

Worship

Catholicism

Protestantism

African-American
  Worship

Judaism

Buddhism

Islam

Historic Churches
  and Religious Sites

Since its very founding, San Antonio has been linked with religion. Named for the Roman Catholic saint whose feast day was the day the first Mass was celebrated here in 1691, San Antonio has long been a religious center. The Spanish missionaries who ventured north from Mexico to covert the Native American population stamped the region with their Catholic beliefs. The tradition persists. Even today, San Antonio is considered one of the nation's largest Catholic cities and serves as a capital of Hispanic Catholicism. But followers of all the world's major religions reside and worship here.

Catholicism

The efforts of the missionaries to convert the region to Catholicism were not completely successful. After establishing a string of missions along the San Antonio River (see our Attractions chapter for more on this Mission Trail), the missionaries worked to convert the Indians, but few converts were won.

When Mexico separated from Spain in 1821, the Catholic Church here was left in disarray. Some bishops returned to Spain; when offices were vacated by movement or death, the Vatican did not replace the

Insiders' Tip
Every Sunday, the *San Antonio Express-News* publishes a religion calendar listing special events scheduled by local houses of worship. The calendar is also available online at www.mysanantonio.com.

bishops because of its hope that Mexico would return to Spain. Soon the region was desperately short of priests and as a result became increasingly self-reliant in terms of religious worship. Upon the establishment of the Republic of Texas in 1836, the Texas Catholics fell under the jurisdiction of the Diocese of Monterrey, Mexico. Soon the Vatican ordered a French cleric to come to the new country and make recommendations regarding the church in Texas. The Pope designated the republic as missionary territory; later it became part of the Diocese of Galveston and a group of French missionaries were dispatched to South Texas. In the ensuing years, these missionaries and other church officials saw the Mexican Texans as a burden to the church.

Because of this prejudice, the Mexican Texans began to interpret Catholicism on their own. As the priests did not offer worship services in Spanish and did not provide financial support, the Texas Mexicans developed their own practices, such as *altarcitos* or home altars.

The rule of the French clerics ended in the late nineteenth century, when priests from Spain began to provide missionary services to the region. In 1910, the Mexican Revolution brought many immigrants from Mexico into Texas and the attention of the Catholic Church again turned to San Antonio. The Tejanos (Mexican Texans) began to build their own churches and parochial schools.

Today almost half the population of San Antonio and Bexar County are Catholic. The Archdiocese of San Antonio oversees 23 counties. The largest parish in San Antonio is St. Matthew's, with 6,000 families.

America's oldest cathedral sanctuary is San Antonio's San Fernando Cathedral, which was founded in 1731 by Canary Islanders. Its 9:00 A.M. Sunday Mass is broadcast across the country; it can also be seen locally on Catholic Television of San Antonio, cable channel 15. The cathedral is also well known among visitors of all denominations for its annual reenactment of the Way of the Cross on Good Friday; the Spanish-language presentation draws thousands of viewers.

Another Mass often attended by visitors of all denominations is the Mariachi Mass at Mission San José. Scheduled for noon on Sunday, the English-language Mass is accompanied by Spanish songs played by mariachi musicians. The Mass is quite popular (often standing room only), and visitors are encouraged to arrive early in appropriate worship dress (no shorts or tank tops).

Along with worship centers, the Catholic church also brought to San Antonio many educational centers. The Ursuline Sisters of Galveston, aided by their counterparts in New Orleans, opened a girls' school in 1851; the next year, they opened St. Mary's School, later to become St. Mary's University. The Sisters of Divine Providence from France opened Our Lady of the Lake Academy in 1895; by 1913 the school was transformed into a four-year college. The Soeurs Hôpitalières, later known as the Sisters of Charity of the Incarnate Word, opened the Santa Rosa Infirmary in 1869; it became Santa Rosa Hospital in 1930. The city's Oblate School of Theology was founded in 1903 by the Oblates of Mary Immaculate; the school trains priests as well as lay ministers.

Catholic education continues to remain an important force on the San Antonio educational scene. Many of the

The Mariachi Mass at Mission San José is a uniquely San Antonio worship experience. PHOTO: RICK HUNTER, COURTESY OF THE SAN ANTONIO CONVENTION AND VISITORS BUREAU

nearly 5,500 Catholic-school teachers live in the Alamo City.

Protestantism

Today, Baptists make up San Antonio's second-largest religious group. More than 200 churches in the region make up the San Antonio Baptist Association, a group representing some 100,000 congregants. Baptist worshippers across the country watch the services of Rev. Buckner Fanning at San Antonio's Trinity Baptist Church.

Other Protestant leaders in San Antonio are also well-known across the nation. Author Max Lucado at the Oak Hills Church of Christ has written numerous inspirational books. Rev. John Hagee at the Cornerstone Church, the city's largest with 17,000 congregants, is seen on television. The nondenominational church seats 5,000 worshippers.

San Antonio is also the home of the Episcopal Diocese of West Texas, overseeing about 30,000 congregants; the Southwest Texas Conference of the Methodist Church, with 115,000 members; and the Southwestern Texas Synod of the Evangelical Lutheran Church in America, with more than 72,000 congregants.

African-American Worship

Brought into the region from the 1820s until the Civil War, African-American slaves followed religious traditions of Africa as well as those practiced at the plantations where they lived. By the 1860s, the black population in Texas reached 30 percent, and many slaves attended worship services in the churches of their masters. In 1860, the Methodist Church of Texas reported some 7,500 black congregants; the Baptist Church recording more than 1,000 members. At that time, black worshippers were restricted to separate pews and the message they received was often one of obedience. In 1866, San Antonio's first African-American church was established. St. Paul United Methodist Church was founded by freed slaves.

In the years following emancipation, most black members left the Methodist faith and worshipped in Baptist churches. By 1916, 72 percent of black churchgoers in Texas were Baptist.

During these years, some African Americans also practiced the Catholic faith. Catholicism was not new to blacks; sub-Saharan Africa had been served by Catholic missionaries, and some enslaved Africans were believed to have brought their faith with them.

In 1888 St. Peter Claver Church was founded in San Antonio by an Irish priest who did not approve of the segregation of the races in church. By 1915 the Alamo City had three predominantly black Catholic churches.

Years later, in the 1940s, San Antonio archbishop Robert E. Lucey worked to integrate the city's Catholic schools. In the 1950s at least 100 black students attended San Antonio Catholic schools.

Judaism

Judaism in Texas dates back to the region's earliest days, although until 1821 all non-Catholic worshippers practiced their religion in secret. By 1838, however, Judaism was being practiced openly in San Antonio and by 1856 the first Jewish cemetery was established in the city.

In 1874, Beth El of San Antonio was established. Soon a number of Jewish associations, such as the International Order of B'nai B'rith, were established throughout the region. In 1889, Rabbi Moses Sadovsky became the city's first rabbi.

The earliest Jews in the region were Sephardic, from North Africa and Spain. Later, Jews from Germany as well as Eastern Europe settled in the city. These worshippers were joined by immigrants from Russia at the turn of the century.

Today the Jewish community in San Antonio numbers about 10,000 people, divided among six congregations.

Agudas Achim Congregation
16550 Huebner Rd., San Antonio
(210) 479–0307

Beth Am Congregation
7150 W. I–10, San Antonio
(210) 492–4014

Beth Simcha Congregation
15805 San Pedro Ave., San Antonio
(210) 493–7482

Chabad Lubavitch
14535 Blanco Rd., San Antonio
(210) 492–1085

Rodfei Sholom Congregation
3003 Sholom Dr., San Antonio
(210) 492–0629

Temple Beth El
211 Belknap Pl., San Antonio
(210) 733–9135

Buddhism

Today there are about 15,000 Buddhists in Texas, many of whom came to the state in the late twentieth century. Although San Antonio's Buddhist community is not as large as that of Houston, the city has several temples as well as the Dharma Study Group, which follows both Tibetan and non-Tibetan Buddhist traditions.

Buddhamahawanaram
425 S. Loop 1604 West, San Antonio
(210) 626–1517

Buddhist Temple of San Antonio
425 S. Loop 1604 West, San Antonio
(210) 626–1517

Rissho Kosei Kai
6083 Babcock Rd., San Antonio
(210) 561–7991

San Antonio Shambhala Center
6233 Evers Rd., San Antonio
(210) 647–1804

Islam

Texas has the eighth-largest Muslim population in the United States, and San Antonio is home to a growing Muslim community. The state has some 140,000 Muslim residents, more than 5,000 of whom reside in the Alamo City.

Mosques Association Muslim Center
1702 Hays St., San Antonio
(210) 224–5767

Historic Churches and Religious Sites

Little Church
La Villita, 508 Villita St., San Antonio
(210) 226–3593

In 1879 German Methodists constructed this Gothic Revival church in the La Villita

Insiders' Tip

A good source of information about San Antonio's many churches, synagogues, temples, and other worship sites is the Chamber of Commerce. The Chamber's Web site is www.thecityof sanantonio.com/church. html.

area. The tiny church features wooden pegs carved by a Norwegian sailor; the building also has lancet-shaped casement windows. The Methodist church was purchased by the Episcopal diocese of West Texas in 1895, then by the City of San Antonio in 1945. Today the church offers nondenominational worship services and is often the site of weddings. The church is open to the public from 10:00 A.M. to 6:00 P.M. daily. Church services are held at 11:00 A.M. and 6:00 P.M. on Sundays.

Oblate Grotto of the Southwest
5722 Blanco Rd., San Antonio
(210) 736–1685
www.oblatemissions.org

This grotto is an exact replica of the grotto in Lourdes, France. Constructed in 1941 by the missionary Oblates of Mary Immaculate, the grotto is carved from limestone and represents the cave in which Mary appeared to St. Bernadette, who is seen kneeling in prayer in the grotto. In the grotto burn many candles; the site is also filled with hundreds of *milagros* or charms.

The grotto is located in a five-acre park, where a path leads to outdoor Stations of the Cross. Throughout the year, the grotto is the site of many special novenas and Masses. The grounds are open 24 hours a day. The chapel here is open daily from 6:30 A.M. to 5:00 P.M. Daily Mass is offered in English on Monday through Saturday at 7:15 A.M. and in Spanish at noon Monday through Friday. Sunday Mass is at 9:00 A.M. in English and at 11:30 A.M. in Spanish.

San Fernando Cathedral
115 Main Plaza, San Antonio
(210) 227–1297
www.sfcathedral.org/

Still an active place of worship, this historic church was constructed in 1738 by Canary Island colonists, making this the oldest cathedral sanctuary in the nation. At this site, Santa Anna raised a flag of no quarter before attacking the Alamo. The

San Fernando Cathedral is a cornerstone of religious life in San Antonio. PHOTO: DAVE G. HOUSER, COURTESY OF THE SAN ANTONIO CONVENTION AND VISITORS BUREAU

Votive candles aglow at San Fernando Cathedral. PHOTO: DAVE G. HOUSER, COURTESY OF THE SAN ANTONIO CONVENTION AND VISITORS BUREAU

cathedral has another link with the Alamo: in the back of the chapel, a sarcophagus holds what many believe to be the remains of the Alamo defenders. The remains were unearthed during a renovation in 1936.

The site suffered a fire in 1873 and the chapel was replaced with what visitors see today. Nonetheless, the site is filled with historic items including a stone baptismal font that is believed to have been a gift from King Charles III of Spain in 1759. The pipe organ is the oldest in the city. The church was visited by Pope John Paul II on his San Antonio visit on September 13, 1987.

For all its history, the cathedral remains a very vital church today. More than 4,000 worshippers attend Mass each Sunday; the cathedral is also the site of more than 900 baptisms and some 100 weddings every year. It is also the seat of the Archdiocese of San Antonio.

The cathedral is open to the public Tuesday through Friday from 9:00 A.M. to 1:00 P.M. and 2:00 P.M. to 4:45 P.M. Mass is celebrated on Saturday at 8:00 A.M. (Spanish) and 5:30 P.M. (bilingual), and Sunday at 6:00 A.M. (Spanish), 8:00 A.M. (a televised bilingual service), 10:00 A.M. (Latin/Spanish/English), 12:00 P.M. (Spanish), 2:00 P.M. (English), and 5:00 P.M. (bilingual). On weekdays, Mass is held at 6:15 A.M. (English) and 12:05 P.M. (bilingual).

Military

Early Years

Statehood and the
    Civil War

Post-War Growth

The Rough Riders

Flight and Forts

World War II

Further Developments

Military Base
    Attractions

From its earliest days as an isolated outpost of Spain, San Antonio has had a long and distinguished history as a military base. Small garrisons of Spanish troops were dispatched to Bexar to guard the first colonists and the early missions. In 1721, the Marques de San Miguel de Aguayo, governor of the "New Philippines," commanded the construction of a permanent barracks of adobe, a fort, and the Plaza de Armas, a parade ground which later became Military Plaza.

These early Spanish regiments were never of sufficient size to end the raids by the Apache and Comanche. The garrison was attacked in 1730 by Apache, and 15 of the soldiers were killed. A desultory war of raid and counterattack was fought for the next 150 years before San Antonio's survival was assured.

Early Years

The colonization of San Antonio by Americans under the leadership of Moses and Stephen F. Austin began a parade of different military forces to the area: Spanish, insurrectionary Mexican Republicans, Mexican Royalists, Texian volunteer militia, and Mexican. Each controlled the city for a time, San Antonio's strategic value being obvious, as the only fort within hundreds of miles in any direction. By the time of the Texian's famous defense against Santa Anna in 1836, the Alamo fortress consisted of an area of some four acres, enclosed by a series of stone walls and fences. Although General Sam Houston had ordered the fort destroyed and its defenders to fall back to Goliad, Santa Anna's forced march across the Rio Grande prevented them from doing so. Although the Texians were killed, their spirited defense from the walls of the Alamo bought precious time for Sam Houston's main army, which defeated the Mexicans at San Jacinto a few weeks later.

Yet, even the founding of an independent Republic of Texas did not allow the frontier town much peace. Range war with

the Comanche intensified as more settlers moved into the area. And there was a continued threat of Mexican troops foraging into what some still believed was their territory. In 1842, a Mexican army under General Woll attacked and captured San Antonio. Many prominent citizens and town officials were taken prisoner, taken to Mexico and jailed. A company of early Texas Rangers stationed in San Antonio were better equipped to deal with the Comanche than with an army of 1,200 Mexicans. Only a reorganized Texas militia checked Woll's advance at the Battle of Salado Creek, 7 miles from San Antonio.

Statehood and the Civil War

With the annexation of Texas by the United States in 1845, a new chapter of military history was written in San Antonio. As Americans chased their Manifest Destiny west, San Antonio became important as a garrison and supply depot for troops and settlers headed toward the Rio Grande and distant California. Army troops were stationed in Military Plaza, in the barracks first built by the Spanish. The

Army also leased the Alamo from Catholic Church authorities, reroofed it in 1849–1850, and used it as a supply warehouse. The city became the principal headquarters for forts extending south and west. The Army became the first big business to locate in San Antonio and its presence, in turn, attracted other businesses to town.

San Antonio's military importance made it a prime target for secessionists at the beginning of the Civil War. On February 6, 1861, more than a month before Texas formally joined the Confederacy, General David E. Twiggs of the U.S. Army's Second Cavalry Regiment surrendered munitions and supplies totaling around $3 million to a secessionist force headed by Army Major Ben McCullough. Robert E. Lee of Virginia, the base's inspector-general, was likewise beset by a mob of secessionists who demanded that he join them or leave town immediately. Lee refused to obey "any revolutionary government of Texas," and returned to Washington without bothering to pack, and then went on to serve his native Virginia. Thus San Antonio passed the Civil War years as a Confederate city; legions of Confederate troops were mustered and trained in Military Plaza. Involuntary conscription into the Confederate army began in 1862 and proved very unpopular, especially with the immigrant German population. These farmers tried to remain neutral to the conflict, but reacted with rebellion against the military draft, some even forming their own militia. A number of serious confrontations erupted between these militia and Confederate forces. One of the most tragic of these conflicts occurred in 1862, when several dozen German Union sympizers were chased and shot down by Confederate troops near the Nueces River. Yet, on the whole, the city was spared many of the horrors of the war, even prospering in a fashion by serving as a shipping point for Mexican goods bound for the Confederate states in defiance of Union blockades.

Post-War Growth

When the U.S. Army reoccupied the town in 1865 at the conclusion of the Civil War, San Antonio resumed its role as headquarters for the great westward expansion. The poet Sidney Lanier, who lived in San Antonio at the time, observed in a historical sketch published in 1873: "The United States Government selected San Antonio as the base for the frontier army below El Paso, and the large quantities of money expended in connection with the supply and transportation of all material for so a long a line of forts have contributed very materially to the prosperity of the town."

San Antonio's growing military population led to the town's development as an American city. Businesses that catered to the military began to establish a presence in the city. During the war between Mexico and the United States, volunteer troops serving under General Zachary Taylor were drilled and trained in San Antonio. In 1875, the city donated 93 acres of land, a parcel known as Government Hill, for a permanent military base called Post San Antonio. Work on the primary walls, forming the original quadrangle, began in 1876. Other facilities were added in the next few years: officers' quarters, post commander's quarters, and a base hospital. The defeated Apache Chief Geronimo was held at the post in 1886.

In 1890, Post San Antonio was renamed Fort Sam Houston, in honor of the hero of the Texas Revolution. Over the next few years, the fort was enlarged several times as U.S. presence in the West increased.

The Rough Riders

One of the most memorable episodes in San Antonio's long military history occurred with the beginning of the Spanish-American War of 1898. The United States sought to increase its ranks by enlisting volunteer cavalry. The only such unit to actually see combat was the First United States Volunteer Cavalry, informally known as the "Rough Riders." The regiment was mustered in San Antonio, where it met its famous leader, Theodore Roosevelt. The group needed strong leadership, as it was composed of many types of individuals from all walks of life: cowboys, Indian fighters, and bandits as well as Ivy Leaguers and society swells. Many arrived from the Wild West, bearing names as colorful as their dispositions—Rocky Mountain Bill, Bronco George, Dead Shot Jim, and Rattlesnake Pete. Others, such as William Tiffany, were Easterners who became known as the "millionaire recruits" for their refined tastes in food and clothing. However, a newspaper of the time saw them all as "one homogeneous mass of patriotism and pluck, representing and illustrating our fierce democracy where every man is equally a sovereign . . . the rough frontiersman, daring but uncouth, and the cultured collegiate, genteel but full of spirit, stand upon a common level and mingle in a common purpose."

The unit was bivouacked in Riverside Park (now Roosevelt Park) where they were drilled and trained to fight using Krag-Jorgensen repeating carbines. Although the nominal commander of the regiment was Col. Leonard Wood, its actual leader was Lt. Col. Roosevelt, who had resigned his post as U.S. Assistant Secretary of the Navy to serve under Wood's command. Roosevelt proved to be a popular leader and was lionized by the press while he was in town. Roosevelt, in turn, was effusive in his praise of his men, especially the recruits from Texas. "We drew a great many recruits from Texas," wrote Roosevelt, "and from nowhere did we get a higher average, for many of them had served in that famous body of frontier fighters, the Texas Rangers. Of course, these rangers needed no teaching. They were trained to obey and to take responsibility. They were splendid shots, horsemen, and trailers. They were accustomed to living in the open, to enduring great fatigue and hardship, and to encountering all kinds of danger."

On May 30, a scant month after the Rough Riders arrived in San Antonio, they were ordered into action in Cuba, the first U.S. troops to land there. After a bloody battle with Spanish forces at Las Guisimas, the Spanish retreated to the well-fortified San Juan Hill. There, on July 1, 1898, the regiment joined other U.S. divisions to successfully storm San Juan Hill in one of the most famous battles in U.S. history. The Rough Riders and their ebullient leader Teddy Roosevelt are memorialized in San Antonio by Roosevelt Park, where the regiment camped; Roosevelt Street; and the Roosevelt Bar of the Menger Hotel, where the Riders frequently stopped to wet their whistles.

Flight and Forts

On Feb. 15, 1910, the U.S. Army's first airplane was moved to Fort Sam Houston by Lt. Benjamin Foulois, who is credited with performing the first flight in U.S. military history. By the time of World War I, Fort Sam Houston was home base for nine air-

Insiders' Tip

At present, approximately 150,000 military and ex-military personnel reside in San Antonio.

planes in addition to its regular contingent of infantry, cavalry, artillery, and military engineers. In all, more than 200,000 army troops bound for the trenches of Europe in World War I were trained at the fort.

Several other military bases were established in San Antonio in the first decades of the twentieth century. Kelly Field, named for Lt. George Kelly, the first U.S. military pilot killed in a crash of a military aircraft, opened in 1917. The base had two initial missions: training of airmen and aircraft maintenance and supply. Nearly all U.S. aviators in World War I were trained here, including some famous pilots such as Charles Lindbergh, Flying Tigers organizer Claire Lee Chennault, and Curtis Lemay, former Air Force Chief of Staff.

The demands of World War I also led to the opening of Brooks Field. Known as Gosport Field when it opened in 1917, it was renamed a year later in honor of Cadet Sidney Johnson Brooks, who died in a training accident at Fort Sam Houston in 1911. In addition to its flight instructor school, Brooks also trained B-25 bomber pilots, airship personnel, and paratroopers. In 1929, it was the scene of the first large paratroop deployment in U.S. military history. The School of Aviation Medicine, first relocated to the base from New York in 1926, was charged with research in the area of aircraft-related health issues such crew airsickness, injury hazard reduction, and cold-related health problems.

The Aviation Medicine School was later moved to nearby Randolph Field, which was founded in 1930 as a facility dedicated to pilot training. Randolph Field began as an Army Air Corps base, and so many future military pilots were trained there that it was once known as "The West Point of the Air." Its exact mission has varied over the years from basic training to advanced programs for bomber and fighter pilots and flight engineers. The base is located about 15 miles northeast of San Antonio, near the city of

Schertz. At the time of the base's construction, 1928–1933, it represented the largest project undertaken by the U.S. Army Corps of Engineers since the Panama Canal. It was designed by Lt. Harold Clark and features Spanish Renaissance–style architecture and more than 30 miles of roads, ramps, and runways, and streets radiating out from the central administrative area like spokes of a wheel.

World War II

A large Army hospital, Brooke Army Medical Center, was built on Fort Sam Houston in 1938, and by 1940, as the country again prepared for war, "Fort Sam" was the largest of all U.S. Army bases. Several important tactical strategies in U.S. military history were devised here, and a number of officers who served at the fort went on to important posts in World War II, among them Lt. General Walter Krueger and Lt. General Courtney Hodges, who served with the U.S. Third Army, and General Dwight D. Eisenhower.

In 1942, Lackland Army Air Field, originally part of Kelly Field, was detached to become a high-volume training facility for aviation personnel, including not only pilots but also navigators, bombardiers, fiscal officers, nurses, medical technicians, even chaplains bound for World War II. As the U.S. war effort accelerated, Lackland's population swelled to 31,000 military personnel. After the war, the name was changed to Lackland Air Force Base when the Air Force became a separate military entity, but Lackland's nickname, "The Gateway to the Air Force" still rang true, as all new Air Force personnel were processed through Lackland during their basic training. In addition to its training mission, the base has expanded its operations to include marksmanship, cryptography, and other programs. Wilford Hall Air Force Medical Center, the Air Force's largest hospital, is also located here.

Also in 1947, Randolph Field became Randolph Air Force Base, and the name of

Kelly Field was officially changed to Kelly Air Force Base. At that time, Kelly assumed responsibility for strategically important aircraft such as the B-29, B47, and B-58 bombers, and fighters such as F-102 and F-106. The world's largest clear-span hanger, covering more than one million square feet was built to accommodate planes such as the C-5 transport, one of the largest aircraft in the world, with its 223-foot wingspan and 270,000-pound payload capacity.

Further Developments

After the war, Fort Sam Houston, then home of the U.S. Fourth Army, continued to expand. The Institute of Surgical Research was added in 1946, and the Burn Center opened in 1949. At that time, the fort's 1,500 buildings covered over 3,000 acres. Fort Sam Houston's large concentration of military medical facilities was further augmented in 1973 with the addition of the Health Services Command. The fort now calls itself "The Home of Army Medicine," and hosts various commands, including the U.S. Army Medical Command, the U.S. Army Medical Department Center and School, Brooke Army Medical Center, and the Fifth U.S. Army and Fifth Recruiting Brigade. The post's National Landmark and Historic Conservation District designations include more than 900 historic structures, including the U.S. Army Medical Department Museum and the Fort Sam Houston Museum. The Fort Sam Houston National Cemetery is also located on the post.

In 1959, The School of Aviation Medicine at Randolph Field was again moved, this time to Brooks Air Force Base as the U.S. Air Force School of Aerospace Medicine. The primary mission of the school, dedicated in 1961 by newly elected President John F. Kennedy, was support of the national space exploration program; all regular flight-training operations having been curtailed the previous year. Researchers here developed many of the discoveries that have enabled both unmanned and manned space missions, such as an early space capsule used in a 1959 flight.

In the early 1980s, other organizations relocated to Brooks AFB. Among them were the Air Force Human Resources Laboratory and the USAF Occupational and Environmental Health Laboratory. Brooks also became home to the Air Force Drug Testing Laboratory and the Air Force Systems Command's Systems Acquisition School. Brooks celebrated its 70th anniversary in November 1987. In 1991, four of its laboratories—the Harry G. Armstrong Aerospace Medical Research Laboratory, the Air Force Drug Testing Laboratory, the Air Force Human Resources Laboratory, and the Air Force Occupational and Environmental Health Laboratory, merged, creating the Armstrong Laboratory, one of the Air Force's "super labs." In 1992, the Air Force Systems Command and the Air Force Logistics Command merged into a new organization called the Air Force Materiel Command. Brooks's Human Systems Division changed its name to the Human Systems Center. Brooks Air Force Base continues to pursue as its mission "the development of combat power and efficiency through the many facets of aerospace medicine.

The demand for additional troops during the Korean and Vietnam Wars forced Lackland Air Force Base to rapidly expand, including construction of the 1,000 person steel and brick Recruit Hous-

---

Insiders' Tip

The picturesque clock tower on Fort Sam Houston's historic Quadrangle was originally designed as a water cistern.

ing and Training (RH&T) facility. Flight training was conducted in shifts around the clock to supply pilots bound for Vietnam and later for Desert Storm. In addition to its training mission, the base also expanded its operations to include marksmanship, cryptography, and other programs. Wilford Hall Air Force Medical Center, the Air Force's largest hospital, is also located here.

At Randolph Air Force Base in the early 1970s, the 12th Tactical Fighter Wing became the 12th Flying Training Wing. Many Air Force pilots in Vietnam trained here. At the end of the Vietnamese conflict, Randolph became the site of Operation Homecoming, in which U.S. military pilots who had been prisonors of war in Vietnam were retrained and requalified to fly. About the same time, another era of training at Randolph began with the formation of the Undergraduate Navigator Training squadrons.

As part of the Base Realignment and Closure process, Kelly Air Force Base was closed in July, 2001. However, "Kelly USA" will continue to serve as a Foreign Trade Zone and an inland port which will service the vast international trade industry.

With the newly privatized Kelly USA, San Antonio has five bases with approximately 36,000 military and an additional 34,000 civilian personnel. San Antonio's military bases are involved in the Afghanistan conflict in many ways, from air support to military medicine.

Military Base Attractions

You don't have to be a military buff to appreciate San Antonio's long military tradition. All of the city's bases have public attractions, although the bases can be closed to visitors during wartime for security reasons. Call for current schedules and restrictions.

Fort Sam Houston
1212 Stanley Rd., San Antonio
(210) 221–1151
www.fshtx.army.mil

The U.S. Army Medical Department Museum is one of Fort Sam Houston's main visitor attractions. PHOTO: AL RENDON, COURTESY OF THE SAN ANTONIO CONVENTION AND VISITORS BUREAU

Now designated a National Historic Landmark, Fort Sam Houston welcomes visitors with several attractions that are fully open to the public. The original Quadrangle features a famous clock tower and resident wildlife such as deer and peacocks. It's the fort's oldest structure. The Fort Sam Houston Museum (210–221–1886) features exhibits that tell the story of the fort's past as well as the more general history of the military in San Antonio. Admission to the museum is free, as is admission to the Gift Chapel, dedicated by President William Howard Taft in 1909. The U.S. Army Medical Department Museum (210–221–6277) traces the development of military medicine in U.S. history. It includes displays of uniforms, medical instruments, army ambulances, even a railroad hospital car. There is also a gift shop and bookshop in the museum. Admission is free. In addition to its public

Lackland Air Force Base, the "Gateway to the Air Force." PHOTO: AL RENDON, COURTESY OF THE SAN ANTONIO CONVENTION AND VISITORS BUREAU

areas, Fort Sam Houston boasts a number of other notable places that are at least worth a drive-by. However, these remain part of the working base so call before visiting sites such as The Pershing House, named for General of the Armies John J. "Blackjack" Pershing; the Infantry Post, built in 1885; and the First Flight Memorial, marking the spot where, in 1910, Lt. Benjamin Foulois made the first U.S. military flight. Also notable are two residences where General Dwight D. Eisenhower lived during two tours of duty at the fort.

Brooks Air Force Base
8008 Inner Circle Rd., Brooks A.F.B., San Antonio
(210) 531–9767
www.brooks.af.mil/

Brooks offerings include Hangar 9, the U.S. Air Force's oldest aircraft hangar. It holds exhibits on the history of Brooks A.F.B., manned flight, and aerospace medicine. The museum includes a gift shop. There is no admission charge, but be sure to call before you go as the museum sometimes operates by appointment only.

Lackland Air Force Base
37th Training Wing
1701 Kenly Ave., Lackland A.F.B., San Antonio
(210) 671–3055
www.lackland.af.mil/homepage/

Lackland is the home of the U.S. Air Force History and Traditions Museum at 2051 George Avenue, Building 5206. The museum is dedicated to the history of military aviation, with 30 aircraft on display covering the period from World War I to the present. There is also a museum gift shop. Admission is free, but groups of more than 15 require an appointment.

Randolph Air Force Base
12 FTW Public Affairs
1 Washington Circle, Suite Four, Randolph AFB, San Antonio
(210) 652–4407
www.randolph.af.mil/

Tours of the "Showplace of the Air Force" must be scheduled at least three weeks ahead of time by writing or calling the above address. Tours normally last approximately two hours.

Index

A

A Beckmann Inn and Carriage House, 67
AAA Limousine and Sedan Service, 27
Abbey Walker Executive Cars & Limousines, 27
Ace, 19
Adams House Bed & Breakfast Inn, 67
Adam's Mark Riverwalk, 42
Addie's Playhouse, 292
Adelante Boutique, 124
Advantage Rent A Car, 20
Ageless Times, 312
AIDS/HIV care, 301–2
airport shuttle service, 20
air travel, 18–21
Alamo, 133–35, 166
Alamo Café, 97
Alamo Cenotaph, 135
Alamo City Men's Chorale, 207
Alamo Country Club, 230
Alamo Heights Independent School
    District, 288
Alamo Irish Festival, 190
Alamo Quarry Mall, 115–16
Alamo Street Restaurant and Theatre, 213
Alamo Travelodge, 42
Aldo's Ristorante Italiano, 92
Alien Worlds, 122
Alzheimer's Association of South Central
    Texas, 307
AMC Theaters, 112
American Association of Retired Persons, 303
AmeriSuites San Antonio Airport, 54
Amtrak, 26–27
amusement parks, 157–59
Anaqua Grill, 93
Angelita's, 124
annual events and festivals, 186–205

Antique Center, The, 119
Antiques at 115 Broadway, 119
antique stores, 119–20
Antlers Lodge, 94
arcades, 164–66
Arden Courts, 310
Arneson River Theater, 213
Around The Carousel, 123
Arrow—The Limousine Co., 27
art classes/workshops for children, 159–60
art galleries, 209
art museums, 209–11
ArtPace, 209
arts. *See* specific art form
Artworks, 159
Asian New Year Festival, 187–88
A-1 Sports Center, 126
assisted living facilities, 310–11
Astro Bowling Center, 225
Atrium, The, 106
attractions
    in & around Loop 410, 141–44
    downtown, 133–41
    historic districts, 149–54
    outside Loop 410, 147–49
    San Antonio Missions, 144–47
    tours, 154–56
    See also kidstuff
Audie L. Murphy Memorial Veterans
    Hospital, 298
Austin day trip, 243–45, 248

B

Babies Make Music Program, 172
Backstage CDs, 125–26
Banana Joe's Island Party, 106
Bandit, The, 229
B and J Bicycle Shop, 225

Baptist Medical Center, 296
Baramerica, 102
Barnes and Noble Booksellers, 120, 160
bars, 102–4, 113, 114
baseball, 224, 238
Baseball SA, 224
basketball, 225, 236–38
Bastrop State Park, 221
Bawdsey Manor British Tea Room, 87
Bayous Riverside, The, 87
Beacon House, The, 310
bed and breakfast inns, 66–73
Beignets Coffee House, 87
Bering's, 121
Best Friends and Best Buddies, 123
Best Homes GMAC Real Estate, 281–82
Bestpresso's, 88
Best Western Continental Inn, 59
Bexar County Medical Society, 300
Bexar County Retired Senior Volunteer
    Program (RSVP), 309
Biga's on the Banks, 93–94
Bill Miller Bar-B-Q, 82
Blanco State Park, 221
Blanco Tavern, 102–3
Bless Your Heart Gift Shop, 121
Blossom Golf Center, 230
Blue Star Art Space, 209
Blue Star Brewing Company Restaurant
    & Bar, 78, 105
Blum Street Cellars, 127
Boccone's Italian Restaurant, 92
Boerne day trip, 261–63
Bolivar Hall, 135
Bonham Exchange, 106
Bonner Garden, The, 68–69
bookstores, 120–21, 160–61
Boot Hill, 130
Boot Town Western Wear, 130
Borders Books and Music, 120, 160
Boudro's, 94
boutiques, 121–22
Bowie Street Blues, 192–93
bowling, 225

Brackenridge House, 69–70
Brackenridge Park, 141, 178, 216–17
Brackenridge Park Golf Course, 226
Bradfield Properties, 282
Brew Moon Cafe & Pub, 113
brewpubs, 105
Bright Kids Day Care/Learning Center, 292
Brighton Gardens by Marriott—San Antonio,
    310
Brooke Army Medical Center, 296
Brooks Air Force Base, 332
Buckhorn Saloon and Museum, 135–36,
    169–70
Bullpepper's Old Towne Café, 78
Bun 'N' Barrel, 82
buses, 24–26
Bussey's Flea Market, 123
Buttons-N-Bows, 292

C
Cabaret Dance Hall, 106–7
Cadillac Bar & Restaurant, 103
Cadillac Lofts, 61
Café Ole!, 97
Cafe Soleil, 90
Calcutta Coffee House, 88
Camp Fair, 161
camps, 161–64
Canary Islands Descendants Museum, 136
Candlelight Coffeehouse, 88
Canyon Lake Golf Club, 229
Canyon Springs Golf Club, 227
Carey/River City Limo, Inc., 27
Caring for Your Aging Parent, 308
Caroling in the Caverns, 202
Carranza Grocery and Market, 82
car rentals, 19–20
carriages, horse-drawn, 28
Carver Community Cultural Center,
    159, 213
Casa Manos Alegres, 125
Casa Navarro State Historical Park, 136
Casa Rio, 97, 99
Casbeers, 108–9

Castle Hills Learning Center and Day Care, 292

Castroville day trip, 259–61

Casual Male—Big and Tall, 124

Catholic Schools of San Antonio, 291

Cavender's Boot City, 130

caves, 174–75

CD Exchange, 126

Cedar Creek Golf Course, 226

Center for Health Care Services, 302

Central Park Mall, 116

Chandler Assisted Living, 310

Chapparal Golf Course, 229

Charlotte's Antiques and Clocks, 119

Chez Ardid, 90–91

child-care centers, 291–94

children, activities for. *See* kidstuff

Children's Festival, 167, 192

Children's Fine Arts Series, 181

Children's World Learning Centers, 292

Childtime Children's Center, 292–93

choirs, 207

Christmas Along the Corridor, 202–4

CHRISTUS Santa Rosa Children's Hospital, 296

CHRISTUS Santa Rosa Hospital, 296–97

churches, 320–25

Cinco de Mayo, 193

CineFestival, 189, 208

Cinemark Theaters, 112

City of San Antonio Elderly and Disabled Services, 303–4

city parks, 216–20

Classic Cruise Along the Corridor, 193

clothing stores, 123–24

Club Agave, 107

Club House Pit Bar-B-Q, The, 83–84

coffeehouses, 87–89

collectible stores, 122–23

Collector's Gallery, 122

colleges and universities, 285–86

Comanche Lookout Park, 217

comedy clubs, 105

Comfort day trip, 256–57

Comfort Inn Airport, 54

Comfort Inn East, 54–55

Comfort Suites, 60

Comfort Suites Airport North, 55

comic book stores, 122–23

Community Care Services to Aged and Disabled (CCAD), 304

community colleges, 286

Contemporary Art Month, 198

Corporate Limousine, 27

Corpus Christi weekend getaway, 267–69

Cos House, 153

Cositas Gift Shop, 122

Country Home Learning Center, 293

country/western clubs, 106

County Line Smokehouse and Grill, 84

Courtyard San Antonio Airport, 55

Courtyard San Antonio Downtown/Market Square, 42

Cowboy Breakfast, 187

Crescent, The, 61

Crossroads Mall, 116

Crumpets Restaurant, 89

Crystal Ice Palace Ice Arena, 230, 231

Crystal Steak House, 95

cycling, 225

D

Daily Commercial Recorder, 313

dance classes, 226

dance clubs, 106–8

dance (performing art), 207–8

Dawn at the Alamo, 189

Dawson Park, 217

Days Inn Northeast, 55

day trips

    Austin, 243–45, 248

    Boerne, 261–63

    Castroville, 259–61

    Comfort, 256–57

    Enchanted Rock State Natural Area, 255–56

    Fredericksburg, 257–59

    Georgetown, 248–50

Gruene, 252

Kerrville, 263–64

Laredo, 265–66

New Braunfels, 253–55

San Marcos, 250–51

Seguin, 264–65

Wimberley, 261

See also weekend getaways

delicatessens, 90

Del Rio weekend getaway, 272–73

Diamond W. Longhorn Ranch Chuckwagon
Supper and Dinner Show, 173

Dick's Last Resort, 78–79

Diez y Seis De Septiembre, 198

Dignowity Hill Historic District, 149–50

Doubletree Club Hotel San Antonio
Airport, 55–56

Doubletree Hotel San Antonio Airport, 56

Downtown YMCA, 226

driver's licenses, 308

Dunnewood Limousine, Inc., 27

Durty Nelly's Irish Pub, 113–14

E

Eagle Quest at Panther Springs, 230

Eagle Quest Precision Golf Center, 230

Earl Abel's, 86

East Central Independent School District, 288

Edgewood Independent School District,
288–89

Educare Child Care Inc., 293

education. *See* schools

Edward Steves Homestead, 151–52

Eisenhauer Road Flea Market, 123

Eisenhower Park, 178–79, 217

El Grito Ceremony, 198

Ellis Alley, 150

Embassy Suites San Antonio International
Airport, 60

emergency services, 296

Enchanted Rock State Natural Area day trip,
221, 255–56

Enterprise Rent-A-Car, 20

Esplanade Gardens, 310

Espuma Coffee and Tea Emporium, 88

Excalibur Comics and Video, 122

extended-stay accommodations, 60–62

F

Fairfield Inn San Antonio Airport, 56

Fairfield Inn San Antonio Downtown, 43–44

Fairmount, The—A Wyndham Historic
Hotel, 42–43

Fatso's Sports Garden, 14, 84, 235

Fat Tuesday, 103

Fay Willie's, 86

festivals, 186–205

Fiesta de Las Luminarias, 168, 204

Fiesta Magazine, 313–14

Fiesta Noche Del Rio, 168, 194–95, 198

Fiesta San Antonio, 190–92

Fiestas Navideñas, 204

Fig Tree Restaurant, 89

film (performing art), 208–9

fine art stores, 119–20

FitKids, 181

fitness centers, 226

flea markets, 123

Flip Side Record Parlor, 126

Floore Country Store, 109

Flying L Golf Course, 229

food (specialty) stores, 127

football, 239

Fort Sam Houston, 331–32

Fort Sam Houston Independent School
District, 289

Forum, The, 116

Four Points Hotel San Antonio Riverwalk, 44

Fredericksburg day trip, 257–59

Friedrich Wilderness Park, 179, 217–18

Fujiya, 81

G

Galeria Ortiz, 209

Galleria II, 119

galleries, art, 209

Galveston weekend getaway, 276–77

GameWorks Studio, 164–65

Gassman's Archery and Air Gun Head-
quarters, 126
Gazebo at Los Patios, 79
Georgetown day trip, 248–50
getaways. *See* weekend getaways
gift shops, 121–22
golf, 226–30
golf tournaments, 239–40
Goodwill Industries of San Antonio, 309
Goodwill Stores, San Antonio, 127, 130
Go Rodeo Roundup, 198
Government Hill, 150
Go Western Gala, 187
Grady's Bar-B-Que, 84–85
Grand Court I, The, 310–11
Grandma's Attic, 122
Gray Line Tours, 155–56
Greek Funstival, 198
Greenhouse Gallery of Fine Art, 209
Green Tree Tennis Club, 161
Greyhound Bus Terminal, 25–26
Grey Moss Inn, 95
Grief Support Group, 308
Growing Room For Kids, 123
Gruene day trip, 252
Gruene Hall, 109–10
Guadalupe River State Park, 221
Guenther House, 86, 152
Gunn Sports Club, 235
Guy Chipman Company Realtors, 282
Gymboree Play and Music, 182

H
Half Price Books Records Magazines, 121
Halsell Conservatory, 142, 177–78, 219,
222–23
Hampton Inn San Antonio Airport, 56
Hampton Inn San Antonio—Downtown,
44–45
handicraft stores, 124–25
Hard Rock Cafe San Antonio, 79
Harlandale Independent School District, 289
Hawthorn Inn & Suites On the River-
walk, 45

health care
AIDS/HIV care, 301–2
emergency services, 296
hospitals, 296–99
mental health care, 302
poison center, 302
public health care, 299–300
referral agencies, 300–301
therapeutic programs, 302
Heche-a-Mano, 204
HemisFair Park, 179
Heroes and Fantasies, 122
Hertz, 20
Hills & Dales Ice House, 103
Hilton Palacio del Rio Hotel, 45–46
Hilton San Antonio Airport, 57
historic districts, 149–54
historic sites, 166–67
history, 29–40, 326–31
hockey, 230, 240
Hogwild Records Tapes and CDs, 126
Holiday Inn Crockett Hotel, 46
Holiday Inn Express Hotel & Suites, 46
Holiday Inn Express San Antonio Airport, 57
Holiday Inn Riverwalk, 47
Holiday Inn San Antonio Downtown, 46–47
Holiday Inn Select San Antonio International
Airport, 57
holiday lights, 200–201
Holiday River of Lights, 168–69, 204–5
Homegate Studios & Suites San Antonio
Airport, 57
Homewood Suites Riverwalk, 47
horse-drawn carriages, 28
horse racing, 241–42
hospitals, 296–99
hotels and motels
beyond Loop 410, 59–60
downtown, 42–54
extended-stay accommodations, 60–62
inside and along loop 410, 54–59
resorts, 62–65
See also bed and breakfast inns
Houston Street Alehouse, 103

Houston weekend getaway, 275–76
Howl at the Moon, 113
Huebner Oaks, 117
Hunan River Garden, 81
Hyatt Regency Hill Country Resort, 62–63, 228
Hyatt Regency Riverwalk, 47–48

I

ice hockey, 230, 240
I-37 Flea Market, 123
Ike and J's Comics, 123
IMAX Theater at Rivercenter Mall, 113, 136, 172
import stores, 124–25
Indian Hollow, 61
Ingram Park Mall, 117
Inn at Los Patios Personal Care Center, The, 311
Institute of Texan Cultures, 136, 170
International San Antonio Inter-American Bookfair and Literary Festival, 199
Italia Ristorante, 92

J

J. Adelman Antiques, 119
Jacala Mexican Restaurant, 99
Japanese Tea Gardens, 141, 179
Jensen's Yamaha Music School, 172
Jewish Community Center, 159
Jim Cullum's Landing, 110–11
Jim's Restaurant, 79–80
J.J. Rodriguez ERA Troy Realtor, 283
Jump Start Performance Company, 212
Jungle Jim's Playland, 165

K

KABB Channel 11, 317–18
Kabuki Japanese Restaurant, 81–82
Kangaroo Court, 80, 86
Kathleen Sommers Retail Store, 124
KCYY FM 100, 315
KENS 5 Channel 5, 318
Kerrville day trip, 263–64

Kerrville Folk Festival, 194
Kiddie Park, 157–58, 165–66
Kids Paint the Town, 159
Kids' Sports Network, 181
Kids' Sports Network Golf Camps, 161
kidstuff
    amusement parks, 157–59
    art classes and workshops, 159–60
    bookstores, 160–61
    camps, 161–64
    games and arcades, 164–66
    historic sites, 166–67
    indoor attractions, 172–73
    kid-friendly festivals, 167–69
    libraries, 169
    museums, 169–72
    music, 172
    outdoor attractions, 173, 175–78
    parks and playgrounds, 178–79
    recreation centers/programs, 179–81
    sports and fitness, 181
    theater, 181
    toy stores and children's shops, 182
    water parks, 182–85
KinderCare, 293–94
King's Attic/About Antiques and Art, A, 119
Kingsley Place, 311
Kingsville weekend getaway, 271–72
King William Fair, 192
King William Historic District, 150–51
Kirby Senior's Thrift Shoppe, 130
KISS FM 99.5, 316
KJ97 FM 97, 315
KLEY-FM 94.1, 317
KLRN Channel 9, 318
KMOL Channel 4, 318
Kosta's Greek Food, 91
KPAC FM 88.3, 315–16
KRRT Channel 35, 318–19
KSAT Channel 12, 318
KSJL FM 96.1, 317
KSLR AM 630, 315
KSMG FM 105.3, 316
KSTX FM 89.1, 316

KTSA AM 550, 316–17
Kuper Realty Corporation, 283
KVDA Channel 60, 319
KXTN 107.5, 317
KYFS FM 90.9, 315
KZEP FM 104.5, 316

L

Laboratory Brewing Co., 105
Labor of Love, 182
La Cantera Golf Club, 228
Lackland Air Force Base, 332
Lackland Independent School District, 289
La Fogata Mexican Restaurant, 99–100
Lakeside Villas, 61
La Mansión del Rio, 48
La Margarita Mexican Restaurant and
    Oyster Bar, 100
Landmark Inn State Historic Park, 221, 224
LandM Bookstore, 121
La Petite Academy, 294
La Prensa de San Antonio, 314
La Quinta Airport East, 57–58
La Quinta Inn San Antonio Convention
    Center, 49
La Quinta San Antonio Airport West, 58
La Quinta San Antonio Market Square, 49
Laredo day trip, 128–30, 265–66
Larry Campbell–Jack Biegger, Inc., Realtors,
    282
LarzLand, 166
Laser Quest, 166
Las Palomas Country Club, 229
Las Posadas, 169, 205
Latino Laugh Festival, 197–98
La Villita, 115, 152–53
L'Etoile, 91
libraries, 169
Lifeway Christian Stores, 121
Lighthouse Coffee and Cafe, 88
Lightning Ranch, 175–76
limousines, 27
Little Church at La Villita, 153–54, 323–24
Little Hipps, 80

Little League District 19, 224
Little League District 20, 224
Little Red Barn Steakhouse, 95–96
Little Rhein Steak House, 96
Lone Star Cafe, 97
Lone Star Carriage, 28
Lone Star Rent A Car, 20
Lone Star Trolley, 156
Los Pastores, 205
Los Patios, 117
Love Creek Orchards, 176
Low and Slow Classic Car Show, 199
Lower Colorado River Authority Parks,
    246–47
Lucchese Boot Company, 130–31
Luv-N-Care, 294
Lyndon B. Johnson State Historical Park, 224
Lyric Opera of San Antonio, 211–12

M

Madhatter's Tea, 89
magazines, 313–14
Magic Time Machine Restaurant, 80–81
Magik Children's Theatre, 181, 212
Magnolia Pancake Haus, 86–87
Majestic Performing Arts Center, 213
Malibu Grand Prix, 166
malls and shopping areas, 115–19
Malt House, 81
Marion Koogler McNay Art Museum, 141,
    209–10
Market Square, 131–32, 137
Mark's on the River, 103
Marriott Rivercenter, 49
Marriott Riverwalk, 49–50
Marshall's Brocante, 119
Martini's, 103
Martin Luther King Jr. March and Rally, 186
McCreless Mall, 117
McFarlin Tennis Center, 234
McNay Art Museum, 141, 209–10
Meadows Retirement Community, The, 311
media. *See* specific type
medical care. *See* health care

Menger Bar, The, 104

Menger Hotel, 43

Mental Health Association, 302

mental health care, 302

Merrill Gardens, 311

Methodist Ambulatory Surgery Hospital, 297

Methodist Children's Hospital of South
Texas, 297–98

Methodist Hospital, 297

Methodist Specialty and Transplant
Hospital, 297

Metropolitan Methodist Hospital, 298

Mexican-American Cultural Center Bookstore
and Gift Shop, 121

Mexican markets, 131–32

Michelino's, 92

Microtel Inn & Suites, 58

Midnight Rodeo, 106

Milam Park, 179

military history, 326–31

Mina and Dimi's Greek House, 91–92

Mission Concepción, 145–46

Mission del Lago Golf Course, 227

Mission 4 Drive-In, 113

Mission Espada, 147

Mission Flea Market, 123

missions, 144–47

Mission San José, 146–47

Mission San Juan Capistrano, 147

Mi Tierra Cafe and Bakery, 100

Mix Night Club, 104

Monterrey Park, 218

Monte Vista Historic District, 154

Morton's of Chicago Steakhouse, 96

motels. See hotels and motels

motorcycle rentals, 28

mountain biking, 225

movie theaters, 112–13

museums, 169–72, 209–11

music, 108–11, 172, 207, 211–12

music stores, 125–26

N

National Car Rental, 20

National Museum of the Pacific War,
The, 220

Natural Bridge Caverns, 147–48, 176

Natural Bridge Wildlife Ranch, 148, 176

New Braunfels day trip, 253–55

New Braunfels Marketplace, 127

New Lifestyles, 312

news media. *See* specific type

newspapers, 313–14

nightlife

bars, 102–4

brewpubs, 105

comedy clubs, 105

country/western clubs, 106

dance clubs, 106–8

live music, 108–11

movie theaters, 112–13

piano bars, 113

pubs, 113–14

sports bars, 114

Tejano clubs, 114

Niles Wine Bar, 104

Norma Pearson Realtor, 283

North Central Baptist Hospital, 298

Northeast Baptist Hospital, 298

North East Independent School District,
289, 308

Northeast Methodist Hospital, 298

Northside Independent School District,
289–90, 308

North Star Mall, 117

Northwest Arts and Crafts Group, 159

Northwest Vista College, 286

Nuevo Laredo (Mexico), shopping in,
128–30

O

Oblate Grotto of the Southwest, 324

Observatory Night Club, 107

Oceans Window Tropical Divers, 231, 233

Offstage, Inc., 212–13

Ogé House on the Riverwalk, The, 70

Olmos Basin Golf Course, 227

Olmos Coffee House, 89

Olmos Pharmacy, 81
Original Mexican Restaurant, The, 101
Our Lady of the Lake University, 285
outlet stores, 127

P

Paesanos, 92–93
Palmetto State Park, 224
Palo Alto College, 286
Palo Alto Pool, 232
Paris Hatters, 131
parks
    children-oriented, 178–79
    city, 216–20
    Lower Colorado River Authority, 246–47
    state, 220–21, 224
Pear Apple County Fair, 158
Pecan Valley Golf Club, 228
Penner's, 124
performing arts venues, 213–14
Peter Rabbit's Great Hill Country Garden
    Party, 167–68
pet licenses, 306
Phyllis Browning Company, 282
piano bars, 113
Pig Stand, 85
Pink Giraffe, The, 122
Place For Kids Christian Learning Center,
    A, 294
Planeta Mexico, 114
Plaza San Antonio, 50
Plaza Wax Museum, 137, 172–73
poison center, 302
Polly Esther's Culture Club, 107–8
Polo Field Driving and Practice Range, 230
Polo Lounge, 104
Polo's at the Fairmount, 94
Port Aransas weekend getaway, 270–71
Posada Car Rental, 20
Prime Outlets, 127
Prime Time Newspapers, 314
private schools, 291
Promised Land Dairy, 176
Promontory Point, 61

Prudential, Don Johnson Company
    Realtors, 283
public health care, 299–300
public schools, 286–90
public transit, 23–25
pubs, 113–14

Q

Quadrangle at Fort Sam Houston, 166–67
Quarry Golf Club, The, 228

R

Racquetball Pros of San Antonio, 126
radio stations, 314–17
Radisson Market Square, 50–51
Ramada Inn Emily Morgan, 51
Randolph Air Force Base, 332
Randolph Field Independent School
    District, 290
R and R Bookstore, 121
real estate
    agencies, 281–83
    current conditions, 280–81
    neighborhoods, 278–79
recreation. *See* specific activity
recreation centers/programs, 179–81
Red Balloon, The, 160–61
Regal Cinemas, 112–13
Regent at Hamilton House, 311
Re/Max Associates 2000, 283
Remembering the Alamo Weekend, 167, 189
Republic of Texas, 97
resale shops, 127, 130
Residence Inn Alamo Plaza, 51
Residence Inn San Antonio Airport, 58
Residence Inn San Antonio Downtown, 51–52
resorts, 62–65
restaurants
    American, 78–81
    Asian, 81–82
    barbecue, 82–86
    breakfast, 86–87
    Cajun/Creole, 87
    coffeehouses, 87–89

continental, 89
delicatessens, 90
French, 90–91
Greek, 91–92
Italian, 92–93
New American, 93–94
overview of local cuisine, 74–77
Southwestern, 94–95
steak, 95–97
Texas, 97
Tex-Mex, 97–101
Retama Park, 241–42
retirement and senior services
community activities, 308–9
employment opportunities, 309
housing, 310–11
lifetime learning, 308
publications, 312
senior centers, 304–7
senior resources, 303–4
support groups, 307–8
transportation, 309–10
volunteer opportunities, 309
Return of the Chili Queens, 193
Rio Grande Valley weekend getaway, 274–75
Ripley's Believe It or Not!, 137, 173
River Art Group Gallery, 120
River Art Show, 199, 202
Rivera's Chili Shop, 127
Rivercenter Comedy Club, The, 105
Rivercenter Mall, 17–18
Riverside Golf Course, 227
Riverside Park, 218
River Walk Arts & Crafts Show, 187
Riverwalk Inn, 71
River Walk Mardi Gras, 188–89
River Walk Mud Festival, 186–87
River Walk (Paseo del Rio), 137–39, 176
Riverwalk Plaza Hotel Resort & Conference Center, 52
Rockport weekend getaway, 269–70
rodeo, 240–41
Rodeway Inn Downtown, 58–59
Rollercade, The, 231

Rolling Oaks Golf Center, 230
Rolling Oaks Mall, 118
Rosario's Mexican Cafe y Cantina, 101
Royal Swan, The, 71–72
Rudy's Country Store and Bar-B-Q, 85
running, 230, 241

S

Saint, The, 108
Salute International Bar, 111
San Antonio
African-American culture, 6–8
cost of living, 9
economy, 9–10, 12–13
ethnic diversity of, 8–9
Hispanic influence, 3, 5–6
history, 29–40
military history, 326–31
overview of activities, 10–11
vital statistics, 13–16
San Antonio Academy, 291
San Antonio Airport Pear Tree Inn, 59
San Antonio Airport Posada Ana Inn, 59
San Antonio Art League Museum, 152
San Antonio Botanical Gardens and Halsell Conservatory, 142, 177–78, 219, 222–23
San Antonio Bowling Association, 225
San Antonio Business Journal, 314
San Antonio Central Library, 169
San Antonio Children's Museum, 161, 170–71
San Antonio City Tours, 156
San Antonio College, 286
San Antonio Conservation Society Foundation Library, 36
San Antonio Current, 314
San Antonio Days Inn, 60
San Antonio District Dental Society, 300–301
San Antonio Express-News, 313
San Antonio Film Commission, 208–9
San Antonio Food and Leisure Magazine, 75
San Antonio Highland Games, 190
San Antonio Iguanas, 240
San Antonio Independent School District, 290

San Antonio International Airport, 18–21

San Antonio Marathon, 241

San Antonio Metropolitan Ballet, 207–8

San Antonio Missions, 238

San Antonio Missions National Historical
Park, 167

San Antonio Museum of Art, 142, 159–60,
210–11

San Antonio Natorium, 232

San Antonio Parks and Recreation Department, 179–81, 225, 226, 231–35, 309

San Antonio Parks and Recreation Department Senior Programming, 308–9

San Antonio Parks and Recreation Mural Project, 160

San Antonio Retirement Guide, 312

San Antonio/Riverwalk Drury Inn &
Suites, 53

San Antonio Spurs, 236–38

San Antonio Stock Show and Rodeo, 167,
188, 240–41

San Antonio Symphony, 212

San Antonio Taxis, 26

San Antonio Thunder, 239

San Antonio Wheelmen, 225

San Antonio Zoological Garden and
Aquarium, 142, 178

San Fernando Cathedral, 139, 324–25

San Marcos day trip, 250–51

San Pedro Driving Range and Par 3, 230

San Pedro Playhouse, 214

San Pedro Springs Park, 218–19

Satel's, 124

SATRANS, 20

S.A.V.E. (San Antonio Vacation Experience), 8

Schilo's Delicatessen, 90

Schlitterbahn, 148, 182–84

schools
colleges and universities, 285–86
community colleges, 286
private, 291
public, 286–90

Scobee Planetarium at San Antonio
College, 173

scuba diving, 231

SeaWorld of Texas, 148–49, 158, 162–63, 184

Seguin day trip, 264–65

senior services. See retirement and senior
services

Sheraton Gunter, 53

shopping
antiques and fine art, 119–20
bookstores, 120–21
boutiques/gift shops, 121–22
clothing, 123–24
comic books/collectibles, 122–23
flea markets, 123
imports and handicrafts, 124–25
in Laredo, Texas and Nuevo Laredo,
Mexico, 128–30
malls and shopping areas, 115–19
Mexican markets, 131–32
music stores, 125–26
outlet shopping, 127
specialty food stores, 127
sporting goods, 126–27
thrift stores and resale shops, 127, 130
toy stores and children's shops, 182
Western gear, 130–31

Silverhorn Golf Club, 228

Six Flags Fiesta Texas, 149, 158–59, 184–85

skating, 231

soccer, 231

Soccer Locker USA, 126

Soccer World, 127

Social Security Administration, 304

softball, 231–32

Southeast Baptist Hospital, 299

South Padre Island weekend getaway, 273–74

South Park Mall, 118

South San Antonio Independent School
District, 290

Southside Independent School District, 290

South Texas Poison Center, 302

Southwest Independent School District, 290

Southwest School of Art and Craft, 139, 160,
163, 208

Spanish Governor's Palace, 139–40

spectator sports. *See* specific sport

"Spirits of San Antonio" Tour, 154–55, 156

Splashtown, 142, 185

sporting goods stores, 126–27

sports. *See* specific sport

sports bars, 114

St. Anthony Catholic High School, 291

St. Anthony Hotel, 52–53

St. Luke's Baptist Hospital, 299

St. Mary's Hall, 291

St. Mary's University, 285

St. Patrick's Day River Parade and Pub Crawl, 190

St. Phillips College, 286

state parks, 220–21, 224

Sterling Heights, 62

Steven Stoli's Backyard Theatre, 182

Stinson Municipal Airport, 21

Stockyards Cafe, 96

Street Eagle of San Antonio, Texas, 28

Studio 794, 108

Super 8 San Antonio Airport, 60

Swig, 104

swimming, 232–24

T

Taco Land, 111

Tanger Factory Outlet Center, 127

Tapatio Springs Resort and Conference Center, 228

Taste of New Orleans, A, 192

taxis, 20–21, 26

Tejano clubs, 114

Tejano Conjunto Festival en San Antonio, 194

Tejano Music Awards, 190

television stations, 317–19

tennis, 234–35

Tequila Mockingbird, 111

Tequila Tree, The, 125

Terrell Castle, 72–73

Texas Adventure, 140, 173

Texas Air Museum—Stinson Chapter, 143

Texas Bach Choir, 207

Texas Folklife Festival, 168, 195, 197

Texas Highway Patrol Association Hall of Fame Museum, 143

Texas Motorcycle Rentals, 28

Texas Parks and Wildlife Magazine, 221

Texas Pioneer Trail Drivers and Rangers Museum, 143

Texas State Arts and Crafts Fair, 168, 194

Texas Thrift Store, 130

Texas Transportation Museum, 143

theatre, 181, 212–13

Therapeutic Recreation Program, 302

thoroughbred racing, 241–42

thrift stores, 127, 130

Thrifty Car Rental, 20

Tomatillos Café y Cantina, 101

Tom's Ribs, 85–86

tours, 154–56

Tower of the Americas, 140–41

Tower of the Americas Restaurant, 96–97

Towers at the Majestic, 62

toy stores and children's shops, 182

trains, 26–27

transportation
    airport shuttle service, 20
    air travel, 18–21
    buses, 24–26
    car rentals, 19–20
    horse-drawn carriages, 28
    limousines, 27
    motorcycle rentals, 28
    public transit, 23–25
    for seniors, 309–10
    taxis, 20–21, 26
    trains, 26–27
    traveling by car, 22–23
    trolleys, 23–24
    walking, 21–22
    water taxis, 27–28

Travis Park, 219

Trident Dive Center, 231

Trinity University, 285

Trinity University Tigers, 239

trolleys, 23–24

Turtle Rock, 62
Tutor Time Child Care/Learning Centers, 294
TV stations, 317–19
2015 Club, 108

U

United Way of San Antonio and Bexar
   County, 301, 309
universities and colleges, 285–86
University of Texas at San Antonio, 285–86
University of Texas Health Science Center,
   286
University of the Incarnate Word, 286

V

VIA Downtown Trolleys, 23–24
VIA Metropolitan Transit Service, 24–25,
   225–26, 309–10
Village Gallery, The, 125
Villager Lodge, 53
Village Weavers, 125
Villita Stained Glass, 125
Vintage, The, 62
Viva Botanica, 190
volleyball, 235

W

Wahooz Seafood Kitchen, 87
Walk Across Texas, 193
Walker Ranch Historic Landmark Park,
   219–20
Warm Springs Rehabilitation Hospital, 299
Waterford at Huebner, The, 311
water parks, 182–85
water taxis, 27–28
weekend getaways
   Corpus Christi, 267–69
   Del Rio, 272–73
   Galveston, 276–77
   Houston, 275–76
   Kingsville, 271–72

Port Aransas, 270–71
   Rio Grande Valley, 274–75
   Rockport, 269–70
   South Padre Island, 273–74
   See also daytrips
Western gear stores, 130–31
Westin La Cantera, 63–65
Westin Riverwalk, The, 54
Westin Texas Open, 239–40
Westlakes Mall, 118
White Rabbit, 111
Widowed Persons Service, 308
wildflower viewing, 196–97
wildlife ranches, 164–65
Wild Planet, 182
Wilford Hall Medical Center, 299
Willow Springs Golf Course, 227
Wimberley day trip, 261
Windsor Park Mall, 118–19
Witte Museum of History and Science/H-E-B
   Science Treehouse, 143–44, 163, 171–72
WOAI AM 1200, 317
Woodlake Golf and Country Club, 228–29
Wreath Laying Ceremony at the Alamo
   Shrine, 189
Wurstfest, 202

Y

Yanaguana Cruises, Inc., 27–28, 156
Yellow Checker Cab, 26
Yellow Rose, A, 73
Yellow Rose Carriage, 28
YMCA Camp Flaming Arrow, 163
Y.O. Adventure Camp, 163–64
Yturri-Edmunds Historic Site, 143

Z

Zany Brainy, 182
Zinc Champagne & Wine Bar, 104
Zuni Bar and Grill, 95

About the Authors

Paris Permenter and John Bigley are a husband-wife team of freelance writers who specialize in travel. Their work has been published in numerous international, national, and statewide publications.

Paris's desire for travel began at an early age. Born in San Francisco, she spent her first years in Sausalito, Angel Island, Louisiana, Illinois, and Missouri, finally settling in Texas in 1969. Her professional writing career began in high school and college, when some of her work appeared in *Seventeen* magazine. Those articles soon were followed by full-length features in *Reader's Digest* and other national publications.

John is a native Texan, born in La Grange, east of San Antonio. John's first forays into professional writing were in the field of poetry; his first book was published in 1973.

After their marriage in 1986, Paris and John realized they shared a talent and interest in the field of nonfiction, specifically travel. Since that time, the couple has reported on travel in the Lone Star State in many aspects. Since 1992, they have coauthored the "Getaways" column for *Fiesta*, the monthly magazine of the *San Antonio Express-News*, covering weekend excursions around the Alamo City. As coauthors of *Day Trips from San Antonio* and *Day Trips from Austin* (both published by The Globe Pequot Press), Paris and John have covered the region extensively.

Their work as freelance travel writers has also taken them much farther afield. Paris and John specialize in romantic travel. The two have traveled extensively on assignment in India, Morocco, Egypt, Cyprus, Israel, Italy, the UK, Malta, Jordan, Mexico, and most islands in the Caribbean. Having visited six continents, the couple continues to seek out new destinations of special interest to romantic travelers.

Much of their travel has been in the Caribbean. The pair have authored more than two dozen guidebooks to the Caribbean islands and have visited most islands in the region. Their Caribbean guidebooks include *Lovetripper.com's Guide to Caribbean Destination Weddings*, *Adventure Guide to Jamaica*, *Adventure Guide to the Cayman Islands*, *Cayman Islands Alive!*, *Jamaica Alive!*, and *Caribbean with Kids*.

Both Paris and John enjoying learning about a region's culture through its cuisine. They have written *Texas Barbecue*, *Jamaica: A Taste of the Island*, *Bahamas: A Taste of the Islands*, and *Gourmet Getaways: North America's Top 75 Resorts*.

Paris and John also edit *Lovetripper.com Romantic Travel Magazine*, an online publication aimed at romantic travelers and honeymooners. The couple writes about romantic resorts, destination weddings, and adventures for two for the publication, which features the work of professional travel writers.

As members of the Society of American Travel Writers, Paris and John appear frequently on local television and radio programs promoting travel. They have spoken on many of the San Antonio television affiliates discussing day trips in the region.

The couple's work has received many accolades from a variety of organizations. In 1994, Paris and John's *Texas Barbecue* guide received the "Best Regional Book" award from the Mid-America Publishers Association. Their *Adventure Guide to the Leeward Islands* was awarded second place in the "Best Book" competition sponsored by the Central States chapter of the Society of American Travel Writers in 1999. In 1995, 1996, and 1997, articles by the couple published in *Fiesta* magazine won them awards of merit from the San Antonio Professional Chapter of Women in Communication. In 1996, the *Austin*

Chronicle readers' poll awarded their *Texas Getaways for Two* guidebook the title "Best Romantic Travel Book." Paris and John have more than 1,400 magazine and newspaper articles to their credit.

Today Paris and John live in Cedar Park, Texas, with their dogs and cats; their daughter, Lauren, is presently enrolled at the University of Texas at Austin and is studying radio, TV, and film. The couple enjoys the outdoors, photography, and travel.